the
slow cooker
recipe book

the
slow cooker
recipe book

Over 220 one-pot dishes for no-fuss preparation
and delicious eating

Catherine Atkinson

JG PRESS

Published by World Publications Group, Inc.

140 Laurel Street, East Bridgewater, MA 02333

www.wrldpub.net

© Anness Publishing Ltd 2004, 2008

Produced by Anness Publishing Ltd, an imprint of Anness Publishing Ltd,

Hermes House, 88–89 Blackfriars Road, London SE1 8HA; tel. 020 7401 2077; fax 020 7633 9499

www.hermeshouse.com; www.annesspublishing.com

If you like the images in this book and would like to investigate using them for publishing, promotions or advertising, please visit our website

www.practicalpictures.com for more information.

Publisher: Joanna Lorenz

Editorial Director: Helen Sudell

Senior Editor: Sarah Ainley

Recipes: Catherine Atkinson, Jane Bamforth, Alex Barker, Valerie Barrett, Judy Bastyra, Jacqueline Clark, Carole Clements, Joanna Farrow, Brian Glover, Nicola Graimes, Juliet Harbutt,

Christine Ingram, Becky Johnson, Lucy Knox, Marlene Spieler, Kate Whiteman, Rosemary Wilkinson, Elizabeth Wolf-Cohen and Jeni Wright

Photography: Karl Adamson, Edward Allwright, Steve Baxter, Nicki Dowey, James Duncan, Michelle Garrett, Amanda Heywood, Janine Hosegood, David King, Don Last, William

Adams-Lingwood, Thomas Odulate, Craig Robertson, Bridget Sargeson and Sam Stowell

Designer: Nigel Partridge

Indexer: Helen Snaith

ETHICAL TRADING POLICY

Because of our ongoing ecological investment programme, you, as our customer, can have the pleasure and reassurance of knowing that a tree is being cultivated on your behalf to

naturally replace the materials used to make the book you are holding. For further information about this scheme, go to www.annesspublishing.com/trees

ISBN10: 1 57215 165 X

ISBN13: 9781572151659

Printed and bound in China

NOTES

Bracketed terms are intended for American readers.

For all recipes, quantities are given in both metric and imperial measures and, where appropriate, in standard cups and spoons. Follow one set of measures,
but not a mixture, because they are not interchangeable.

Standard spoon and cup measures are level. 1 tsp = 5ml, 1 tbsp = 15ml, 1 cup = 250ml/8fl oz.

Australian standard tablespoons are 20ml. Australian readers should use 3 tsp in place of 1 tbsp for measuring small quantities.

American pints are 16fl oz/2 cups. American readers should use 20fl oz/2.5 cups in place of 1 pint when measuring liquids.

Electric oven temperatures in this book are for conventional ovens. When using a fan oven, the temperature will probably need to be reduced by about 10–20°C/20–40°F.
Since ovens vary, you should check with your manufacturer's instruction book for guidance.

The nutritional analysis given for each recipe is calculated per portion (i.e. serving or item), unless otherwise stated. If the recipe gives a range, such as Serves 4–6, then
the nutritional analysis will be for the smaller portion size, i.e. 6 servings. Measurements for sodium do not include salt added to taste.

Medium (US large) eggs are used unless otherwise stated.

CONTENTS

The Principles of Slow Cooking

The Story of Slow Cooking 6

Slow Cooker Basics 8

Useful Equipment 10

Ingredients:

Beef 12

Lamb 14

Pork 15

Poultry and Game 16

Fish and Shellfish 20

Vegetables 22

Grains, Pasta and Beans 24

Fruits 26

Herbs, Spices and Flavourings 28

Basic Techniques:

Making Stock 30

Making Soups 34

Making Marinades 36

Making Stews and Casseroles 38

Braising 42

Toppings 44

Pot-roasting 46

Poaching 48

Using the Slow Cooker as a Bain-marie 50

Making Steamed Puddings and Desserts 52

Making Cakes 54

Making Savoury Sauces 56

Making Sweet Sauces 58

Making Fondues 60

Making Preserves 62

Slow Cooker Safety 64

Slow Cooker Recipes

Soups and Appetizers 66

Fish and Shellfish 96

Poultry and Game 120

Meat Dishes 148

Vegetarian and Side Dishes 182

Desserts and Cakes 206

Preserves and Drinks 236

Useful Addresses 252

Index 253

THE STORY OF SLOW COOKING

Long, slow cooking techniques have been used for centuries. From the earliest times, cooks discovered that meat roasted in the dying embers of the fire, or in a pot of gently bubbling stock suspended well above the flames, produced the tenderest results with rich, well-balanced flavours.

Cooking methods have developed and improved over the years, but no drastic changes were seen until the reduction of staff employed in richer households meant that very few people still had a cook who would spend the entire day preparing food, thus leading to changes in the types of food prepared.

Along with the gradual introduction of controllable range cookers and, eventually, the introduction of modern gas and electric ovens came an increased demand for dishes requiring less cooking time. In the latter half of the 20th century, more women went out to work, and time-saving became all-important.

Food manufacturers thrived on the sale of prepared ingredients that could

Below: *The gentle heat of the slow cooker means that delicate fish cooks beautifully.*

reduce the number of hours spent in the kitchen. Canned and dried soups, dehydrated prepared vegetables, main meals and "instant" desserts were all the rage at the end of the 1960s and throughout the 1970s.

The rise and fall of the slow cooker

In the mid-1970s, the slow cooker was invented. It was originally designed for making baked beans and was marketed to the public as an appliance that would cook a wholesome meal unattended, ready to be served after a hard day's work. As such it caught the attention of those with busy working lives. It lived up to its promise, and busy working mothers, families and students soon discovered its delights. The slow cooker's popularity continued for a decade.

However, with the booming economy years in the late 1980s and 1990s, the demand for economical cuts of meat fell. They were replaced by lean prime cuts, such as chicken breast portions and beef steak, which were more suited to fast cooking methods, such as grilling, broiling and stir-frying. Time-saving

Above: *Impressive terrines can be made using the slow cooker as a bain-marie.*

appliances appeared on the scene, including the microwave – and with their arrival, many slow cookers were left to gather dust.

Changing attitudes

Towards the end of the 20th century and in the new millennium, there has been a change in attitudes towards food and a reverse in eating trends. Many people now demand natural food, with fewer artificial chemicals and more nutrients and flavour, rather than instant, quick-fix food. Genetically modified produce has not been welcomed and sales of organic food have rocketed, along with requests for less tender, tastier cuts of meat. Slow-simmered casseroles, home-made soups and traditional desserts are back in fashion, and so are slow cookers.

From tasty, wholesome family food to sophisticated entertaining, a slow cooker is a superb way to create wonderfully tender and flavour-packed meals. Its reputation for making delicious soups and succulent stews is well known, and the slow cooker is far more versatile than many people realize.

Because the slow cooker cooks gently, without the vigorous bubbling or fierce heat of some other cooking methods, delicate food, such as fish, fruit and

vegetables, won't break up even after long cooking. Used as a bain-marie the slow cooker can produce divine creamy "baked" custards, the lightest sponge desserts, and tasty terrines and pâtés. The constant temperature makes it perfect for keeping party punches steaming hot and simmering preserves so that the flavours mingle, making ready-to-eat preserves that don't need to be left to mature.

There are many advantages to using a slow cooker. Not only does it produce delicious dishes with well-developed flavours, but once the food is in the slow cooker you can usually turn it on and forget about it. Because the slow cooker uses less electricity than a light bulb, it can be left unattended, which means you can be away from the kitchen all day and return when ready to serve.

Some slow cookers have timers that automatically switch to the warm setting when the food is cooked, and this is ideal for households who eat at different times. The remaining portions will still be deliciously moist for latecomers, and won't be overcooked or dry. As an added bonus, little steam or smell escapes from slow cookers.

You will be pleasantly surprised at the range of uses of the slow cooker. Although traditionally associated with

Below: Pastry toppings for traditional pies are oven-cooked to retain their crispness.

cold weather foods, such as warming casseroles, soups and stews, you can also make delicious hot weather dishes, such as chilled pâtés and terrines, light fish dishes and summery Mediterranean-style pasta meals. The slow cooker really is invaluable when it is warm outside and you don't want to be confined to a steamy kitchen, with the oven pumping out heat. Simply switch on the slow cooker and leave it to it.

Below: Individual servings can be cooked in single-portion ramekins in the slow cooker.

Above: The slow cooker makes excellent steamed chocolate and fruit puddings.

Using this book

This book is ideal for the first-time slow cooker user, as well as the more experienced slow cooker fan. It contains a wonderfully detailed reference section with everything you need to know about ingredients, equipment and techniques, so that you can feel confident about every aspect of slow cooking.

Once you have mastered the basics, turn to the recipe chapters for a selection of all-time classics as well as unusual recipes that are sure to become household favourites. Step-by-step photographs show the key preparation stages of each recipe to give successful results every time.

Most recipes are based on a family of four people, but if you have a small or large slow cooker the quantities can easily be halved to serve two, or doubled for eight. All recipes have been thoroughly tested, but it is important to get to know your slow cooker, as times can vary from one model to another. After trying a few recipes, you will know whether your slow cooker is faster or slower, and you will be able to adjust the recipe cooking times accordingly.

SLOW COOKER BASICS

The basic principle behind the slow cooker is that it cooks food very slowly at a low temperature. The heat gradually builds up and is then maintained at an even temperature throughout cooking, to give perfect, tender results. Slow cookers are very simple and economical to use. They have a low wattage that consumes about the same amount of electricity as a light bulb, which makes them environmentally friendly as well.

Choosing a slow cooker

There is a very wide selection of slow cookers available. They come in a range of sizes, shapes, colours and prices, and it is these factors that you will need to think about before you decide which type of slow cooker is right for you.

When slow cookers were first manufactured, the earthenware or ceramic pots were permanently fixed into the heat-resistant plastic or aluminium outer casing. While it is still possible to buy models made this way, most modern versions have a removable cooking pot that fits snugly into an inner metal casing. The heating elements are safely situated between the inner and outer casings. This newer style not only simplifies washing up, but allows the cooking pot to be lifted out and taken to the table as a serving dish. In addition, food can be browned in the oven or under the grill (broiler) without causing damage to the outer casing.

The heat-resistant lid may be made of toughened glass or ceramic. The former has the advantage of allowing you to monitor the food's cooking progress without lifting off the lid and losing heat and moisture, although this may be hindered to some extent by steam and condensation gathering on the inside of the lid.

The range of designs and colours of slow cookers has increased in recent years. The original round-shaped rustic cream and brown design with ceramic lid is still available, but alongside it you will now find much more contemporary-looking white, stainless steel and brightly coloured models that will fit well in a bright, modern kitchen.

Slow cookers may be round or oval in shape. Round ones are superb for cooking casseroles, steaming desserts and cooking cakes in round tins (pans), while the oval version is better for pot-roasted meats and for use with loaf tins (pans) and terrines.

The size of different slow cookers can vary enormously — from a small 600ml/ 1 pint/2½ cup cooking pot to a huge 6.5 litre/11¼ pint/26¼ cup one. Of all the sizes, the most popular size is probably 3.5 litres/6 pints/14¼ cups, which will enable you to cook a wide range of dishes and easily cater for four people. However, the smaller versions, intended for cooking just one or two portions at a time, are a great asset for single people and couples and take up less space in the kitchen. They are also perfect for making hot dips and fondues.

Below: Oval-shaped slow cookers are perfect for cooking certain types of food, such as pot-roasted joints of meat, long, loaf-shaped terrines, and small whole fish.

Temperature settings

The cooking temperatures and settings on slow cookers vary slightly from model to model. The most basic (but perfectly adequate) models have three settings: off, low and high. When the slow cooker is switched to low, the food will barely simmer, and at the highest setting it will cook at a simmer or even boil.

Other models have an additional medium setting and some also have an auto setting. The auto setting is thermostatically controlled, so that the cooking temperature builds up to high, maintains it for a short time, then automatically switches to low to maintain the heat. It normally takes about an hour for the slow cooker to reach the "high" temperature, but this depends on the quantity of food being cooked and its initial temperature.

Most slow cooker models also have a power indicator light that remains on constantly during cooking – although in a few models it may switch off to indicate that the optimum temperature has been reached, so check the instructions.

Using a new slow cooker

Every model of slow cooker varies slightly, so it is important to read the manufacturer's instructions carefully before using. Even when using the same settings, some cookers will cook slower or faster than others.

To cover all models of slow cooker, the recipes in this book offer a range of cooking times. Depending on whether your own model cooks more slowly or quickly, you will either need to use the longer or shorter timing, or somewhere in between. Once you have used your new cooker a few times, it will be easy to know at a glance which cooking time you need to use.

Preheating

Some slow cookers need to be preheated on high for 15–20 minutes before cooking. However, always check the instructions first because some models heat up quickly, making this step unnecessary, and the manufacturer may advise against heating the slow cooker when empty.

To preheat the slow cooker, place the empty cooking pot and lid in the slow cooker base and switch the temperature on to the high setting. While the slow cooker heats up, prepare the ingredients for the recipe.

Slow cooker care

Always remove any labels and tags from a new slow cooker, then wash the ceramic cooking pot well in hot soapy water, rinse and dry thoroughly.

After use, the slow cooker should be switched off before removing the ceramic cooking pot. If you don't want to wash the pot immediately after serving the food, it can be filled with warm water and left to soak for as long as necessary. However, do not immerse the entire pot in water for long periods of time because the base is usually porous and soaking may damage the pot. Very few cooking pots are dishwasher-proof, but it is worth checking the manufacturer's instructions; these should also inform you whether the cooking pot can be used on the stovetop or in the oven, microwave or freezer.

Never plunge the hot cooking pot into cold water immediately after use, or pour boiling water into an empty cold cooking pot. Subjecting it to a sudden change in temperature could cause it to crack. As with all electrical appliances, never immerse the outer casing in water or fill it with water. Nor should you use the metal inner casing without the ceramic cooking pot.

Scouring pads and abrasive cleaners will damage the outside of the cooker, so use a damp soapy cloth to clean it.

Above: Smaller slow cookers intended for cooking just one or two portions at a time are an asset for single people and couples.

During cooking, the cooking pot and lid will become very hot, so always use oven gloves when handling. The outer casing may also become hot after long cooking, so care should be taken when touching this, too.

The first few times you use a slow cooker, you may notice a slight odour. This is caused by the burning off of manufacturing residues, which is normal, and will lessen and disappear after time. After several months, the glaze on the cooking pot may become crackled; this is common with glazed stoneware and will not affect the slow cooker's efficiency.

Adapting your own recipes

Conventional recipes can be adapted for cooking in a slow cooker. The easiest way to adapt a recipe is to find a similar one in this book and use it as a guide to adapt the original recipe. As a general rule, the liquid content of a dish cooked conventionally can be reduced by as much as half in a slow cooker. Check towards the end of cooking time and add more hot liquid if necessary.

Tips for success

During cooking, steam will condense on the lid of the slow cooker, then slowly trickle back into the pot. This helps to form a seal around the lid, retaining heat, flavour and cooking smells. If possible, avoid lifting the lid during cooking because this will cause heat loss and lengthen the cooking time. Unless a recipe states otherwise, the slow cooker should be left undisturbed. There is no need to stir food frequently because the even cooking and low temperature help to prevent food from sticking or bubbling over. Should you need to lift the lid though, add an extra 15–20 minutes to the cooking time to make up for the heat lost.

If at the end of the cooking time the food is not quite ready, replace the lid and switch the slow cooker to high to speed up the cooking process. Once ready, many dishes can be kept hot for an hour or so without risk of spoiling, by switching the slow cooker to low.

Guide to cooking times

You can often introduce some flexibility to the total cooking time by adjusting the temperature setting. Certain foods, however, are only successful if cooked at the specified setting. Cakes, for example, should always be cooked on high for the entire cooking time, and pot-roasted meats and egg-based recipes should usually be started on high (or auto) for the first hour of cooking, then reduced. For dishes such as soups and casseroles, the cooking time may be shortened or extended to suit your needs by cooking on a higher or lower setting. As a rough guide, the cooking time on high is just over half that on low.

Low	Medium	High
6–8 hours	4–6 hours	3–4 hours
8–10 hours	6–8 hours	5–6 hours
10–12 hours	8–10 hours	7–8 hours

USEFUL EQUIPMENT

To make most recipes in this book, you will only need a slow cooker. Stocks, soups, stews, casseroles, compotes and pot roasts can all simply be cooked in the ceramic cooking pot. However, to make other dishes, such as cakes and pâtés that are cooked in a bain-marie, you will need suitable cookware that is watertight and which will fit inside the ceramic cooking pot.

Cake tins/pans

When cooking cakes in the slow cooker, always use cake tins that have a fixed, non-removable base, rather than loose-based or springform tins. Before use, check that the tin is completely watertight by filling it with water and leaving it to stand for an hour; if it leaks it is not suitable. You should also check that the tin will fit inside the ceramic cooking pot before you prepare and fill it with mixture.

While it is important that the tin has a strong rigid shape, heat will penetrate more quickly if lighter, thinner tins are used. When using heavy-gauge metal tins, you will need to allow an extra 15–20 minutes cooking time.

Generally, round slow cookers can accommodate larger round and square cake tins than oval cookers. A 20cm/8in round tin or a 17.5cm/6½in square tin should fit comfortably in a 5 litre/ 8¾ pint/20 cup round cooker, providing the sides of the tins are straight and

there is no protruding lip or side handle. Oval cookers can also be used for round and square tins, if necessary, but the size will obviously be more limited.

The recipes in this book state which size and shape of tin to use. Try to stick to these as closely as possible – if the tin is too large you will end up with a shallow cake; if it is too small the mixture may overflow. Bear in mind, too, that the length of cooking time and the texture of the cake may be affected if the wrong tin is used.

Loaf tins/pans

Perfect for making terrines, pâtés and loaf-shaped cakes, these sturdy long, narrow metal tins are better suited to cooking in an oval-shaped slow cooker, which will accommodate their shape conveniently. A 3.5 litre/6 pint/14 cup oval slow cooker will hold a straight-sided 900g/2lb loaf tin or Balmoral – a barrel-shaped ridged tin.

Ring tins/pans

Kugelhopf tins and deep, ring-shaped tins that are not too wide, are excellent for using in a slow cooker. The hollow tube in the centre conducts heat into the middle of the cake, helping it to cook quickly and evenly. Ideally choose

Below: Classic rectangular loaf tins are very useful for making terrines and chunky, country-style cooked pâtés.

Above: Rectangular, round and heart-shaped tins can be used in the slow cooker as long as they fit comfortably inside the pot.

a tin with a central tube that is just a little higher than the outer rim of the tin. However, you should also check that the tin fits inside the slow cooker, and that the cooker lid can still fit tightly on top of the ceramic cooking pot when the tin is inside.

Other shaped tins/pans

There are many other shapes of tin that may also be used in the slow cooker. These include small heart-, petal-, oval-, and hexagon-shaped tins. Before buying a tin to use in a slow cooker, it may be worth taking the internal measurement of the ceramic cooking pot first, to be sure the tin will fit inside.

Dariole moulds

These little sandcastle-shaped tins are usually made of matt aluminium and come in various sizes, although moulds with a 65mm/2½in diameter are the most popular. Dariole moulds are useful for making single-portion sized cakes, desserts and timbales, and are particularly good for making individual baked custards.

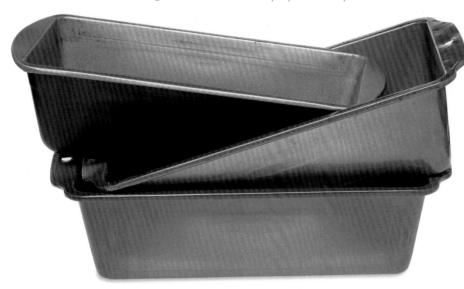

Soufflé and ramekin dishes

These pretty round dishes can be used as an alternative to metal cake tins, as well as for cooking pâtés and mousses. They are always straight-sided and may be made of glass, heatproof porcelain or stoneware. Glass or porcelain are preferable because they conduct heat more quickly to the food inside. When using these dishes for cake making, it is better to choose one with a perfectly flat base; occasionally they are slightly domed. Individual soufflé and ramekin dishes are miniature versions and can be used to make small, individual cakes, pâtés and desserts such as baked custards.

Terrines

Usually rectangular in shape, these dishes may be made of porcelain, cast iron or earthenware. When used to make pâté, they may double up as a serving dish. Some earthenware terrines aren't glazed, so are unsuitable for use in a bain-marie in a slow cooker. A loaf tin makes a good substitute.

Left: Meat thermometers are used to check that meat is cooked through.

Pudding bowls

Traditionally made of white earthenware, but also made of toughened glass, aluminium or polypropylene, pudding bowls have sloping sides, which make the top much wider than the base. They are ideal for making sweet and savoury steamed puddings and can also be used to melt chocolate, butter and similar ingredients in a bain-marie in the slow cooker. Bowls made from aluminium may have a clip-on lid with a handle attached. They are very good for making steamed meat and plain sponge puddings, because heat is conducted quickly. They are unsuitable for making acidic fruit desserts or similarly acidic recipes because the acid will react with the metal.

Below: Soufflé dishes and ramekins can be used inside the slow cooker to make steamed desserts, custards and pâtés.

Above: Metal pudding bowls with a clip-on lid and handle for easy lifting are great for making steamed meat puddings.

Meat thermometers

These useful instruments are the most reliable way of checking that meat is thoroughly cooked – this is particularly important for poultry, which can pass on the salmonella bacteria when raw or partially cooked. Most thermometers have a stainless steel body and a glass dial. By piercing the meat near the centre towards the end of the cooking time, you can check the temperature inside the meat. The meat is ready to eat when the pointer on the dial reaches the appropriate wording; there are indications for types of meat including chicken, beef, lamb and pork, as well as readings within some of those categories for rare, medium and well-cooked meat. Choose a thermometer with a thin probe, so that it doesn't make large holes in the meat, causing juices to be lost. Do not leave the thermometer inside the meat during cooking because exposure to steam in the slow cooker could damage the dial. Immediately after use, rinse the probe in hot soapy water and wipe it clean; don't immerse the thermometer in water.

12

INGREDIENTS: BEEF

Enjoyed all over the world, there are dozens of classic beef dishes, from the British Sunday roast, to French boeuf bourguignonne, German sauerbraten and Russian stroganoff. Beef's popularity is partly due to its versatility. There are many different cuts of beef, and many of these are suitable for a range of cooking methods. Tender fillet, for example, is perfect for cutting into steaks for grilling (broiling), strips for stir-frying, or baked whole, wrapped in pastry. Other cuts, such as the less expensive shin of beef, are unsuitable for roasting or grilling but are wonderful in stews and braised dishes – and are perfect for slow cooker cooking.

Buying and storing

As with all meat, the flavour and texture of beef is determined by the breed of the animal, its feed, the environment in which it is reared and, ultimately, by the process of slaughtering and the treatment of meat before it is cooked. While pork and lamb tend to come from very young animals, beef usually comes from those aged between 18 months and 2 years.

Beef should be hung to allow the flavour to develop and the texture to improve, preferably for at least two weeks. Well-matured beef has a deep, rich burgundy colour, not a bright red hue, and the fat is a creamy colour, or yellow, if the animal was grass-fed. Maturing is an expensive process because some water content will be lost through evaporation, so expect to pay a little more for well-hung meat. The leanest looking joint isn't always the best: for pot-roasting, casseroling

Above: Topside, also known as top round or top rump, is a fairly lean cut of beef that is best slowly braised or pot-roasted.

and braising, a marbling of fat running through the meat will provide flavour and basting to keep the meat moist.

Beef should be kept on a low shelf in the refrigerator, below any cooked foods and ingredients that will be eaten raw. When buying pre-packed meat, check and observe the eat-by date. Whether pre-packed or loose, minced (ground) and cubed beef should be used within 1–2 days of buying; chops and small joints should be used within 3 days, and larger joints within 4–5 days.

Cuts of beef

Butchering techniques differ according to regional and cultural traditions, and also from country to country. Good butchers and larger supermarkets offer a range of cuts and it is worth asking for their advice when buying.

Generally, cuts from the top of the animal, along the middle of the back, are tender because the muscles in this area do relatively little work. These are prime cuts that are good for quick cooking techniques, such as grilling (broiling) and pan-frying, and tend to be the most expensive. Cuts from the neck, shoulders and lower legs are full of flavour, but the texture is coarser and tougher because these are the parts of the animal that work the hardest. They require longer cooking by moist methods to ensure tender results – it is these cuts that are perfectly suited to cooking in the slow cooker. Slow, gentle stewing results in meltingly tender meat and a further developed flavour.

Left (from top): Thick flank makes good braising steak; thin flank produces rich-flavoured steaks and is best suited to slow, moist methods of cooking. Skirt and onglet, which is taken from the skirt area, are lean cuts with a coarse texture that become moist and tender when slowly braised.

Below: Neck is one of the less tender beef cuts but is delicious braised or stewed.

Blade or chuck These cuts come from the top forequarter and are relatively lean, marbled with just a little fat that keeps the meat moist. They are usually boned and sold together as braising steak. The long, gentle cooking of a slow cooker helps to tenderize the meat and intensifies its flavour. These cuts suit pot-roasting, casseroling and braising.

Brisket This may be bought on the bone or boned and rolled and comes from the lower part of the shoulder. It can be a fatty and somewhat tough cut of meat, but is excellent pot-roasted, braised or stewed in the slow cooker. It may also be salted or spiced before cooking, and served cold in thin slices.

Clod and neck Sometimes referred to as "sticking", these cuts come from the neck area and are fairly lean. They are often sold cut up as "stewing" steak. Slightly leaner than blade or chuck, they may also be sold minced (ground).

Fillet/tenderloin, rump/round, sirloin steak These lean, tender cuts from the back are usually cut into steaks for grilling (broiling) or frying, or into strips for stir-frying, and occasionally they are used for roasting. They may be included in braised slow cooker recipes, particularly those cooked on a high setting, but there is little point in using such cuts in casseroles and similar long-cooked dishes, where less expensive cuts produce more flavourful results.

Flank Lean thick flank, or top rump, comes from the hindquarter. In a whole piece, it is ideal for pot-roasting in the slow cooker. It is also sold thickly sliced as braising steak. Thin flank can be fatty and gristly. It can be stewed but is often sold minced (ground).

Leg and shin/foreshank The leg cut comes from the hind legs of the animal and the shin from the forelegs. The shin is a tough cut that responds well to slow cooking. It is usually sold in slices with the bone in the centre and sinews and connective tissue running though; these and the marrow from the bones give the cooked meat a rich, gelatinous quality.

Minced/ground beef This is made from meat from any part of the animal, which has been passed through a mincer. It can be used to make meat sauces and meatballs in the slow cooker. As a general rule, the paler the meat the higher the fat content, so look for dark meat with less fat.

Rib Fore rib and wing, or prime rib, are expensive joints, best served roasted. For the slow cooker, choose middle rib. It is a fairly lean joint, and best boned before braising or pot-roasting.

Silverside/round pot roast This is lean, but tough, and is excellent for pot-roasts and braised dishes. It is often salted and gently cooked, then pressed and served cold.

Skirt/flank steak This thin braising cut can also be pot-roasted. It has a lean but somewhat coarse texture, and can be fast-fried or cooked very slowly, making it an ideal cut for the slow cooker.

VEAL

This meat comes from young calves so is very tender and lean. Most cuts are not well suited to cooking in the slow cooker. Exceptions are shoulder of veal, also known as the oyster, which is sometimes cut into chunks for casseroles; and the knuckle, the bonier end of the hind leg, which can be cut into slices and used to make the Italian stew osso bucco.

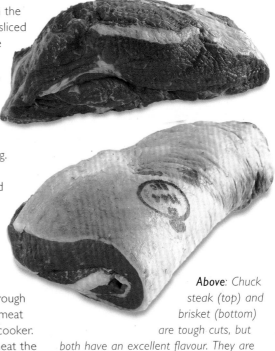

***Above**: Chuck steak (top) and brisket (bottom) are tough cuts, but both have an excellent flavour. They are perfectly suited to long, slow stewing, which gives deliciously moist results.*

***Below**: Knuckle (top) and shoulder (bottom) are two of the few cuts of veal suitable for slow cooker cooking.*

BRING OUT THE TASTE

Beef is a well-flavoured meat that is delicious cooked with robust ingredients and served with spicy accompaniments. Peppery mustards and spicy horseradish are classic accompaniments, while wasabi, a sharp-tasting Japanese horseradish gives a more unusual twist. Other Asian flavourings, such as soy sauce and ginger, also work well. Perfect vegetable partners include potatoes, leeks, onions, parsnips, celery and celeriac.

LAMB

Though lamb cuts do not usually need tenderizing, the fragrant flavour of the meat is intensified by slow cooking. It is enjoyed around the world in a wealth of pot-roasts, casseroles, stews, tagines, curries and braised dishes.

Buying and storing

Lamb comes from animals that are less than a year old; spring lamb comes from animals that are between five and seven months old. Meat from older sheep is known as mutton and has a darker colour and stronger flavour; it is rarely available. Look for firm, slightly pink lamb with a fine-grained texture. The younger the animal, the paler the meat. The fat should be creamy white, firm and waxy. Avoid any meat that looks dark, dry or grainy.

Lamb should be kept covered on a low shelf in the refrigerator. Pre-packed meat can be left in its packaging and used by the date given on the packet. When buying loose meat, steaks and chops will keep for 2–3 days, while larger joints will keep for up to 5 days.

Above: Tender chump chops are good pan-fried, grilled or braised.

Below: A small leg of lamb can be pot-roasted in the slow cooker; steaks cut from the leg are good for braises and casseroles.

Cuts of lamb

The lean, tender prime cuts are taken from the top of the lamb along the middle of the back and are often grilled (broiled), fried or roasted. However, they may also be cooked using slow, moist methods. Tougher cuts from the neck and lower legs respond well to slow cooker methods.

Breast This inexpensive cut is fairly fatty and is often served boned and rolled, sometimes with stuffing. It can be braised in the slow cooker, but trim off the visible fat.

Chops and cutlets Chump or loin chops and leg chops are thick tender chops. Best-end chops or cutlets and middle neck cutlets are thinner and should be trimmed of fat before slow cooking.

Leg This is the prime roasting joint and is often divided into two pieces: the knuckle or shank end, and the leg fillet. The shank is a flavourful cut and is good pot-roasted or gently braised. A small leg of lamb may be pot-roasted on the bone in a large or oval slow cooker, or it can be boned and stuffed. It may also be cut into leg steaks or cubed.

Middle neck and scrag end Relatively cheap and made tender by long, slow cooking, these are used in dishes such as Lancashire hot-pot and Irish stew.

Saddle of lamb Also called a double loin of lamb, this tender roasting joint is too big to cook in a slow cooker.

Shoulder This roasting joint from the forequarter is fattier than the leg, so should be trimmed before pot-roasting on or off the bone. Boneless shoulder can be cubed for casseroles.

Above: Tender noisettes cut from the rolled, boned loin (top) are better suited to quick cooking techniques, while lamb cutlets (bottom) are great for braised dishes.

PERFECT PARTNERS

Fragrant herbs and fruity flavours go well with lamb. Dried fruit is a common addition to lamb dishes all over the world; rosemary, thyme and mint are popular herbs; and garlic and salty additions, such as anchovies and olives, are widely used in Mediterranean dishes. Vegetables that go well with lamb include new potatoes, peas, carrots and beans such as haricot (navy) and flageolet.

Below: Dried prunes make a tasty addition to a Moroccan lamb tagine.

PORK

This light meat is rich-tasting and very versatile. It is also particularly good for slow cooking: whole joints can be pot-roasted, bacon and gammon can be poached, chops can be braised, and cubes of meat stewed. Pork products, such as sausages and minced (ground) pork, are also fabulous cooked in the slow cooker, in dishes such as hearty stews and chunky pâtés and terrines.

Buying and storing

Traditionally, fresh pork was a food for late autumn. Pigs were fattened through the summertime to provide fresh and cured meats during the colder months. However, with modern storage techniques, pork is no longer a seasonal meat and is available all the year round.

Pork should be a pale brownish-pink in colour with a smooth, moist, fine-grained texture. The fat should look white and firm. In older animals, the meat darkens to a deeper colour and the flesh is coarser and less tender.

Hygiene is very important when handling pork, and great care should be taken not to contaminate other foods with the meat juices. Store pork on a low shelf in the refrigerator, below any food that will be eaten raw. Keep pre-packed meat in its packaging and observe the use-by dates. Minced (ground) pork can be kept for up to 2 days, while pork chops and joints can be kept for 3 days.

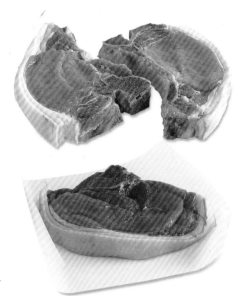

Above: Loin chops (top) and chump chops (bottom) are very good for braising.

Cuts of pork

Belly/side This cut can be rolled and tied to make a neat joint and pot-roasted, or used for mincing and making sausages or terrines. Once a very fatty cut, today's belly pork tends to be leaner.
Chops Large and bony chump chops come from the hind loin, and leaner loin chops from the foreloin. Both are good for braising. (A loin joint is better suited to oven-roasting than slow cooking.)
Leg/ham Often weighing more than 4.5kg/10lb, this cut is too big to be cooked in the slow cooker. However, it can be cut into two joints: the knuckle (shank) and the fillet. The knuckle can be pot-roasted, but is better oven-roasted. Leg fillet is cut across the top of the leg and is very tender. Leg steaks, cut from the top of the leg, are good for braising.
Neck end Cuts from this area include the spare rib, which is often cut into spare rib chops (different from Chinese-style spare ribs, which are cut from the belly). They are good for braising.
Shoulder/blade Taken from the fore end and sold on or off the bone, this can be pot-roasted, but is usually trimmed, cubed and casseroled.
Tenderloin/fillet This lean, boneless, fine-textured piece of meat can be sliced into medallions or split lengthways, stuffed and tied. It may be cooked on a high setting in the slow cooker.

CLASSIC FLAVOURINGS
Pork is widely eaten in Europe, Asia and South and Central America. Because of its rich taste and texture, it goes well with fruity and acidic accompaniments. In England, Germany and France, apples are a popular choice, while in New England, cranberries are favoured. In other cuisines, peaches, apricots and pineapple are all used. Pungent herbs and spices, such as sage, rosemary, thyme and juniper, are often added to pork dishes, and throughout Europe cabbage is a popular vegetable accompaniment.

OFFAL
Known as variety meats in the United States, offal refers to all the offcuts from the carcass, including the organs, tail, feet and head. Most offal is rich and highly flavoured; it may be eaten on its own in a dish, but is often used together with other meats — for example, in steak and kidney pie and in terrines and pâtés. Many types of offal are good cooked in a slow cooker, particularly heart, tongue and pig's trotters, which become deliciously tender with slow, moist, gentle cooking. Unlike meat, which is often hung and matured for several weeks before using, offal does not keep well and should be bought very fresh and used quickly.

Bacon, ham and gammon

These are cured cuts of pork. Bacon is usually cured meat taken from the back and sides of the pig. Ham is the hind leg of a pig cut from the whole side, then cured separately. Gammon is the name of the whole hind leg cut from a side of bacon after curing. Cooked gammon is now often referred to as ham. These joints respond well to poaching in the slow cooker, as long cooking makes them very tender. Bacon chops and gammon steaks are also good braised. Strips of bacon are often fried in a pan before adding to slow cooker stews.

Above: Rolled belly of pork is perfect for pot-roasting in the slow cooker.

POULTRY and GAME

The term poultry covers domesticated birds, including chicken, turkey, duck, goose and guinea fowl, while game refers to wild birds and animals hunted for food, including pheasant, quail, wild rabbit and venison. However, many game birds and animals are now farmed.

SMALL POULTRY

Chicken is probably the most popular of all small poultry, but there are many other types that are just as good.

Buying and storing

When buying fresh or chilled poultry, choose birds with soft blemish-free skin. Because poultry is highly susceptible to bacterial growth, keep poultry well chilled. Place loose poultry in a deep dish and cover loosely, check pre-packed poultry to make sure that the packs are sealed and place on a plate, then store in the coldest part of the refrigerator. Check inside whole birds and remove any giblets. Always wash hands, utensils and surfaces after handling poultry.

When using frozen poultry, the safest way to thaw it is in the refrigerator. Place in a suitable container and leave to defrost: for a 900g–1.3kg/2–3lb bird, allow about 30 hours in the refrigerator, or 8 hours at room temperature; for a 2.25kg/5lb chicken, allow about 48 hours in the refrigerator, or 10 hours at room temperature. Once thawed or partially thawed, it should not be refrozen.

Below (from left to right):
Corn-fed, free-range and
organic chickens are
widely available.

Types of small poultry

Poussin This is the French name for a young chicken that is only four to six weeks old and weighs 350–675g/12oz–1½lb. These are very tender, with little fat, and will serve one or two people. They are ideal for pot-roasting, which gives moist, tender results.

Spring chicken These are sometimes called double poussins and will easily serve two. They are slightly larger birds, between six and ten weeks old, and weigh about 900g/2lb.

Roasting chicken Sometimes known as a roaster, these prime birds are about 12 weeks old. They usually weigh about 1.3kg/3lb but they may be as big as 3kg/6–7lb. The larger the bird, the better its value, because the proportion of meat to bone will be higher. They can be pot-roasted whole or in portions, poached, braised or stewed.

Stewing or boiling chicken Rarely available from supermarkets, these birds are over one year old and tend to be large. Too tough for roasting, they are full of flavour and perfect for the slow cooker as they need slow simmering. Either poach or use for soups and stews.

Guinea fowl These domestic fowl originated from the coast of Guinea in West Africa, hence their name. These birds are about the same size as a spring chicken. The flesh is delicate with a slightly gamey flavour. They can be cooked in the same way as chicken, but because they are quite dry, they respond best to moist cooking such as pot-roasting, braising and stewing.

Cuts of chicken

A wide range of chicken portions are available fresh and frozen and are sold either individually, or in large, more economical packs. They may be sold on or off the bone.

Chicken quarters may be either leg joints or wing joints that have a portion of breast meat attached. The leg joint may be divided into thighs, small well-flavoured dark meat joints, and drumsticks. Both need relatively long cooking in the slow cooker because the meat is compact.

Tender breast portions are entirely white meat; they are sold on or off the bone and may be skinned or unskinned. Portions on the bone have the most flavour when stewed or braised. Boneless chicken breast portions are sometimes referred to as fillets. The very small strips of chicken that can be found under the chicken breast are often sold separately. Supremes are chicken breast portions that include the wingbone, while part-boned breasts still have the short piece of bone leading into the wing and the fine strip of breastbone.

Jointing small poultry

This method of jointing can also be used for game birds, such as pheasant.

1 With the breast uppermost, use a sharp knife to remove the leg between the thigh and carcass. Cut, angling the knife inwards, through the ball and socket joint. Repeat with the other leg.

2 Using poultry shears, cut along the breastbone, between the breast sections. Turn the bird over and cut out the backbone. Using poultry shears, cut off the wing tips at the first joint.

3 Cut each breast section in half, leaving a portion of the breast attached to the wing. Next, cut each leg through the knee joint to separate the thigh and drumstick, making eight portions in all.

TURKEY

These substantial birds have dense meat that is lean and succulent. Fully grown, a turkey can weigh over 9kg/20lb and feed over twenty people. Whole birds won't fit in a slow cooker, but prepared joints and cuts are perfect for slow cooking.

Skinless, boneless breast fillets can be used in many different dishes. Turkey drumsticks can be large enough to provide a meal for three to four people. They can be pot-roasted, but are better braised or stewed until tender. Diced turkey is usually darker meat from the thigh or leg, and is ideal for casseroles and pâtés. Minced (ground) turkey can be used as an alternative to minced beef.

DUCK

Flavourful, juicy and rich, duck is much fattier than chicken or turkey, with a higher proportion of bone to meat. Birds under 2 months old are called ducklings and are slightly leaner and more tender, but with less flavour. Wild duck has a stronger, more gamey taste than farmed duck, but can be cooked in the same way. The slow cooker is unsuitable for cooking whole birds because of their awkward shape and fat content. However, duck breast portions can be used, providing the thick layer of fat is removed. Breast portions weigh about 225g/8oz, making a generous serving for one. Skinned duck portions are ideal for braising, especially in citrus or fruit sauces, which tenderize and flavour.

Jointing a duck

Because ducks have a high proportion of bone to meat, it is better to cut the bird into four portions, dividing an equal amount of meat between them.

1 Place the duck, breast side up, on a board. Using poultry shears, trim off the wing tips at the first joint. Pull back the skin at the neck end and cut out the wishbone. Cut the breast in half from the tail end to the neck.

Above: Turkey is a versatile as well as economical meat.

2 Separate the bird into two halves by cutting along each side of the backbone. Remove the backbone and discard.

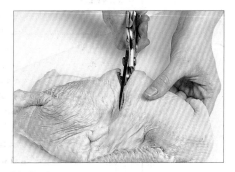

3 Cut each portion in half, sharing the meat as evenly as possible between the four portions.

GOOSE

These large, fatty birds are difficult to rear intensively, so fresh birds are usually only available from the late autumn until Christmas. Goose is much better suited to oven-roasting than cooking gently in the slow cooker.

GAME

Once hard to come by, game is now readily available from the supermarket. Fresh wild game remains seasonal and is only available during the months when hunting is allowed. Many types of game are now farmed and available year-round, while wild game is available frozen. Game can be divided into two types: game birds and furred game, which includes rabbit, hare, wild boar and venison.

Buying and storing

Larger supermarkets and specialist butchers offer a good choice of game when in season and should be able to offer you advice on preparation and cooking. Game birds will not look as perfect as poultry, but check that they are not too damaged. Pheasant should be even in shape with a pleasant gamey aroma. Partridge will have a slightly stronger game smell and soft pale flesh. When buying grouse and quail, look for a moist fresh skin and choose birds with a high proportion of meat to bone.

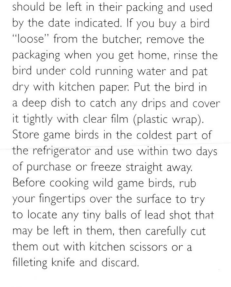

Right: A brace of pheasant.

Below: Tiny quail are often farmed.

Below: Mallard is the most commonly available wild duck.

Birds that are sold in sealed packaging should be left in their packing and used by the date indicated. If you buy a bird "loose" from the butcher, remove the packaging when you get home, rinse the bird under cold running water and pat dry with kitchen paper. Put the bird in a deep dish to catch any drips and cover it tightly with clear film (plastic wrap). Store game birds in the coldest part of the refrigerator and use within two days of purchase or freeze straight away. Before cooking wild game birds, rub your fingertips over the surface to try to locate any tiny balls of lead shot that may be left in them, then carefully cut them out with kitchen scissors or a filleting knife and discard.

Types of game bird

Very young and tender birds are often roasted or spatchcocked and grilled (broiled), but most older game birds benefit from moist cooking techniques, such as pot-roasting, stewing or braising. When pot-roasting dry game birds, such as cock pheasant, wrap rashers (slices) of streaky (fatty) bacon around the bird, then tie in place with string. This will help to baste and flavour the meat.

Below: Pigeon.

Pheasant One of the most plentiful of game birds, these are usually raised on managed estates in a similar manner to free-range farming. Traditionally they were sold in pairs, known as a brace (one male and one female). The tender hen pheasant would be roasted and the cock pheasant hung and stewed. In practice, supermarket pheasants are always young and tender. For the best results, pot-roast or stew pheasants. One bird should serve three or four people.

Grouse Native to Scotland, these birds feed on highland heather, which gives them a rich gamey flavour. They are quite small and

will serve one or two people. Ptarmigan and capercaillie are members of the grouse family, but are considered to have an inferior flavour compared to grouse. Young birds may be pot-roasted, but need to be kept moist with a layer of fat or streaky bacon over the breast. They are good stewed.

Partridge There are two main types: French or red-legged partridge, and the smaller English or grey-legged partridge, which has a better flavour. At their prime (around three months old), they weigh about 450g/1lb and it is usual to serve one per person. Older birds should always be casseroled or braised.

Wild duck These are less fatty than farmed ducks, so smaller ones may be cooked whole in a large slow cooker. Choose inland ducks because those from saltwater areas may have a fishy flavour.

Pigeon Wild and wood pigeon has a strong flavour and can be stewed slowly to tenderize the meat. Another traditional way of cooking an older bird is in a steamed pudding, often with beef steak inside a suet crust. Young pigeon is known as squab. They are reared commercially, although they are usually only available in the spring.

Quail This is now a protected species, so quail on sale will have been farmed. They are tiny, so you will need two per person for a main course. They may be pot-roasted whole.

FURRED GAME

Most game needs to be hung before cooking to tenderize the flesh and develop the flavour. However, this is usually done by the butcher, so the meat is ready for cooking when you buy it.

Game is cooked in the same way as other meats and recipes for similar types of meat are usually interchangeable. For example, wild boar can often be used instead of pork, farmed rabbit instead of chicken, and venison in place of beef in many recipes. Mature game should always be cooked using gentle, moist heat, such as braising and stewing, making it ideal for the slow cooker.

Deer

The word venison was once used to describe the meat of any animal killed for food by hunting. Today, in Britain and Australia, the term venison only refers to the meat from deer, although in North America it also includes meat from the reindeer, moose, caribou, elk and antelope. Venison from deer is a lean, dark, close-textured meat. Much of it is now farmed and is more tender, with a slightly milder flavour, than venison from wild deer. Prime cuts, such as loin and fillet, are best roasted and served rare. Other cuts, such as shin, neck and shoulder, benefit from marinating (red wine and juniper is traditional); they then need long and gentle cooking to tenderize and bring out the flavour of the meat.

Wild boar

Although hunted to extinction in Britain in the 17th century, wild boar is still found in Europe, central Asia and North Africa. The meat is dark-coloured with a strong flavour and little fat, so it benefits from marinades with a little added oil. It can be cooked in exactly the same way as pork, but care must be taken because the meat is dry and can easily become tough. Moist cooking methods work best.

Rabbit and hare

Although these animals belong to the same family, the meat is very different. Rabbit, especially if it has been farmed, is a paler, milder meat, similar to chicken. Hare, or jack rabbit as it is known in the United States, has a very strong, dark gamey flesh. The saddle of both can be roasted, but other cuts are best slowly stewed. Boneless rabbit and hare meat can be used in steamed puddings, terrines and pâtés. Older hares are traditionally jugged (cooked in a casserole set over a pan of simmering water to temper the heat) to give deliciously tender results. Cooking gently in the slow cooker gives similar results.

Above and right: Rabbit saddle is best roasted. Other rabbit cuts should be stewed.

Above and left: Cultivated hare has lean, dark meat and is available whole or in pieces.

Jointing a rabbit

A whole rabbit can be jointed into five pieces or more, depending on its size.

1 To joint a skinned and cleaned rabbit, use a large filleting knife to cut between the ball and socket joint at the top of each thigh to remove the hind legs.

2 Cut the body into three pieces. This will give you five pieces – two forelegs, two hind legs and the saddle.

Above and left: Venison cuts that benefit from long, slow cooking include shin, shoulder and neck (above left to right) and haunch (left).

FISH and SHELLFISH

The slow cooker is great for cooking fish, allowing the subtle flavour to develop slowly and also helping to retain the fish's shape as it cooks. Fish dishes that can be made in the slow cooker include terrines, soups, risottos and pasta dishes, as well as simple steamed and poached fish. The slow cooker is also good for cooking many dishes containing raw and cooked shellfish. However, it is not suitable for cooking live shellfish, such as mussels and lobsters, because these require brief, fast boiling.

Most shellfish benefit from short cooking and should be added towards the end of cooking time, particularly when using pre-cooked shellfish. One exception is squid, which requires either very brief or very long, slow cooking; anything in between gives tough results.

Buying and cooking

Always buy the freshest fish and shellfish available, from a supplier with a high turnover, and prepare and cook it within 24 hours. Fish and shellfish should smell fresh; if it has an unpleasant fishy or ammoniac odour, it is past its best. Most fish and shellfish from the supermarket has already been frozen, so shouldn't be refrozen; check this when you buy.

PREPARING FISH

Fish can be divided into two types: white and oily. These, in turn, can be divided into round and flat fish, which require slightly different preparation and cooking.

Round fish

This group includes white-fleshed fish such as cod, coley and haddock, and oily fish such as salmon and mackerel. They have rounded bodies and eyes on either side of the head. The flesh is usually firm with largish flakes when cooked. Many are too big to be cooked whole in the slow cooker, so need to be sliced into steaks or filleted. A good fishmonger will often do this for you.

I To remove the scales, place the fish on a large sheet of newspaper. Scrape a fish scaler or knife against the skin, working from the tail to the head.

2 Using a filleting knife or thin, sharp knife, slit the fish open along the belly from the gills to the tail vent. Carefully scrape out the innards with a spoon, then rinse well under running water, inside and out. Cut off the head using a sharp knife.

3 To fillet the fish, lay it on its side, tail away from you. Make an incision along the backbone from head to tail, cutting through behind the gills. Starting at the head end, slide the knife between the fillet and bones to release the fillet.

4 To skin the fillet, lay it skin side down. Make a cut at the tail end, cutting through the flesh, but not the skin, so that the fillet can be lifted away slightly. Hold the tail firmly and "saw" the knife between the skin and flesh.

Flat fish

This group includes sole and plaice. Both eyes lie on their upper side and, because they lead an inactive life on the seabed, the flesh tends to be very delicate.

I Place the fish, light side down, on a board. Make a cut down the centre using a sharp filleting knife, following the backbone, then make a second cut round the head.

2 Slide the knife under one fish fillet, inserting the blade between the flesh and bones. Holding the loosened corner, cut the flesh from the bones. Remove the second fillet in the same way, then turn the fish over and repeat.

3 The skins may be removed in the same manner as for round fish.

PREPARING SHELLFISH

You can often ask the fishmonger to prepare shellfish for you, but it is also easy to prepare at home.

Prawns/shrimp

Raw prawns may be cooked in their shells or peeled first. The dark intestinal vein is usually removed.

1 To peel, grip the head between your forefinger and thumb. Holding the body with your other hand, gently pull until the head comes off. Remove the legs and peel the shell from the body. The tail may be pulled away or left on.

2 To remove the dark intestinal vein, make a shallow cut down the centre of the back and pull out the vein using a knife blade or a cocktail stick (toothpick).

Preparing squid

Unlike other shellfish, which have their protective shell on the outside, the shell of the squid is found inside its body.

1 Hold the body of the squid in one hand and the tentacles in the other and gently pull apart. Cut the tentacles away from the head just below the eyes and discard the head.

2 Remove the "quill" and soft innards from the body and discard. Peel off the thin membrane, then rinse the body and tentacles under cold running water.

3 Using a sharp knife, slice the body into rings, or cut it into large pieces and lightly score in a criss-cross pattern.

COOKING FISH

Fish is well suited to simple cooking methods that retain its natural juices. Unlike meat, fish should be removed from the slow cooker as soon as it is done, otherwise it will become dry. It is ready when the flesh is still slightly translucent when eased away from the bone, and flakes easily.

Poaching

This is a good method for cooking large, fairly firm pieces of fish, such as steaks or chunky fillets. It can also be used for small whole fish. Fish stock, wine, water and milk can all be used for poaching.

1 Lightly grease the base of the ceramic cooking pot. Place four 175–225g/6–8oz salmon fillets or similar in the base, leaving space between each one.

2 Pour over 150ml/¼ pint/⅔ cup dry white wine and 300ml/½ pint/1¼ cups of boiling fish stock or water. Add a pinch of salt, 2 black peppercorns, a few slices of onion, 1 bay leaf and a sprig of fresh parsley.

3 Cover the pot with the lid and switch the slow cooker to high. Cook for 45 minutes–1½ hours, or until cooked. Serve with melted butter or a sauce, or leave to cool and serve with salad.

Braising

This method cooks the fish in a small amount of liquid, so that it is partly poached and partly steamed. It is a good technique for delicate flat fish fillets. Rolling the fish fillets helps to protect them during cooking and allows you to add a filling for extra flavour.

1 Pour slightly less than 5mm/¼in white wine, cider or fish stock into the ceramic cooking pot and switch the slow cooker to high. Cover with the lid.

2 Blend 25g/1oz butter with lemon or orange rind, salt and pepper. Place four large, skinned lemon sole fillets on a board and spread each with the butter.

3 Roll up the fillet to enclose the filling and carefully place in the base of the ceramic cooking pot, with the loose end tucked underneath.

4 Sprinkle the fish with 15ml/1 tbsp lemon juice. Cover with the lid and cook for 45 minutes–1½ hours, or until the fish is opaque and cooked. Transfer to serving plates. Stir a little sour cream and chopped fresh parsley, dill or coriander (cilantro) into the cooking juices and spoon over the fish.

VEGETABLES

Cooking vegetables in the slow cooker is a good way to ensure they are tender without being overcooked, which can spoil their texture and subtle flavours.

Onions

An essential ingredient in many slow cooker recipes, they take a long time to cook so are often fried in oil before adding to the slow cooker.

Different types of onion have varying degrees of pungency. Large, yellow onions (often called Spanish or Bermuda onions) are mild. Smaller, white onions, the most common type, have a stronger flavour; red onions are mild and sweet. Leeks are part of the onion family and have a milder flavour than onions; they cook more quickly. Garlic adds

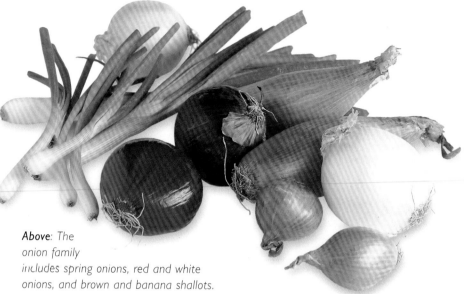

Above: The onion family includes spring onions, red and white onions, and brown and banana shallots.

flavour; the taste it imparts is milder when whole or sliced, and stronger when crushed or chopped. Slow cooking tames the pungency, so you may need to increase the amount in dishes cooked for more than 4 hours. Spring onions (scallions) are usually used raw, but have a delicate flavour when cooked.

Roots and tubers

These vegetables, which include carrots, swedes (rutabagas), turnips, parsnips and potatoes, have a dense, sometimes starchy flesh. They take the longest time to cook in the slow cooker.

Cut roots and tubers into small pieces, no larger than 2.5cm/1in thick, and place in the base of the ceramic cooking pot, which is the hottest part during cooking. The vegetables should be immersed in the cooking liquid to ensure they soften, and to protect those roots and tubers, such as potatoes, that will discolour if exposed to air.

In braised dishes that use only a little liquid, it may be necessary to layer the ingredients. It does not matter if some of the meat on the surface is not covered with cooking liquid, as it will cook in the steam. If the dish contains ingredients that do not require long cooking, such as fish, sauté the root vegetables first.

Mushrooms

These add a deep colour and rich taste to many dishes. They give off a lot of liquid, so if you add extra mushrooms to a recipe, adjust the liquid content.

Button (white), chestnut and flat mushrooms are the most common cultivated types. Button mushrooms have a mild taste; small whole ones are good in casseroles. Flat mushrooms have a stronger flavour and are usually sliced or left whole and stuffed. Chestnut mushrooms have a darker brown skin, firmer texture and a stronger, nuttier taste than buttons. Large ones are known as field (portabello) mushrooms and have a meaty taste.

Field mushrooms, field blewitts, ceps, morels and shiitake mushrooms are wild varieties with intense flavours. Delicate mushrooms, such as oyster and enoki, should be added to the slow cooker near the end of cooking. Dried mushrooms are used to thicken dishes by absorbing liquid. They should be pre-soaked in boiling water for a few minutes before adding, to remove any grit or dirt.

CLEANING LEEKS

Leeks usually need careful cleaning to remove grit and dirt in the leaves.

1 Trim the root and coarse green tops and discard. Remove any damaged or tough outer leaves.

2 Slit the top green part lengthways about a third of the way down. Rinse well under cold running water, separating the layers as you do so.

Above: *Mushrooms have a distinctive taste and meaty texture.*

Pumpkins and squashes

These come in many shapes, sizes and colours. Cooking in the slow cooker helps to develop their flavour and retain their firm texture. They tend to produce a lot of liquid during cooking, so don't add too much extra liquid to braised dishes containing pumpkins or squashes.

Squashes can be divided into two varieties: summer and winter. Winter squashes have a dense, fibrous flesh and include pumpkins and butternut and acorn squashes. They all have sweet-tasting, deep-orange flesh. Summer squashes include patty pans and courgettes (zucchini). They are picked young and have a high water content and delicate flesh that cooks quickly, so be careful not to overcook.

Below (from left): *Butternut, acorn and patty pan squashes make a great addition to slow cooked dishes.*

Shoot vegetables

This category covers a large number of vegetables, which vary widely in appearance and characteristics. Some, such as fennel, chicory and celery, respond well to slow cooking, while others, such as asparagus and globe artichokes, are better cooked using conventional methods.

VEGETABLE FRUITS

Although tomatoes, (bell) peppers and aubergines (eggplant) are all used as vegetables, botanically they are fruits.

Tomatoes

Great for slow cooking, these add a rich colour and flavour to many dishes. They are juicy, so can be used as part of the cooking liquid. Long cooking can make the skins tough and seeds bitter, so these are best removed before cooking.

Sweet peppers

Known as bell peppers in the United States, these come in many colours, including red, orange, yellow, green and purple. Green peppers are the unripe stage of peppers of other colours, such as red. Green peppers tend to lose their colour and become bitter in slow cooked dishes, unless they are cut into very small pieces and added towards the end of cooking.

Aubergines/eggplant

There are many types of aubergine, from large, glossy, dark-purple ones to the small, creamy-white egg-shaped ones that gave rise to the American name "eggplant". Very large aubergines may be slightly bitter, so should be salted after slicing or cubing and left for half an hour, then rinsed well. This process is also useful for drawing out liquid that would dilute the sauce of the dish.

Brassicas and green leafy vegetables

Brassicas, such as broccoli and cauliflower, should be broken or cut into small sprigs to ensure they cook evenly in the slow cooker. When using leafy vegetables, such as cabbage and spinach, shred them very finely and always add to hot liquid so they cook in the shortest possible time to retain their taste and texture.

CANNED AND FROZEN VEGETABLES

These make a useful last-minute addition to many dishes. They are particularly good time-savers because they require no further preparation. Cooked, canned vegetables should be well drained, then simply added 15 minutes before the end of cooking time.

Frozen vegetables, such as peas and corn, should be defrosted first and need a little more cooking. (For speedy defrosting, they can be placed in a strainer under cool running water.) Once added to the slow cooker, they should be cooked for 15–20 minutes.

GRAINS, PASTA and BEANS

Cereal grains, pasta and beans are all very versatile and can be used as a main ingredient or an accompaniment. Classic slow cooker dishes that use grains, pasta and beans as the main ingredient include risottos, pilaffs, lasagne, pasta bakes and bean stews and curries.

RICE

Ordinary long grain rice doesn't cook well in the slow cooker, but easy-cook (converted) rice gives excellent results. Also known as par-boiled rice, it is soaked in water and then steamed under pressure, making it difficult to overcook. The grains remain separate during cooking, so it is particularly good for slow cooking, where the water bubbles very gently, if at all. The dry grains may appear more yellow than normal rice, but this coloration disappears during cooking, and when fully cooked the rice becomes bright white.

TYPES OF EASY-COOK RICE

As well as white, long grain easy-cook (converted) rice, there are several other varieties, all with their own unique cooking properties.

Easy-cook brown rice Also known as easy-cook wholegrain rice, this is the whole rice grain complete with bran. It has a chewier texture and nuttier flavour than white long grain rice, and stands up best of all to long, slow cooking, still holding its shape after several hours on high.

Easy-cook basmati rice Basmati rice is grown in northern India, the Punjab, parts of Pakistan and in the foothills of the Himalayas. It has a unique taste and texture, and the word *basmati* means "fragrant one" in Hindi. Basmati is particularly good in pilafs and for serving with spicy Indian-style dishes.

Easy-cook Italian rice Sometimes labelled easy-cook risotto rice, this rice has short plump grains and a high proportion of starch, which gives a rich, creamy texture to dishes such as risotto.

Making slow cooker rice

A simple savoury rice dish can be made easily in the slow cooker, and makes a good accompaniment for four people.

1 Grease the bottom of the ceramic cooking pot with 15g/½oz/1 tbsp butter, or 15ml/1 tbsp sunflower oil. Sprinkle 4–6 very finely chopped spring onions (scallions) over the butter or oil. Switch the slow cooker to high and leave to cook for 20 minutes.

2 Add 1.5ml/¼ tsp ground turmeric or a pinch of saffron strands and 750ml/1¼ pints/3 cups boiling vegetable stock to the pot. If the stock is unseasoned, add a pinch of salt as well.

3 Sprinkle 300g/10oz/generous 1½ cups easy-cook rice over the stock and stir well. Cover and cook for about 1 hour, or until the rice is tender and the stock has been absorbed. Serve hot, or put into a shallow dish, stir in 30ml/2 tbsp vinaigrette, and serve warm or cold.

Making risotto

A good risotto should be creamy and moist. Cooked conventionally, this is achieved by adding the cooking liquid gradually and stirring constantly. The gentle heat of the slow cooker and the use of easy-cook Italian rice means that the liquid can be added in one go to produce a creamy risotto. This recipe for Risotto alla Milanese serves 3–4 people.

1 Gently fry 1 finely chopped onion in 15g/½oz/1 tbsp butter and 15ml/1 tbsp olive oil in a frying pan until soft. Pour in 120ml/4fl oz/½ cup dry white wine and heat until steaming but not boiling.

2 Transfer the mixture to the ceramic cooking pot and switch the slow cooker to high. Cover with the lid and cook for about 30 minutes, until boiling.

3 Sprinkle 225g/8oz/1¼ cups easy-cook Italian rice and a pinch of saffron strands into the pot. Pour in 750ml/1¼ pints/3 cups boiling stock. Stir well, re-cover and cook for about 45 minutes, stirring once halfway through cooking. The rice should be almost tender and most of the stock absorbed.

4 Turn off the slow cooker. Sprinkle 50g/2oz/¾ cup freshly grated Parmesan cheese into the risotto and stir, then season with freshly ground black pepper.

5 Cover the pot and leave to stand for about 5 minutes to allow the risotto to finish cooking. Taste and adjust the seasoning if necessary, then serve with fine shavings of Parmesan.

COOK'S TIP

This recipe is for the classic Risotto alla Milanese, but the ingredients can be varied to create other risotto dishes. Try stirring pan-fried mushrooms or chopped cooked chicken into the risotto 15 minutes before the end of cooking.

OTHER GRAINS

As well as rice, there are many other grains that can be cooked successfully in a slow cooker. Whole grains, such as barley, quinoa and whole wheat, can be served as an accompaniment instead of rice or potatoes, or as part of a main course. Whole rye grains need to be soaked in cold water overnight before cooking. This is not necessary for most grains, although pre-soaking will shorten the cooking time.

Cooking grains

The cooking times vary from grain to grain; quinoa and millet take the least time, while grains such as barley and rye take much longer. To speed up cooking and enhance the flavour, fry grains in a little oil for 2–3 minutes, before transferring to the slow cooker.

1 Allow about 75g/3oz per person for part of a main course. If the quantity of cooking liquid is not indicated on the packet, place the grains in a measuring jug (cup) to check their volume, then measure three parts boiling water or stock to one part grain (millet is the exception, and needs four parts water).

2 Rinse the grains in a sieve under cold running water, then place in the ceramic cooking pot and pour over the water or stock. Cover and cook on high for 40 minutes–2 hours, or until tender.

PASTA

Both ordinary and easy-cook pastas can be used in the slow cooker. The latter gives the best results, but is not suitable for "all-day cooking"; the final result will be soft and soggy. As a general rule, pasta made from 100 per cent durum wheat holds its shape better than the varieties made with eggs (all'uova). Fresh pasta is not suitable for slow cookers because it requires fast boiling in a large quantity of water. There is a huge range of pasta shapes, and the shape and size will affect cooking times.

"Pre-cooked" lasagne sheets layered with meat or vegetables and white or cheese sauces, and stuffed cannelloni tubes, covered with white or cheese sauce, will take about 2 hours on high, or 1 hour on high followed by 2 hours on low. The time taken will also be affected by the initial temperature of the sauces; the hotter they are to start with, the quicker the pasta will cook.

Large and medium shapes added to almost-cooked casseroles or near-boiling sauces will take 30–45 minutes on high. They will take less time if there is plenty of free cooking liquid, and if the sauce is thin. Wholemeal (whole-wheat) pasta will take 10 minutes longer than white.

Small shapes, such as soup pasta, will take about 20 minutes on high. These can also be used to thicken casseroles or soups towards the end of cooking; the pasta absorbs some of the liquid.

BEANS

The slow cooker was invented for the commercial cooking of baked beans, cooking haricot beans until perfectly tender, while still keeping their shape. The slow cooker is therefore great for cooking all dried beans, peas and lentils.

Cooking beans

Most beans, peas and lentils need to be soaked before cooking, but soaking times depend on the variety and also the age of the beans. Red lentils and split peas need no soaking; most beans should be soaked for at least 6 hours and some, such as chickpeas, for 8–12 hours. Beans should not be left to soak for more than 24 hours. When they are fully soaked, the skin should look plump and smooth.

1 Put the beans in a large bowl, cover with at least twice their volume of cold water and leave to soak.

2 Drain the beans, then rinse under cold running water. Place the pulses in a large pan and cover with cold water. Pour over enough cold water to come about 4cm/1½in above the beans. Bring to the boil and boil rapidly, uncovered, for 10–15 minutes. (All beans, except for lentils and gunga peas, should be boiled fast before being transferred to the slow cooker to destroy toxins.)

3 Remove the pan from the heat and skim off any froth on the surface. Leave to cool for 5 minutes, then transfer the beans and cooking liquid to the ceramic cooking pot. The liquid should cover the pulses by at least 2cm/¾in; if necessary, top up with a little boiling water.

4 Add flavouring ingredients, such as bay leaves or sprigs of thyme, but do not add salt or acidic ingredients, such as tomato juice – these will toughen the beans and prevent them cooking properly. Cover with the lid and cook on high for 1¼–5 hours. (Cooking times vary according to the type of bean: kidney beans take about 1½ hours and soya beans take 4½–5 hours. Canned beans or peas only need to be added to a dish about 30 minutes before the end of cooking time to warm through.)

FRUITS

The gentle simmering of the slow cooker makes it ideal for cooking all kinds of fruit to perfection. It is particularly good for poaching delicate fruits that have a tendency to break up during cooking, including soft fruits, such as currants and rhubarb. It can also be used to make desserts, such as cobblers and crumbles.

PREPARING FRUIT
Many fruits need only simple preparation, such as washing, while others need to be peeled, cored, seeded or stoned (pitted) before they are cooked.

Peeling
Fruits such as apples, pears and peaches should be peeled before cooking.

To peel fruits such as apples and pears, use a vegetable peeler or a small paring knife to pare off the skin in thin strips. Apples can also be peeled in one single, spiral strip.

To peel fruits such as peaches and apricots, loosen the skins first. Make a tiny nick in the skin, then place in a bowl. Pour over boiling water to cover and leave for 20–30 seconds. Lift out using a slotted spoon, rinse under cold water, and the skin should peel off easily.

Coring
Tough cores, pips and stems should be removed from fruit before cooking so that they do not spoil the dish.

When cooking chunks of fruit, first cut the fruit lengthways into quarters. Remove the central core and pips using a small knife, then peel and chop into smaller pieces as required.

When cooking whole fruits (for example, baked apples) you will need a special corer. Place the sharp "blade" of the corer over the stem end of the fruit, press down firmly and twist. The core will come out with the corer.

Removing stones/pits
Hard stones should always be removed from fruit before cooking, since they will become loose as the fruit cooks.

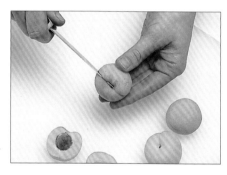

To stone larger fruits such as plums and apricots, cut around the crease in the fruit. Twist the halves apart, then carefully lever out the stone using the point of a small knife.

To stone cherries, it is easiest to use a special cherry stoner. Put the fruit in the stoner, with the end where the stalk was facing upwards. Push the bar into the fruit to eject the stone.

COOKING FRUIT
Fruit can be cooked in all kinds of ways in a slow cooker, which is good for stewing and poaching, and can be used for "baking" as well.

Poaching and stewing
These techniques are slightly different. Poaching cooks fruit in a hot syrup, and is good for pears, stone fruits, and figs. Stewing is used for fruit such as apples, berries and rhubarb.

1 To stew rhubarb, cut 900g/2lb rhubarb into 2.5cm/1in pieces. Put into the ceramic cooking pot with 150–200g/5–7oz/¾–1 cup caster (superfine) sugar, sprinkling it between the layers. Pour over the juice of 1 large orange and 120ml/4fl oz/½ cup water.

2 Switch the slow cooker to high and cook for 1½ hours, or until the rhubarb is tender but still holds its shape. Stir gently halfway through cooking.

Baking
Fruits such as whole apples, halved peaches and figs can be "baked" in the slow cooker, with just a tiny amount of liquid to start the cooking process.

1 To make baked apples, you can use either cooking or eating apples. Keeping the fruits whole, remove the cores, then score the skin around the circumference.

2 Blend together 115g/4oz/½ cup soft light brown sugar and 50g/2oz/¼ cup finely chopped dried fruit and use to fill the apples. Top each with a piece of butter and place in the ceramic pot on a square of foil shaped to form a saucer.

3 Pour 150ml/¼ pint/⅔ cup very hot water around the foil squares. Cover and cook on high for 2–3 hours. If using cooking apples, check frequently and remove as soon as they are tender; if overcooked, they may collapse.

To bake nectarines, figs and oranges, place the halved fruits in the buttered ceramic cooking pot. Sprinkle a little lemon juice and sugar over each one and dot with butter. Pour 75ml/5 tbsp water around the fruit, cover and cook on high for 1½–2 hours, or until tender.

Making compotes

Compotes can be made with a single fruit, or several different types, cooked in a flavoured syrup. They may be served hot or cold, as a dessert or for breakfast. The fruits should be ripe but still firm.

When using a slow cooker, all the fruits can be added at the same time, rather than in order of their cooking time. When using dried fruit, less extra sugar is needed because the fruit is already very sweet.

I Put 200g/7oz/1 cup sugar in the ceramic cooking pot with 300ml/½ pint/ 1¼ cups cold water. Add flavouring ingredients such as lemon rind.

2 Switch the slow cooker to high and heat for about 30 minutes, then stir until the sugar dissolves completely. Cover the cooking pot with the lid and heat for a further 30–45 minutes.

3 Add the fruit to the syrup. This could be 450g/1lb each prepared peaches, apricots and cherries, or 450g/1lb each halved pears, plums and apple slices. Cover and cook for 1–3 hours, or until the fruit is tender. Serve hot or allow to cool and transfer to a bowl before chilling. The compote will keep for several days in the refrigerator.

Making cobblers

Stewed and canned fruit are perfect for making these traditional baked desserts. Adding a little of the juice or syrup with the fruit produces steam and helps the cobbler to rise.

I Lightly grease the ceramic cooking pot with unsalted (sweet) butter. Add the fruit, cover the cooking pot with the lid and switch the slow cooker to high. Canned fruit, such as peaches and berries, should be cooked for about 1 hour until hot and steaming; uncooked fruit, such as apple slices, should be cooked for 2–3 hours until tender.

2 When the fruit is nearly ready, make the cobbler topping. Sift 50g/2oz/½ cup plain (all-purpose) flour, 5ml/1 tsp baking powder and a pinch of salt into a bowl. Rub in 40g/1½oz/3 tbsp butter, then add the finely grated rind of ½ lemon. Stir in 75ml/2½fl oz/⅓ cup milk to make a thick batter and spoon over the fruit. Cover and cook on high for 45 minutes–1 hour, or until a skewer inserted into the topping comes out clean.

Making crumbles

Crumbles made in a slow cooker do not brown in the same way as conventional crumbles, but using brown flour, oats, butter and crunchy sugar and a fairly dry fruit mixture gives similar results.

I Combine prepared fruit such as apple and peach slices with a little sugar and 5ml/1 tsp cornflour (cornstarch). Add 30ml/2 tbsp fruit juice or water and switch the slow cooker to high.

2 Place 75g/3oz/¾ cup wholemeal (whole-wheat) flour and 50g/2oz/½ cup jumbo oats in a mixing bowl. Rub in 75g/ 3oz/6 tbsp butter. Stir in 50g/2oz/¼ cup demerara (raw) sugar, then sprinkle over the fruit. Cover and cook for 3–4 hours, or until the fruit and topping are cooked.

HERBS, SPICES and FLAVOURINGS

The judicious use of flavourings is the key to successful cooking. Some dishes require just a subtle hint, while others need more robust flavourings.

HERBS

While fresh herbs are usually considered superior, for slow cooker dishes dried herbs are often better. Delicate fresh leaves lose their pungency and colour with long cooking, whereas dried herbs release their flavour slowly. As a general rule, fresh herbs should be added about 30 minutes before the end of cooking, or just before serving.

Some herbs dry more successfully than others. Thyme, marjoram, oregano and sage dry very well, while parsley and chives lose their potency and colour; it is better to use these herbs fresh at the end of cooking. Dried herb mixtures are often well flavoured and worth using.

Buy dried herbs from a reliable source with a quick turnover and look for small packets. "Freeze dried" herbs have a good fresh flavour. Store dried herbs in a cool, dark place for 6–9 months. Try to buy fresh herbs on the day you need them. They will keep for several days stored in the refrigerator.

Below: Robustly flavoured rosemary and sage should be used sparingly.

Tender herbs

These herbs have soft, fragile leaves and need careful handling. They should be added in the last few minutes of cooking time, or to the finished dish. Popular tender herbs include pungent basil, which goes well with tomatoes and Mediterranean-style dishes; anise-scented chervil, dill and tarragon, which go well with fish, eggs and cream sauces; strong, refreshing mint; aromatic coriander (cilantro); lovage with its mild taste of celery; and the great all-rounder, parsley.

Robust herbs

These usually have tough, woody stems and pungent leaves and can withstand long cooking. They should be added at the start of slow cooking to extract and mellow their flavour, then removed just before serving. Popular robust herbs include richly flavoured bay leaves, which are used in stocks, casseroles, marinades and some sweet dishes; fragrant, aromatic oregano, marjoram and thyme, which are very good in Mediterranean-style dishes; robust rosemary, which goes well with lamb; pungent sage, which complements pork; and aromatic kaffir lime leaves, which are used in Thai and Malaysian dishes.

SPICES

Warm, fragrant spices are usually added at the beginning of cooking time. However, some may become bitter if cooked for many hours, and should be added partway through cooking. Most spices are better used whole, rather than ground, in slow cooker dishes. Store spices in a cool, dark place and check the sell-by date before using; they lose their taste and aroma with age. Whole spices will keep for up to 1 year; ground spices start to lose their pungency after about 6 months.

Left: Delicate dill has a mild aniseed flavour that goes well with fish.

BOUQUET GARNI

This simple bunch of herbs is a classic flavouring and is used in soups, casseroles and sauces.

Using a long piece of string, tie together a bay leaf with sprigs of parsley and thyme. Add to the slow cooker and tie the string to the handle for easy removal.

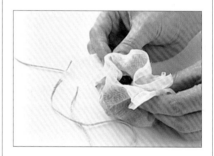

Alternatively, place the herbs in a square of muslin (cheesecloth) and tie into a loose bag. Flavourings such as peppercorns can also be added.

Hot spices

Many spices add heat to dishes – some give just a hint of warmth, others a fierce heat. The main hot spices are chilli, ginger, pepper and mustard.

There are more than 200 types of chilli, with varying shape, size, colour and potency. They can be bought fresh, dried, flaked or ground. Chilli powder may be hot or mild – from red hot cayenne pepper to mild, sweet paprika. There are also chilli sauces, such as Tabasco or Thai chilli sauce. All chillies and chilli products can become bitter with long cooking and should be added partway through cooking.

Sweet, peppery ginger is used in both sweet and savoury dishes and is available fresh, dried, ground and preserved in syrup. Its close relative, galangal, is used in many South-east Asian dishes. Warm, spicy fresh turmeric looks similar to fresh root ginger and is used in curries.

Black, white and green peppercorns add a peppery bite to dishes. Black are the most aromatic. Black, brown and white mustard seeds have a much more pungent aroma and kick, with the black seeds being the hottest. The heat diminishes with cooking, so add towards the end of cooking time.

Fragrant spices
Some plants are grown for their fragrant, aromatic seeds. These are sold whole and ground. Long, slow cooking softens the whole seeds and releases their taste. Popular seed spices include warm, aromatic cumin and coriander, which are used in Indian, North African and Middle Eastern dishes; pungent caraway seeds, which feature in many European dishes, especially pork- and cabbage-based ones, as well as baked recipes such as rye bread and sweet seed cake; and poppy seeds, which are often used in desserts in eastern Europe, and are also a popular topping for crusty bread. Other fragrant spices include warming allspice, cinnamon, cassia and nutmeg; aromatic cardamom pods; pungent cloves; scented star anise; vanilla, which is mainly used in sweet dishes; gin-scented juniper berries, which go well with pork, game and cabbage; delicate, bitter-sweet saffron, which is often used in rice and fish dishes; and sour tamarind, which is widely used in Indian and South-east Asian cooking.

Above: There are many different varieties of chilli.

Spice mixtures
As well as individual spices, there are a number of ground spice mixes that are widely used in both sweet and savoury dishes. Popular mixes include mixed spice (apple pie spice), which is used in cakes and desserts; Chinese five-spice powder, which is used in many savoury Chinese and Asian dishes; garam masala, a popular Indian spice mix that is added towards the end of cooking; and a wide variety of curry powders that vary in strength from mild to very hot. Jars of curry paste are also available.

OTHER FLAVOURINGS
As well as herbs and spices, there are many other flavourings that can be used to enliven dishes – ranging from pungent sauces to delicate flower waters.

Savoury sauces
There are many savoury sauces that can be used to boost the flavour of dishes. They are strongly flavoured and often salty, so usually only a splash or two is required. Mushroom ketchup and Worcestershire sauce can add a rich, rounded flavour to stews and casseroles. Dark and light soy sauce and other soy-based sauces, such as hoisin, are good in Asian-style braised dishes and soups. Fermented fish sauces are common in many cuisines and include anchovy sauce, oyster sauce and nam pla (Thai fish sauce). They should be added at the beginning of cooking.

Sweet essences/extracts
These have a rich, fragrant aroma and are usually used to flavour sweet dishes. You only need a little, sometimes just a few drops, to flavour a whole dish. Look for the real thing, and avoid artificial flavourings. Almond and vanilla essence (extract) are used to flavour cakes and desserts. Orange flower water and rose water have a delicate fragrance and should be added towards the end of cooking for the best flavour.

Alcohol
Because of the gentle heat, alcohol evaporates more slowly in a slow cooker, resulting in a stronger flavour. When adapting conventional recipes, the amount of alcohol should be reduced slightly. Beer, cider and wine can be used in marinades and casseroles. Fortified wines, such as sherry, port, Marsala and Madeira, can be used to enrich both sweet and savoury dishes; a few spoonfuls should be added towards the end of cooking. Colourless fruit spirits, such as kirsch, and sweet liqueurs, such as amaretto, can be used to flavour desserts and sweet dishes.

GRINDING SPICES
Where ground spices are called for in a recipe, it is better to use whole spices and grind them yourself.

1 Dry-fry whole spices in a heavy frying pan, shaking the pan over a medium-high heat for 1–2 minutes until the aroma is released.

2 Place the spices in a mortar and grind to a powder. To grind a larger quantity of spices, it is easier to use an electric spice grinder or a coffee grinder used solely for the purpose.

BASIC TECHNIQUES: MAKING STOCK

A good stock forms the foundation of many dishes, from simple soups and classic sauces to warming casseroles and pot-roasts. Although ready-made stocks are available from supermarkets, making your own is easy and inexpensive. Most butchers and fishmongers will supply meat and fish bones and trimmings.

Making stock in a large pan on the stovetop is a simple process, but using a slow cooker is even easier because it can be left to bubble unattended for hours. A good stock must be simmered gently (rapid boiling will make it go cloudy) so the slow cooker comes into its own, keeping the stock at a bare simmer.

There are two types of stock: brown stock, where the bones and vegetables are roasted in the oven first, and white stock, where ingredients are only boiled. Clean vegetable peelings, celery leaves and the stalks from fresh herbs are useful additions, providing extra flavour.

Always start making a stock with cold water; ideally this and any vegetables should be at room temperature. Use whole peppercorns because long cooking makes ground pepper taste bitter. If you make stock without salt, it can be used in dishes that include salty ingredients, such as smoked meats and fish, and as a base for reduced sauces.

Below: The ingredients used for stock can be varied according to what is available.

A good stock should be beautifully clear. Fat and other impurities will make it cloudy, so it is important to skim these off as the stock comes to simmering point, and at least once during cooking. Strain the stock through a sieve placed over a bowl and leave to drip slowly, rather than squeezing the vegetables, which will spoil the clarity.

For the following recipes, you will need a slow cooker with a capacity of at least 3.5 litres/6 pints/10¼ cups. If your slow cooker is too small, the recipes can be halved, but the cooking times remain the same.

Basic meat stock

Used for meat dishes, such as casseroles, and as a base for light soups, basic meat stock is traditionally made from veal bones. Beef bones will also make a good stock but with a stronger flavour. Lamb bones may also be used, but this stock can only be used for lamb dishes. Some recipes include lean stewing meat, such as shin of beef, which gives a much meatier flavour. For this option, you will need 450g/1lb each bones and meat.

MAKES ABOUT 1.2 LITRES/2 PINTS/5 CUPS

675g/1½lb beef or veal bones
1 onion, unpeeled and quartered
1 carrot, sliced
1 stick celery, sliced
6 black peppercorns
1 fresh bouquet garni
about 1.2 litres/2 pints/5 cups cold water

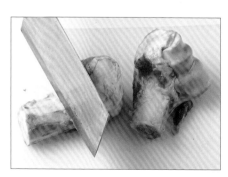

1 Using a meat cleaver, chop any large bones, so that they will fit into the slow cooker. (Cutting the bones into pieces will increase the flavour of the stock.)

2 Place the vegetables in the ceramic cooking pot. Add the peppercorns and bouquet garni, then place the bones on top, packing them tightly so that they fit in a single layer. Pour over the water, adding a little more, if necessary, to cover the bones, but leaving a space of at least 4cm/1½in between the water and the top of the pot. Cover and cook on high or auto for 2 hours.

3 Using a slotted spoon, skim off any scum and turn the temperature to low or leave on auto and cook for 5 hours.

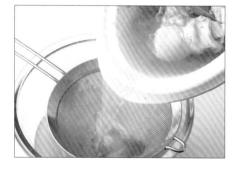

4 Strain the stock through a fine strainer and leave to cool. This should be done quickly, ideally over a bowl of iced water.

5 Chill the stock for at least 4 hours, then remove the fat from the surface.

Brown meat stock

This stock is used as the base for classic beef consommé and other clear soups such as French onion soup. It also adds depth to the colour and flavour of casseroles and braised meat dishes. The secret to the stock's rich colour and flavour lies in the way the onion and bones are caramelized before simmering. However, take care not to let them burn, or the final stock will taste bitter.

MAKES ABOUT 1.2 LITRES/2 PINTS/5 CUPS

675g/1½lb beef or veal bones
1 onion, unpeeled and quartered
1 carrot, sliced
1 stick celery, sliced
6 black peppercorns
1 fresh bouquet garni
about 1.2 litres/2 pints/5 cups cold water

1 Preheat the oven to 220°C/425°F/ Gas 7. Using a meat cleaver, chop up the large bones, then place in a large, heavy roasting pan. Roast for 15 minutes, turning several times during cooking.

2 Add the vegetables to the pan and cook for 15 minutes more, until the bones are well browned and the vegetables lightly tinged with colour.

3 Transfer the bones and vegetables to the slow cooker, adding the peppercorns and bouquet garni. Pour in enough water to just cover, allowing a space of at least 4cm/1½in between the water and the top of the cooking pot. Cover with the lid and cook on high or auto for 2 hours.

4 Using a slotted spoon, skim off any scum, then reduce the temperature to low or leave on auto. Cook for 4 hours.

5 Strain the stock through a fine strainer into a bowl and cool quickly. Cover and chill or freeze. Remove the fat from the surface of the stock before using.

STORING STOCK

Fresh stock should be covered and stored in the refrigerator as soon as it is cool, then used within 3 days. If it will not be needed in this time, freeze it in small quantities – 300ml/ ½ pint/1¼ cups is ideal. Line square-sided containers with freezer bags, leaving plenty overhanging the sides. Pour the measured stock into the bags, then freeze until solid. Remove the bags of stock, seal, label and stack the blocks in the freezer.

White poultry stock

Raw poultry bones, chicken wings or a cooked poultry carcass can be used to make this stock. It makes an excellent base for soups, white sauces and for braising or stewing white meats. Including the onion skins does not add a great deal of extra flavour, but gives the stock a lovely, rich golden colour.

MAKES ABOUT 1 LITRE/1¾ PINTS/4 CUPS

1 fresh or cooked poultry carcass
1 onion, unpeeled and roughly chopped
1 leek, roughly chopped
1 celery stick, sliced
1 carrot, sliced
6 white peppercorns
2 sprigs fresh thyme
2 bay leaves
about 1 litre/1¾ pints/4 cups cold water

1 Using poultry shears, cut the carcass into pieces, so that they will fit into the slow cooker. (This will also help to extract the flavour from the bones.)

2 Place the chopped onion, leek, celery and carrot in the base of the ceramic cooking pot. Sprinkle over the peppercorns, then add the herbs and top with the chopped poultry carcass.

3 Pour over the water, adding a little more to cover the chicken carcass, if necessary, but leaving a space of at least 4cm/1½in between the water and the top of the ceramic cooking pot. Cover the pot with the lid, then cook on high or auto for 2 hours.

4 Using a slotted spoon, skim off any scum that has risen to the surface of the stock. Reduce the temperature to low or leave on auto, re-cover and cook for a further 3–4 hours.

5 Strain the stock through a fine strainer into a bowl and cool quickly, ideally over a bowl of iced water.

6 Cover the stock and store in the refrigerator, or freeze. Before using, remove the fat that has risen to the surface of the stock.

TURKEY GIBLET STOCK
This stock can be made in exactly the same way as white poultry stock. Use the giblets (including the liver) and neck of the turkey in place of the poultry carcass and pour over 900ml/1½ pints/3¾ cups water.

Fish Stock
This light broth can be used as the base for delicate fish soups and hearty stews, as well as for poaching. It is the quickest and most easily made of all stocks.

Unlike other stocks, fish stock should not be simmered for very long, otherwise it will become bitter. Once the stock has come to simmering point (which will take about 1 hour), it should be kept at a bare simmer for no more than 1 hour.

Use only the bones of white fish such as sole and plaice. (The bones of oily fish such as mackerel are unsuitable.) Heads may be added, but the eyes and gills should be removed because these will spoil the final flavour. You can also use prawn (shrimp) shells. The vegetables should be sliced finely to extract as much flavour as possible during cooking. To make a stock with a richer flavour, you can replace about 150ml/¼ pint/⅔ cup of the water with dry white wine.

MAKES ABOUT 900ML/1½ PINTS/3¾ CUPS

900g/2lb fish bones and trimmings
2 carrots, finely sliced
1 onion, peeled and sliced
6 white peppercorns
1 bouquet garni
900ml/1½ pints/3¾ cups water

1 Rinse the fish bones and trimmings well under cold water and cut any larger bones or pieces into several chunks so that they will easily fit inside the ceramic cooking pot.

2 Arrange the vegetables in the base of the cooking pot. Sprinkle over the peppercorns, add the bouquet garni and place the fish bones on top.

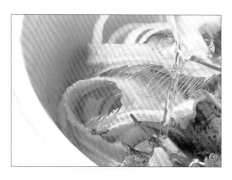

3 Pour the cold water into the pot, adding a little more to cover the bones, if necessary, but leaving a space of at least 4cm/1½in between the water and the top of the cooking pot. Cover with the lid, then cook on high or auto for 1 hour until simmering.

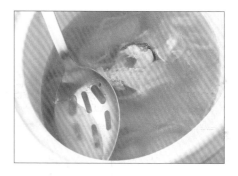

4 Using a slotted spoon, skim off any scum that has risen to the surface. Reduce the temperature to low or leave on auto, re-cover and cook for 1 hour. (Do not cook for longer than this.)

5 Using a fine sieve – or a course sieve lined with muslin (cheesecloth) that has been briefly held under running water – pour the stock into a bowl, then cool quickly, ideally in a bowl of iced water. Cover with clear film (plastic wrap) and store in the refrigerator, or freeze.

Vegetable stock

You can vary the vegetables used in this recipe, but be sure to wash them well and chop fairly small. Strong-tasting vegetables, such as turnips and parsnips, should be used in small quantities; their flavour will dominate otherwise. Starchy vegetables, such as potatoes, should be avoided; they will make the stock cloudy.

MAKES ABOUT 1.5 LITRES/2½ PINTS/ 6¼ CUPS

1 large onion, left unpeeled
   and chopped
1 leek, roughly chopped
2 carrots, thinly sliced
1 celery stick, thinly sliced
2 bay leaves
1 sprig fresh thyme
a few fresh parsley stalks
6 white peppercorns
about 1.5 litres/2½ pints/6¼ cups water

1 Put the vegetables, herbs and peppercorns in the ceramic cooking pot and pour over the water. Cover and cook on high or auto for 2 hours.

2 Using a slotted spoon, skim off any scum. Reduce the temperature to low, or leave on auto, and cook for 2 hours.

3 Strain the stock through a fine sieve into a bowl and leave to cool. Cover and store in the refrigerator, or freeze.

Removing fat

Before using stock, the fat should be removed. The easiest way to do this is by cooling, then chilling the stock.

Pour the stock into a bowl, cover and leave undisturbed in the refrigerator for at least 4 hours, or overnight. The fat will rise to the surface, setting in visible globules or a single layer if there is a lot of fat in the stock. Simply lift the fat from the top, or scoop off with a spoon.

1 If you don't have time to let the stock cool, let it settle for a few minutes, then skim off as much fat as possible, using a slotted spoon.

2 Next, draw a sheet of absorbent kitchen paper across the top to soak up any remaining surface fat. You may need to use two or three pieces of paper to remove the fat completely.

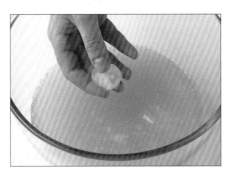

Another way to remove the fat is to leave the stock to cool, then lower several ice cubes into it. Gently move the ice cubes around for a few seconds, then remove. The fat will solidify and cling to the ice cubes, making it easy to remove. (This method will only work if the stock is cool.)

Reducing stocks

After straining and removing the fat from stock, it can be concentrated by returning it to the slow cooker and cooking uncovered on high for several hours to allow some of the water to evaporate. However, if you need a very concentrated stock, for a reduced sauce for example, the slow cooker is not suitable. To make very concentrated stocks, pour the stock into a pan and boil rapidly on the stovetop.

READY-MADE STOCKS

If you do not have time to make your own stock, cartons of fresh stock can be found in the chiller cabinets of many supermarkets. These make a good substitute. Good-quality bouillon powders and liquid stocks may also be used, but take care with stock cubes because they are often strongly flavoured and high in salt. Make them only in the recommended strength and use in robustly flavoured dishes.

MAKING SOUPS

Although many slow cooker soup recipes have lengthy cooking times, the actual preparation time for most is minimal, and they can then be left simmering on a low setting all day or overnight. Most soups benefit from long, gentle cooking, so there is no need to worry if they are left for a little longer than intended.

A good home-made stock forms the base of many soups so it is well worth making large batches of stock and freezing it in convenient quantities. Alternatively, use good-quality ready-made stock from the supermarket.

There are two basic techniques for making slow cooker soups. The easiest is to place the prepared ingredients in the ceramic cooking pot with either cold or near-boiling stock. This produces a fresh-flavoured soup with a low fat content and is a good method for vegetable soups. However, it is less suitable for recipes containing onions, which take a long time to soften. The second, more usual, method is to sauté or fry onions, other vegetables and/or meat in a frying pan before placing in the cooking pot. In some recipes, vegetables are simply softened, but in others they may be lightly browned, giving a richer flavour and deeper colour.

Mixed vegetable soup

Almost any vegetable can be made into soup, but for the best results, use the freshest, seasonal ingredients.

SERVES 4–6

675g/1½lb mixed vegetables, such as
    carrots, celery, parsnips, potatoes
25g/1oz/2 tbsp butter
1 onion, finely chopped
5ml/1 tsp dried mixed herbs
900ml/1½ pints/3¾ cups near-boiling
    vegetable stock
150ml/¼ pint/⅔ cup milk or single
    (light) cream (optional)
salt and ground black pepper

1 Prepare the mixed vegetables, then cut them into 5mm/¼in slices, sticks or dice to ensure that they cook evenly and within the recommended time.

2 Melt the butter in a frying pan, add the onion and fry gently, stirring frequently, for 10 minutes, until softened, but not coloured.

3 Add the chopped vegetables to the pan and fry for 2–3 minutes. Transfer the vegetables to the ceramic cooking pot and switch the slow cooker to low.

4 Sprinkle over the dried mixed herbs, then pour in the stock. If you are using vegetables with a high water content, such as courgettes (zucchini) or squash, reduce the quantity of liquid. Others, such as potatoes and dried vegetables, soak up cooking juices, so add a little more liquid to compensate. (Bear in mind that it is easier to dilute the soup at the end of cooking, than to try to thicken a watery soup.)

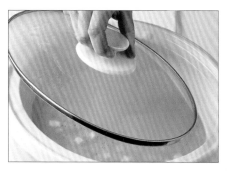

5 Make sure that there is a gap of at least 2cm/¾in between the liquid and the top of the slow cooker, then cover with the lid and cook for 7–12 hours, or until the vegetables are tender.

6 If using milk or cream, stir this in and cook for a further 30 minutes to bring the soup back to boiling point. (Do not heat for longer than this because long heating may cause the soup to separate.) Season to taste, then serve.

ADAPTING SOUP RECIPES

Use this simple mixed vegetable soup recipe as a guide for making other soups. If you want to add meat or poultry to the soup, add it to the ceramic cooking pot at the start of cooking and cook on high for at least 1 hour before reducing the heat to low. If you want to use fresh rather than dried herbs, stir in twice the quantity at the end of cooking time. Rather than using plain stock, use a mixture of stock and tomato juice, or a moderate amount of white wine or cider. Instead of stirring in cream, try adding crème fraîche instead.

Above: *Using a hand blender is one of the easiest ways to make smooth soups, but be sure to keep the blade submerged in the soup to avoid spattering.*

Puréeing soups

A few ladlefuls of soup can be puréed, then stirred back into the remaining soup to thicken it, or the entire soup can be puréed to make a wonderfully smooth, velvety soup. When making chilled puréed soup, it is best to adjust the consistency after chilling because the soup will thicken considerably as it cools.

The simplest way to make puréed soup is using a hand-held blender. It can be puréed while still in the slow cooker, and will not need reheating. You can also use a food processor or blender, but do not over-fill it because it may flood over the top. Most soups will need to be processed in two or more batches and, unless being served cold, will need to be reheated in the slow cooker or in a pan on the stovetop.

Soft vegetable soups can be puréed by hand. Press the mixture through a fine stainless steel or plastic sieve, using a wooden "mushroom" or a large spoon. Alternatively, press the vegetables through a mouli-légumes, then stir in the cooking liquid. The soup will need to be reheated if serving hot.

Thickening soups

There are several ways to thicken soups. Cornflour (cornstarch) or arrowroot are probably the simplest. They can be blended with a little cold water to make a smooth paste, then stirred or whisked into the hot soup. Cornflour will thicken boiling liquid instantly, but takes about 10 minutes to lose its raw flavour. Arrowroot thickens as soon as it reaches boiling point, but will become slightly thinner with prolonged cooking, so add in the last few minutes of cooking.

Plain (all-purpose) flour can be sprinkled over fried onions before stirring in the stock, or blended with an equal quantity of softened butter or double (heavy) cream and whisked into the finished soup a little a time, cooking for a few minutes to thicken. Allow the soup to cook for at least 5 minutes to avoid a raw flour flavour.

Beaten eggs, egg yolks or a mixture of eggs and cream can be used to thicken and enrich smooth soups. Always turn off the heat and allow the soup to cool slightly before whisking in the egg mixture, otherwise it may curdle.

Breadcrumbs are sometimes used to thicken rustic and chilled soups. The breadcrumbs are stirred into the finished soup to soak up and thicken the liquid.

Garnishing soups

Adding a pretty garnish gives the final flourish as you serve soup, and can be as simple or complex as you like. A swirl of cream, crème fraîche or yogurt, followed by a sprinkling of paprika or ground black pepper, can look great with smooth soups. Fresh chopped herbs make another simple but stylish garnish, adding colour, flavour and texture. Use strong herbs, such as sage and rosemary, in moderation.

For a richly flavoured garnish, try adding a spoonful or swirl of pesto. It works especially well with Italian and Mediterranean soups. Grated, shaved or crumbled cheeses also work well and are particularly good with vegetable and bean soups. Strongly flavoured cheeses, such as Parmesan, Cheddar or a crumbly cheese, such as Stilton, are ideal.

To add more substance, flavour and texture to soups, try sprinkling over croûtons or fried breadcrumbs. These are a classic soup garnish and they add a crunchy texture that works with both smooth and chunky soups. To make croûtons, cut thick slices of day-old bread (any type will do) into cubes. Shallow-fry in hot olive oil, turning them continuously, so that the cubes brown evenly, then drain on kitchen paper. Fried breadcrumbs can be made in the same way, but need less cooking time. To oven-bake croûtons, toss them in a little oil, then bake in a shallow roasting pan at 200°C/400°F/Gas 6 for 12–15 minutes.

Grilled cheesy croûtes are the classic topping for French onion soup and can make a dramatic impact floating on top of a bowl of steaming hot soup. Simply rub thin slices of day-old baguette with peeled garlic cloves, then lightly toast both sides under a hot grill (broiler). Sprinkle one side with grated Cheddar or Parmesan cheese, or sliced goat's cheese, and put under a hot grill until melted. Float one or two croûtes on top of the soup just before serving.

Below: *Crispy croûtes coated in melted, bubbling cheese make an impressive garnish for a simple blended soup.*

MAKING MARINADES

Marinating tenderizes and flavours meat, poultry, game, fish and even vegetables and cheese. Although tenderizing may not be necessary when using a slow cooker, it is worth doing for the flavour. There are three basic types of marinade: moist, dry and paste. Always use a non-metallic dish for marinating.

Basic moist marinade

Moist marinades are usually made with oil and vinegar, or other acidic ingredients, such as wine, fruit juice or yogurt. They add moisture as well as flavour.

Red meat, poultry and game can be marinated for up to 2 hours at room temperature, or up to 24 hours in the refrigerator; small pieces of meat, such as steaks, chops and cutlets, should be marinated for no more than 2 hours at room temperature, or 12 hours in the refrigerator; whole fish, fish fillets and steaks should be marinated for up to 30 minutes at room temperature, or 2 hours in the refrigerator; vegetables need 30 minutes at room temperature, or 2 hours in the refrigerator; cheeses and tofu can be marinated for 1 hour at room temperature, or about 8 hours in the refrigerator.

SUFFICIENT FOR 900G/2LB MEAT OR FISH OR 675G/1½LB VEGETABLES

90ml/6 tbsp olive oil
15–30ml/1–2 tbsp cider vinegar
1 garlic clove, crushed
5ml/1 tsp dried thyme
2.5ml/½ tsp crushed peppercorns

1 Combine all the ingredients, using 15ml/1 tbsp vinegar for fish and 30ml/2 tbsp vinegar for meat or vegetables.

2 If you are marinating meat or fish with skin, make several shallow slashes in each piece, then place in a shallow dish.

3 Drizzle or brush the marinade over the food, making sure the pieces are completely covered, then leave to marinate, turning the pieces regularly.

Other moist marinades

You can make several other marinades, using the same techniques and timings as for the basic moist marinade.

Spicy yogurt marinade: Combine 175ml/6fl oz/1 cup plain yogurt, 2 crushed garlic cloves, 2.5ml/½ tsp each ground cumin and cinnamon and crushed black peppercorns, a pinch each of ground ginger, ground cloves, cayenne pepper and salt. Use for chicken, lamb and fish.

Hoisin marinade: Combine 175ml/6fl oz/1 cup hoisin sauce, 30ml/2 tbsp each sesame oil, dry sherry and rice vinegar, 4 finely chopped garlic cloves, 2.5ml/½ tsp soft light brown sugar, 1.5ml/¼ tsp five-spice powder. Use this Chinese marinade for chops and chicken pieces.

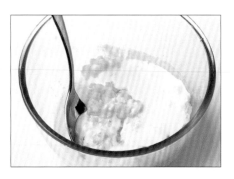

Coconut and pineapple: Blend ¼ peeled, chopped pineapple, juice of ½ lime and 150ml/¼ pint/⅔ cup coconut milk in a food processor. Use for chicken and pork.

Thai: Soak 30ml/2 tbsp tamarind pulp in 45ml/3 tbsp boiling water until softened, then press through a fine sieve into a pan. Finely chop 1 lemon grass stalk, 2.5cm/1in piece fresh galangal or ginger, 2 shallots, 2 garlic cloves, 2 seeded green chillies and 2 kaffir lime leaves and place in a blender with 30ml/2 tbsp each groundnut (peanut) oil and dark soy sauce. Blend to a paste and add to the pan. Bring to the boil, then leave to cool. Use for beef, pork or chicken.

Wine: Combine 75ml/5 tbsp wine, 30ml/2 tbsp olive oil, 2 finely chopped shallots, a pinch of dried herbs or 10ml/2 tsp chopped fresh herbs, such as rosemary. Use red wine for red meat and duck, and white wine for chicken and fish.

Basic dry marinade

Also known as dry rubs, these herb and spice mixtures are rubbed into food shortly before cooking. They are used purely for flavouring and so are best used on fattier pieces of meat, oily fish, or for braised dishes. You can vary the flavour by using different spices, such as cardamom, dry-roasted cumin seeds or a little chilli powder, or try a dried herb mixture with some grated citrus rind.

SUFFICIENT FOR 900G/2LB MEAT OR FISH

15ml/1 tbsp dried thyme
15ml/1 tbsp dried oregano
15ml/1 tbsp garlic granules
15ml/1 tbsp ground cumin
15ml/1 tbsp ground paprika
2.5ml/½ tsp cayenne pepper
2.5ml/½ tsp ground black pepper

1 Combine the ingredients in a bowl, then transfer the mixture to a shallow dish and spread out in an even layer.

2 Press each piece of meat or fish into the mixture to coat evenly, then gently shake off any excess. Arrange on a dish, cover with clear film (plastic wrap) and leave to marinate at room temperature for 30 minutes, or use immediately.

Paste marinades

Because these coat the food, it should be cooked above the level of the liquid – such as on a bed of vegetables.

Herb paste: Heat 50g/2oz/¼ cup butter in a frying pan and gently fry 115g/4oz finely chopped shallots and 1.5ml/¼ tsp fennel seeds until the shallots are soft. Remove from the heat and stir in 2.5cm/1in piece grated fresh ginger, 30ml/2 tbsp each chopped fresh dill and parsley and 15ml/1 tbsp finely chopped capers. Stir in 15–30ml/1–2 tbsp sunflower oil to make a paste. Spread over chicken pieces or tuck under the skin, or use to fill the cavity of whole fish. Marinate for up to 1 hour at room temperature, or cook straight away. Use for food with a short cooking time.

Mexican chilli paste: Combine the finely grated rind of 1 lime, 4 crushed garlic cloves, 30ml/2 tbsp mild chilli powder, 15ml/1 tbsp ground paprika, 5ml/1 tsp ground cumin, 2.5ml/½ tsp dried oregano and a pinch each of ground cinnamon and salt. Stir in 15ml/1 tbsp olive oil and enough lime juice to make into a paste. Use for chicken and pork. Marinate for up to 1 hour at room temperature, or cook straight away.

Tandoori paste: Mix together 30ml/ 2 tbsp each ground coriander, cumin and garlic powder, 15ml/1 tbsp each paprika and ground ginger and 10ml/2 tsp each ground turmeric and chilli powder with enough groundnut (peanut) oil to make a paste. Use for lamb, beef, chicken and oily fish. Marinate for up to 2 hours at room temperature, or cover and leave overnight in the refrigerator. Scrape off the excess paste before cooking.

Fruit marinades

Certain fruits contain enzymes that soften the fibres of meat and tougher seafood, such as squid. Papaya, pineapple and kiwi fruit all contain papain, which breaks down protein and is used in commercial tenderizers. Add a little of the juice to a marinade, or slice the fruit and place on top of the meat or fish and leave for no longer than 15 minutes.

MARINATING TIPS

• The thicker a piece of food is, the longer it will need to marinate.
• When marinating meats such as game and white fish that can become dry during cooking, choose marinades containing less vinegar, wine or fruit juice. These are suitable for fattier meats, such as lamb, and oily fish.
• During humid weather or in a warm kitchen, it is safer to marinate meat and fish in the refrigerator. In cooler weather, or for short marinating times, it is safe to leave the food at room temperature.
• As a general rule, dry herbs are better than fresh for marinades. When using fresh woody herbs, such as rosemary and thyme, crush the leaves to release their aroma.
• If you are frying or grilling (broiling) marinated food before adding it to the slow cooker, pat it dry on kitchen paper first.
• Avoid adding salt to marinades; this will draw moisture from the food. If you want to season with salt, do so after marinating.

MAKING STEWS and CASSEROLES

The slow cooker's gentle, constant heat makes it perfect for making stews and casseroles. The lengthy cooking allows all cuts of meat to become tender and succulent, and even the toughest pieces can be turned into a flavoursome meal.

Stews, casseroles, carbonnades, hot-pots and navarins are all names for what is, essentially, the same type of dish – meat and/or vegetables cooked in liquid in a cooking pot. Originally, the word stew described such dishes cooked on the stovetop, while casserole described dishes cooked in the oven, but now the names are largely interchangeable.

Choosing the right cut

Ideal meats for slow cooking are the cheaper cuts, such as brisket, chuck steak, blade-bone, shank and knuckle. These cuts come from the part of the animal (usually the front) that has worked hardest, so have a looser texture and a good marbling of fat. During cooking, the connective tissues and fat dissolve to create a rich gravy and the fibres open up and allow moisture to penetrate, making them juicy. These cuts also have far greater flavour than very lean ones.

More expensive cuts of meat, such as fine-grained and densely-textured sirloin steak and pork fillet, are delicious when cooked to rare or medium by quick-frying or grilling (broiling). However, they are less suitable for slow cooking because the tightness of the fibres prevents them absorbing the liquid around them. This means that although they become tender when cooked in a slow cooker, the final stew will lack succulence and flavour.

Cutting meat into cubes

Tougher cuts of meat, such as stewing steak, cook more evenly and quickly if they are cut into small, even-size cubes; 2.5cm/1in is ideal. They should be slightly larger than the vegetables being cooked in the stew because these will take a little longer to cook than the meat. Although excess fat should be removed, some marbling is useful for keeping the meat moist. Any excess fat can be skimmed off after cooking.

1 Trim the meat, cutting off the excess fat and any gristle, sinew or membranes while it is in one piece.

2 Using a large sharp knife, cut the meat across the grain into 2.5cm/1in thick slices. These slices can be used for stews and casseroles. Cutting across the grain makes the fibres shorter so that the meat is more tender.

3 To cut the meat into cubes, first cut the slices lengthways into thick strips. Remove any fat or gristle as you go.

4 Cut each strip crossways into 2.5cm/1in cubes. (When preparing meats such as shoulder of lamb, it may not be possible to cut into perfect cubes. Simply cut into evenly-sized pieces, removing any fat or gristle as you go.)

Preparing chops

These are usually sold ready-prepared and fairly lean, but it is usually worth trimming a little before cooking. This will help them cook, look and taste better.

1 Using sharp kitchen scissors or a sharp knife, remove the excess fat, cutting around the contours of the chop and leaving a little less than 5mm/¼in fat on the edge of each chop.

2 If you are going to pre-fry chops, such as bacon or gammon, before adding to the slow cooker, make shallow cuts with the knife all around the edge. The edge of the meat will then fan out during frying, preventing the meat curling up, so that it stays in constant contact with the frying pan.

Preparing poultry

A variety of chicken and game portions can be used in stews and casseroles – from whole or diced breast portions, to drumsticks and thighs. Leaving the bones in the meat during cooking will enhance the flavour, or you may remove them (saving to use for stock) if you prefer. Generally, it is better to remove poultry skin before casseroling because it won't crispen during the moist cooking.

To skin breast fillets, carefully pull the skin and thin membrane away from the meat. If you like, use a small, sharp knife to cut the meat off the rib bone and any remaining breastbone. Turn the breast portion over and remove the thin, white central tendons from the meat.

To prepare escalopes (scallops), cut the breast in half horizontally, holding your hand on top of the chicken breast as you cut. A chicken breast portion will yield two escalopes, a duck breast portion three, and turkey four or more.

To skin and bone chicken thighs, use a sharp knife to loosen the skin, then pull it away from the meat. Carefully cut the flesh lengthways along the main thigh bone, then cut the bone out, trimming the meat close to it.

Preparing vegetables

One of the unusual characteristics of slow cooking is that many types of vegetables take longer to cook than meat. To ensure that they cook within the recommended time, they should be cut into even-size pieces slightly smaller than the meat.

When preparing onions, slice them thinly or chop finely. If you want to have chunkier pieces, fry them until they are soft before adding to the slow cooker, because onion takes a long time to cook in a slow cooker.

Hard root vegetables such as carrots, potatoes and turnips take the longest time to cook in the slow cooker. Cut them into 5mm/¼in dice, slices or sticks. (Potatoes discolour when exposed to air, so make sure they are covered with liquid during cooking.)

COOK'S TIP

Some vegetables, such as (bell) peppers, become bitter if cooked too long and some types, especially green peppers, may discolour. They cook fairly quickly, so add these to the slow cooker 45 minutes– 1 hour before the end of cooking time.

LIQUIDS FOR CASSEROLES AND STEWS

The finished sauce is provided by a mixture of the juices from the meat and vegetables and the liquid that is added at the start of cooking. The long cooking time ensures plenty of flavour if you use water, although other liquids will give the dish a richer finish. You may need to adjust the quantity of liquid used, according to the main ingredients in the dish; vegetables such as mushrooms, for example, will give out a lot of moisture that will thin the sauce.

Stock Home-made stock is preferable, but you can use ready-made fresh stock, or good-quality stock cubes or bouillon powder. Make these to the correct strength (you may only need a small portion of stock cube) because too much can produce an over-salty, artificial flavour. Try to use the flavour of stock that matches the dish. If you haven't got the appropriate meat stock, use vegetable stock instead.

Wine Red or white wine will add extra flavour and its acidity will help to tenderize the meat. Choose a wine that you enjoy drinking because a really cheap, acidic wine will spoil the finished dish. Generally, it is preferable to use a mixture of wine and stock, rather than wine alone.

Cider This flavours and tenderizes meat in the same way as wine, and is excellent in chicken and pork dishes, especially ones containing fruit. Unless you require a very sweet finish, use dry (hard) or medium cider.

Beer Pale or brown ale or stout makes a rich dark sauce and cooks without a hint of its original bitterness. Too much can be overpowering, though, so use a mixture of beer and stock.

Tomatoes These add flavour to the dish. You can use chopped fresh or canned tomatoes, passata (bottled strained tomatoes), concentrated purée (paste), or tomato juice.

BASIC TECHNIQUES

There are two basic ways of making slow cooker stews and casseroles: a simple one-step method, where cold raw ingredients are placed in the ceramic cooking pot, and a second method in which the meat and some or all of the vegetables are fried beforehand.

Making a one-step stew

Irish stew is a classic one-step stew, and the recipe given here is a perfect guide to cooking any stew using this technique. All the ingredients are placed in the ceramic cooking pot without pre-frying. This reduces preparation time and is also suitable for those on a reduced-fat diet.

The stock or cooking liquid is usually cold, but may be hot to speed up the cooking process. For the tenderest results, casseroles should be cooked on a low setting. However, when the ingredients are cold to begin with, and especially if cooking larger pieces of meat, it is better to start the cooking on the high or auto setting for 1–2 hours.

SERVES 4

900g/2lb boned shoulder of lamb
   or 8 neck of lamb chops
450g/1lb onions
900g/2lb potatoes
1 carrot, sliced (optional)
sprig of thyme or bay leaf (optional)
about 600ml/1 pint/2½ cups lamb
   or vegetable stock
salt and ground black pepper

1 Using a sharp knife, trim all excess fat from the lamb, then cut the meat into 3cm/1¼in pieces. (If using lamb chops, these may be left whole.)

2 Using a sharp knife, slice the onions and potatoes as thinly as possible.

3 Place the onions at the bottom of the ceramic cooking pot, then arrange the potatoes, carrot and herbs, if using, on top and finally the meat. Lightly season each layer with salt and pepper.

4 Pour the stock over the meat. If necessary, add a little more stock to cover the meat. Cover the slow cooker with the lid and cook on auto or high for 2 hours.

5 Using a large spoon, skim off any scum that has risen to the surface. Re-cover the pot and leave on auto or switch to low and cook for a further 4–6 hours, or until the meat and vegetables are very tender and juicy.

Making a pre-fried stew

This method is used for the majority of stews and casseroles, because it adds colour and an intense rich flavour. The natural sugars in the ingredients are broken down by pre-frying and the sweet, complex flavours are released. While pre-cooking meat improves the taste and appearance of the cooked casserole, it is also useful to give vegetables the same treatment, especially onions because they take much longer to tenderize than meat in a slow cooker.

SERVES 4–6

900g/2lb lean stewing steak
45ml/3 tbsp plain (all-purpose) flour
50g/2oz/¼ cup butter
30ml/2 tbsp oil
12 baby (pearl) onions, peeled
115g/4oz button (white) mushrooms
1 garlic clove, crushed
300ml/½ pint/1¼ cups red wine
150ml/¼ pint/⅔ cup near-boiling
   beef stock
1 bay leaf
30ml/2 tbsp chopped fresh parsley
salt and ground black pepper

1 Trim the meat and cut into 2.5cm/1in cubes. Season the flour with salt and black pepper and either spread out on a plate or place in a plastic bag. Roll the meat in the flour, or add a few cubes at a time to the bag, shaking until coated, then remove and coat the next batch. Shake off any excess and reserve.

2 Melt half the butter with half of the oil in a large frying pan. (If you prefer, you can reduce the fat slightly by using a non-stick frying pan.)

3 When the butter sizzles, fry the meat in two or three batches. (Do not try to cook too much meat at once because it will start to stew, rather than brown.) Turn the meat frequently, so that it browns on all sides. Lift the meat out of the pan with a slotted spoon and transfer to the ceramic cooking pot.

4 Heat the remaining butter and oil in the frying pan, then add the onions and cook until glazed and golden brown. Transfer to the ceramic cooking pot using a slotted spoon. Add the mushrooms and garlic to the pan and cook for 2–3 minutes until browned, then transfer to the cooking pot.

5 Sprinkle any remaining flour into the pan juices and stir to mix. Gradually mix in the red wine, followed by the stock.

6 Stir the sauce to loosen any sediment from the base of the pan and heat to simmering point. Pour over the meat and vegetables, and add the bay leaf, pressing it down into the liquid.

7 Cover the slow cooker with the lid and switch to high or auto. Cook for 1 hour, then leave on auto or switch to low and cook for a further 6–8 hours, or until the meat and vegetables are tender. Alternatively, cook on high throughout for 4–5 hours. Sprinkle over the parsley just before serving.

Thickening stews
There are many different ways to thicken the sauces of stews and casseroles.
Flour Meat is often fried before being put in the ceramic cooking pot, and can be first dusted in flour, which will act as a thickener for the juices as the meat cooks. Do not over-brown the flour as this gives it a bitter flavour; only fry until light brown.

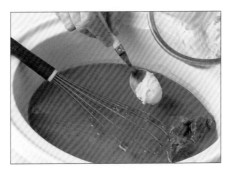

Alternatively, you can add flour towards the end of cooking time by whisking in a paste made from equal quantities of flour and butter. Allow extra cooking time to allow the flour to cook and lose its "raw" flavour.

Cornflour/cornstarch or arrowroot
These very fine flours can both be used as thickeners. They should be blended with a little water or other cold liquid before being stirred into the stew.

Pasta and rice If it becomes obvious part-way through cooking that the stew or casserole will be too thin, you can stir in a little pasta or easy-cook (converted) rice, which will absorb some of the liquid. These should be added about 45 minutes before the end of cooking time. (Lentils and grains, such as pearl barley, will also act as thickeners, but these must be added early in the cooking time to cook thoroughly.)
Reduction If the sauce is too thin when cooking is complete, lift out the meat and vegetables with a slotted spoon and set aside. Pour the liquid into a wide pan or frying pan and boil fast to reduce the liquid. Add the meat and vegetables to the reduced sauce and gently reheat. This is a useful technique with delicate fish and chicken, which may break up if overcooked.

Skimming off fat
If the dish has produced a lot of fat during cooking, you may wish to remove it before serving. Most will rise to the surface so that you can simply skim it off the top, using a large kitchen spoon. Further fat can be removed using absorbent kitchen paper. Simply rest the kitchen paper on the surface of the stew and remove as soon as it has soaked up the fat. If you have made the dish in advance, chill it in the refrigerator so that the fat solidifies on the top of the stew or casserole. It can then be lifted or scooped off.

BRAISING

This technique involves slow cooking in very little liquid in a dish with a tight-fitting lid; the trapped steam keeps the food moist during cooking. Instead of cutting meat into small chunks, it is sliced into larger, even-size pieces, or in some cases, such as chops or lamb shanks, left whole. Braising also works well for large pieces of firm, meaty fish which can be placed on a bed of vegetables, with just enough liquid to cover these. The slow cooker is perfect for braising because the heat is so gentle, and the lid forms a tight seal, so that any steam condenses on the inside of the lid and trickles back into the pot.

Preparing meat for braising

Always trim excess fat from meat before braising, then skim any fat from the surface before serving. To ensure even cooking, all the pieces of meat should be of a similar thickness.

1 Cut the meat into slices about 2cm/¾in thick. At the narrower end cut slightly thicker slices.

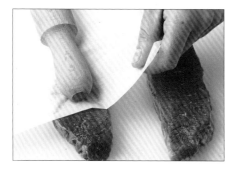

2 Place the thicker slices on a chopping board, cover with a sheet of greaseproof (waxed) paper and gently beat with a rolling pin or meat mallet to flatten.

If you want to pound all the meat, to help tenderize it, you can start by cutting it all into thick slices, about 3cm/1in thick, then pounding it to flatten.

Braising lamb shanks

On the whole lamb joints are tender and quite fatty and do not benefit from being braised. Lamb shanks, however, are lean and tough so benefit from long, slow, moist cooking. Thickly sliced meat, such as braising steak, and small joints, such as topside, can be cooked in the same way.

SERVES 4

4 lamb shanks
1 red onion, very finely chopped
1 garlic clove, crushed
sprig of fresh thyme
5ml/1 tsp chopped fresh rosemary
5ml/1 tsp ground paprika
15ml/1 tbsp balsamic vinegar
60ml/4 tbsp olive oil
175ml/6fl oz/¾ cup red wine
150ml/¼ pint/⅔ cup lamb
   or vegetable stock
chopped fresh parsley
salt and ground black pepper

1 Using the point of a sharp knife, gently prick the shanks at intervals all over.

2 Combine the onion, garlic, thyme, rosemary, paprika, vinegar and 30ml/2 tbsp of the oil. Brush over the shanks, place in a shallow, non-metallic dish, cover and leave to marinate for 2 hours at room temperature, or up to 24 hours in the refrigerator. (Marinating starts the tenderizing process, but is not essential.)

3 Brush the marinade off the lamb and set aside. Heat the remaining 30ml/2 tbsp oil in a frying pan and lightly brown the shanks all over. Transfer to the ceramic cooking pot and season with salt and pepper.

4 Add the reserved marinade to the frying pan and pour in the wine and stock. Bring almost to the boil, stirring, then pour over the shanks.

5 Cover with the lid and switch to high or auto. Cook for 1 hour, then leave on auto or reduce to low and cook for a further 6–8 hours, or until very tender, turning the meat halfway through.

6 Using a slotted spoon, transfer the lamb shanks to a warmed serving plate. Skim off any fat from the cooking juices, then check the seasoning. Stir in the parsley and spoon over the shanks.

Braising red cabbage

Many types of vegetable respond well to braising, becoming meltingly tender with an intense flavour. Red cabbage is used here, but fennel and celery are also very good braised. Fennel should be cut into thin, even slices from the top through the root end; sticks of celery can be left whole or cut into shorter pieces.

SERVES 4–6

1 red cabbage, about 900g/2lb
450g/1lb cooking apples, peeled, cored and chopped
30ml/2 tbsp soft light or dark brown sugar
30ml/2 tbsp red wine vinegar
175g/6fl oz/¾ cup near-boiling water
salt and ground black pepper

1 Discard the tough outer leaves of the cabbage, cut it into quarters and remove the hard stalk. Shred the cabbage finely.

2 Put the cabbage, apples, sugar, vinegar, salt and pepper into the ceramic cooking pot and toss together. Pack down firmly, then pour over the water.

3 Cover with the lid and switch to high for 3–4 hours, or to low for 6–8 hours, stirring halfway through.

Reheating braised dishes, casseroles and stews

Braised dishes, casseroles and stews are often served the day after they are made because their flavour improves with keeping and reheating. The improvement in taste is less obvious in dishes made in the slow cooker because the long gentle cooking has already allowed the flavours to develop and mingle. However, if you do plan to reheat a dish, it is important to cool it as quickly as possible – but you should never plunge the hot ceramic cooking pot into cold water because this may cause it to crack.

1 When cooking is complete, remove the ceramic cooking pot from the slow cooker, and place on a pot stand for at least 10 minutes, taking off the lid to allow steam to escape. (Do not remove the lid for braised vegetables; you want to retain the moisture with these.)

2 Place the ceramic cooking pot in a washing-up bowl of cool but not very cold water. Leave for about 15 minutes, or until the surrounding water starts to feel warm. (Don't overfill the bowl or the water may overflow into the prepared dish; the water should come just over halfway up the cooking pot.)

3 Remove the ceramic cooking pot and pour away the warmed water. Refill the bowl with very cold water, replace the ceramic cooking pot and add a few ice cubes or frozen ice packs to speed up the cooling process. Leave until the food is completely cool.

4 Cover the ceramic cooking pot with the lid and place in the refrigerator until needed, or transfer the contents to another container, if you prefer.

5 The slow cooker is not suitable for reheating the dish. It will take too long for the contents to reheat to ensure food safety. Check whether the ceramic cooking pot is suitable for use on the stovetop or in the oven. Remove the dish from the refrigerator at least 30 minutes before reheating.

6 If necessary, transfer the food to a suitable pan or casserole dish, then reheat gently over a low heat on the stovetop, or in the oven at 170°C/325°F/Gas 3, until simmering. For safety, meat dishes must come to a gentle simmer and be maintained at that temperature for at least 30 minutes. Any fresh herbs should be added at this stage, a few minutes before serving.

TOPPINGS

Adding a topping to casseroles and braised dishes can transform them into a special meal. It is also an easy way to create a one-pot meal with no need for extra accompaniments. Many toppings are arranged on top of the casserole or braise and cooked as an integral part of the dish. Others are cooked separately, then served with the dish.

Dumplings

These are ideal for casseroles and stews, but are unsuitable for braised dishes because they need plenty of simmering liquid to cook in. If the casserole is cooking on a low setting, increase the temperature to high about 30 minutes before adding the dumplings. This recipe makes enough to serve four.

1 Sift 115g/4oz/1 cup self-raising (self-rising) flour and a little salt and pepper into a mixing bowl. Stir in 50g/2oz shredded beef or vegetable suet. Mix in about 75ml/5 tbsp chilled water to make a soft but not sticky dough.

2 Using floured hands, shape the mixture into 8 medium or 12 small round dumplings. Alternatively, roll out into a "rope" with a diameter of about 2.5cm/1in and cut off 2.5cm/1in pieces.

3 Remove the lid from the slow cooker. Working quickly so that heat isn't lost, lower the dumplings into the casserole, spacing them slightly apart. Cover and cook on high for 45 minutes–1 hour, or until well risen and firm. Do not lift the lid during cooking, or the dumplings won't rise properly. (Alternatively, the dumplings can be cooked separately in a covered shallow pan of simmering stock for 30 minutes. Lift out using a slotted spoon and serve with the casserole.)

FLAVOURING DUMPLINGS

Dumplings can be flavoured in many ways. Good choices include herbs or flavoured liquids, such as stock, white wine or cider, instead of water.

Herb and mustard dumplings go well with rich beef casseroles. Sift 5ml/1 tsp mustard powder with the flour and stir in 30–45ml/2–3 tbsp chopped fresh parsley.

Lemon and tarragon dumplings are good with chicken, turkey and fish casseroles. Stir in the finely grated rind of ½ lemon and 45ml/3 tbsp chopped fresh tarragon.

Caraway and sour cream dumplings work well with beef and veal goulash. Stir in 5ml/1 tsp caraway seeds and mix the dry ingredients together with a mixture of half sour cream and half chilled water.

Mushroom dumplings go well with beef and pork casseroles. Stir 50g/2oz very finely chopped mushrooms into the dumpling mixture.

Rosemary dumplings are good with lamb casseroles. Stir in 2.5–5ml/½–1 tsp chopped fresh rosemary.

Potato toppings

Sliced, grated and mashed potatoes make a good topping for casseroles and some braised dishes. If you like, they can be browned in the oven or under a grill (broiler) before serving. Sliced and grated potatoes are usually added at the beginning of cooking; mashed potatoes are added towards the end. All these recipes make enough to serve four.

Sliced potato topping: Thinly slice 675g/1½lb potatoes and arrange over the top of the casserole at the beginning of cooking. Make sure there is just enough liquid to cover the potatoes. Cover with the lid and cook on low for 8–10 hours, or on high for 4–5 hours, until tender. To brown the top before serving, brush the potatoes with a little melted butter and place under a hot grill (broiler) for 3–4 minutes.

Grated potato topping: Grate 675g/1½lb potatoes, then blanch in boiling salted water for 5 minutes. Drain well and squeeze out any excess liquid. Stir in 15ml/1 tbsp melted butter or olive oil, then sprinkle evenly over the surface of the casserole. Cook on low for 4–6 hours, or on high for 2–3 hours. If you like, brown under the grill.

Creamy mashed potato topping: Boil 900g/2lb peeled floury potatoes (such as King Edward or Maris Piper) until tender. Drain well, return to the pan and add 50g/2oz/¼ cup butter, or 30ml/2 tbsp olive oil. Mash with a potato masher until smooth, then beat in 75ml/5 tbsp hot milk or cream, salt, pepper and grated nutmeg. Spoon on top of the casserole or braised dish, spreading out evenly. Cover and cook in the slow cooker for 1 hour. Alternatively, bake in an oven preheated to 190°C/375°F/ Gas 5 for 30 minutes, or brown the top under a medium grill (broiler).

Polenta toppings

This golden-yellow cornmeal topping goes well with Mediterranean-style stews. Mixed with flour, milk and egg, polenta makes a cornbread topping.

Basic polenta topping: Bring 2 litres/ 3½ pints/8 cups water with 5ml/1 tsp salt to the boil in a large, heavy pan. Remove the pan from the heat and pour in 375g/13oz/3 cups fine polenta, whisking continuously. Return the pan to the heat and stir for 15 minutes, until thick. Season well with salt and pepper. This soft polenta can be used in the same way as mashed potato topping.

Polenta triangles: Spoon the basic polenta mixture on to a wet board and spread out to 1cm/½in thick. Leave to set for 1 hour, then cut into triangles. One hour before the end of cooking time, arrange the polenta on top of the casserole. To serve, brush with olive oil, sprinkle with grated Parmesan cheese and grill.

Cornbread topping: Mix 175g/6oz/ 1½ cups fine cornmeal with 15ml/1 tbsp wholemeal (whole-wheat) flour and 5ml/1 tsp baking powder. Make a well in the centre and add 1 beaten egg and 175ml/6fl oz/¾ cup milk. Mix, then quickly spoon over the top of the casserole. Cover and cook for 1 hour until firm. If you like, brown under a grill.

Crumble toppings

These can be cooked in the slow cooker, but are much better baked in the oven. They work well with braised dishes and chunky casseroles with only a little sauce or gravy. This recipe serves four.

1 Sift 175g/6oz/1½ cups plain (all-purpose) white or wholemeal (whole-wheat) flour and a pinch of salt into a bowl. Rub in 90g/3½oz/7 tbsp butter or margarine until the mixture resembles very fine breadcrumbs.

2 Stir in 50g/2oz/½ cup chopped nuts, or 30–45ml/2–3 tbsp porridge oats, 25g/1oz grated mature (sharp) Cheddar cheese, or 25g/1oz sunflower seeds.

3 Preheat the oven to 190°C/375°F/ Gas 5. Sprinkle the topping over the casserole in an even layer, then bake uncovered for 30 minutes until golden.

Bread toppings

Sliced, cubed or crumbled, many types of bread may be used, from sliced white to textured wholegrain.

Breadcrumb topping: Preheat the oven to 150°C/300°F/Gas 2. Combine 75g/3oz/1½ cups breadcrumbs with 30ml/2 tbsp chopped fresh parsley and 2 finely chopped garlic cloves. Sprinkle over the casserole and bake for about 30–40 minutes until golden.

Cheesy French bread topping: Lightly toast 6–12 thick slices of day-old baguette on both sides. Rub one side of each slice with a halved garlic clove, then spread with a little French mustard. Sprinkle over 115g/4oz/1 cup coarsely grated Gruyère cheese and grill until the cheese bubbles. Arrange on top of the casserole and serve immediately.

POT-ROASTING

This method of cooking small or large joints of meat and whole poultry in a small amount of liquid, usually with herbs and vegetables, is ideal for less tender cuts of meat, poultry and game that are low in natural fat. It makes them wonderfully succulent and tender and minimizes shrinkage. The meat is nearly always browned before being placed in the slow cooker with a little liquid and other ingredients. Sometimes the meat is marinated before cooking, especially beef and game, which can be dry.

When choosing joints of meat for pot-roasting, small pieces weighing no more than 1.2kg/2½lb are ideal. If the meat is irregularly shaped it will cook less uniformly and may be awkward to carve, so boned joints such as sirloin, silverside and topside should be tied; shoulder of lamb should be both boned and tied before pot-roasting.

Tying a boneless joint

You will need fine string for tying joints of meat. Store it in a plastic bag or box, rather than leaving loose in a drawer, so that it does not get dirty.

1 Roll or arrange the meat joint into a neat shape. Tie it lengthways with a piece of string. This should be pulled tightly and double-knotted because the meat will shrink a little during cooking. (You may need to ask someone to help you do this.)

2 Tie the joint widthways at regular intervals about 2.5cm/1in apart, knotting and trimming the ends of string as you go. Apply even pressure when tying each length of string to keep the shape of the joint as neat as possible.

Boning a shoulder of lamb

Lamb shoulder is made up of three bones: the flat blade bone, the thin arm bone and the knuckle.

1 Place the shoulder on a board and trim off any excess fat. Insert a sharp knife into the larger end of the lamb joint, then slice it along the flat blade bone, working towards the centre. Turn the meat over and repeat on the other side. Twist out the blade bone.

2 Put the lamb, skin side down, on the board. Cut along the line of the arm and knuckle bones, scraping the meat off the bones, then remove them.

3 Cut through the flesh where the blade bone was and open out the meat. It can now be stuffed, then rolled and tied.

Tying a shoulder *en ballon*

As an alternative to rolling and tying a shoulder of lamb, it can be tied *en ballon*; this is a round cushion shape that is served sliced into wedges.

1 Lay the meat out flat, skin side down. If you like, spoon stuffing into the middle. Pull one corner of the joint into the centre and secure it with a skewer.

2 Do the same with the other four corners, tucking in the remains of the shank and securing them by tying a loop of string around the "ballon".

3 Turn the joint over and continue tying loops of string at even spaces around the ballon, to make six or eight sections. Tie a knot at the crossover point on each side as you go.

Pot-roasting brisket of beef

Other cuts of beef, such as silverside and topside of beef, can be cooked in this way. Stuffed breast or shoulder of lamb also work very well.

SERVES 4–6

1.2kg/2½ lb rolled brisket
25g/1oz/2 tbsp beef dripping
   or white vegetable fat
2 onions, cut into 8 wedges
2 carrots, quartered
2 sticks celery, cut into 5cm/2in lengths
2 bay leaves
2 sprigs of fresh thyme
300ml/½ pint/1¼ cups near-boiling
   beef stock
salt and ground black pepper

1 Season the meat well with salt and pepper. Heat the dripping or vegetable fat in a large, heavy pan until hot. Add the meat and turn frequently using two spoons until browned. If the fat gets too hot before the meat is browned, add a little cold butter to cool it. Lift out the meat and transfer to a plate.

2 Pour away some of the fat, leaving about 15ml/1 tbsp in the pan. Add the onions, carrots and celery and cook for a few minutes or until lightly browned and beginning to soften. Browning the vegetables will add flavour and colour to the pot-roast, but take care not to darken them too much or the stock will become bitter. Arrange a single layer of vegetables in the base of the cooking pot, then place the meat on top, adding any juices from the plate. Put the remaining vegetables around the sides of the meat and tuck in the fresh herbs.

3 Pour the stock into the pan and bring to the boil, stirring in any sediment.

4 Pour the stock over the meat and vegetables; it should barely cover them, leaving most of the meat exposed.

5 Cover the slow cooker with the lid and switch to high. Cook for 4 hours, then reduce the temperature to low and cook for a further 2–3 hours, or until the meat is cooked through and very tender. Once or twice during cooking, turn the meat and baste. Avoid using any sharp utensils when doing so because they may puncture the outer layer and allow juices to escape.

6 Lift out the meat and place on a warmed serving dish. Cover with a piece of foil and leave it to rest; 15 minutes will be sufficient to allow the fibres to relax and let the juices settle, making the meat easier to carve.

7 Meanwhile, skim any fat from the juices and stock in the cooking pot. Serve as a gravy with the meat. (If you like, thicken the juices with cornflour or arrowroot first.) Normally the vegetables are discarded, but these may be served with the meat as well.

Pot-roasting chicken

A whole chicken can be pot-roasted in exactly the same way as a joint of beef or lamb, but this technique is unsuitable for large chickens weighing more than 1.6kg/3½lb. Avoid stuffing the cavity, although you may add a quartered onion or lemon for flavouring.

SERVES 4

150ml/¼ pint/⅔ cup dry white wine
   or dry (hard) cider
2 bay leaves
1.2–1.3kg/2½–3lb chicken
1 lemon, quartered
15ml/1 tbsp sunflower oil
25g/1oz/2 tbsp unsalted (sweet) butter
150ml/¼ pint/⅔ cup boiling chicken stock
15ml/1 tbsp cornflour (cornstarch) blended
   with 30ml/2 tbsp water or wine
salt and ground black pepper

1 Pour the wine into the ceramic cooking pot. Add the bay leaves and switch the slow cooker to high. Meanwhile, rinse or wipe the chicken and pat dry using kitchen paper. Season the cavity, then add the lemon quarters.

2 Heat the oil and butter in a heavy frying pan. Brown the chicken on all sides, then transfer it to the ceramic cooking pot. If the chicken has been trussed, untie it before placing in the cooking pot. This will allow the heat to penetrate more easily.

3 Pour the stock over the chicken, then cover with the lid and cook on high for 3½–4½ hours, or until the juices run clear when pierced with a thin knife or skewer, or a meat thermometer inserted into the thickest part of the thigh reads 77°C/170°F. (Chicken and other poultry must be cooked on high throughout.)

4 Lift the chicken out of the cooking pot, place on a warmed serving dish, cover with foil and leave to rest for 10–15 minutes before serving. Meanwhile, skim the juices, stir in the cornflour mixture and cook on high for 10 minutes, then serve as a sauce.

POACHING

This gentle method of cooking keeps food wonderfully moist. It differs from boiling because the heat is so low that only the occasional bubble breaks the surface of the liquid. It is ideal for delicate meats, such as poultry and fish, which can overcook and disintegrate if fiercely boiled. Poaching also allows you to skim off the scum and fat that faster boiling would bubble back into the liquid, making it cloudy and spoiling the flavour. The slow cooker is perfect for poaching because it keeps the heat constant and steady and needs little attention.

Poaching chicken

Unlike pot-roasting, the slow cooker can be used for poaching large chickens and other poultry, although it is important to check that it will fit comfortably in the ceramic cooking pot. There should be enough space for it to be completely immersed in liquid and room for liquid to circulate around the sides. Because the cavity of the bird will be filled with poaching liquid, the bird will be cooked from the inside and the outside.

SERVES 4

1.3kg/3lb oven-ready chicken
1 onion
2 carrots
2 leeks
2 celery sticks
a few fresh parsley stalks
2 bay leaves
6 black peppercorns
2.5ml/½ tsp salt

1 Remove any trussing string from the chicken. Remove any loose pieces of fat from inside the chicken, then rinse the cavity under cold water and place the chicken in the ceramic cooking pot.

2 Trim the onion at the stem and root end, but do not peel (the skin will add a rich golden colour to the stock). Cut the onion into six or eight wedges. Wash and trim the carrots, leeks and celery, then roughly chop or slice them and add to the cooking pot, packing them in around the chicken.

3 Tie the herbs together and add to the pot with the peppercorns and salt.

4 Pour in enough near-boiling water to just cover the chicken, pouring it over the vegetables and the chicken. Cover with the lid, switch the slow cooker to high and cook for 1 hour.

5 Skim off any scum and fat using a slotted spoon. Re-cover the pot and cook for 2–2½ hours, or until the chicken is cooked and tender. To check the chicken is cooked, insert a meat thermometer into the thickest part, where the thigh joins the body; it should read 77°C/170°F. (Alternatively, insert a skewer into the thickest part; the juices should show no traces of pink. If they are clear, lift the chicken out of the pot and double-check on the other side.)

6 Remove the chicken from the pot, using a large fork inserted into the cavity to lift it up. Leave the chicken to rest for 10 minutes before carving. Alternatively, if you plan to eat the chicken cold, leave it to cool completely on a wire rack placed over a large plate to catch any drips. (The wire rack will allow air to circulate around the chicken, helping it to cool more quickly.)

7 Leave the cooking liquid to cool for a few minutes, then ladle into a colander set over a large bowl. Leave to drip; do not press the vegetables or the stock will become cloudy. Cool the stock quickly by placing the bowl in cold water.

8 If you plan to eat the chicken cold, as soon as it is cool, cover with clear film (plastic wrap) and store in the refrigerator. (Leave the skin on because this will help to keep the meat moist.) Use within 2 days of cooking.

9 When the stock is cool, cover with clear film (plastic wrap) and place in the refrigerator. Any fat in the stock will rise to the surface and can be removed easily and discarded. The stock can be kept for up to 3 days, or it can be frozen in airtight containers for up to 6 months.

Poaching gammon

Gammon is the cured hind leg of the bacon pig. Once cooked, it is known as ham. When serving the meat in slices, poaching is the best cooking method, producing tender, juicy results. However, if you wish to serve it whole, it can be glazed after poaching and briefly baked.

SERVES 6–8

1.8kg/4lb boned middle gammon joint
1 onion
6 whole cloves
2 carrots, halved
1 bouquet garni
10 black peppercorns
dry (hard) cider (optional)

1 Place the meat in the ceramic cooking pot, cover with cold water and leave to soak for 2–24 hours to remove the salt. (Mild cured gammon shouldn't need long soaking, but it is preferable to soak smoked gammon for the longer time.)

2 Drain the gammon, then return it to the cooking pot. Peel the onion, stud with the cloves and add to the pot with the carrots, herbs and peppercorns. If you find it difficult to squeeze the onion down the side of the gammon, halve it.

3 Pour in enough cold water, or cider or a mixture of the two, to just cover the gammon. Switch the slow cooker to high, cover with the lid and cook for 1 hour. Skim off any scum using a slotted spoon, then re-cover and cook for a further 4–5 hours. Check and skim the surface once or twice during cooking.

4 Lift the ham out of the pot and place on a board. Slice and serve hot, or allow to cool, then wrap in foil and store in the refrigerator for up to 5 days.

5 Strain the cooking liquid into a bowl and leave to cool. (Taste the stock when hot; if it is very salty, use sparingly in dishes and do not add additional salt.) Chill the stock and remove any fat from the surface. Store in the refrigerator and use within 2 days. Alternatively, freeze for up to 6 months.

GLAZING HAMS

After poaching, lift the ham into a foil-lined baking dish and leave to cool for 15 minutes. Snip the string off the ham, then slice off the rind, leaving a thin, even layer of fat. Score the fat in diagonal lines, then score in the opposite direction to make a diamond pattern. Brush the warm joint with about 45ml/3 tbsp lime marmalade and sprinkle with 45ml/3 tbsp demerara (raw) sugar. Push whole cloves into the corners of the diamond shapes after glazing, if you like. Bake at 220°C/425°F/Gas 7 for about 20 minutes, until the fat is brown and crisp. Serve hot or cold.

Poaching fish

The delicate texture of fish benefits from simple cooking. Poaching brings out its flavour and keeps it moist. Both whole fish and fillets can be poached in the slow cooker, but first check that there is enough room for the fish, as well as space to manoeuvre a fish slice (spatula).

Fish can be poached in cold liquid, but it will retain its shape and texture if added to hot liquid. Larger pieces of fish, such as steaks or cutlets, will take no more than 45 minutes on high, or 1½–2 hours on low, but take care not to overcook and check frequently. Fish is ready when the flesh is only slightly translucent when eased away from the bone, or flakes easily when tested with the point of a sharp knife or skewer.

Poaching fruit

Apples, pears, stone fruits, such as plums, and soft fruit, such as figs, can be poached whole, halved or sliced. Even fragile fruit, such as rhubarb, will retain its shape when cooked in a slow cooker. Cooking times will depend on the size and ripeness of the fruit, but as a rough guide, tender fruit, such as figs and rhubarb, will take about 1½ hours on high; ripe or near-ripe fruit, such as plums or apples, will take about 2 hours on high; and harder, less ripe fruit, such as pears, will take 3–5 hours on high, or 6–8 hours on low.

The classic poaching liquid is syrup and usually consists of 1 part sugar to 2 parts water. Flavouring ingredients such as a pared strip of lemon rind or spices can be added to the liquid, as can red or white wine, cider or fruit juice sweetened with sugar.

1 Put the sugar, poaching liquid and any flavourings into the ceramic cooking pot and switch the slow cooker to high. Cook for 1 hour, stirring occasionally to dissolve the sugar.

2 Add the fruit, cover and cook until the fruit is barely tender. Leave the fruit to cool in the syrup, or remove and place in a serving dish. Strain the syrup over the fruit, or simmer gently to thicken.

USING the SLOW COOKER as a BAIN-MARIE

While many dishes are cooked directly in the ceramic cooking pot, others may be cooked in a bain-marie – in a tin (pan) or dish placed inside the cooking pot and surrounded by barely simmering water. This technique is good for making pâtés, terrines, cakes, steamed puddings and custard-based desserts. To allow the water to move freely around the cooking container, an upturned saucer or metal pastry ring is often placed on the base of the cooking pot. This is important if the cooking pot has a slightly concave base.

MAKING PÂTÉS AND TERRINES

When raw meat and eggs are used, make sure that the depth of the mixture is no greater than 6cm/2¼in, otherwise the pâté may not cook thoroughly. This is especially important with pork and chicken. A 450g/1lb terrine or loaf tin measuring about 20 × 10 × 5.5cm/ 8 × 4 × 2¼in and holding a volume of 900ml/1½ pints/3¾ cups is an ideal size.

Making classic pork pâté

You can use this recipe as a guide for making other pâtés. You can vary the proportions of the main ingredients, and can use lean minced (ground) beef or pork in place of the veal.

SERVES 6

225g/8oz rindless smoked streaky
   (fatty) bacon rashers (strips)
225g/8oz boneless belly of pork
175g/6oz veal
115g/4oz chicken livers
45ml/3 tbsp dry white wine
15ml/1 tbsp brandy
2.5ml/½ tsp dried thyme
2.5ml/½ tsp dried rosemary
1 garlic clove, crushed
2.5ml/½ tsp salt
1.5ml/¼ tsp ground mace
ground black pepper

1 Place an upturned saucer or metal pastry cutter in the base of the ceramic cooking pot. Pour in about 2.5cm/1in of very hot water, then turn the slow cooker to high.

2 Taking 150g/5oz of the bacon, stretch one rasher at a time on a board using the back of a large knife. Use to line a 450g/1lb loaf tin, or a 900ml/1½ pint/ 3¾ cup round dish, leaving the bacon overhanging the sides.

3 Finely chop the remaining bacon and place in a large bowl. Trim the belly of pork, veal and chicken livers, then mince (grind) using the medium blade of a mincer, or place in a food processor and chop roughly. Add to the bowl.

4 Spoon the white wine and brandy over the meat. Add the herbs, garlic and seasonings, then mix well. Transfer the mixture to the tin or dish, pressing down lightly. Fold the overhanging bacon over the top of the filling, then cover with a piece of foil.

5 Place the pâté in the slow cooker, then pour enough very hot water around it to come nearly to the top. Cook on high for 4–6 hours. To test whether the pâté is cooked, push a thin skewer into the centre and press lightly around the edges of the hole; the liquid should be clear, not cloudy or pink.

6 Carefully remove the pâté from the slow cooker and leave to cool on a wire rack. Cover and chill for several hours, then unmould and keep covered until ready to serve. (If you like, the pâté can be pressed before chilling.)

PRESSING PÂTÉS

After cooling the cooked pâté, you may "press" it to give it a slightly firmer texture and to make it easier to slice. Cover the pâté with greaseproof (waxed) paper or clear film (plastic wrap). Top with a board that fits exactly inside the tin (pan) and place several weights or cans on the board. (Alternatively, use bags of rice or lentils, which can be moulded to fit into the top of the tin.) Leave until completely cool, then chill overnight (still weighted if you want a really firm texture).

Making mousseline pâté

A mousseline pâté has a light, smooth, creamy texture. Allow plenty of time to prepare it because you will need to chill the mixture between each stage. Mousseline pâtés are extremely rich, so serve thinly sliced with bread or salad.

SERVES 8

15g/½oz/1 tbsp butter
1 shallot, finely chopped
15ml/1 tbsp brandy or sherry
225g/8oz skinless chicken breast portion
50g/2oz chicken livers, trimmed
15ml/1 tbsp fresh white breadcrumbs
1 egg, separated
300ml/½ pint/1¼ cups double (heavy) cream
salt and ground white pepper

1 Lightly oil and line a 450g/1lb loaf or terrine tin (pan), or a 900ml/1½ pint/ 3¾ cup baking dish, with baking parchment. Melt the butter in a small pan, add the shallot and cook for about 5 minutes until soft. Turn off the heat, then stir in the brandy or sherry. Place the mixture in a bowl and leave to cool.

2 Meanwhile, roughly chop the chicken breast portion and livers, then place in a food processor and purée for about 30 seconds. Add the shallot mixture and breadcrumbs to the chicken and process until very smooth. Return the mixture to the bowl and chill for 30 minutes.

3 Meanwhile, place an upturned saucer or metal pastry cutter in the bottom of the ceramic cooking pot. Pour in about 2.5cm/1in of very hot water, then turn the slow cooker to high.

4 Set the bowl of chicken purée over a larger bowl filled with crushed ice and water. Lightly whisk the egg white with a fork until frothy and beat into the purée, a little at a time. Beat in the egg yolk.

5 Gradually add the cream, mixing well between each addition. Season with salt and white pepper, then spoon the mixture into the prepared tin and level the top. Cover with clear film (plastic wrap) or foil.

6 Place the tin or terrine in the slow cooker, then pour enough hot water around to come nearly to the top. Cook on high for 3–4 hours, or until firm.

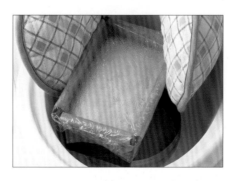

7 Carefully remove the pâté from the slow cooker and leave to cool on a wire rack. Chill well before slicing and serving.

Making a studded terrine

Attractive terrines can be made using the mousseline mixture and studding it with vegetables or layering it with other meats, such as strips of chicken or ham.

SERVES 8

75g/3oz fine asparagus stalks
75g/3oz green beans, topped and tailed
115g/4oz carrots, peeled and cut into matchstick strips
½ quantity mousseline pâté mixture

1 Lightly oil and line a 450g/1lb loaf tin or terrine, or a 900ml/1½ pint/3¾ cup baking dish, with baking parchment. Cook the vegetables, one type at a time, in boiling water for 1 minute. Drain, plunge into cold water, then drain again.

2 Spread a layer of the mixture in the bottom of the tin. Arrange the asparagus lengthways, with gaps between each, then cover with a thin layer of the pâté.

3 Repeat the layers using the beans and carrots and finishing with the remaining pâté mixture. Smooth the top. Cover with clear film (plastic wrap) or foil and cook in the same way as the chicken mousseline for 2½–3½ hours.

MAKING STEAMED PUDDINGS and DESSERTS

The slow cooker is perfect for cooking sticky steamed sponges and custards. It keeps the water at a very gentle simmer, reducing the risk of the water bubbling up and spoiling the dish.

Making a steamed sponge

Sponge puddings cooked in steam have a surprisingly light, moist texture. They were traditionally made using shredded beef or vegetarian suet, but this modern version uses a creamed cake mixture. Make sure that all the ingredients are at room temperature before you start.

SERVES 4–6

115g/4oz/½ cup butter, at room
   temperature
115g/4oz/generous ½ cup caster
   (superfine) sugar
2.5ml/½ tsp vanilla essence
   (extract)
2 eggs, lightly beaten
175g/6oz/1½ cups self-raising
   (self-rising) flour
about 45ml/3 tbsp milk

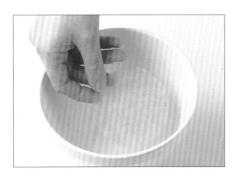

1 Place an upturned saucer or metal pastry cutter in the bottom of the ceramic cooking pot. Pour in 2.5cm/1in very hot water, then preheat the slow cooker on high. Grease a 900ml/ 1½ pint/3¾ cup pudding bowl and line the base with a piece of greaseproof (waxed) paper or baking parchment.

2 Cream the butter, sugar and vanilla essence together in a large mixing bowl until pale and fluffy. Add the eggs, a little at a time, beating thoroughly. If the mixture begins to curdle, beat in a spoonful of the flour.

3 Sift half the flour over the creamed mixture and fold in using a large metal spoon. Sift over the rest and fold in with 30ml/2 tbsp of the milk. If necessary, add the remaining milk to make a soft dropping (pourable) consistency, then spoon into the pudding bowl.

4 Cover the pudding with greaseproof paper and foil and tie with string. Lower into the slow cooker, then pour enough water around the bowl to come halfway up the sides. Cover with the lid and cook on high for 4–5 hours, or until well risen and springy to the touch. Lift out of the slow cooker and remove the foil. Turn out on to a serving plate, peel off the paper and serve.

**HOW TO COVER A
STEAMED PUDDING**

1 Brush a sheet of greaseproof (waxed) paper with softened butter, then place the unbuttered side on a sheet of foil. Make a pleat about 2cm/¾in wide in the middle to allow the pudding to rise. (If fresh fruit is included in the pudding, you must use greaseproof paper; otherwise, a double piece of foil may be used.)

2 Cover the bowl with the pleated greaseproof paper and foil, allowing it to overlap the rim by 2.5cm/1in. Tie the foil securely with fine string.

3 Make a loop with the string at the top of the bowl to make a secure handle. This will enable the bowl to be lifted in and out of the ceramic cooking pot easily.

Making baked egg custard

A lightly set, creamy-textured custard is ideal for serving hot or cold. It can be enjoyed on its own or with all manner of desserts, such as fruit pies, steamed sponges and crumbles.

SERVES 4–6

butter or flavourless oil, for greasing
475ml/16fl oz/2 cups milk
3 eggs
45ml/3 tbsp caster (superfine) sugar
pinch of freshly grated nutmeg

1 Place an upturned saucer or metal pastry cutter in the bottom of the ceramic cooking pot. Pour in about 2.5cm/1in of very hot water, then turn the slow cooker to high.

2 Lightly grease the base and sides of a 900ml/1½ pint/3¾ cup heatproof dish. Heat the milk in a pan until it is steaming hot, without letting it boil.

3 Whisk the eggs and sugar lightly in a bowl, then slowly pour over the hot milk, whisking all the time. Strain the mixture through a fine sieve (strainer) into the prepared dish and sprinkle the top with a little grated nutmeg.

4 Cover the dish with clear film (plastic wrap) and place in the slow cooker. Pour in enough near-boiling water to come just over halfway up the sides of the dish. Put the lid on the slow cooker, then switch to the low setting and cook for 4 hours, or until the custard is lightly set. Serve hot or cold.

Making crème brûlée

You can use the basic baked egg custard mixture to make other custard-based desserts, such as crème brûlée, which is a rich, creamy baked custard topped with a crisp layer of caramelized sugar.

1 Make the custard, whisking 5ml/1 tsp vanilla essence (extract) into the egg and sugar mixture, then use 150ml/¼ pint/ ⅔ cup double (heavy) cream and 300ml/ ½ pint/1¼ cups single (light) cream in place of the milk.

2 Strain the custard into a jug (pitcher), then pour into four or six individual ramekins (custard cups), first making sure that the ramekins will fit inside the cooking pot in a single layer.

3 Cover each dish with clear film (plastic wrap), then place in the ceramic cooking pot. Pour enough near-boiling water around the dishes to come three-quarters of the way up the sides. Cover with the lid and cook on low for about 3 hours, or until set.

4 Remove the custards from the slow cooker and leave to cool. Sprinkle the tops with 115g/4oz/½ cup caster (superfine) sugar. Place under a hot grill (broiler) and cook until the sugar melts and caramelizes. Cool, then chill.

Making bread and butter pudding

This favourite dessert can be made using the classic baked custard mixture.

1 Make the custard using 300ml/½ pint/ 1¼ cups milk and 75ml/2½fl oz/⅓ cup double (heavy) cream.

2 Butter 8 medium slices of bread, then cut each in half diagonally. Arrange the slices in a 1 litre/1¾ pint/4 cup, buttered baking dish, first making sure that it will fit in the cooking pot.

3 Pour the custard over the bread and sprinkle 30ml/2 tbsp demerara (raw) sugar and a little grated nutmeg over the top. Cover with clear film (plastic wrap) and put the dish in the cooking pot. Pour enough near-boiling water around the dish to come two-thirds up the sides. Cover with a lid and cook on high for 3–4 hours, or until the custard has set. Serve the pudding warm.

Making cheese and vegetable strata

This savoury bread and butter pudding can be made using the baked custard mixture. Simply leave out the sugar and season well with salt and black pepper.

1 Cook 1 thinly sliced leek and 1 large finely chopped onion in 25g/1oz/2 tbsp butter until soft. Stir in 30ml/2 tbsp chopped fresh chives or parsley.

2 Remove the crusts from 8 slices of bread, then cut into fingers. Arrange one-third of the bread fingers in a buttered 1.75 litre/3 pint/7½ cup soufflé dish. Top with half the vegetable mixture. Repeat the layers, ending with bread.

3 Pour the custard mixture over the strata, then sprinkle 75g/3oz/¾ cup finely grated Cheddar cheese over the top. Cover with buttered foil, then put in the ceramic cooking pot and pour enough near-boiling water around the dish to come halfway up the sides. Cover and cook on high for 3–4 hours until lightly set. Cut into wedges and serve warm.

Making rice pudding

Cooked in the slow cooker, rice pudding is wonderfully rich and creamy. Unlike baked versions it doesn't form a thick skin on the top. Add flavourings such as grated nutmeg at the beginning, or part-way through cooking.

SERVES 4–6

25g/1oz/2 tbsp softened butter
75g/3oz/generous ⅓ cup pudding rice, rinsed and drained
50g/2oz/4 tbsp caster (superfine) sugar
750ml/1¼ pints/3 cups milk
175ml/6fl oz/¾ cup evaporated (unsweetened condensed) milk

1 Thickly butter the ceramic cooking pot, taking it about half-way up the sides. Add the rice, sugar, milk, evaporated milk and any flavourings and stir to mix.

2 Cover with the lid and cook on high for 3–4 hours, or on low for 5–6 hours, until the rice is cooked and most of the milk has been absorbed.

3 Stir the pudding at least twice during the last 2 hours of cooking. If the mixture gets too thick towards the end, stir in a little more milk.

MAKING CAKES

Many cakes can be made successfully in a slow cooker – in particular, moist cake mixtures, such as carrot cake and gingerbread, that normally require long cooking at low temperatures. These types of cake usually benefit from being left to mature before eating, but this is not necessary when they are cooked in the slow cooker. The slow cooker is also good for making lightly textured, rich-flavoured sponge cakes. However, it is not suitable for whisked sponges and cakes because these need fast cooking at a high temperature.

Cakes can be cooked either in a tin (pan) with a fixed base or in a straight-sided soufflé dish. Before you line a tin and fill it with cake mixture, make sure it will fit in the ceramic cooking pot. It is a good idea to test that the tin is watertight: fill it with water and leave for a few minutes to check for leakages.

The baking tin should be lined with greaseproof (waxed) paper that has been greased with a little flavourless oil, or baking parchment. This makes it easier to remove the cake from the tin.

Base-lining
Some recipes only require the base of the tin (pan) to be lined. This technique can be used to line any shape of tin, whether round, square or rectangular.

Place the tin on a sheet of greaseproof (waxed) paper or baking parchment and, using a pencil, draw round the tin. Cut just inside the line so that the paper will fit neatly inside the tin. Using a sheet of kitchen paper drizzled with a flavourless oil, grease the inside of the tin and place the lining paper in the base, pressing it right into the corners.

Lining round cookware
The sides, as well as the base, of a tin or soufflé dish will often need to be lined.

1 Place the tin (pan) or soufflé dish on a sheet of greaseproof (waxed) paper and draw round it. Cut inside the line. Cut strips of paper, about 1cm/½in wider than the depth of the tin or dish. Fold up the bottom edge by 1cm/½in, then make cuts about 1cm/½in apart from the edge of the paper to the fold.

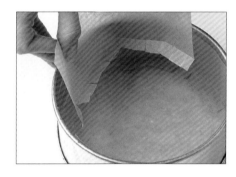

2 Brush the inside of the tin or dish with oil, then position the paper strips around the side of the tin so that the snipped edge sits on the base. Place the paper circle in the base.

Lining a square tin
You can line a square tin (pan) with a single piece of greaseproof paper.

Put the tin on a square of greaseproof paper, which allows the depth of the tin on all four sides. Draw around the base of the tin. Cut in from the edge to each corner of the square. Fold in each side along its pencil line, making a firm crease. Lightly brush the inside of the tin with oil, then fit the paper inside, making sure it fits well into the corners.

Lining a loaf tin
Unlike a square tin (pan), it is easier to line a loaf tin with two strips of paper.

1 Cut a strip of greaseproof paper the length of the tin base and wide enough to cover the base and long sides. Cut another strip of paper, the same width as the tin base and long enough to cover the base and ends of the tin.

2 Lightly brush the inside of the tin with oil, then press the two pieces of paper into position, creasing it where it meets the edges of the base of the tin.

Making dark chocolate cake
Steaming in the slow cooker gives this rich cake a deliciously moist crumb.

SERVES 8–10

175g/6oz/¾ cup butter, at room temperature
115g/4oz/½ cup soft light brown sugar
50g/2oz/¼ cup clear honey
3 eggs, lightly beaten
150g/5oz/1¼ cups self-raising (self-rising) flour
25g/1oz/¼ cup unsweetened cocoa powder
10ml/2 tsp milk
5ml/1 tsp vanilla essence (extract)
whipped cream, for the filling (optional)

1 Place an upturned saucer or metal pastry cutter in the ceramic cooking pot. Pour in 2.5cm/1in of very hot water, then switch the slow cooker to high.

2 Grease and line a 16cm/7in fixed-base round cake tin (pan) or soufflé dish, at least 7.5cm/3in deep.

3 Put the butter, sugar and honey in a bowl and cream together until pale and fluffy. Beat the eggs into the creamed mixture a little a time, beating well after each addition. If the mixture curdles, mix in a little of the measured flour.

4 Sift the flour and cocoa over the cake mixture. Using a large metal spoon, gently fold in with the milk and vanilla essence. Spoon the mixture into the prepared tin and level the surface.

5 Loosely cover the cake tin with lightly oiled foil. Put the tin in the ceramic cooking pot and then pour enough near-boiling water around the tin to come just over halfway up the sides.

6 Cover with the lid and cook on high for 3 hours. To test if the cake is cooked, insert a skewer into the centre of the cake. Leave for a few seconds, then remove; it should come away clean. If any mixture sticks to the skewer, re-cover and cook for 30 minutes more.

7 Remove the cake from the ceramic cooking pot and place on a wire rack for 10 minutes before turning out of the tin. Leave to cool, then cut in half and fill with whipped cream, if you like.

DECORATING CAKES

Cakes cooked in a slow cooker darken in colour but they do not brown in the same way as an oven-baked cake. As a result, many will benefit from decorating.

Decorating uncooked cakes

Many cakes can be decorated before they are cooked in the slow cooker. Note that light sponges and wet cake mixtures cannot hold heavy decorations.

Glistening sugar is an easy and effective way of decorating cakes. Different types of sugar can be sprinkled over the top of an uncooked cake. Good choices include caster (superfine) sugar, larger crystals of granulated or demerara (raw) sugar, and brown sugar crystals.

Chopped and flaked (sliced) nuts can be sprinkled over cakes in the same way as sugar. Toast them first.

Halved nuts and glacé (candied) fruits can be arranged in decorative patterns on fruit cakes and stiff cake batters. After cooking, brush over a little warmed honey or sugar syrup to glaze.

Decorating cooked cakes

After cooking, cakes can be decorated in a number of different ways.

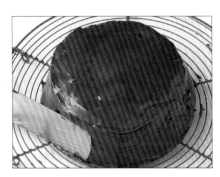

Icing or frosting can transform a simple cake into something special. To make fudge frosting, break 50g/2oz plain (semisweet) chocolate into the cooking pot and add 225g/8oz/2 cups sifted icing (confectioners') sugar, 50g/2oz/¼ cup butter, 45ml/3 tbsp milk and 5ml/1 tsp vanilla essence (extract). Switch the slow cooker to high for 15–25 minutes, or until the chocolate has melted. Remove the cooking pot, stir to mix, then beat until thick and spread over the cake.

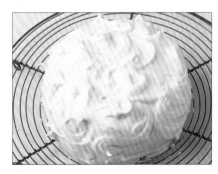

American frosting can be made by placing a bowl in the ceramic cooking pot, then pouring enough near-boiling water around the bowl to come just over halfway up the sides. Switch the slow cooker to high. Place 350g/12oz caster (superfine) sugar in the bowl with 2.5ml/½ tsp cream of tartar and 2 egg whites. Whisk continuously until the mixture holds its shape. Spread over the cake in peaks.

MAKING SAVOURY SAUCES

Sauces add flavour, colour, texture and moisture to food. Many can be made in the slow cooker, from classic simmered sauces to emulsions that are made by using the slow cooker as a bain-marie. Here are just a selection of classic sauces that can be used for cooking or for serving with other dishes.

Making fresh tomato sauce

This sauce can be used as the base for pasta dishes, or can be combined with meat or poultry to make a rich cooking sauce. You can use 2 × 400g/14oz cans chopped plum tomatoes instead of fresh, if you prefer. This recipe will make about 475ml/16fl oz/2 cups.

I Pour 15ml/1 tbsp olive oil into the ceramic cooking pot. Add 2 crushed garlic cloves and the finely grated zest of ½ lemon. Stir, then cover with the lid and switch the slow cooker to high. Cook for 15 minutes.

2 Peel and roughly chop 900g/2lb ripe tomatoes and add to the cooking pot with 60ml/4 tbsp vegetable stock or red wine, 5ml/1 tsp dried oregano and a pinch of caster (superfine) sugar. Stir to combine, then cover with the lid and cook on low for 3 hours.

3 Stir in 30–45ml/2–3 tbsp chopped fresh basil and season to taste with salt and ground black pepper.

Making white sauce

To make white sauce in a slow cooker, heat the milk, then whisk in a mixture of butter and flour. This recipe will make about 475ml/16fl oz/2 cups.

I Pour 400ml/14fl oz/1⅔ cups milk into the ceramic cooking pot. Add flavouring ingredients (such as a bay leaf, a blade of mace, a few parsley stalks, half a peeled onion and 4 black peppercorns). Switch the slow cooker to high and heat for 1 hour, or until simmering.

2 Blend 20g/¾oz/1½ tbsp softened butter with 20g/¾oz/scant ¼ cup plain (all-purpose) flour to make a paste.

3 Remove the flavouring ingredients from the milk using a slotted spoon. Add the paste in small spoonfuls and whisk into the hot milk until thickened.

4 Cover with the lid and cook for about 30 minutes, stirring occasionally. Season with salt and extra pepper if needed.

HOT EMULSION SAUCES

These rich, creamy sauces can be made very successfully using the slow cooker as a bain-marie.

Making hollandaise sauce

The rich flavour of hollandaise sauce goes well with fish, shellfish and many vegetables. Take your time making it because it may curdle if the butter is added too quickly. This recipe will make about 300ml/½ pint/1¼ cups.

I About 30 minutes before making the sauce, remove 150g/5oz/¾ cup unsalted (sweet) butter from the refrigerator. Cut into tiny cubes and leave to come to room temperature.

2 Pour about 5cm/2in near-boiling water into the ceramic cooking pot. Cover the slow cooker with the lid to retain the heat and switch to high.

3 Put 60ml/4 tbsp white wine vinegar in a pan with 4 black peppercorns, 1 bay leaf and 1 blade of mace (optional). Bring to the boil and simmer until reduced to 15ml/1 tbsp. Remove from the heat and dip the base of the pan into cold water to prevent further evaporation.

4 Beat 3 egg yolks with 15g/½oz/1 tbsp of the butter and a pinch of salt in a heatproof bowl that will fit in the slow cooker. Strain in the reduced vinegar. Place the bowl in the ceramic cooking pot and pour enough boiling water around the bowl to come just over halfway up the sides. Whisk for about 3 minutes until beginning to thicken.

5 Beat in the remaining butter a little at a time, making sure that each addition of butter is completely incorporated before adding the next. The mixture will slowly thicken and emulsify. Season with salt and ground black pepper. Switch the slow cooker to low and keep the hollandaise warm for up to 1 hour. (If the sauce starts to curdle, add an ice cube and whisk vigorously; the sauce should combine. If this doesn't work, whisk 1 egg yolk with 15ml/1 tbsp lukewarm water and slowly whisk into the separated sauce.)

Making beurre blanc

This simple butter sauce is served with poached or grilled (broiled) fish and poultry. It can be varied by adding chopped fresh herbs, such as chives or chervil, to the finished sauce. It is extremely rich, and only a small amount is needed per serving. This recipe will make about 250ml/8fl oz/1 cup.

1 Pour about 5cm/2in of near-boiling water into the ceramic cooking pot. Cover with the lid and switch the slow cooker to high.

2 Pour 45ml/3 tbsp each of white wine and white wine vinegar into a pan. Add 2 finely chopped shallots and bring to the boil. Simmer until reduced to about 15ml/1 tbsp liquid.

3 Strain the mixture into a heatproof bowl that will fit in the slow cooker, then pour enough boiling water around the bowl to come halfway up the sides.

4 Whisk in 225g/8oz/1 cup chilled diced butter, adding it piece by piece and making sure that each addition is completely incorporated before adding the next. Season with salt and ground black pepper before serving.

Making a sabayon sauce

Light and airy sabayon sauce is thickened with egg. It goes well with vegetable and pastry dishes. This recipe will make about 300ml/½ pint/1¼ cups.

1 Half-fill the ceramic cooking pot with near-boiling water, cover with the lid and switch to high.

2 Place a heatproof bowl over the water in the slow cooker; the base should just touch the water but the rest of the bowl should be above the water. Place 4 egg yolks with 15ml/1 tbsp white wine vinegar in the bowl and whisk until pale. Add 90ml/6 tbsp red or white wine or stock and whisk again.

3 When the sauce is thick and frothy, season to taste and serve immediately.

MAKING SWEET SAUCES

A sweet sauce adds the finishing touch to a dessert, and the slow cooker is excellent for making fruit purées, creamy custards and rich chocolate sauces.

Making fresh fruit coulis

Cooking soft fruits, such as raspberries, blackberries, blueberries, blackcurrants, plums, cherries and apricots, brings out their natural flavour. This recipe will make about 350ml/12fl oz/1½ cups.

1 Put 350g/12oz/3 cups prepared fruit in the ceramic cooking pot with 45ml/ 3 tbsp water. Stir in a little sugar and add a dash of lemon juice. Cover with the lid and cook on high for 1–1½ hours or until very soft.

2 Remove the cooking pot from the slow cooker and leave to cool slightly. Pour the fruit into a food processor or blender and process until smooth. Press the purée through a sieve (strainer) to remove any seeds or skins.

3 Taste the sauce and stir in a little more sugar or lemon juice, if needed. Cover and chill until required. If you like, stir in 45ml/3 tbsp liqueur, such as Kirsch, before serving. The coulis can be stored in the refrigerator for up to 5 days.

Making dried fruit sauce

Dried fruits, such as apricots, can also be made into sauces. This recipe will make about 600ml/1 pint/scant 2½ cups.

1 Place 175g/6oz dried apricots in the ceramic cooking pot, pour over 475ml/ 16fl oz/2 cups orange juice, cover and leave to soak overnight.

2 Place the ceramic pot in the slow cooker and cook on high for 1 hour, or until the apricots are tender. Purée in a food processor or blender and serve warm or cold. If necessary, dilute the sauce with a little extra fruit juice.

Making custard

Custard is the classic dessert sauce and can also be used as the basis for many desserts. The slow cooker maintains a gentle, constant heat, so the custard can be made directly in the ceramic cooking pot, rather than in a bain-marie. It can be served hot or cold, and can also be flavoured: try stirring 75g/3oz chopped plain (semisweet) chocolate or 45ml/ 3 tbsp rum or brandy into hot custard. For extra richness, replace some of the milk with single (light) or double (heavy) cream. This recipe will make about 600ml/1 pint/2½ cups.

1 Pour 475ml/16fl oz/2 cups of milk into the ceramic cooking pot. Split a vanilla pod (bean) lengthways and add it to the milk. Heat on high for 1 hour, or until the milk reaches boiling point.

2 Meanwhile, whisk together 5 egg yolks and 90g/3½ oz/scant ½ cup caster (superfine) sugar in a bowl until the mixture is pale and thick.

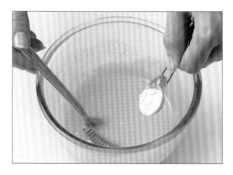

3 Whisk 5ml/1 tsp cornflour (cornstarch) into the egg mixture. (This will help the custard to thicken and prevent curdling.)

4 Remove the vanilla pod and pour the hot milk over the egg mixture, whisking all the time. Pour the mixture back into the ceramic cooking pot and stir until slightly thickened. Bring the custard to simmering point; do not let it boil or it may curdle. Cook until it is thick enough to coat the back of a wooden spoon.

Making sabayon sauce

This frothy sauce goes well with elegant desserts and dainty pastries. This recipe makes about 450ml/¾ pint/scant 2 cups.

1 Pour about 5cm/2in near-boiling water into the ceramic cooking pot. Cover with the lid and switch to high.

2 Put 4 eggs and 50g/2oz/¼ cup caster (superfine) sugar in a heatproof bowl, first checking that it will fit comfortably in the slow cooker. Beat well until the mixture becomes a paler colour, then whisk in 100ml/3½fl oz/generous ½ cup sweet white wine.

3 Place the bowl in the ceramic cooking pot and pour enough boiling water around it to come just over halfway up the sides. Continue whisking the sauce for 10 minutes until it is very thick and frothy. Serve hot or cold.

Making creamy chocolate sauce

This dark, velvety smooth sauce should be served with desserts that can stand up to its deep, rich flavour.

1 Pour 200ml/7fl oz/scant 1 cup double (heavy) cream, 60ml/4 tbsp milk and 2.5ml/½ tsp vanilla essence (extract) into the ceramic cooking pot. Switch the slow cooker to high and heat for about 45 minutes.

2 Turn off the slow cooker. Add 150g/5oz chopped dark (bittersweet) chocolate and stir continuously until it has melted. Serve warm.

Making glossy chocolate sauce

This sweet pouring sauce is ideal for serving with profiteroles and ice cream.

Put 225g/8oz chopped plain (semisweet) chocolate, 60ml/4 tbsp golden (light corn) syrup, 60ml/4 tbsp water and 25g/1oz/ 2 tbsp unsalted (sweet) butter into the ceramic cooking pot. Switch the slow cooker to high and heat, stirring, for 30 minutes until melted. Serve warm.

Making white chocolate sauce

This sweet creamy sauce is good served warm with fresh summer fruits.

1 Pour about 5cm/2in very hot water into the cooking pot. Cover with the lid and switch the slow cooker to high.

2 Put 200g/7oz white chocolate and 30ml/2 tbsp double (heavy) cream into a heatproof bowl. Place in the cooking pot and pour enough near-boiling water around the bowl to touch the base.

3 Stir until melted, then stir in 60ml/ 4 tbsp double (heavy) cream and 60ml/4 tbsp milk. Heat for 5 minutes, then remove from the heat and whisk.

Making caramel sauce

This rich, creamy sauce is delicious poured over sweet pastries and pastry desserts.

1 Put 25g/1oz/2 tbsp unsalted (sweet) butter and 75g/3oz/6 tbsp soft dark brown sugar in the ceramic cooking pot. Switch the slow cooker to high and heat for about 20 minutes, stirring occasionally, until the butter has melted and the sugar has dissolved.

2 Stir 150ml/¼ pint/⅔ cup double (heavy) cream into the sauce and cook for 20 minutes, stirring occasionally, until smooth. Serve warm or cold.

Making butterscotch sauce

This buttery sauce is very sweet and rich and should be served in small quantities.

1 Put 50g/2oz/¼ cup unsalted (sweet) butter, 75g/3oz/6 tbsp soft light brown sugar, 50g/2oz/¼ cup caster (superfine) sugar and 150g/5oz/scant ½ cup golden (light corn) syrup into the ceramic cooking pot. Heat on high for 20 minutes, stirring, until the sugar has dissolved.

2 Gradually stir in 150ml/¼ pint/⅔ cup double (heavy) cream and 5ml/1 tsp vanilla essence (extract). Serve warm.

MAKING FONDUES

Fondues are tremendous fun for informal entertaining, and if you already own a slow cooker you won't need a special fondue set to keep the dip warm at the table. The smaller models of slow cooker are ideal for fondue-making because they are deeper and the mixture needs to be at least 5cm/2in deep for dipping. Cheese, chocolate and butterscotch fondues can all be made in the slow cooker. Meat fondues cooked in hot oil are unsuitable because the slow cooker does not reach a high enough temperature.

Making cheese fondue

There are many versions and variations of this hot cheese dip. The classic Swiss cheese fondue, traditionally enjoyed after an exhausting day of Alpine skiing, usually uses hard cheeses, such as Emmenthal and Gruyère, and slightly softer ones, such as Appenzeller.

This basic recipe serves four to six people and can be used as a guide for creating your own variations. Try using beer, cider, ale or milk in place of the white wine, or add brandy in place of Kirsch. Alternatively, you can vary the cheese, using mature (sharp) Cheddar or Monterey Jack. You can buy packets of cheese mixtures for fondues but check the label carefully; *fromage fondu* is a term for a blended cheese product and not a cheese for fondue-making.

1 Rub the inside of the ceramic cooking pot with the cut half of a clove of garlic. This will impart a subtle flavour to the fondue. Pour in 150ml/¼ pint/⅔ cup dry white wine. Cover with the lid, then switch the slow cooker to high and heat for 45 minutes.

2 In a small bowl, blend 10ml/2 tsp cornflour (cornstarch) with 15ml/1 tbsp Kirsch to make a smooth paste, then stir in a pinch of freshly grated nutmeg and season well with ground black pepper.

3 Stir the cornflour mixture into the hot wine until thickened and smooth. (The cornflour will help to prevent the fondue separating once the cheese is added.)

4 Sprinkle 225g/8oz grated Gruyère or Emmenthal cheese over the wine and stir until completely melted. Switch the slow cooker to low and continue stirring until the fondue is thoroughly blended and smooth. Add a little more wine if the mixture seems too thick. The fondue is now ready to serve, or can be kept warm on low for up to an hour.

SPECIALITY FONDUES

While the Swiss fondue is classic, other countries have their own versions. *Fonduta* is a creamy fondue made with Fontina cheese from the Piedmontese region of Italy.
The Dutch *kaasdoop* is a similar hot cheese dip. The French make fondue using Comte and Beaufort cheese.

SAVOURY DIPPERS

Savoury fondues are usually served with cubes of crusty bread, which are speared on to long-handled forks for dipping: Swiss tradition has it that anyone who loses their piece of bread in the fondue has to pay a forfeit. There are lots of other foods that can be dipped into the fondue as an alternative to bread:

• Crispy bacon rolls: rinded streaky (fatty) bacon rashers (strips) cut in half widthways, rolled and skewered, then grilled (broiled) or oven-baked. Cooked cocktail sausages.

• Small whole mushrooms, grilled (broiled) or lightly fried.

• Vegetable crudités such as florets of raw cauliflower.

Making chocolate fondue

This smooth, not-too-sweet fondue makes a deliciously indulgent dessert. It is made using equal quantities of chocolate and cream, so you can easily increase the quantities to feed more people, if necessary. This recipe makes enough to serve four people.

If you prefer, you can use other types of chocolate, such as milk or white; be sure to choose a good quality chocolate that is intended for melting because many brands of eating chocolate are difficult to melt.

This recipe can also be used as a guide for a fudge fondue. Simply omit the liqueur and add 65g/2½oz chopped caramel chocolate bars in place of the dark (bittersweet) chocolate.

1 Pour 150ml/¼ pint/⅔ cup double (heavy) cream into the ceramic cooking pot and switch the slow cooker to high. Stir in 15ml/1 tbsp orange or coffee liqueur, then cover with the lid and heat for about 30 minutes.

2 Finely chop 150g/5oz dark (bittersweet) chocolate and sprinkle over the hot cream mixture. Stir with a wooden spoon until melted and well blended, then switch the slow cooker to low.

3 Keep the chocolate fondue warm for up to 30 minutes, or serve immediately. For a thicker fondue, turn off the slow cooker and leave to cool for 10 minutes.

Butterscotch fondue

This rich, creamy fondue is especially good served with sweet fruits, such as pineapples, pears and bananas. This recipe will serve four to six people.

1 Cut 115g/4oz/½ cup unsalted (sweet) butter into small cubes and place in the ceramic cooking pot. Add 115g/4oz/ 1 cup dark muscovado (molasses) sugar and heat on high for about 15 minutes, until the butter starts to melt.

2 Pour in 200ml/7fl oz/scant 1 cup double (heavy) cream and stir until the sugar dissolves.

3 Stir in 2.5ml/½ tsp vanilla essence (extract), then cover with the lid and cook on high for 30 minutes, stirring occasionally, until the sauce is smooth and creamy. Switch the slow cooker to low and keep warm for up to 1 hour.

4 Before serving, turn off the slow cooker and leave for 10 minutes to allow the sauce to cool and thicken slightly.

SWEET DIPPERS

As with savoury fondues, there are all manner of sweet and fruity treats that you can dip into hot chocolate or butterscotch fondues.

• Pink and white marshmallows, bitesize strawberries and marzipan cut into small shapes.

• Fresh fruits such as seedless grapes, tangerine segments, pineapple cubes, sliced figs and kiwis. (Toss any fruits that are likely to discolour, such as apples, in a little orange juice.)

• Plain cake, such as Madeira or fruit cake, cut into small cubes. Cut up the cake a few hours before serving to allow it to dry out and firm up.

MAKING PRESERVES

The slow cooker is excellent for making chutneys, curds and syrups. Although it is unsuitable for making jams and jellies because the temperatures reached are too low to achieve setting point, it can be used for softening fruits at the start of many of these recipes. It is particularly useful for the long simmering needed to soften citrus fruits for marmalades.

Making chutney

Long, gentle cooking in the slow cooker produces chutneys with a well-developed flavour. As a result, slow cooker chutneys can often be eaten immediately and do not need to be matured before eating. Because the slow cooker allows little evaporation, only chutneys with a relatively low liquid content are suitable. Those whose main ingredients contain a lot of liquid, such as rhubarb, tomatoes and marrows (large zucchini), should be avoided because the juices will not evaporate sufficiently to make a thick, spoonable preserve.

You can use the following fruity apple chutney recipe as a guide to making other chutneys. Vary the ingredients, depending on your preference, seasonal availability and the dried fruits that you have to hand.

MAKES JUST OVER 1.3KG/3LB

225g/8oz onions
675g/1½lb cooking apples
25g/1oz fresh root ginger
3 garlic cloves, crushed
450g/1lb/2 cups soft light brown sugar
175ml/6fl oz/¾ cup cider vinegar
450g/1lb mixed dried fruit, such as
    apricots, peaches, figs, dates, prunes
    or sultanas (golden raisins)
5ml/1 tsp salt

1 Peel and finely chop the onions and place in the ceramic cooking pot. Quarter, core, peel and roughly chop the apples into even-size pieces and add to the onions. Peel the ginger, then finely chop and add to the pot. (If the ginger is tough and fibrous, grate it rather than chopping, squeeze the juices into the pot, then discard the fibres.)

2 Add the garlic, sugar and cider vinegar to the ceramic cooking pot and switch the slow cooker to high.

3 Heat, uncovered, for 30 minutes, then stir until the sugar has completely dissolved. Cover with the lid and cook for 6 hours, stirring occasionally.

4 Towards the end of cooking time, chop the dried fruit into small, even-size pieces and stir into the chutney with the salt. Cover and cook for 2–3 hours, or until the chutney is thick, stirring once or twice towards the end of cooking.

5 Spoon the chutney into hot sterilized jars and seal with vinegar-proof tops. Label and store in a cool dark place. Use within 6 months of making and once opened, store in the refrigerator.

Making fruit curd

Using the slow cooker as a bain-marie is a great way to make fruit curds because the temperature of the water won't get too hot and spoil the preserve. You can use this basic citrus fruit curd recipe as a base for other fruit curds. To make a passion fruit curd, use 30ml/2 tbsp less citrus juice and stir in the seeds and pulp of 2 passion fruits at the end of cooking. If you prefer a richer, firmer preserve, replace some of the beaten egg with 2 egg yolks.

MAKES ABOUT 675G/1½LB

finely grated rind of 3 lemons,
    4 limes or 2 oranges (preferably
    unwaxed or organic)
150ml/¼ pint/⅔ cup lemon, lime
    or orange juice
350g/12oz/1¾ cups caster
    (superfine) sugar
115g/4oz/8 tbsp unsalted (sweet)
    butter, diced
150ml/¼ pint/⅔ cup beaten eggs

1 Pour 5cm/2in hot water into the ceramic cooking pot and switch the slow cooker to high. Put the citrus rind and juice, sugar and butter into a large heatproof bowl, first checking that it will fit in the slow cooker.

2 Put the bowl in the slow cooker and pour enough near-boiling water around the bowl to come just over halfway up the sides. Leave for 15 minutes, stirring occasionally, until the sugar has dissolved and the butter has melted. Remove the bowl from the ceramic cooking pot and leave to cool for a few minutes. Turn the slow cooker to low.

3 Pour the beaten eggs through a sieve (strainer) into the fruit mixture and whisk to combine. Cover the bowl with foil, then return it to the slow cooker.

4 Cook on low for 1–1½ hours, stirring every 15 minutes, until the curd thickens and lightly coats the back of the spoon.

5 Remove the bowl from the slow cooker and pour the curd into small warmed sterilized jars. If you prefer a smooth curd, strain through a sieve before potting.

6 Cover each jar with a waxed disc and cellophane, then label. Store in a cool, dark place or the refrigerator and use within 3 months. Once opened, store in the refrigerator and use within 1 week.

Making marmalade

Although the slow cooker can't be used to bring marmalade to setting point, it is ideal for the long simmering of the peel. This recipe will fit in a 3.4 litre/6 pint/14¼ cup slow cooker, but you can double or halve the quantities as necessary.

MAKES ABOUT 2.75KG/6LB

900g/2lb Seville (Temple) oranges
1.5 litres/2½ pints/6¼ cups
    near-boiling water
juice of 2 lemons
1.8kg/4lb/9 cups sugar

1 Wash and scrub the oranges. Cut them in half, squeeze out the juice and reserve. Remove the pips and membrane from the peel and tie them in a piece of muslin (cheesecloth). Slice the orange peel thinly or thickly, as preferred.

2 Put the peel and muslin bag in the ceramic cooking pot, then pour over the water and lemon juice. Cover the pot with the lid and switch the slow cooker to high. Cook for 4–6 hours, or until the peel is tender. (The peel must be really soft before adding the sugar.)

3 Remove the muslin bag and leave until cool enough to handle. Squeeze the liquid from it into a large, heavy pan. Transfer the rind and cooking liquid from the slow cooker to the pan. Add the orange juice and sugar and heat gently, stirring until the sugar has dissolved.

4 Bring the mixture to the boil and boil rapidly for about 15 minutes until the marmalade reaches 105°C/220°F on a sugar thermometer. (Alternatively, place a spoonful of the marmalade on a chilled saucer and leave to cool for 1 minute. Press gently with your finger and it should wrinkle; if not, continue boiling.)

5 Remove the pan from the heat and skim off any scum using a slotted spoon. Leave to stand for 15 minutes, then stir to distribute the peel evenly. Ladle the marmalade into hot sterilized jars, seal and label. Store in a cool, dark place and use within one year of making.

Making cordial

The slow cooker is the perfect vehicle for infusing flavours such as citrus rind and spices. It brings the liquid very slowly to the boil and maintains it at a constant, low temperature, ensuring that maximum flavour is extracted. It is therefore perfect for making cordials, as well as syrups for fruit compotes. This recipe is for lemon cordial, but you can use the same method to make other flavours. Try using the rind of 2 oranges and the juice of 1 lemon. Alternatively, omit the lemon rind and use 10 scented rose petals, 1 split vanilla pod (bean) and the juice of 1 lemon.

MAKES ABOUT 1.2 LITRES/2 PINTS/5 CUPS

3 large juicy lemons, preferably
    unwaxed or organic
350g/12oz/1¾ cups caster
    (superfine) sugar
sparkling mineral water and ice, to serve

1 Wash the lemons, then thinly pare off the rind, leaving the bitter white pith behind. Put the rind in the cooking pot with the sugar and 1 litre/1¾ pints/4 cups cold water. Cover and switch the slow cooker to high.

2 Heat for 30 minutes, then stir until the sugar has dissolved. Cook for a further 1½ hours, then leave to cool.

3 Halve the lemons and squeeze out the juice. Stir into the syrup, then strain through a stainless steel or plastic sieve. Pour into sterilized bottles, seal and label. Store in the refrigerator for up to 10 days. To serve, dilute to taste with mineral water and serve over ice.

SLOW COOKER SAFETY

The slow cooker is an extremely efficient and safe way to cook food. It is however an electrical appliance, and some basic common-sense safety precautions should be followed. Because slow cooker models vary, always take the time to read the instruction manual supplied by the manufacturer before use.

Cooker care

Looking after your cooker is simple but very important. When you first unwrap and remove your slow cooker from its box, check that it isn't damaged in any way, that the plug (which has hopefully been provided) is attached properly and, if you bought your slow cooker in another country, that the voltage on the rating plate of the appliance corresponds with your house electricity supply. If you are in any doubt, consult a qualified electrician before using the slow cooker.

Before you use the slow cooker for the first time, wash the ceramic cooking pot in warm soapy water and dry it thoroughly. Stand the slow cooker on a heat-resistant surface when in use, making sure that the mains lead is tucked away safely; the slow cooker should not touch anything hot or hang over the edge of the table or work-top in case it falls off accidentally.

Take extra care if you have young children (or curious pets) and position the slow cooker out of reach. After an hour or so of cooking, the slow cooker can become very hot; not just the

Below: Do not submerge the slow cooker in water. If it needs cleaning, make sure it is unplugged and use a damp, soapy sponge.

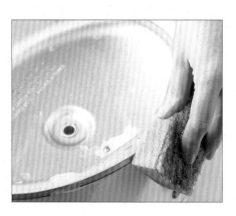

Above: Protect your hands from the hot cooker and escaping steam with a pair of padded oven gloves.

ceramic cooking pot, but the outer casing and the lid as well. Always use oven gloves when lifting the lid (do this away from you to prevent scalding from steam or drips), and when removing the cooking pot from inside the slow cooker.

Do not switch on the slow cooker if the ceramic cooking pot is empty (the only exception to this would be if the manufacturer recommends preheating). As soon as you have finished cooking, remove the plug from the socket to prevent the slow cooker being switched on accidentally.

Never immerse the outer casing of the slow cooker in water – this would be extremely dangerous, risking electric shock and fatal injury, because the outer casing contains the electrical elements that heat the ceramic cooking pot.

You should never use the outer casing for cooking without the ceramic cooking pot in place. If you need to clean the casing, do so with warm soapy water and a damp cloth, and be absolutely sure that the appliance is unplugged before you put it in contact with water.

Ensuring food safety

Slow cookers cook food slowly using a gentle heat – the precise temperature will vary from model to model but the average is from about 90°C/200°F on the low setting to about 150°C/300°F on the high setting. Bacteria in food is destroyed at a temperature of 74°C/165°F, so as long as the food is cooked

for the appropriate length of time, as stated in the recipe, this temperature will be reached quickly enough to ensure that the food is safe to eat. However, additional factors may affect the slow cooker's ability to reach the desired temperature and you should be aware of the following to ensure food safety:
• Avoid placing the slow cooker near an open window or in a draught.
• Do not lift the lid during cooking time unless instructed to do so in the recipe.
• Do not add ingredients that are frozen or part-frozen to the ceramic cooking pot because they will increase the length of time needed to reach the required cooking temperature, and the timings given in the recipe will not be sufficient.
• Increase the cooking time in extreme cold temperatures, where the kitchen temperature is considerably lower than normal, and check food is cooked before serving, particularly poultry and pork.

Checking meat is cooked

When it comes to food safety, one of the main things to look out for is that meat is properly cooked – in particular, poultry and pork. A meat thermometer is a worthwhile investment if you are planning to cook whole joints of meat and poultry in your slow cooker. It is the most reliable way to ensure that the inside of the meat has reached a high enough temperature to kill any potentially harmful bacteria, without losing its juices and becoming dry and overcooked.

Below: A meat thermometer is easy to use and gives an accurate temperature reading to let you know when meat is safe to eat.

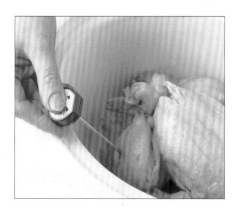

Above*: A skewer or the tip of a sharp knife can be inserted into a thick part of a meat joint to check that it is thoroughly cooked*

When using a meat thermometer, the tip of the stainless steel probe should be inserted as near the centre of the meat as possible, but not touching any bone. Meat thermometers have different markings for various meats, indicating rare and pinkish lamb and beef, through to medium and well cooked. Pork and poultry must always be cooked thoroughly to avoid the risk of food poisoning as they can pass on harmful bacteria when raw or partially cooked; always err on the side of caution and go for well cooked, rather than risk the meat being underdone and therefore unsafe.

To check that meat is cooked without a thermometer, insert the tip of a thin sharp knife or skewer into the thickest part of the meat joint and hold it there for 20 seconds. For medium to well-cooked lamb or beef, the juices will be almost clear and the knife will feel hot on the back of the hand. When cooking pork or poultry, it is essential that the meat juices should be completely clear. If there is any trace of pink, the meat is not ready to eat and should be cooked for a further 30 minutes; check again with the skewer or knife before serving.

With poultry, you can double check by giving the leg a tug – it should have some give in it and not be resistant. If you are still unsure, make a deep cut where the thigh joins the body; there should be no visible trace of pink meat. If there is, cook the meat for a further 30 minutes, then check again.

FOOD SAFETY TIPS

Basic food safety recommendations should be followed when preparing or using food in the slow cooker.

• Food should always be at room temperature when it is added to the slow cooker, otherwise it will take longer to reach the safe cooking temperature. However, ingredients such as meat and fish should not be left out of the refrigerator for longer than is necessary, so remove from the refrigerator just to take off the chill and keep covered with cling film or plastic wrap.

• Marinating food in the ceramic cooking pot before cooking saves on washing up, but the cooking pot will become cold in the refrigerator, so remove it at least 1 hour before you plan to start cooking.

• Large joints of meat and whole poultry should be cooked at a high temperature for the first 1–2 hours to accelerate the cooking process. Switch the slow cooker to low for the remaining cooking time.

• Avoid lifting the lid of the ceramic cooking during the cooking time, especially in the early stages. It takes 15–20 minutes to recover the lost heat each time the lid is removed, so it will take much longer to reach a safe temperature.

• Don't be tempted to partially cook meat or poultry, then refrigerate for subsequent cooking. Also avoid reheating pre-cooked dishes in the slow cooker.

• Frozen foods should always be thoroughly thawed before being placed in the slow cooker. If added when frozen, they will increase the time the food takes to reach a safe temperature. If adding frozen vegetables towards the end of cooking time, thaw them first under cold running water.

• Soak dried beans, in particular red kidney beans, overnight and then fast-boil them on the stovetop for 10 minutes in a pan of fresh cooking water to destroy toxins before adding to the slow cooker.

SOUPS AND APPETIZERS

The slow cooker truly excels when it comes to soup-making – the long, gentle cooking allows the flavours to develop fully over time, giving rich, flavoursome results. It is great for making appetizers too, particularly pâtés and terrines, which work exceptionally well. This chapter draws on recipes from around the world and offers dishes for every occasion – from North African spiced soup and Galician broth for a hearty lunch to delicate Greek avgolemono for an elegant start to a meal. There are pretty fish terrines, along with chicken mousselines and divine poached pears stuffed with cheese, which are perfect for a special dinner party.

FRENCH ONION SOUP with CHEESE CROÛTES

Probably the most famous of all onion soups, this hearty, warming dish was traditionally served as a sustaining early morning meal to the porters and workers of Les Halles market in Paris. Use large yellow Spanish onions for the best result.

3 Add the sugar and stir well. Cover again with the lid and folded dish towel and continue cooking on high for 4 hours, stirring two or three times, to ensure the onions are colouring evenly. At the end of this time, they should be a dark golden colour.

4 Sprinkle the flour over the onions and stir to mix. Next, stir in the vinegar followed by the brandy, then slowly blend in the wine. Stir in the stock and thyme and season with salt and pepper. Cook on high for a further 2 hours, or until the onions are very tender.

5 For the croûtes, place the bread slices under a low grill (broiler) and cook until dry and lightly browned. Rub the bread with the cut surface of the garlic and spread with mustard, then sprinkle the grated Gruyère cheese over the slices.

6 Turn the grill to high and cook the croûtes for 2–3 minutes, until the cheese melts, bubbles and browns. Ladle the soup into warmed bowls and float a Gruyère croûte on top of each. Serve straight away.

SERVES 4

40g/1½oz/3 tbsp butter
10ml/2 tsp olive oil
1.2kg/2½lb onions, peeled and sliced
5ml/1 tsp caster (superfine) sugar
15ml/1 tbsp plain (all-purpose) flour
15ml/1 tbsp sherry vinegar
30ml/2 tbsp brandy
120ml/4fl oz/½ cup dry white wine
1 litre/1¾ pints/4 cups boiling beef, chicken or duck stock
5ml/1 tsp chopped fresh thyme
salt and ground black pepper

For the croûtes
4 slices day-old French stick or baguette, about 2.5cm/1in thick
1 garlic clove, halved
5ml/1 tsp French mustard
50g/2oz/½ cup grated Gruyère cheese

1 Put the butter and olive oil in the ceramic cooking pot and heat on high for about 15 minutes until melted.

2 Add the onions to the pot and stir to coat well in the melted butter and oil. Cover with the lid, then place a folded dish towel over the top to retain all the heat and cook for 2 hours, stirring halfway through cooking time.

Nutritional information per portion: Energy 418Kcal/1747kJ; Protein 11.5g; Carbohydrate 51.8g, of which sugars 19.4g; Fat 15.9g, of which saturates 8.2g; Cholesterol 33mg; Calcium 209mg; Fibre 5.3g; Sodium 1195mg.

CARROT and CORIANDER SOUP

Root vegetables, such as carrots, are great for slow cooker soups. Their earthy flavour becomes rich and sweet when cooked slowly over a gentle heat and goes perfectly with robust herbs and spices, and their texture becomes beautifully smooth when puréed.

SERVES 4

450g/1lb carrots, preferably young
   and tender
15ml/1 tbsp sunflower oil
40g/1½oz/3 tbsp butter
1 onion, chopped
1 stick celery, plus 2–3 pale leafy tops
2 small potatoes, peeled
900ml/1½ pints/3¾ cups boiling
   vegetable stock
10ml/2 tsp ground coriander
15ml/1 tbsp chopped fresh coriander
   (cilantro)
150ml/¼ pint/⅔ cup milk
salt and ground black pepper

3 Pour the boiling vegetable stock over the vegetables, then season with salt and ground black pepper. Cover the pot with the lid and cook on low for 4–5 hours until the vegetables are tender.

4 Reserve 6–8 tiny celery leaves from the leafy tops for the garnish, then finely chop the remaining celery tops. Melt the remaining butter in a large pan and add the ground coriander. Fry for about 1 minute, stirring constantly, until the aromas are released.

5 Reduce the heat under the pan and add the chopped celery tops and fresh coriander. Fry for about 30 seconds, then remove the pan from the heat.

6 Ladle the soup into a food processor or blender and process until smooth, then pour into the pan with the celery tops and coriander. Stir in the milk and heat gently until piping hot. Check the seasoning, then serve garnished with the reserved celery leaves.

1 Trim and peel the carrots and cut into chunks. Heat the oil and 25g/1oz/2 tbsp of the butter in a pan and fry the onion over a gentle heat for 3–4 minutes until slightly softened. Do not let it brown.

2 Slice the celery and chop the potatoes, and add them to the onion in the pan. Cook for 2 minutes, then add the carrots and cook for a further 1 minute. Transfer the fried vegetables to the ceramic cooking pot.

Nutritional information per portion: Energy 168Kcal/697kJ; Protein 3g; Carbohydrate 11.9g, of which sugars 9.2g; Fat 12.4g, of which saturates 6g; Cholesterol 24mg; Calcium 94mg; Fibre 3.1g; Sodium 758mg.

TOMATO and FRESH BASIL SOUP

Peppery, aromatic basil is the perfect partner for sweet, ripe tomatoes – and it is easy to grow at home in a pot on a sunny kitchen windowsill. Make this soup in late summer when fresh tomatoes are at their best and most flavoursome.

SERVES 4

15ml/1 tbsp olive oil
25g/1oz/2 tbsp butter
1 onion, finely chopped
900g/2lb ripe tomatoes, roughly chopped
1 garlic clove, roughly chopped
about 600ml/1 pint/2½ cups
    vegetable stock
120ml/4fl oz/½ cup dry white wine
30ml/2 tbsp sun-dried tomato paste
30ml/2 tbsp shredded fresh basil
150ml/¼ pint/⅔ cup double
    (heavy) cream
salt and ground black pepper
whole basil leaves, to garnish

1 Heat the oil and butter in a large saucepan until foaming. Add the onion and cook gently for about 5 minutes, stirring, until the onion is softened but not brown, then add the chopped tomatoes and garlic.

2 Add the stock, white wine and sun-dried tomato paste to the pan and stir to combine. Heat until just below boiling point, then carefully pour the mixture into the ceramic cooking pot.

3 Switch the slow cooker to the high or auto setting, cover with the lid and cook for 1 hour. Leave the slow cooker on auto or switch to low and cook for a further 4–6 hours, until tender.

4 Leave the soup to cool for a few minutes, then ladle into a food processor or blender and process until smooth. Press the puréed soup through a sieve (strainer) into a clean pan.

5 Add the shredded basil and the cream to the soup and heat through, stirring. Do not allow the soup to reach boiling point. Check the consistency and add a little more stock if necessary. Season, then pour into warmed bowls and garnish with basil. Serve immediately.

Nutritional information per portion: Energy 335Kcal/1387kJ; Protein 3.1g; Carbohydrate 11.7g, of which sugars 10.8g; Fat 28.9g, of which saturates 16.4g; Cholesterol 65mg; Calcium 50mg; Fibre 3g; Sodium 168mg.

CHILLED TOMATO and SWEET PEPPER SOUP

Inspired by the classic Spanish soup, gazpacho, which is made with raw salad vegetables, this soup is cooked first and then chilled. Grilling the peppers gives a slightly smoky flavour, but you can leave out this step to save on preparation time, if you like.

SERVES 4

2 red (bell) peppers
30ml/2 tbsp olive oil
1 onion, finely chopped
2 garlic cloves, crushed
675g/1½lb ripe, well-flavoured
    tomatoes
120ml/4fl oz/½ cup red wine
450ml/¾ pint/scant 2 cups vegetable
    or chicken stock
2.5ml/½ tsp caster (superfine) sugar
salt and ground black pepper
chopped fresh chives, to garnish

For the croûtons
2 slices white bread, crusts removed
45ml/3 tbsp olive oil

1 Cut each pepper into quarters and remove the core and seeds. Place each quarter, skin side up, on a grill (broiler) rack. Grill (broil) until the skins are blistered and charred, then transfer to a bowl and cover with a plate.

2 Heat the oil in a frying pan. Add the onion and garlic and cook gently for about 10 minutes until soft, stirring occasionally. Meanwhile, remove the skin from the peppers and roughly chop the flesh. Cut the tomatoes into chunks.

3 Transfer the onions to the ceramic cooking pot and add the peppers, tomatoes, wine, stock and sugar. Cover and cook on high for 3–4 hours, or until the vegetables are very tender. Leave the soup to stand for about 10 minutes to cool slightly.

4 Ladle the soup into a food processor or blender and process until smooth. Press through a fine sieve (strainer) into a bowl. Leave to cool before chilling in the refrigerator for at least 3 hours.

5 Meanwhile, make the croûtons. Cut the bread into cubes. Heat the oil in a frying pan, add the bread and fry until golden. Drain well on kitchen paper.

6 Season the soup to taste with salt and pepper, then ladle into chilled bowls. Serve topped with a few croûtons and a sprinkling of chopped chives.

Nutritional information per portion: Energy 262Kcal/1090kJ; Protein 3.5g; Carbohydrate 17.6g, of which sugars 11.5g; Fat 18g, of which saturates 2.6g; Cholesterol 0mg; Calcium 47mg; Fibre 3.4g; Sodium 499mg.

SPICY PUMPKIN SOUP

This stunning golden-orange soup has a smooth velvety texture, and a delicate taste, which is subtly spiced with cumin and garlic. Long, slow cooking really gives the flavours time to develop and come together to make a wonderful autumnal dish.

SERVES 4

900g/2lb pumpkin, peeled
   and seeds removed
30ml/2 tbsp olive oil
2 leeks, trimmed and sliced
1 garlic clove, crushed
5ml/1 tsp ground ginger
5ml/1 tsp ground cumin
750ml/1¼ pints/3 cups near-boiling
   chicken stock
salt and ground black pepper
60ml/4 tbsp natural (plain) yogurt, to serve
coriander (cilantro) leaves, to garnish

COOK'S TIP
To save time, reheat the soup on the stovetop rather than in the slow cooker.

1 Using a sharp knife, cut the pumpkin into large chunks. Place the chunks in the ceramic cooking pot.

2 Heat the oil in a large pan and add the leeks and garlic. Cook gently until softened but not coloured.

3 Add the ginger and cumin to the pan and cook, stirring, for a further minute. Tip the mixture into the ceramic cooking pot, pour over the chicken stock and season with salt and black pepper.

4 Cover the slow cooker with the lid, switch to low and cook for 6–8 hours, or until the pumpkin is very tender.

5 Ladle the soup, in batches if necessary, into a food processor or blender and process until smooth. Return the soup to the rinsed out cooking pot, cover and cook on high for 1 hour, or until piping hot. Serve in warmed individual bowls, with a swirl of natural yogurt and a few coriander leaves.

Nutritional information per portion: Energy 89Kcal/372kJ; Protein 2.3g; Carbohydrate 6.2g, of which sugars 4.7g; Fat 6.3g, of which saturates 1.1g; Cholesterol 0mg; Calcium 75mg; Fibre 3.1g; Sodium 127mg.

WILD MUSHROOM SOUP

*This robust, creamy soup is ideal for a simple lunch or supper, served with chunks of
nutty wholegrain bread spread with fresh butter. The rich flavour and colour of the soup
are further enhanced by the addition of dried wild mushrooms and a dash of Madeira.*

SERVES 4

15g/½oz/¼ cup dried wild mushrooms,
    such as morels, ceps or porcini
600ml/1 pint/2½ cups hot chicken
    or vegetable stock
25g/1oz/2 tbsp butter
1 onion, finely chopped
1 garlic clove, crushed
450g/1lb button (white) or other
    cultivated mushrooms, trimmed
    and sliced
15ml/1 tbsp plain (all-purpose) flour
fresh nutmeg
1.5ml/¼ tsp dried thyme
60ml/4 tbsp Madeira or dry sherry
60ml/4 tbsp crème fraîche or
    sour cream
salt and ground black pepper
chopped fresh chives, to garnish

1 Put the dried mushrooms in a sieve
(strainer) and rinse under cold running
water to remove any grit, then place in
the ceramic cooking pot. Pour over half
of the hot chicken or vegetable stock
and cover with the lid. Switch the slow
cooker to the auto or high setting.

2 Place the butter in a large pan and melt
over a medium heat. Add the chopped
onion and cook for 5–7 minutes until
softened and just golden.

3 Add the garlic and fresh mushrooms
to the pan and cook for 5 minutes.
Sprinkle over the flour, then grate some
nutmeg into the mixture and add the
thyme. Cook for 3 minutes more,
stirring all the time, until blended.

4 Stir in the Madeira or sherry and the
remaining stock, and season with salt and
pepper. Bring to the boil, then transfer
to the ceramic cooking pot. Cook for
1 hour, then switch to low or leave on
auto and cook for a further 3–4 hours,
or until the mushrooms are very tender.

5 Ladle the soup into a food processor
or blender and process until smooth.
Strain it back into the pan, pressing it
with the back of a spoon to force the
purée through the sieve.

6 Reheat the soup until piping hot, then
stir in half the crème fraîche or sour
cream. Ladle into warmed bowls, swirl
a little of the remaining crème fraîche
or sour cream on top of each and
sprinkle with chives.

COOK'S TIP
Dried mushrooms have a rich, intense
flavour and are perfect for boosting the
flavour of cultivated mushrooms, which
can often be rather bland.

Nutritional information per portion: Energy 143Kcal/592kJ; Protein 3.7g; Carbohydrate 8.2g, of which sugars 3.2g; Fat 9g, of which saturates 5.3g; Cholesterol 22mg; Calcium 41mg; Fibre 2g; Sodium 174mg.

GENOESE MINESTRONE

In the Italian city of Genoa, pesto is stirred into minestrone to add extra flavour and colour. This tasty version is packed with vegetables and makes an excellent vegetarian supper dish when served with bread. To save time, you can use ready-made bottled pesto.

SERVES 4

30ml/2 tbsp olive oil
1 onion, finely chopped
2 celery sticks, finely chopped
1 large carrot, finely chopped
1 potato, weighing about 115g/4oz,
  cut into 1cm/½in cubes
1 litre/1¾ pints/4 cups vegetable stock
75g/3oz green beans, cut into 5cm/
  2in pieces
1 courgette (zucchini), thinly sliced
2 Italian plum tomatoes, peeled
  and chopped
200g/7oz can cannellini beans, drained
  and rinsed
¼ Savoy cabbage, shredded
40g/1½oz dried "quick-cook" spaghetti
  or vermicelli, broken into short lengths
salt and ground black pepper

For the pesto
about 20 fresh basil leaves
1 garlic clove
10ml/2 tsp pine nuts
15ml/1 tbsp freshly grated
  Parmesan cheese
15ml/1 tbsp freshly grated Pecorino cheese
30ml/2 tbsp olive oil

1 Heat the olive oil in a pan, then add the chopped onion, celery and carrot and cook, stirring, for about 7 minutes, until the vegetables begin to soften.

2 Transfer the fried vegetables to the ceramic cooking pot. Add the potato cubes and vegetable stock, cover the cooking pot with the lid and cook on high for 1½ hours.

3 Add the green beans, courgette, tomatoes and cannellini beans to the pot. Cover and cook for 1 hour, then stir in the cabbage and pasta and cook for a further 20 minutes.

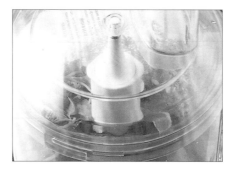

4 Meanwhile, place all the pesto ingredients in a food processor. Blend to make a smooth sauce, adding 15–45ml/1–3 tbsp water through the feeder tube to loosen the mixture if necessary.

5 Stir 30ml/2 tbsp of the pesto sauce into the soup. Check the seasoning, adding more if necessary. Serve hot, in warmed bowls, with the remaining pesto spooned on top of each serving.

Nutritional information per portion: Energy 263Kcal/1098kJ; Protein 8.5g; Carbohydrate 25.1g, of which sugars 7g; Fat 14.9g, of which saturates 2.8g; Cholesterol 5mg; Calcium 103mg; Fibre 5.4g; Sodium 1034mg.

GALICIAN BROTH

This classic Galician soup from the north coast of Spain needs long, slow cooking to give the flavours time to develop fully. Traditionally it would be made with young, green leafy turnip tops, but in this version tasty spring greens are used instead.

SERVES 6

450g/1lb gammon, in one piece, soaked
   overnight in cold water
2 bay leaves
2 onions, sliced
10ml/2 tsp paprika
675g/1½lb baking potatoes, cut into
   2.5cm/1in chunks
225g/8oz spring greens (collards)
425g/15oz can haricot (navy) or cannellini
   beans, drained
ground black pepper

COOK'S TIP
Bacon knuckles can be used instead of
the gammon. The bones will give the
stock a delicious flavour. If there is any
broth left over, you can freeze it and use
it as stock for another soup.

1 Drain the gammon and put it in the ceramic cooking pot with the bay leaves and onions. Pour over just enough fresh cold water to cover the gammon. Switch to high, cover and cook for 1 hour.

2 Skim off any scum, then re-cover and cook for 3 hours. Check and skim the broth once or twice if necessary.

3 Using a slotted spoon and a large fork, carefully lift the gammon out of the slow cooker and on to a board. Add the paprika and potatoes to the broth and cook for 1 hour.

4 Meanwhile, discard the skin and fat from the gammon and cut the meat into small chunks. Add it to the slow cooker and cook for a further 2 hours, or until the meat and potatoes are tender.

5 Remove the cores from the greens, then roll up the leaves and cut into thin shreds. Add to the slow cooker with the beans and cook for 30 minutes.

6 Remove the bay leaves from the broth, season with black pepper to taste and serve piping hot.

Nutritional information per portion: Energy 273Kcal/1147kJ; Protein 21.4g; Carbohydrate 33.7g, of which sugars 5.3g; Fat 6.7g, of which saturates 2g; Cholesterol 17mg; Calcium 113mg; Fibre 6.7g; Sodium 974mg.

SEAFOOD CHOWDER

The word chowder takes its name from the French chaudière *– a pot traditionally used for making soups and stews. Like most chowders, this is a substantial dish, and could be served with crusty bread for a tasty lunch or supper.*

3 Sprinkle the flour over the leek mixture and stir in. Gradually add the remaining milk, stirring after each addition. Stir in the stock, followed by the corn mixture. Cover the slow cooker with the lid and cook for 2 hours.

4 Add the rice to the pot and cook for 30 minutes. Meanwhile, pull the corals away from the scallops and slice the white flesh into 5mm/¼in slices. Cut the fish fillet into bitesize chunks.

5 Add the scallops and fish to the chowder and gently stir to combine. Cover and cook for 15 minutes.

SERVES 4

25g/1oz/2 tbsp butter
1 small leek, sliced
1 small garlic clove, crushed
1 celery stalk, chopped
2 rindless smoked streaky (fatty) bacon
    rashers (strips), finely chopped
200g/7oz/generous 1 cup drained, canned
    corn kernels
450ml/¾ pint/scant 2 cups milk
5ml/1 tsp plain (all-purpose) flour
450ml/¾ pint/scant 2 cups boiling chicken
    or vegetable stock
115g/4oz/generous ½ cup easy-cook
    (converted) rice
4 large scallops, preferably with corals
115g/4oz white fish fillet, such as monkfish
15ml/1 tbsp chopped fresh parsley, plus
    extra to garnish
pinch of cayenne pepper
45ml/3 tbsp single (light) cream (optional)
salt and ground black pepper

1 Melt the butter in a frying pan, add the leek, garlic, celery and bacon and cook, stirring frequently, for 10 minutes, until soft but not browned. Transfer the mixture to the ceramic cooking pot and switch the slow cooker on to high.

2 Place half the corn kernels in a food processor or blender. Add about 75ml/2½fl oz/⅓ cup of the milk and process until the mixture is well blended and fairly thick and creamy.

6 Stir the corals, parsley and cayenne pepper into the chowder and cook for 5–10 minutes, or until the vegetables, rice and fish are cooked through. Stir in the cream, if using, ladle into bowls, sprinkle with a little chopped parsley and serve immediately.

Nutritional information per portion: Energy 355Kcal/1497kJ; Protein 18.5g; Carbohydrate 45.9g, of which sugars 10.8g; Fat 12.1g, of which saturates 5.8g; Cholesterol 49mg; Calcium 179mg; Fibre 1.5g; Sodium 655mg.

AVGOLEMONO

This light, delicate soup is a great favourite in Greece and is a fine example of a few carefully chosen ingredients combining to make a delicious dish. It is essential to use a stock that is well flavoured, so use home-made if you can.

SERVES 4

900ml/1 ½ pints/3¾ cups near-boiling
    chicken stock
50g/2oz/⅓ cup easy-cook (converted)
    white rice
3 egg yolks
30–60ml/2–4 tbsp lemon juice
30ml/2 tbsp finely chopped fresh parsley
salt and ground black pepper
lemon slices and parsley sprigs, to garnish

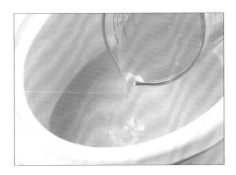

1 Pour the stock into the ceramic cooking pot. Cover with a lid and cook on high for 30 minutes, or until it reaches boiling point.

2 Stir in the rice, cover and cook for 45 minutes, or until the rice is tender. Season to taste with salt and pepper. Switch off the slow cooker, remove the lid and leave to stand for 5 minutes.

3 Meanwhile, whisk the egg yolks in a bowl, then add about 30ml/2 tbsp of the lemon juice, whisking constantly until the mixture is smooth and bubbly. Add a ladleful of the hot soup to the egg mixture, whisking continuously.

4 Slowly add the egg mixture to the soup in the ceramic cooking pot, whisking all the time. The soup will thicken slightly and turn a pretty yellow.

5 Taste and add more lemon juice and seasoning if necessary. Stir in the parsley and serve immediately, garnished with lemon slices and parsley sprigs.

COOK'S TIP
When adding the egg mixture, you need to be careful not to let the soup curdle. You should avoid whisking the mixture into boiling liquid, so allow the soup to cool very slightly before whisking in the egg mixture in a slow, steady stream. Do not reheat the soup.

Nutritional information per portion: Energy 98Kcal/410kJ; Protein 3.3g; Carbohydrate 11.1g, of which sugars 0.3g; Fat 4.8g, of which saturates 1.3g; Cholesterol 151mg; Calcium 26mg; Fibre 0.1g; Sodium 211mg.

CABBAGE, BEETROOT and TOMATO BORSCHT

There are numerous versions of this classic soup, which originates in eastern Europe.
Beetroot and soured cream are the traditional ingredients in every borscht, but other
ingredients tend to be many and varied. This version has a deliciously sweet and sour
taste and can be served piping hot or refreshingly chilled.

SERVES 6

1 onion, chopped
1 carrot, chopped
6 raw or vacuum-packed (cooked, not
   pickled) beetroot (beets), 4 diced
   and 2 coarsely grated
400g/14oz can chopped tomatoes
6 new potatoes, cut into bitesize pieces
1 small white cabbage, thinly sliced
600ml/1 pint/2½ cups vegetable stock
45ml/3 tbsp sugar
30–45ml/2–3 tbsp white wine vinegar
   or cider vinegar
45ml/3 tbsp chopped fresh dill
salt and ground black pepper
sour cream and dill, to garnish
buttered rye bread, to serve

1 Put the onion, carrot, diced beetroot, tomatoes, potatoes and cabbage into the ceramic cooking pot and pour over the vegetable stock. Cover the cooking pot with the lid and cook on high for about 4 hours, or until the vegetables are just tender.

2 Add the grated beetroot, sugar and vinegar to the pot and stir to combine. Cook for a further hour until the beetroot is cooked.

3 Taste the soup, checking for a good sweet/sour balance, and add more sugar and/or vinegar if necessary. Season to taste with plenty of salt and freshly ground black pepper.

4 Just before serving, stir the chopped dill into the soup and ladle into warmed soup bowls. Garnish each serving with a generous spoonful of sour cream and plenty more fresh dill, then serve with thick slices of buttered rye bread.

VARIATIONS
• Borscht is often served cold in summer. To serve chilled, leave it to cool at room temperature, then chill in the refrigerator for at least 4 hours. Ladle into bowls, each containing an ice cube, and top with a large spoonful of soured cream.
• For a different garnish, try scattering finely chopped hard-boiled egg or spring onions (scallions) over the top.

Nutritional information per portion: Energy 125Kcal/531kJ; Protein 3.5g; Carbohydrate 27.8g, of which sugars 7g; Fat 0.7g, of which saturates 0.1g; Cholesterol 0mg; Calcium 58mg; Fibre 3.2g; Sodium 357mg.

CHICKEN SOUP with KNAIDLACH

This famous Jewish soup is often made using a whole chicken cut into portions and slowly simmered in a huge stockpot. If you have a very large slow cooker you can double the quantities given here, using a small whole chicken; the cooking times will remain the same. The knaidlach are cooked separately, so that the clarity of the soup is retained.

SERVES 4

2 chicken portions, about 275g/10oz each
I onion
1.2 litres/2 pints/5 cups boiling
    chicken stock
2 carrots, thickly sliced
2 celery sticks, thickly sliced
I small parsnip, cut into large chunks
small pinch of ground turmeric
30ml/2 tbsp roughly chopped fresh parsley,
    plus extra to garnish
15ml/I tbsp chopped fresh dill
salt and ground black pepper

For the knaidlach
175g/6oz/¾ cup medium matzo meal
2 eggs, lightly beaten
45ml/3 tbsp vegetable oil
30ml/2 tbsp chopped fresh parsley
½ onion, finely grated
pinch of chicken stock cube (optional)
about 90ml/6 tbsp water
salt and ground black pepper

I Rinse the chicken pieces and put them in the ceramic cooking pot. Peel the onion, keeping it whole. Cut a small cross in the stem end and add to the pot with the stock, carrots, celery, parsnip, turmeric, salt and pepper.

2 Cover with the lid and cook on high for I hour. Skim off the scum that comes to the surface. (Scum will continue to form but it is only the first scum that rises that will detract from the appearance and flavour of the soup.)

3 Cook for a further 3 hours, or until the chicken is tender. Remove the chicken, discard the skin and bones and chop the flesh. Skim the fat off the soup, then return the pieces of chicken. Stir in the parsley and dill and continue cooking while you make the knaidlach.

4 Put the matzo meal, eggs, oil, parsley, onion, chicken stock, if using, and water in a large bowl. Mix together well; it should be the consistency of a thick, soft paste. Cover and chill for 30 minutes, until the mixture has become firm.

5 Bring a pan of water to the boil and have a bowl of cold water next to the stove. Dip two tablespoons into the cold water, then take a spoonful of the matzo batter. With wet hands, roll it into a ball, then slip it into the boiling water and reduce the heat so that the water simmers. Continue with the remaining matzo batter, then cover the pan and cook for 15–20 minutes.

6 Remove the knaidlach from the pan with a slotted spoon and divide between individual serving bowls. Leave them to firm up for a few minutes. Ladle the hot soup over the knaidlach and serve sprinkled with extra chopped parsley.

VARIATIONS
• Instead of knaidlach, the soup can be served over cooked rice or noodles.
• To make knaidlach with a lighter texture, separate the eggs and add the yolks to the matzo mixture. Whisk the whites until stiff, then fold into the batter.

Nutritional information per portion: Energy 586Kcal/245IkJ; Protein 38.2g; Carbohydrate 42.6g, of which sugars 6.3g; Fat 30.3g, of which saturates 7.7g; Cholesterol 272mg; Calcium 131mg; Fibre 3.7g; Sodium 802mg.

POTAGE of LENTILS

In this soup, red lentils and vegetables are cooked slowly until very soft, then puréed to give a rich and velvety consistency. On a hot day, serve chilled with extra lemon juice.

SERVES 4

45ml/3 tbsp olive oil
I onion, chopped
2 celery sticks, chopped
I carrot, sliced
2 garlic cloves, peeled and chopped
I potato, peeled and diced
250g/9oz/generous I cup red lentils
750ml/1 ¼ pints/3 cups near-boiling
   vegetable stock
2 bay leaves
I small lemon
2.5ml/½ tsp ground cumin
cayenne pepper or Tabasco sauce, to taste
salt and ground black pepper
lemon slices and chopped fresh flat leaf
   parsley, to serve

I Heat the oil in a frying pan. Add the onion and cook, stirring frequently, for 5 minutes, or until beginning to soften. Stir in the celery, carrot, garlic and potato. Cook for a further 3–4 minutes.

2 Tip the fried vegetables into the ceramic cooking pot and switch to high. Add the lentils, vegetable stock, bay leaves and a pared strip of lemon rind and stir briefly to combine.

3 Cover the slow cooker with a lid and cook on auto or high for I hour.

4 Leave the cooker on auto or switch to low and cook for a further 5 hours, or until the vegetables and lentils are soft and tender.

5 Remove and discard the bay leaves and lemon rind. Process the soup in a food processor or blender until smooth. Tip the soup back into the cleaned cooking pot, stir in the cumin and cayenne pepper or Tabasco, and season.

6 Cook the soup on high for a further 45 minutes, or until piping hot. Squeeze in lemon juice to taste and check the seasoning. Ladle into warmed bowls and top each portion with lemon slices and a sprinkling of chopped fresh parsley.

Nutritional information per portion: Energy 300Kcal/1265kJ; Protein 15.8g; Carbohydrate 40.1g, of which sugars 3.6g; Fat 9.6g, of which saturates 1.3g; Cholesterol 0mg; Calcium 47mg; Fibre 3.9g; Sodium 456mg.

SPINACH and ROOT VEGETABLE SOUP

This is a typical Russian soup, traditionally prepared when the first vegetables of spring appear. You will need to use a large slow cooker to accommodate the spinach.

SERVES 4

1 small turnip, cut into chunks
2 carrots, diced
1 small parsnip, cut into large dice
1 potato, peeled and diced
1 onion, chopped
1 garlic clove, finely chopped
¼ celeriac bulb, diced
750ml/1¼ pints/3 cups boiling vegetable
    or chicken stock
175g/6oz fresh spinach, roughly chopped
1 small bunch fresh dill, chopped
salt and ground black pepper

For the garnish
2 hard-boiled eggs, sliced lengthways
1 lemon, sliced
30ml/2 tbsp fresh parsley and dill

COOK'S TIP
For best results, use a really good-quality vegetable or chicken stock.

1 Put the turnip, carrots, parsnip, potato, onion, garlic, celeriac and stock into the ceramic cooking pot. Cook on high or auto for 1 hour, then either leave on auto or switch to low and cook for a further 5–6 hours, until the vegetables are soft and tender.

2 Stir the spinach into the cooking pot and cook on high for 45 minutes, or until the spinach is tender but still green and leafy. Season with salt and pepper.

3 Stir in the dill, then ladle the soup into warmed bowls and serve garnished with egg, lemon and a sprinkling of fresh parsley and dill.

Nutritional information per portion: Energy 67Kcal/280kJ; Protein 3g; Carbohydrate 11.5g, of which sugars 7g; Fat 1.3g, of which saturates 0.1g; Cholesterol 0mg; Calcium 121mg; Fibre 3.9g; Sodium 499mg.

ASIAN-STYLE DUCK CONSOMMÉ

*The Vietnamese community in France has had a profound influence on French cooking.
As a result, you will find many classic French dishes brought together with Asian flavours.*

SERVES 4

1 small carrot
1 small leek, halved lengthwise
4 shiitake mushrooms, thinly sliced
soy sauce
2 spring onions (scallions), thinly sliced
finely shredded watercress
    or Chinese cabbage
ground black pepper

For the consommé
1 duck carcass (raw or cooked), plus
    2 legs or any giblets, trimmed of fat
1 large onion, unpeeled, with root
    end trimmed
2 carrots, cut into 2.5cm/1in pieces
1 parsnip, cut into 2.5cm/1in pieces
1 leek, cut into 2.5cm/1in pieces
2 garlic cloves, crushed
15ml/1 tbsp black peppercorns
2.5cm/1in piece fresh root ginger,
    peeled and sliced
4 thyme sprigs or 5ml/1 tsp dried thyme
1 small bunch fresh coriander (cilantro)

3 Line a sieve (strainer) with muslin (cheesecloth) and strain the consommé into a bowl, discarding the bones and vegetables. Leave to cool, then chill for several hours or overnight. Skim off any congealed fat and blot the surface with kitchen paper to remove all traces of fat.

4 Cut the carrot and leek into 5cm/2in pieces. Cut each piece lengthways into thin slices, then stack and slice into thin julienne strips. Place the julienne strips in the clean ceramic cooking pot with the sliced shiitake mushrooms.

5 Pour over the consommé and add a few dashes of soy sauce and some ground black pepper. Cover and cook on high for about 45 minutes, or until piping hot, skimming off any foam that rises to the surface with a slotted spoon.

6 Adjust the seasoning and stir in the spring onions and watercress or Chinese cabbage. Ladle into warmed bowls and sprinkle with the fresh coriander leaves.

1 To make the consommé, put the duck carcass, legs or giblets, onion, carrots, parsnip, leek and garlic in the ceramic cooking pot. Add the peppercorns, ginger, thyme and coriander stalks (reserve the leaves) and enough cold water to cover the bones, leaving at least 4cm/1½in space at the top of the pot.

2 Cover the pot with the lid and cook on high or auto for 2 hours. Skim off any surface scum, then reduce the temperature to low or leave on auto. Cover and cook for a further 4 hours, removing the lid for the last hour.

Nutritional information per portion: Energy 96Kcal/406kJ; Protein 7.1g; Carbohydrate 12.1g, of which sugars 7.9g; Fat 2.5g, of which saturates 0.6g; Cholesterol 28mg; Calcium 51mg; Fibre 4g; Sodium 47mg.

HOT and SOUR PRAWN SOUP

This salty, sour, spicy hot Thai soup, known as Tom Yam Kung, *is a real classic. Cooking the stock in the slow cooker maximizes the flavour before the final ingredients are added.*

SERVES 4

450g/1lb raw king prawns (jumbo shrimp),
   thawed if frozen
900ml/1½ pints/3¾ cups near-boiling light
   chicken stock or water
3 lemon grass stalks
6 kaffir lime leaves, torn in half
225g/8oz straw mushrooms, drained
45ml/3 tbsp Thai fish sauce
60ml/4 tbsp fresh lime juice
30ml/2 tbsp chopped spring onion
   (scallion)
15ml/1 tbsp fresh coriander
   (cilantro) leaves
4 fresh red chillies, seeded and
   thickly sliced
salt and ground black pepper

1 Peel the prawns, reserving the shells. Using a sharp knife, make a shallow cut along the back of each prawn and use the point of the knife to remove the thin black vein. Place the prawns in a bowl, cover and place in the refrigerator until ready to use.

2 Rinse the reserved prawn shells under cold running water, then put them in the ceramic cooking pot and add the chicken stock or water. Cover with the lid and switch the slow cooker to high.

3 Using a pestle, bruise the bulbous end of the lemon grass stalks. Lift the lid of the ceramic pot and quickly add the lemon grass stalks and half the torn kaffir lime leaves to the stock. Stir well, then re-cover with the lid and cook for about 2 hours until the stock is fragrant and aromatic.

4 Strain the stock into a large bowl and rinse out the ceramic cooking pot. Pour the stock back into the cleaned pot. Add the drained mushrooms and cook on high for 30 minutes.

5 Add the prawns to the soup and cook for a further 10 minutes until the prawns turn pink and are cooked.

6 Stir the fish sauce, lime juice, spring onion, coriander, chillies and remaining lime leaves into the soup. Taste and adjust the seasoning if necessary. The soup should be sour, salty, spicy and hot.

Nutritional information per portion: Energy 127Kcal/536kJ; Protein 27g; Carbohydrate 1.4g, of which sugars 1.2g; Fat 1.4g, of which saturates 0.3g; Cholesterol 315mg; Calcium 133mg; Fibre 0.7g; Sodium 2715mg.

NORTH AFRICAN SPICED SOUP

The great advantage of cooking soup in the slow cooker is that all the flavours have a chance to develop and mingle. This technique is particularly well suited to richer soups with complex spicing, such as this version of the Moroccan national soup harira.

3 Mix together the cinnamon, turmeric, ginger, cayenne pepper and 30ml/2 tbsp of stock to form a paste, then add to the pot with the carrots, celery and remaining stock. Stir well and season. Cover and cook for 1 hour.

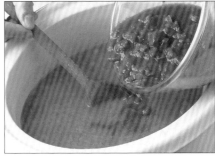

4 Add the chopped tomatoes, potatoes, chickpeas and saffron to the pot. Cook for 4–5 hours until the vegetables are tender. Stir in the coriander and lemon juice, then check the seasoning and adjust if necessary. Ladle into warmed bowls and serve piping hot, with fried wedges of lemon, if you like.

SERVES 6

1 large onion, very finely chopped
1 litre/1¾ pints/4 cups near-boiling
   vegetable stock
5ml/1 tsp ground cinnamon
5ml/1 tsp ground turmeric
15ml/1 tbsp grated fresh root ginger
pinch cayenne pepper
2 carrots, finely diced
2 celery sticks, finely diced
400g/14oz can chopped tomatoes
450g/1lb potatoes, finely diced
400g/14oz can chickpeas, drained
5 strands saffron
30ml/2 tbsp chopped fresh coriander
   (cilantro)
15ml/1 tbsp lemon juice
salt and ground black pepper
fried wedges of lemon, to serve (optional)

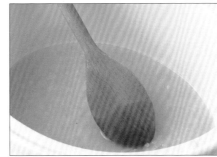

1 Place the chopped onion in the ceramic cooking pot and add 600ml/ 1 pint/2½ cups of the nearly-boiling vegetable stock.

2 Switch the slow cooker to high or auto, cover with the lid and cook for about 1 hour, until the onion is soft and translucent.

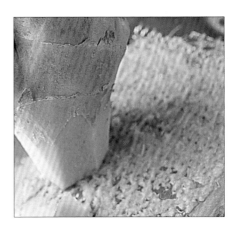

Nutritional information per portion: Energy 166Kcal/705kJ; Protein 7.5g; Carbohydrate 30.3g, of which sugars 7.4g; Fat 2.5g, of which saturates 0.3g; Cholesterol 0mg; Calcium 62mg; Fibre 5.3g; Sodium 335mg.

SPICED CARROT DIP

When carrots are cooked over a slow, gentle heat, their flavour intensifies and becomes deliciously sweet, making them the perfect partner for hot, spicy flavourings. Serve this tasty dip with wheat crackers or fiery tortilla chips.

SERVES 4

1 onion
3 carrots, plus extra grated carrot
    to garnish (optional)
grated rind and juice of 1 orange
15ml/1 tbsp hot curry paste
150ml/¼ pint/⅔ cup plain yogurt
handful of fresh basil leaves
15ml/1 tbsp fresh lemon juice
dash Tabasco sauce (optional)
salt and ground black pepper

4 Add the yogurt to the cooled carrot purée. Tear the basil leaves roughly into small pieces, then stir them into the mixture until thoroughly combined.

5 Stir in the lemon juice and Tabasco, if using, then season to taste with salt and pepper. Serve at room temperature, within a few hours of making.

1 Chop the onion very finely. Peel and grate the carrots. Put the onion, carrots, orange rind and juice, and curry paste in the ceramic cooking pot and stir well to combine. Cover with the lid and cook on high for 2 hours, or until the carrots are soft and tender.

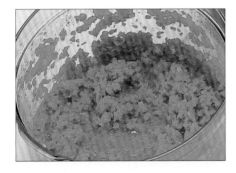

2 Uncover the pot and leave to cool for about 10 minutes, then tip the mixture into a food processor or blender and process until smooth.

3 Transfer the carrot purée to a mixing bowl and leave, uncovered, for about 1 hour to cool completely.

Nutritional information per portion: Energy 58Kcal/241kJ; Protein 2.5g; Carbohydrate 9.5g, of which sugars 8.4g; Fat 1.3g, of which saturates 0.4g; Cholesterol 0mg; Calcium 80mg; Fibre 1.3g; Sodium 34mg.

CHEESE-STUFFED PEARS

These pears, with their scrumptious creamy topping, make a sublime dish when served with a simple salad. If you don't have a very large slow cooker, choose short squat pears rather than long, tapering ones, so that they will fit in a single layer.

SERVES 4

50g/2oz/¼ cup ricotta cheese
50g/2oz/¼ cup dolcelatte cheese
15ml/1 tbsp honey
½ celery stick, finely sliced
8 green olives, pitted and
    roughly chopped
4 dates, stoned and cut into
    thin strips
pinch of paprika
2 medium barely ripe pears
150ml/¼ pint/⅔ cup apple juice
salad leaves, to serve (optional)

4 Pour the apple juice around the pears, then cover with the lid. Cook on high for 1½–2 hours, or until the fruit is tender. (The cooking time will depend on the ripeness of the pears.)

5 Remove the pears from the slow cooker. If you like, brown them under a hot grill (broiler) for a few minutes. Serve with salad leaves, if you like.

COOK'S TIP
These pears go particularly well with slightly bitter and peppery leaves, such as chicory and rocket. Try them tossed in a walnut oil dressing.

1 Place the ricotta cheese in a bowl and crumble in the dolcelatte. Add the honey, celery, olives, dates and paprika and mix together well until creamy and thoroughly blended.

2 Halve the pears lengthways. Use a melon baller or teaspoon to remove the cores and make a hollow for the filling.

3 Divide the ricotta filling equally between the pears, packing it into the hollow, then arrange the fruit in a single layer in the ceramic cooking pot.

Nutritional information per portion: Energy 236Kcal/992kJ; Protein 6.9g; Carbohydrate 35.6g, of which sugars 35.6g; Fat 8.2g, of which saturates 5.0g; Cholesterol 24mg; Calcium 141mg; Fibre 4.1g; Sodium 261mg.

FISH TERRINE

This colourful layered terrine makes a spectacular appetizer or main course on a special occasion. It is particularly good for entertaining because it can be made in advance, chilled until ready to serve, then arranged on plates at the last minute.

SERVES 6

450g/1lb skinless white fish fillets
225g/8oz thinly sliced smoked salmon
2 egg whites, chilled
1.5ml/¼ tsp each salt and ground
    white pepper
pinch of freshly grated nutmeg
250ml/8fl oz/1 cup double (heavy) cream
50g/2oz small tender fresh spinach leaves
lemon mayonnaise, to serve

1 Cut the white fish fillets into 2.5cm/ 1in pieces, removing any bones. Spread out the fish pieces on a plate, cover with clear film (plastic wrap) and chill in the freezer for 15 minutes until very cold.

2 Lightly oil a 1.2 litre/2 pint/5 cup terrine or loaf tin (pan). Line the base and sides of the tin with the smoked salmon slices, making sure they overlap each other all the way around and letting them hang over the edges of the tin.

3 Remove the white fish from the freezer, then place in a food processor and blend to make a very smooth purée. (You may need to stop the machine and scrape down the sides two or three times as you do this.)

4 Add the egg whites, one at a time, processing after each addition, then add the salt, pepper and nutmeg. With the machine running, pour in the cream and stop as soon as it is blended. (If over-processed the cream will thicken.)

5 Transfer the fish mixture to a large glass bowl. Put the spinach leaves into the food processor and process to make a smooth purée. Add one-third of the fish mixture to the spinach and process briefly until just combined, scraping down the sides once or twice.

6 Pour about 2.5cm/1in of very hot water into the ceramic cooking pot. Place an upturned saucer or metal pastry ring in the base, then turn the slow cooker on to high.

7 Spread half the plain fish mixture in the base of the tin. Spoon the green fish mixture over the top and smooth it level, then cover with the remaining plain mixture. Fold the overhanging pieces of smoked salmon over the top to enclose the mixture. Tap the tin to settle the mixture and remove any air pockets, then cover the tin with a double layer of lightly oiled foil.

8 Put the tin in the slow cooker and pour in enough boiling water to come just over halfway up the sides. Cook for 3–3½ hours, or until a skewer inserted into the terrine comes out clean. Leave the terrine to cool in the tin, then chill in the refrigerator until firm.

9 To serve the terrine, turn out on to a board, remove the lining paper and slice. Arrange the slices on individual plates and serve with lemon mayonnaise.

Nutritional information per portion: Energy 340Kcal/1409kJ; Protein 23.2g; Carbohydrate 0.8g, of which sugars 0.8g; Fat 27.1g, of which saturates 14.7g; Cholesterol 110mg; Calcium 50mg; Fibre 0.2g; Sodium 201mg.

HADDOCK and SMOKED SALMON TERRINE

This substantial terrine makes a superb dish for a summer buffet. It is very good served with dill mayonnaise or a tangy mango salsa instead of the crème fraîche or sour cream.

SERVES 6

15ml/1 tbsp sunflower oil, for greasing
350g/12oz smoked salmon
900g/2lb haddock fillets, skinned
2 eggs, lightly beaten
105ml/7 tbsp low-fat crème fraîche
    or sour cream
30ml/2 tbsp drained bottled capers
30ml/2 tbsp drained soft green or pink
    peppercorns
salt and ground white pepper
low-fat crème fraîche or sour cream,
    peppercorns, fresh dill and rocket
    (arugula), to serve

1 Pour about 2.5cm/1in of warm water into the ceramic cooking pot. Place an upturned saucer or metal pastry ring in the base, then turn the slow cooker on to high. Lightly grease a 1 litre/1¾ pint/ 4 cup loaf tin (pan) or terrine. Use some of the smoked salmon slices to line the tin or terrine, letting them hang over the edge. Reserve the remaining salmon.

2 Cut two long slices of the haddock the length of the tin or terrine, and cut the remaining haddock into small pieces. Season with salt and pepper.

3 Combine the eggs, crème fraîche or sour cream, capers and soft peppercorns in a bowl. Season with salt and pepper, then stir in the small pieces of haddock. Spoon half the mixture into the mould and smooth the surface with a spatula.

4 Wrap the long haddock fillets in the reserved smoked salmon. (Don't worry if there isn't enough salmon to cover them completely.) Lay the wrapped haddock fillets on top of the fish mixture in the tin or terrine.

5 Spoon the rest of the fish mixture into the tin or terrine and smooth the surface. Fold the overhanging pieces of smoked salmon over the top and cover tightly with a double thickness of foil.

6 Tap the terrine to settle the contents, then place in the slow cooker and pour in enough boiling water to come just over halfway up the sides. Cook for 3–4 hours, or until a skewer inserted into the terrine comes out clean.

7 Remove the terrine from the slow cooker, but do not remove the foil cover. Place two or three large heavy cans on the foil to weight it, and leave until cold. Chill in the refrigerator for 24 hours.

8 About 1 hour before serving, remove the terrine from the refrigerator, lift off the weights and carefully remove the foil. Gently invert the terrine on to a serving plate and lift off the mould.

9 Cut the terrine into thick slices using a sharp knife. Serve with crème fraîche or sour cream, peppercorns, dill sprigs and rocket leaves.

Nutritional information per portion: Energy 316Kcal/1326kJ; Protein 46.1g; Carbohydrate 0.4g, of which sugars 0.4g; Fat 14.5g, of which saturates 6.2g; Cholesterol 170mg; Calcium 653mg; Fibre Nil g; Sodium 1228mg.

MUSHROOM and BEAN PÂTÉ

This light and tasty pâté is delicious served on wholemeal toast or with crusty French bread and makes an excellent vegetarian appetizer or light lunch served with salad.

SERVES 8

450g/1lb/6 cups mushrooms, sliced
1 onion, finely chopped
2 garlic cloves, crushed
1 red (bell) pepper, seeded and diced
30ml/2 tbsp vegetable stock
30ml/2 tbsp dry white wine
400g/14oz can red kidney beans, rinsed
    and drained
1 egg, beaten
50g/2oz/1 cup fresh wholemeal
    (whole-wheat) breadcrumbs
10ml/2 tsp chopped fresh thyme
10ml/2 tsp chopped fresh rosemary
salt and ground black pepper
salad leaves, fresh herbs and tomato
    wedges, to garnish

VARIATION

To make a lighter, milder-tasting pâté, use cannellini or flageolet beans in place of the kidney beans.

1 Put the mushrooms, onion, garlic, red pepper, vegetable stock and wine in the ceramic cooking pot. Cover and cook on high for about 2 hours, or until the vegetables are almost tender, then set aside for about 10 minutes to cool.

2 Tip the vegetable mixture into a food processor or blender and add the rinsed kidney beans. Process to make a smooth purée, stopping the machine once or twice to scrape down the sides.

3 Lightly grease and line a 900g/2lb loaf tin. Put an inverted saucer or metal pastry ring in the bottom of the ceramic cooking pot. Pour in about 2.5cm/1in of hot water, and switch the slow cooker on to high.

4 Transfer the mushroom mixture to a bowl. Add the egg, breadcrumbs and herbs, and season with salt and pepper. Mix together thoroughly, then spoon the mixture into the prepared tin and cover with cling film (plastic wrap) or foil.

5 Put the tin in the slow cooker and pour in enough boiling water to come just over halfway up the sides of the tin. Cover with the lid and cook on high for 4 hours, or until lightly set.

6 Remove the tin from the ceramic cooking pot and place on a wire rack until completely cool. Refrigerate for several hours, or overnight if preferred. Turn out of the tin, remove the lining paper and serve in slices, garnished with salad leaves, herbs and tomato wedges.

Nutritional information per portion: Energy 85Kcal/358kJ; Protein 5.5g; Carbohydrate 12.3g, of which sugars 3.8g; Fat 1.6g, of which saturates 0.4g; Cholesterol 28mg; Calcium 47mg; Fibre 3.7g; Sodium 187mg.

RED LENTIL and GOAT'S CHEESE PÂTÉ

The slightly smoky, earthy flavour of red lentils provides a perfect partner to tangy goat's cheese, making a pâté that will be a hit with vegetarians and non-vegetarians alike.

SERVES 8

225g/8oz/1 cup red lentils
1 shallot, very finely chopped
1 bay leaf
475ml/16fl oz/2 cups near-boiling
   vegetable stock
115g/4oz/½ cup soft goat's cheese
5ml/1 tsp ground cumin
3 eggs, lightly beaten
salt and ground black pepper
melba toast and rocket (arugula) leaves,
   to serve

1 Place the lentils in a sieve (strainer) and rinse well under cold running water. Drain, then tip the lentils into the ceramic cooking pot and add the shallot, bay leaf and hot vegetable stock.

2 Switch the slow cooker to high, cover and cook for 2 hours, or until all the liquid has been absorbed and the lentils are soft and pulpy. Stir once or twice towards the end of cooking time to prevent the lentils sticking to the pot.

3 Turn off the slow cooker. Tip the lentil mixture into a bowl, remove the bay leaf and leave to cool uncovered, so that the steam can evaporate. Meanwhile, wash and dry the ceramic cooking pot.

4 Lightly grease the base of a 900ml/ 1½ pint/3¾ cup loaf tin (pan) with oil and line the base with greaseproof (waxed) paper. Put an upturned saucer or metal pastry ring in the bottom of the ceramic cooking pot and pour in about 2.5cm/1 in of hot water. Turn the slow cooker to high.

5 Put the goat's cheese in a bowl with the cumin and beat together until soft and creamy. Gradually mix in the eggs until blended. Stir in the lentil mixture and season well with salt and pepper.

6 Tip the mixture into the prepared tin. Cover with clear film (plastic wrap) or foil. Put the tin in the slow cooker and pour in enough boiling water to come just over halfway up the sides. Cover the slow cooker with the lid and cook for 3–3½ hours, until the pâté is lightly set.

7 Carefully remove the tin from the slow cooker and place on a wire rack to cool completely. Chill in the refrigerator for several hours, or overnight.

8 To serve, turn the pâté out of the tin, peel off the lining paper and cut into slices. Serve with melba toast and rocket.

Nutritional information per portion: Energy 136Kcal/573kJ; Protein 9.8g; Carbohydrate 16g, of which sugars 0.9g; Fat 4.1g, of which saturates 2.6g; Cholesterol 13mg; Calcium 34mg; Fibre 1.4g; Sodium 97mg.

COUNTRY-STYLE TERRINE with LEEKS

Traditionally, this sort of French pork terrine contains pork liver and egg to bind the mixture together. This version uses leeks instead to give a lighter result. In France, cornichons (small dill pickles or gherkins) and mustard are served as accompaniments.

3 Reserve two of the bacon rashers (strips) for the garnish, then finely chop the remaining bacon. Add to the pork mixture along with the leeks, herbs, spices, salt and pepper. Mix together, using a wooden spoon or your fingertips, until thoroughly combined.

4 Lightly grease the base and sides of a 1.2 litre/2 pint/5 cup heatproof dish or loaf tin (pan) with oil and line with greaseproof (waxed) paper. Put an upturned saucer or metal pastry ring in the base of the ceramic cooking pot and pour in 2.5cm/1in of hot water. Turn the slow cooker to high.

5 Spoon the meat mixture into the prepared dish or tin, pressing it into the corners. Tap firmly to settle the mixture, and smooth the top. Arrange the bay leaves and reserved bacon (trimmed to size) on top, then cover with foil.

6 Place the dish or tin in the slow cooker and pour in enough boiling water to come just over halfway up the sides. Cover with the lid and cook for 4–5 hours or until cooked; the juices of the pâté should run clear when pierced with a skewer. Lift out of the ceramic cooking pot and leave to cool in the dish or tin.

7 Put the dish or tin on a tray, then place a foil-covered plate or board (just smaller than the size of the dish or tin) on top of the pâté. Weight the plate or board with two or three large cans or other heavy objects, and chill for several hours, or preferably overnight.

SERVES 8

350g/12oz trimmed leeks
25g/1oz/2 tbsp butter
2 garlic cloves, finely chopped
900g/2lb lean pork leg or shoulder
115g/4oz rinded smoked streaky
   (fatty) bacon
5ml/1 tsp chopped fresh thyme
3 sage leaves, finely chopped
1.5ml/¼ tsp quatre épices (see Cook's Tip)
1.5ml/¼ tsp ground cumin
2.5ml/½ tsp salt
2.5ml/½ tsp ground black pepper
3 bay leaves

COOK'S TIP

Quatre épices is a classic French spice mix containing ground cloves, cinnamon, nutmeg and pepper.

1 Cut the leeks lengthways, wash well and slice thinly. Melt the butter in a large heavy pan, add the leeks, then cover and cook over medium-low heat for about 10 minutes, stirring occasionally. Add the garlic and continue cooking for a further 10 minutes until the leeks are very soft. Set aside to cool.

2 Trim off any excess fat and gristle from the pork, then cut the meat into 2.5cm/1in cubes. Working in two or three batches, put the meat into a food processor fitted with a metal blade; the bowl should be about half-full. Pulse to chop the meat to a coarse purée. Alternatively, pass the meat through the coarse blade of a meat grinder. Transfer the meat to a large mixing bowl and remove any white stringy pieces.

Nutritional information per portion: Energy 211Kcal/884kJ; Protein 27.5g; Carbohydrate 1.3g, of which sugars 1g; Fat 10.7g, of which saturates 4.4g; Cholesterol 87mg; Calcium 20mg; Fibre 1.0g; Sodium 395mg.

CARDAMOM CHICKEN MOUSSELINES

These light chicken mousselines, served with a tangy tomato vinaigrette, make an elegant
appetizer. They should be served warm rather than hot, so as soon as they are cooked,
turn off the slow cooker and leave to cool for half an hour before eating.

SERVES 6

350g/12oz skinless, boneless
   chicken breast portions
1 shallot, finely chopped
115g/4oz/1 cup full-fat soft cheese
1 egg, lightly beaten
2 egg whites
crushed seeds of 2 cardamom pods
60ml/4 tbsp white wine
150ml/¼ pint/⅔ cup double (heavy) cream
oregano sprigs, to serve

For the tomato vinaigrette
350g/12oz ripe tomatoes
10ml/2 tsp balsamic vinegar
30ml/2 tbsp olive oil
sea salt and ground black pepper

1 Roughly chop the chicken and put in a food processor with the finely chopped shallot. Process until the mixture becomes fairly smooth.

2 Add the soft cheese, beaten egg, egg whites, crushed cardamom seeds and white wine to the chicken mixture and season with salt and ground black pepper. Process again until the ingredients are thoroughly blended.

3 Gradually add the cream, using the pulsing action, until the mixture has a smooth and creamy texture. Transfer the mixture to a bowl, cover with clear film (plastic wrap) and chill in the refrigerator for about 30 minutes.

4 Meanwhile, prepare six 150ml/¼ pint/⅔ cup ramekins or dariole moulds, checking first that they will all fit in the slow cooker. Lightly grease the base of each one, then line. Pour about 2cm/¾in hot water into the ceramic cooking pot and switch the cooker to high.

5 Divide the chicken mixture among the prepared dishes and level the tops. Cover each with foil and place in the ceramic cooking pot. Pour in a little more near-boiling water to come half-way up the dishes. Cover and cook for 2½–3 hours, or until the mousselines are firm; a skewer or thin knife inserted into the middle should come out clean.

6 Meanwhile, peel, quarter, seed and finely dice the tomatoes. Place them in a bowl, sprinkle with balsamic vinegar and season with a little salt. Stir well.

7 To serve, unmould the mousselines on to warmed plates. Place small spoonfuls of the tomato vinaigrette around each plate, then drizzle over a little olive oil and grind over a little black pepper. Garnish with sprigs of fresh oregano.

Nutritional information per portion: Energy 191Kcal/795kJ; Protein 18.1g; Carbohydrate 2g, of which sugars 2g; Fat 11.6g, of which saturates 5g; Cholesterol 96mg; Calcium 30mg; Fibre 0.7g; Sodium 130mg.

CHICKEN and PISTACHIO PÂTÉ

This easy version of a classic French charcuterie can be made with white chicken breast portions or a mixture of light and dark meat for a more robust flavour. Serve it as an elegant appetizer for a special dinner, or with salad for a light lunch.

SERVES 8

oil, for greasing
800g/1¾lb boneless chicken meat
40g/1½oz/¾ cup fresh white breadcrumbs
120ml/4fl oz/½ cup double (heavy) cream
1 egg white
4 spring onions (scallions) finely chopped
1 garlic clove, finely chopped
75g/3oz cooked ham, cut into small cubes
75g/3oz/½ cup shelled pistachio nuts
30ml/2 tbsp green peppercorns
  in brine, drained
45ml/3 tbsp chopped fresh tarragon
pinch of grated nutmeg
salt and ground black pepper
French bread and salad, to serve

1 Line the base of a 1.2 litre/2 pint/ 5 cup round or oval heatproof dish (such as a soufflé dish) with greaseproof (waxed) paper, then lightly brush the base and sides with oil.

2 Put an upturned saucer or metal pastry ring in the base of the ceramic cooking pot and pour in about 2.5cm/ 1in of hot water. Switch the slow cooker to high.

3 Cut the chicken meat into cubes, then put in a food processor and blend until fairly smooth. (You may need to do this in batches depending on the capacity of your food processor.) Alternatively, pass the meat through the medium blade of a food mill. Remove any white stringy pieces from the minced (ground) meat.

4 Place the breadcrumbs in a large mixing bowl, pour over the cream and leave to soak.

5 Meanwhile, lightly whisk the egg white with a fork, then add it to the soaked breadcrumbs. Add the minced chicken, spring onions, garlic, ham, pistachio nuts, green peppercorns, tarragon, nutmeg, salt and pepper. Using a wooden spoon or your fingers, mix thoroughly.

6 Spoon the mixture into the prepared dish and cover with foil. Place the dish in the ceramic cooking pot and pour a little more boiling water around the dish to come just over halfway up the sides. Cover the slow cooker with the lid and cook for about 4 hours until the pâté is cooked through.

7 To check whether the pâté is cooked, pierce with a skewer or fine knife – the juices should run clear. Carefully lift out of the slow cooker and leave the pâté to cool in the dish. Chill in the refrigerator, preferably overnight.

8 To serve, turn out the pâté on to a serving dish and cut into slices. Serve with crusty French bread and salad.

VARIATIONS
• You can use turkey breast fillet in place of some or all of the chicken, and serve with a tangy cranberry sauce.
• Pale green pistachio nuts look very pretty in this pâté but you can use hazelnuts instead; they are equally good.
• This pâté also makes a perfect dish for a special picnic or a cold buffet. Serve with a delicately flavoured herb mayonnaise.

Nutritional information per portion: Energy 321Kcal/1344kJ; Protein 36.6g; Carbohydrate 3.7g, of which sugars 1.2g; Fat 17.9g, of which saturates 7.7g; Cholesterol 125mg; Calcium 37mg; Fibre 0.7g; Sodium 379mg.

FISH AND SHELLFISH

Delicious, healthy and perfectly suited to cooking in a slow cooker, fish and shellfish can be used in a fabulous range of dishes. The gentle heat of this method cooks the delicate flesh to perfection every time. Although large whole fish, such as salmon, are too big for the slow cooker, smaller fish, such as herring and red mullet, and fish steaks, fillets and shellfish are perfect. Unlike meat, fish cooks relatively quickly in the slow cooker, so is ideal for combining with rice or pasta. It is incredibly versatile and can be cooked in all manner of ways, to make both light and hearty dishes. Try salmon risotto with cucumber for a light and sophisticated summer dish, or comforting fish pie as a winter warmer.

CREAMY ANCHOVY and POTATO BAKE

This classic Scandinavian dish of potatoes, onions and anchovies cooked with cream makes a hearty winter lunch or simple supper, served with a refreshing salad. In Norway and Sweden, it is often served as a hot appetizer.

2 Use half of the butter to grease the base and sides of the ceramic cooking pot, and layer half the potatoes and onions in the base of the dish.

3 Drain the anchovies, reserving 15ml/ 1 tbsp of the oil. Cut the anchovies into thin strips and lay these over the potatoes and onions, then layer the remaining potatoes and onions on top.

4 Combine the single cream and anchovy oil in a small jug (pitcher) and season with a little ground black pepper. Pour the mixture evenly over the potatoes and dot the surface with butter.

5 Cover and cook on high for 3½ hours, or until the potatoes and onions are tender. Brown under a hot grill (broiler), if you like, then drizzle over the double cream and sprinkle with parsley and pepper. Serve with fresh crusty bread.

SERVES 4

1kg/2¼ lb maincrop potatoes
2 onions
25g/1oz/2 tbsp butter
2 x 50g/2oz cans anchovy fillets
150ml/¼ pint/⅔ cup single (light) cream
150ml/¼ pint/⅔ cup double (heavy) cream
15ml/1 tbsp chopped fresh parsley
ground black pepper
fresh crusty bread, to serve

COOK'S TIP
This recipe can also be served as an appetizer for six, or as a side dish to accompany a main meal.

1 Peel the potatoes and cut into slices slightly thicker than 1cm/½in. Cut the slices into strips slightly more than 1cm/½in wide. Peel the onions and cut into very thin rings.

Nutritional information per portion: Energy 378Kcal/1580kJ; Protein 11.3g; Carbohydrate 37.9g, of which sugars 6.4g; Fat 21.2g, of which saturates 11.4g; Cholesterol 54mg; Calcium 1460mg; Fibre 11.5g; Sodium 133mg.

SALMON RISOTTO with CUCUMBER

A classic risotto is time-consuming to make because the stock needs to be added very gradually and requires constant attention from the cook. Here, the wine and stock are added in one go, making it far easier, yet still giving a delicious, creamy texture.

SERVES 4

25g/1oz/2 tbsp butter
small bunch of spring onions (scallions),
    finely sliced
½ cucumber, peeled, seeded
    and chopped
225g/8oz/generous 1 cup easy-cook
    (converted) Italian rice
750ml/1¼ pints/3 cups boiling vegetable
    or fish stock
120ml/4fl oz/½ cup white wine
450g/1lb salmon fillet, skinned
    and diced
45ml/3 tbsp chopped fresh tarragon
salt and ground black pepper

1 Put the butter in the ceramic cooking pot and switch the slow cooker to high. Leave to melt for 15 minutes, then stir in the spring onions and cucumber. Cover and cook for 30 minutes.

2 Add the rice to the pot and stir, then pour in the stock and wine. Cover with the lid and cook for 45 minutes, stirring once halfway through cooking.

3 Stir the diced salmon into the risotto and season with salt and pepper. Cook for a further 15 minutes, or until the rice is tender and the salmon just cooked. Switch off the slow cooker and leave the risotto to stand for 5 minutes.

4 Remove the lid, add the chopped tarragon and mix lightly. Spoon the risotto into individual warmed serving bowls or plates and serve immediately.

COOK'S TIP
Frozen peas can be used instead of cucumber, if you like. These should be defrosted and stirred into the risotto at the same time as the salmon.

Nutritional information per portion: Energy 506Kcal/2122kJ; Protein 28.4g; Carbohydrate 51.3g, of which sugars 2.8g; Fat 20g, of which saturates 5.9g; Cholesterol 70mg; Calcium 91mg; Fibre 1.4g; Sodium 266mg.

SPECIAL FISH PIE

Fish pie topped with melting, cheesy breadcrumbs is the ultimate comfort food and is always a firm family favourite. Serve with plenty of lightly steamed green vegetables such as asparagus spears, green beans or sugar snap peas.

SERVES 4

350g/12oz haddock fillet, skinned
30ml/2 tbsp cornflour (cornstarch)
175g/6oz/1 cup drained, canned corn
115g/4oz/1 cup frozen peas, defrosted
115g/4oz peeled cooked prawns (shrimp)
115g/4oz/½ cup cream cheese
150ml/¼ pint/⅔ cup milk
15g/½oz/¼ cup wholemeal (whole-wheat)
  breadcrumbs
50g/2oz/½ cup grated Cheddar cheese
salt and freshly ground black pepper

1 Cut the haddock into bitesize pieces and place in a mixing bowl. Sprinkle with the cornflour and toss thoroughly to coat the pieces evenly.

2 Add the corn, peas and prawns to the coated haddock pieces and mix together well. In a separate mixing bowl, blend together the cream cheese and milk, season with salt and ground black pepper and pour over the fish mixture. Stir well to combine.

3 Spoon the fish mixture into the ceramic cooking pot. Switch the slow cooker to high, cover with the lid and cook for 2 hours.

4 Meanwhile, combine the breadcrumbs and grated cheese. Spoon the mixture evenly over the top of the dish. Remove the ceramic cooking pot from the slow cooker and brown the top under a moderate grill (broiler) for 5 minutes until golden and crisp. Serve hot.

COOK'S TIP
To make a more economical dish, you can leave out the prawns and replace them with the same weight of haddock. Alternatively, to make a more extravagant dish, use more shellfish, replacing some of the haddock with the same weight of scallops and shelled mussels.

Nutritional information per portion: Energy 306Kcal/1283kJ; Protein 31.3g; Carbohydrate 12.2g, of which sugars 2.1g; Fat 15.1g, of which saturates 9.2g; Cholesterol 153mg; Calcium 224mg; Fibre 0.6g; Sodium 736mg.

SMOKED TROUT CANNELLONI

This delicious dish makes a great change to the classic meat or spinach and cheese cannelloni that are usually served. You can also buy smoked trout ready-filleted, which can save on preparation time. If you buy fillets you will need only about 225g/8oz.

SERVES 4

25g/1oz/2 tbsp butter, plus extra
    for greasing
1 large onion, finely chopped
400g/14oz can chopped tomatoes
2.5ml/½ tsp dried mixed herbs
1 smoked trout, weighing
    about 400g/14oz
75g/3oz/¾ cup frozen peas, thawed
75g/3oz/1½ cups fresh white breadcrumbs
16 cannelloni tubes
15g/½oz/1½ tbsp freshly grated
    Parmesan cheese
salt and ground black pepper
mixed salad, to serve (optional)

For the sauce
40g/1½oz/3 tbsp butter
40g/1½oz/⅓ cup plain (all-purpose)
    flour
550ml/18fl oz/2½ cups milk
1 bay leaf
freshly grated nutmeg

VARIATION
To make a more economical dish, use a drained 200g/7oz can of tuna in oil in place of the trout.

1 Melt the butter in a frying pan, add the onion and cook gently for about 10 minutes until soft, stirring frequently. Stir in the chopped tomatoes and dried herbs and simmer uncovered for a further 10 minutes, or until the sauce is very thick.

2 Meanwhile, skin the smoked trout using a sharp knife. Carefully flake the flesh and discard all the bones. Add the fish to the tomato sauce, then stir in the peas and breadcrumbs and season with plenty of salt and black pepper.

3 Lightly grease the base and halfway up the sides of the ceramic cooking pot. Carefully spoon the trout filling into the cannelloni tubes and arrange the filled tubes in the base of the slow cooker, placing them side by side.

4 To make the sauce, melt the butter in the pan and add the flour. Cook for 1 minute, stirring, then gradually whisk in the milk and add the bay leaf. Cook over a medium heat, whisking constantly until the sauce thickens, then simmer for 2–3 minutes, continuing to stir. Remove the bay leaf and season to taste with salt, pepper and nutmeg.

5 Pour the sauce over the cannelloni and sprinkle with grated Parmesan. Cover and cook on high or auto for 1 hour.

6 Switch the slow cooker to low or leave on auto and cook for 1–1½ hours, or until the cannelloni is tender. If you like, brown the top under a moderate grill (broiler) before serving. Serve with a mixed salad, if using.

Nutritional information per portion: Energy 669Kcal/2811kJ; Protein 41.5g; Carbohydrate 74.5g, of which sugars 15.1g; Fat 24.9g, of which saturates 11.9g; Cholesterol 116mg; Calcium 353mg; Fibre 3.1g; Sodium 390mg.

CANNELLONI SORRENTINA-STYLE

There is more than one way of making cannelloni. For this fresh-tasting dish, sheets of cooked lasagne are rolled around a tomato, ricotta and anchovy filling. You can, of course, use traditional cannelloni tubes, if you prefer.

SERVES 4–6

15ml/1 tbsp olive oil, plus extra for
   greasing
1 small onion, finely chopped
900g/2lb ripe Italian tomatoes, peeled and
   finely chopped
2 garlic cloves, crushed
5ml/1 tsp dried mixed herbs
150ml/¼ pint/⅔ cup vegetable stock
150ml/¼ pint/⅔ cup dry white wine
30ml/2 tbsp sun-dried tomato paste
2.5ml/½ tsp sugar
16 dried lasagne sheets
250g/9oz/generous 1 cup ricotta cheese
130g/4½oz packet mozzarella cheese,
   drained and diced
30ml/2 tbsp shredded fresh basil, plus
   extra basil leaves to garnish
8 bottled anchovy fillets in olive oil,
   drained and halved lengthways
50g/2oz/⅔ cup freshly grated Parmesan
   cheese
salt and ground black pepper

1 Heat the oil in a pan, add the onion and cook gently, stirring, for 5 minutes until softened. Transfer to the ceramic cooking pot and switch on to high. Stir in the tomatoes, garlic and herbs. Season with salt and black pepper to taste, then cover the slow cooker with the lid and cook for 1 hour.

2 Ladle about half of the tomato mixture out of the cooking pot, place in a bowl and set aside to cool.

3 Stir the vegetable stock, white wine, tomato paste and sugar into the tomato mixture remaining in the slow cooker. Cover with the lid and cook for a further hour. Turn off the slow cooker.

4 Meanwhile, cook the lasagne sheets in batches in a pan of salted boiling water for 3 minutes or according to the instructions on the packet. Drain the sheets of lasagne. Separate them, and lay them out on a clean dishtowel until needed.

5 Add the ricotta and mozzarella to the tomato mixture in the bowl. Stir in the shredded fresh basil and season to taste with salt and black pepper. Spread a little of the mixture over each lasagne sheet. Place one halved anchovy fillet across the width of each sheet, close to one of the short ends. Starting from the end with the anchovy, roll up each lasagne sheet to form a tube.

6 Transfer the tomato sauce in the slow cooker to a food processor or blender, and purée until smooth. Wash and dry the ceramic cooking pot, then lightly grease the base and halfway up the sides with a little oil.

7 Spoon about a third of the puréed sauce into the ceramic cooking pot, covering the base evenly. Arrange the filled cannelloni seam-side down on top of the sauce. Spoon the remaining sauce over the top.

8 Sprinkle with the Parmesan. Cover the slow cooker with the lid and cook on high or auto for 1 hour, then switch to low or leave on auto and cook for a further hour until the cannelloni is tender. Brown under the grill (broiler), if you like, then serve garnished with basil.

Nutritional information per portion: Energy 546Kcal/2293kJ; Protein 25.5g; Carbohydrate 54.3g, of which sugars 9.7g; Fat 24.1g, of which saturates 13.4g; Cholesterol 58mg; Calcium 301mg; Fibre 3.5g; Sodium 282mg.

TUNA LASAGNE

This delicious, comforting dish is perfect for a family supper or casual entertaining, and is incredibly simple to make. Use pre-cooked sheets of lasagne, breaking them into smaller pieces as necessary to fit the shape of your slow cooker.

SERVES 6

65g/2½oz/5 tbsp butter, plus extra
   for greasing
1 small onion, finely chopped
1 garlic clove, finely chopped
115g/4oz mushrooms, thinly sliced
40g/1½oz/⅓ cup plain (all-purpose)
   flour
50ml/2fl oz/¼ cup dry white wine
150ml/¼ pint/⅔ cup double (heavy) cream
600ml/1 pint/2½ cups milk
45ml/3 tbsp chopped fresh parsley
2 × 200g/7oz cans tuna in oil
2 canned pimientos, cut into strips
115g/4oz/1 cup mozzarella cheese, grated
8–12 sheets pre-cooked lasagne
25g/1oz/3 tbsp freshly grated
   Parmesan cheese
salt and ground black pepper
Italian-style bread, such as ciabatta,
   and green salad, to serve

1 Lightly grease the base and halfway up the sides of the ceramic cooking pot.

2 Melt 25g/1oz/2 tbsp of the butter in a large pan, add the onion and fry gently for 5 minutes until almost soft but not coloured. Add the garlic and mushrooms and cook for a further 3 minutes, stirring occasionally. Tip the vegetables into a bowl and set aside.

3 Melt the remaining 40g/1½oz/3 tbsp of butter in the pan. Sprinkle over the flour and stir in. Turn off the heat, then gradually blend in the wine, followed by the cream and milk. Gently heat, stirring constantly, until the mixture bubbles and thickens. Stir in the parsley and season well with salt and ground black pepper.

4 Reserve 300ml/½ pint/1¼ cups of the sauce, then stir the mushroom mixture into the remaining sauce.

5 Drain the tuna well and tip into a bowl. Flake the fish with a fork, then gently mix in the pimiento strips, grated mozzarella and a little salt and pepper.

6 Spoon a thin layer of the mushroom sauce over the base of the ceramic cooking pot and cover with 2–3 lasagne sheets, breaking them to fit. Sprinkle half of the tuna mixture over the pasta. Spoon half of the remaining sauce evenly over the top and cover with another layer of lasagne sheets. Repeat, ending with a layer of lasagne. Pour over the reserved plain sauce, then sprinkle with the Parmesan cheese.

7 Cover the slow cooker with the lid and cook on low for 2 hours, or until the lasagne is tender.

8 If you like, brown the top of the lasagne under a medium grill (broiler) and serve with bread and a green salad.

Nutritional information per portion: Energy 554Kcal/2315kJ; Protein 32.2g; Carbohydrate 28.9g, of which sugars 7.4g; Fat 34.7g, of which saturates 18.5g; Cholesterol 110mg; Calcium 371mg; Fibre 0.6g; Sodium 616mg.

POACHED FISH in SPICY TOMATO SAUCE

This traditional Jewish dish is known as Samak. It is usually served with flatbreads, such as pitta or matzos, but you can serve it with plain boiled rice or noodles, if you prefer.

SERVES 4

15ml/1 tbsp vegetable or olive oil
1 onion, finely chopped
150ml/¼ pint/⅔ cup passata (bottled
    strained tomatoes)
75ml/2½fl oz/⅓ cup boiling fish
    or vegetable stock
2 garlic cloves, crushed
1 small red chilli, seeded and
    finely chopped
pinch of ground ginger
pinch of curry powder
pinch of ground cumin
pinch of ground turmeric
seeds from 1 cardamom pod
juice of 1 lemon, plus extra if needed
900g/2lb mixed firm white fish fillets
30ml/2 tbsp chopped fresh
    coriander (cilantro)
30ml/2 tbsp chopped fresh parsley
salt and ground black pepper

1 Heat the oil in a frying pan, add the onion and cook gently, stirring, for 10 minutes until soft but not coloured.

2 Transfer the onions to the ceramic cooking pot, then stir in the passata, stock, garlic, chilli, ginger, curry powder, cumin, turmeric, cardamom, lemon juice, salt and pepper. Cover and cook on high or auto for 1½ hours, until the mixture is just simmering.

3 Add the fish to the pot, cover and continue cooking on auto or low for 45 minutes–1 hour, or until the fish is tender. (The flesh should flake easily.)

4 Lift the fish on to warmed serving plates. Stir the fresh herbs into the sauce, then taste and adjust the seasoning, adding more lemon juice, if necessary. Spoon the sauce over the fish and serve immediately.

Nutritional information per portion: Energy 224Kcal/942kJ; Protein 42g; Carbohydrate 4.1g, of which sugars 3.1g; Fat 4.4g, of which saturates 0.6g; Cholesterol 104mg; Calcium 34mg; Fibre 0.8g; Sodium 151mg.

COCONUT SALMON

*Salmon is quite a robust fish, and responds well to being cooked with this fragrant blend
of spices, garlic and chilli. Coconut milk adds a mellow touch and a creamy taste.*

SERVES 4

15ml/1 tbsp oil
1 onion, finely chopped
2 fresh green chillies, seeded and chopped
2 garlic cloves, crushed
2.5cm/1in piece fresh root ginger, grated
175ml/6fl oz/¾ cup coconut milk
10ml/2 tsp ground cumin
5ml/1 tsp ground coriander
4 salmon steaks, each about 175g/6oz
10ml/2 tsp chilli powder
2.5ml/½ tsp ground turmeric
15ml/1 tbsp white wine vinegar
1.5ml/¼ tsp salt
fresh coriander (cilantro) sprigs, to garnish
rice tossed with spring onions (scallions),
    to serve

VARIATION
Trout fillets go well with spices and can
be used instead of salmon in this dish.

1 Heat the oil in a pan, add the onion,
chillies, garlic and ginger and fry for 5-6
minutes, until fairly soft. Place in a food
processor with 120ml/4fl oz/½ cup of
the coconut milk and blend until smooth.

2 Tip the paste into the ceramic cooking
pot. Stir in 5ml/1 tsp of the cumin, the
ground coriander and the rest of the
coconut milk. Cover and cook on high
for 1½ hours.

3 About 20 minutes before the end of
cooking time, arrange the salmon steaks
in a single layer in a shallow glass dish.
Combine the remaining 5ml/1 tsp cumin,
the chilli powder, turmeric, vinegar and
salt in a bowl to make a paste. Rub the
mixture over the salmon steaks and
leave to marinate at room temperature
while the sauce finishes cooking.

4 Add the salmon steaks to the sauce,
arranging them in a single layer and
spoon some of the coconut sauce over
the top to keep the fish moist while it
cooks. Cover with the lid, reduce the
temperature to low and cook for
45 minutes–1 hour, or until the salmon
is opaque and tender.

5 Transfer the fish to a serving dish,
spoon over the sauce and garnish with
fresh coriander. Serve with the rice.

MIXED FISH JAMBALAYA

As with the Spanish paella, the ingredients used to make this classic Creole dish can be varied according to what is available. The name jambalaya is thought to have come from the French word for ham – jambon – and the Creole word for rice – à la ya.

SERVES 4

30ml/2 tbsp oil
6 rashers (strips) rinded smoked streaky (fatty) bacon, chopped
1 onion, chopped
2 sticks celery, sliced
2 garlic cloves, crushed
5ml/1 tsp cayenne pepper
2 bay leaves
5ml/1 tsp dried oregano
2.5ml/½ tsp dried thyme
4 tomatoes, skinned, seeded and chopped
750ml/1¼ pints/3 cups boiling vegetable or fish stock
15ml/1 tbsp tomato purée (paste)
300g/10oz/1½ cups easy-cook (converted) rice
225g/8oz firm white fish, such as haddock, skinned, boned and cubed
115g/4oz cooked prawns (shrimp)
salt and ground black pepper
4 spring onions (scallions) and 4 cooked prawns (shrimp) in their shells, to garnish

1 Heat the oil in a frying pan and cook the bacon over a medium-high heat for 2 minutes. Reduce the heat, add the onion and celery and cook for a further 5–10 minutes, or until soft and beginning to turn brown.

2 Transfer the mixture to the ceramic cooking pot and switch the slow cooker to high. Add the garlic, cayenne pepper, bay leaves, oregano, thyme, tomatoes, boiling stock and tomato purée. Stir well to mix, then cover with the lid and cook for about 1 hour.

3 Sprinkle the rice over the tomato mixture, followed by the cubes of fish. Season with salt and pepper and stir. Re-cover and cook for 45 minutes.

4 Add the prawns and stir, then cook for 15 minutes, or until the fish and rice are tender and most of the liquid has been absorbed. Serve garnished with spring onions and prawns in their shells.

COOK'S TIP

If you like a really hot, spicy bite to your jambalaya, serve with a little hot chilli sauce for sprinkling over at the table.

Nutritional information per portion: Energy 243Kcal/1015kJ; Protein 23.2g; Carbohydrate 6.5g, of which sugars 5.4g; Fat 14g, of which saturates 3.4g; Cholesterol 126mg; Calcium 64mg; Fibre 1.6g; Sodium 1303mg.

HOKI BALLS in TOMATO SAUCE

This simple fish dish is ideal for serving to young children because there is no risk of bones. For adults, it can be spiced up with a dash of chilli sauce. It is low in fat and therefore ideal for anyone on a low-fat or low-cholesterol diet.

2 Meanwhile, cut the fish into large chunks and place in a food processor. Add the breadcrumbs and the chives or spring onions and season with salt and pepper. Process until the fish is finely chopped, but still has some texture.

3 Divide the mixture into 16 even-size pieces, then roll them into balls with damp hands. Put the fish balls on a plate and chill in the refrigerator until needed.

4 About 30 minutes before the end of the sauce's cooking time, take the fish balls out of the refrigerator and leave them to stand at room temperature.

5 Add the fishballs to the sauce in a single layer. Cook for 1 hour on high, then reduce the temperature to low and cook for a further hour, or until the fish balls are thoroughly cooked. Serve hot, garnished with chives and accompanied by steamed green vegetables.

SERVES 4

400g/14oz can chopped tomatoes
50g/2oz button mushrooms, sliced
450g/1lb hoki or other firm white fish
    fillets, skinned
15g/½oz/¼ cup wholemeal
    (whole-wheat) breadcrumbs
30ml/2 tbsp chopped fresh chives or
    spring onions (scallions)
salt and ground black pepper
chopped fresh chives, to garnish
steamed green vegetables, to serve

COOK'S TIP
If hoki is not available, you can use the same weight of cod, haddock or whiting.

1 Pour the chopped tomatoes into the ceramic cooking pot, then add the sliced mushrooms and a little salt and ground black pepper. Cover with the lid, switch the slow cooker to high and cook for about 2 hours.

Nutritional information per portion: Energy 116Kcal/490kJ; Protein 22.2g; Carbohydrate 4.6g, of which sugars 2.9g; Fat 1.0g, of which saturates 0.1g; Cholesterol 52mg; Calcium 27mg; Fibre 1.0g; Sodium 125mg.

RED MULLET BRAISED on a BED of FENNEL

These pretty pink fish have a wonderful firm flesh and sweet flavour. They are usually cooked whole, but you can remove the heads if there is not enough room in your slow cooker to fit them all in a single layer. Other small whole fish, such as sardines, or fish fillets, such as salmon, cod and hake, can also be cooked in this way.

SERVES 4

10ml/2 tsp fennel seeds
5ml/1 tsp chopped fresh thyme
30ml/2 tbsp chopped fresh parsley
1 clove garlic, crushed
10ml/2 tsp olive oil
4 red mullet, weighing about
   225g/8oz each
lemon wedges, to serve

For the fennel
8 ripe tomatoes
2 fennel bulbs
30ml/2 tbsp olive oil
120ml/4fl oz/½ cup boiling fish
   or vegetable stock
10ml/2 tsp balsamic vinegar
salt and ground black pepper

1 Crush the fennel seeds using a mortar and pestle, then work in the chopped thyme and parsley, garlic and olive oil.

2 Clean and scale the fish and trim off the fins. Use a sharp knife to make deep slashes on each side of the fish.

3 Push the herb paste into the cuts in the fish and spread any excess inside the body cavities. Place the fish on a plate, loosely cover with clear film (plastic wrap) and leave to marinate. On a warm day, it is best to place the marinating fish in the refrigerator and then bring to room temperature about 20 minutes before cooking.

4 Meanwhile, prepare the bed of fennel. Put the tomatoes in a heatproof bowl, add boiling water to cover and leave to stand for 1 minute. Drain and cool under cold running water and peel off the skins. Quarter the tomatoes, seed and cut into small dice.

5 Trim the feathery fronds from the fennel (these can be kept for garnishing), then cut the bulbs into 1cm/½ in slices from the top to the root end.

6 Heat the olive oil in a frying pan and cook the fennel slices over a medium heat for about 10 minutes, or until just starting to colour.

7 Transfer the fennel to the ceramic cooking pot. Add the diced tomatoes, hot stock, balsamic vinegar, salt and pepper, cover with the lid and cook on high for 2 hours.

8 Give the fennel sauce a stir, then place the red mullet on top in a single layer. Cover and cook for 1 hour, or until the fish is cooked through and tender. Serve immediately, with lemon wedges for squeezing over.

COOK'S TIP
Red mullet is highly perishable, so be sure to buy very fresh fish. Look for specimens with bright eyes and skin, and that feel firm. The liver is considered a delicacy, so if your fishmonger will clean them for you, ask for the liver along with the fish.

Nutritional information per portion: Energy 194Kcal/816kJ; Protein 26.5g; Carbohydrate 4.2g, of which sugars 4.1g; Fat 8.1g, of which saturates 1.2g; Cholesterol 63mg; Calcium 95mg; Fibre 3.0g; Sodium 239mg.

HADDOCK with SPICY PUY LENTILS

Dark brown Puy lentils have a delicate taste and texture and hold their shape during cooking, which makes them particularly good for slow cooker dishes. Red chilli pepper and ground cumin add a hint of heat and spice without overpowering the flavour of the fish.

SERVES 4

175g/6oz/¾ cup Puy lentils
600ml/1 pint/2½ cups near-boiling
    vegetable stock
30ml/2 tbsp olive oil
1 onion, finely chopped
2 celery sticks, finely chopped
1 red chilli, halved, seeded
    and finely chopped
2.5ml/½ tsp ground cumin
four thick 150g/5oz pieces of haddock
    fillet or steak
10ml/2 tsp lemon juice
25g/1oz/2 tbsp butter, softened
5ml/1 tsp finely grated lemon rind
salt and ground black pepper
lemon wedges, to garnish

1 Put the lentils in a sieve (strainer) and rinse under cold running water. Drain well, then tip into the ceramic cooking pot. Pour over the hot vegetable stock, cover with the lid and switch the slow cooker on to high.

2 Heat the oil in a frying pan, add the onion and cook gently for 8 minutes. Stir in the celery, chilli and cumin, and cook for a further 2 minutes, or until soft but not coloured. Add the mixture to the lentils, stir, re-cover and cook for about 2½ hours.

3 Meanwhile, rinse the haddock pieces and pat dry on kitchen paper. Sprinkle them with the lemon juice. In a clean bowl, beat together the butter, lemon rind, salt and a generous amount of ground black pepper.

4 Put the haddock on top of the lentils, then dot the lemon butter over the top. Cover and cook for 45 minutes–1 hour, or until the fish flakes easily, the lentils are tender and most of the stock has been absorbed. Serve immediately, garnished with the lemon wedges.

COOK'S TIP
Any firm white fish can be cooked in this way. Both cod and swordfish give particularly good results.

Nutritional information per portion: Energy 366Kcal/1538kJ; Protein 38.9g; Carbohydrate 25.2g, of which sugars 3.2g; Fat 12.8g, of which saturates 4.3g; Cholesterol 82mg; Calcium 64mg; Fibre 4.7g; Sodium 353mg.

SKATE with TOMATO and OLIVE SAUCE

The classic way of serving skate is with a browned butter sauce, but here it is given a Mediterranean twist with tomatoes, olives, orange and a dash of Pernod. If time allows, soak the skate in salted water for a few hours before cooking, to firm up the flesh.

SERVES 4

15ml/1 tbsp olive oil
1 small onion, finely chopped
2 fresh thyme sprigs
grated rind of ½ orange
15ml/1 tbsp Pernod
400g/14oz can chopped tomatoes
50g/2oz/1 cup stuffed green olives
1.5ml/¼ tsp caster (superfine) sugar
4 small skate wings
plain (all-purpose) flour, for coating
salt and ground black pepper
15ml/1 tbsp basil leaves, to garnish
lime wedges, to serve

COOK'S TIP
Pernod gives this dish a deliciously distinctive taste of aniseed, but for those who don't like the flavour, use 15ml/ 1 tbsp vermouth instead.

1 Heat the oil in a pan, add the onion and fry gently for 10 minutes. Stir in the thyme and orange rind and cook for 1 minute. Add the Pernod, tomatoes, olives, sugar and a little salt and pepper, and heat until just below boiling point.

2 Tip the mixture into the ceramic pot and switch on to high. Cover with the lid and cook for 1½ hours.

3 Meanwhile, rinse the skate wings under cold water and pat dry on kitchen paper. Sprinkle the flour on a large, flat dish and season well with salt and ground black pepper. Coat each skate wing in the flour, shaking off any excess, then place on top of the tomato sauce.

4 Re-cover the ceramic cooking pot and reduce the temperature to low. Cook for 1½–2 hours, or until the skate is cooked and flakes easily.

5 Place the fish on to warmed serving plates and spoon over the sauce. Sprinkle over the basil leaves and serve with a wedge of lime for squeezing over.

Nutritional information per portion: Energy 144Kcal/606kJ; Protein 15.5g; Carbohydrate 8.1g, of which sugars 3.7g; Fat 4.8g, of which saturates 0.7g; Cholesterol 35mg; Calcium 37mg; Fibre 1.4g; Sodium 366mg.

LEMON SOLE and PARMA HAM ROULADES

*In this elegant dish, Parma ham and delicately textured lemon sole are rolled around
a subtle herb and lemon stuffing. Serve this dish for a special dinner party with new
potatoes tossed in butter, and lightly steamed asparagus.*

2 Remove most of the fat from the
Parma ham. Lay two overlapping slices
on a board and place a sole fillet on top,
skinned side up.

3 Mix the walnuts, breadcrumbs, parsley,
eggs, lemon rind and pepper together
and spread a quarter of the mixture
over the fish fillet, then press down
gently. Starting at the thicker end of
the fillet, carefully roll up the fish and
ham to enclose the filling.

4 Repeat with the remaining Parma ham,
fish and filling, then secure each roll with
a cocktail stick (toothpick).

5 Place the fish seam-side down in the
ceramic cooking pot. Cover with the lid,
then turn the temperature down to low.
Cook for 1½–2 hours, or until the fish
flakes easily. Remove the cocktail sticks
and serve straight away with freshly
cooked vegetables.

SERVES 4

10ml/2 tsp unsalted (sweet) butter,
    at room temperature
120ml/4fl oz/½ cup dry white wine
4 large lemon sole fillets, about
    150g/5oz each
8 thin slices of Parma ham, about
    130g/4½oz in total
50g/2oz/½ cup chopped toasted walnuts
75g/3oz/1½ cups fresh white breadcrumbs
30ml/2 tbsp finely chopped fresh parsley
2 eggs, lightly beaten
5ml/1 tsp finely grated lemon rind
ground black pepper
new potatoes and steamed green
    vegetables, to serve

1 Smear the inside of the ceramic
cooking pot with the butter. Pour in the
wine and switch the slow cooker to high.
Skin the fish fillets and check that all the
bones have been removed, then pat dry
with kitchen paper.

Nutritional information per portion: Energy 363Kcal/1521kJ; Protein 38g; Carbohydrate 9.6g, of which sugars 1.5g; Fat 17.3g, of which saturates 3.6g; Cholesterol 201mg; Calcium 134mg; Fibre 0.8g; Sodium 714mg.

BASQUE-STYLE TUNA

In Spain, this traditional fisherman's stew is known as marmitako. *It used to be cooked at sea on the fishing boats, and takes its name from the cooking pot, known in France as a* marmite. *The rich flavourings go perfectly with the robust taste of chunky tuna.*

SERVES 4

30ml/2 tbsp olive oil
1 onion, finely chopped
1 clove garlic, finely chopped
75ml/2½fl oz/⅓ cup white wine,
    preferably Spanish
150ml/¼ pint/⅔ cup boiling fish
    or vegetable stock
200g/7oz can chopped tomatoes
5ml/1 tsp paprika
2.5ml/½ tsp dried crushed chillies
450g/1lb waxy new potatoes, cut into
    1cm/½in chunks
1 red and 1 yellow (bell) pepper, seeded
    and chopped
1 small sprig of fresh rosemary
1 bay leaf
450g/1lb fresh tuna, cut into 2.5cm/
    1in chunks
salt and ground black pepper
crusty bread, to serve

3 Stir the chunks of tuna into the sauce. Cover and cook for 15–20 minutes, or until the fish is firm and opaque.

4 Remove the rosemary and bay leaf, then ladle the stew into warmed dishes, grind over a little more black pepper and serve with crusty bread.

1 Heat the oil in a large frying pan, add the onion and fry gently for 10 minutes until soft and translucent. Stir in the garlic, followed by the wine, stock, tomatoes, paprika and chillies. Bring to just below boiling point, then carefully pour the mixture into the ceramic cooking pot.

2 Add the chunks of potato, red and yellow pepper, rosemary and bay leaf to the pot and stir to combine. Cover the slow cooker with the lid and cook on high for 2–2½ hours, or until the potatoes are just tender, then season the sauce to taste with salt and a little ground black pepper.

Nutritional information per portion: Energy 297Kcal/1256kJ; Protein 30.1g; Carbohydrate 27.5g, of which sugars 9.6g; Fat 6.g, of which saturates 1.2g; Cholesterol 57mg; Calcium 39mg; Fibre 3.2g; Sodium 397mg.

COD with CARAMELIZED ONIONS

After very long slow cooking, sliced onions become caramelized and turn a deep golden colour with a fabulously rich, sweet flavour, which is further enhanced here by the addition of balsamic vinegar. Tangy caper and coriander butter adds a fresh, sharp contrast.

SERVES 4

40g/1½oz/3 tbsp butter
10ml/2 tsp olive oil
1.2kg/2½lb yellow onions, peeled
    and finely sliced
5ml/1 tsp caster (superfine) sugar
30ml/2 tbsp balsamic vinegar
30ml/2 tbsp vegetable stock, white wine
    or water
4 x 150g/5oz thick cod fillets

For the butter
115g/4oz/½ cup butter, softened
30ml/2 tbsp capers, drained and chopped
30ml/2 tbsp chopped fresh
    coriander (cilantro)
salt and ground black pepper

1 Put the butter and oil in the ceramic cooking pot and heat on high for about 15 minutes, until melted.

2 Add the sliced onions and stir to coat well in the butter and oil. Cover the pot with the lid, then place a folded dish towel over the top to retain all the heat. Cook for 2 hours, stirring halfway through cooking time.

3 Sprinkle the sugar over the onions and stir well to mix. Replace the lid and folded dish towel and cook on high for 4 hours, stirring two or three times, to ensure the onions colour evenly. At the end of the cooking time, they should be a dark golden colour.

4 Add the vinegar to the onions and stir in the stock, wine or water. Cover again and cook for 1 hour; the onions should now be fairly tender. Season with a little salt and pepper and stir well. Arrange the cod fillets on top of the onions and cook for a final 45 minutes–1 hour, or until the fish flakes easily.

5 Meanwhile, make the caper and coriander butter. Cream the butter in a small bowl until soft, then beat in the capers, coriander, salt and pepper. Roll up the butter in foil, clear film (plastic wrap) or greaseproof (waxed) paper to form a short log shape, twisting the ends to secure them. Chill in the refrigerator or freezer until firm.

6 To serve, spoon the onions and fish on to warmed serving plates. Slice off discs of the butter and top each piece of fish with one or two slices. Serve immediately, with the butter melting over the hot fish.

Nutritional information per portion: Energy 534Kcal/2213kJ; Protein 31.3g; Carbohydrate 25g, of which sugars 18.1g; Fat 35g, of which saturates 20.6g; Cholesterol 152mg; Calcium 96mg; Fibre 4.2g; Sodium 334mg.

SWORDFISH in BARBECUE SAUCE

This is an ideal way to cook any firm fish steaks. The warmly spiced smoky sauce goes particularly well with meaty fish, such as swordfish, shark and tuna. Choose smaller, thicker fish steaks rather than large, thinner ones, so that they will fit in the slow cooker.

SERVES 4

15ml/1 tbsp sunflower oil
1 small onion, very finely chopped
1 garlic clove, crushed
2.5ml/½ tsp chilli powder
15ml/1 tbsp Worcestershire sauce
15ml/1 tbsp soft light brown sugar
15ml/1 tbsp balsamic vinegar
15ml/1 tbsp American mustard
150ml/¼ pint/⅔ cup tomato juice
4 swordfish steaks, about 115g/4oz each
salt and ground black pepper
fresh flat leaf parsley, to garnish
boiled or steamed rice, to serve

1 Heat the oil in a frying pan, add the onion and cook gently for 10 minutes, until soft. Stir in the garlic and chilli powder and cook for a few seconds, then add the Worcestershire sauce, sugar, vinegar, mustard and tomato juice. Heat gently, stirring, until nearly boiling.

2 Pour half the sauce into the ceramic cooking pot. Rinse the swordfish steaks, pat dry on kitchen paper and arrange in a single layer on top of the sauce. Top with the remaining sauce.

3 Cover the slow cooker with a lid and switch on to high. Cook for 2–3 hours, or until the fish is tender and cooked.

4 Carefully transfer the fish to warmed serving plates and spoon the barbecue sauce over the top. Garnish with sprigs of flat-leaf parsley and serve immediately with boiled or steamed rice.

COOK'S TIP
For a really smoky barbecue flavour use a crushed dried chipotle chilli instead of the chilli powder.

Nutritional information per portion: Energy 158Kcal/670kJ; Protein 27.3g; Carbohydrate 4.9g, of which sugars 4.5g; Fat 3.5g, of which saturates 0.6g; Cholesterol 59mg; Calcium 21mg; Fibre 0.2g; Sodium 414mg.

SPINACH and NUT STUFFED HERRINGS

It is difficult to cook large whole fish in a slow cooker, but smaller fish, such as sardines and herrings, are ideal. Their slightly oily flesh is perfectly suited to slow cooking, too, because it helps to keep the fish wonderfully moist.

SERVES 4

40g/1½oz/3 tbsp unsalted (sweet) butter
5ml/1 tsp sunflower oil
25g/1oz/¼ cup pine nuts
1 small onion, finely chopped
175g/6oz frozen spinach, thawed
50g/2oz/1 cup white breadcrumbs
25g/1oz/⅓ cup grated Parmesan cheese
pinch of freshly grated nutmeg
75ml/5 tbsp fish or vegetable stock
    or white wine
4 small herrings, heads removed,
    and boned
salt and ground black pepper
lemon wedges, to serve

4 Put the onion and spinach in the mixing bowl with the pine nuts and add the breadcrumbs, cheese, nutmeg, salt and pepper. Mix the ingredients with a fork until thoroughly combined.

7 Arrange the fish on the base of the ceramic cooking pot in a single layer. Cover the pot with the lid and cook for 1½–2½ hours, or until the fish is cooked. (Test the flesh with a fork; it should flake easily when ready.)

8 Carefully lift the stuffed fish out of the slow cooker on to warmed serving plates, and serve with lemon wedges.

COOK'S TIP

This dish is perfect for a simple, tasty supper, but it is great for entertaining, too. Serve with a tasty couscous salad tossed with plenty of herbs and raisins. The sweetness of the dried fruit goes particularly well with the spinach and pine nut stuffing, and complements the rich flavour of the fish.

1 Heat 25g/1oz/2 tbsp of the butter and sunflower oil in a frying pan until melted. Add the pine nuts and gently fry for 3–4 minutes until golden. Lift them from the pan with a slotted spoon, leaving the fat behind, and place in a mixing bowl.

2 Add the finely chopped onion to the pan and cook gently for 10 minutes, stirring frequently, until soft.

3 Meanwhile, place the thawed spinach in a fine sieve (strainer) and press out as much liquid as possible. (Use your hands to squeeze out the liquid, or press firmly with the back of a spoon.)

5 Smear the remaining 15g/½oz/1 tbsp of butter over the base of the ceramic cooking pot and pour in the stock or wine. Cover with the lid and switch the slow cooker on to high.

VARIATIONS
• Other kinds of nuts can be used in place of pine nuts in the stuffing. Try chopped hazelnuts or walnuts instead.
• As an alternative to nuts, add 15ml/1 tbsp chopped dried apricots to the stuffing.

6 Using a sharp knife, make three shallow cuts down each side of the fish, then spoon the stuffing into the cavities, packing it in quite firmly. Bring the edges of the fish together and secure with wooden cocktail sticks (toothpicks).

Nutritional information per portion: Energy 351Kcal/1462kJ; Protein 24g; Carbohydrate 7.6g, of which sugars 1.9g; Fat 23.9g, of which saturates 6.9g; Cholesterol 78mg; Calcium 619mg; Fibre 1.5g; Sodium 624mg.

NORTHERN THAI FISH CURRY

Thin, soupy, strongly flavoured curries are typical of the northern region of Thailand. Fragrant lemon grass, zesty galangal and salty Thai fish sauce come together to give this dish its characteristic Thai flavour. Serve with lots of sticky rice to soak up the juices.

5 Add the shallots, garlic, galangal or ginger, lemon grass, chilli flakes, fish sauce and sugar to the pot and stir to combine. Cover with the lid and cook for 2 hours.

6 Add the cubes of salmon to the stock and cook for 15 minutes. Turn off the slow cooker and leave to stand for a further 10–15 minutes, or until the fish is cooked through. Serve immediately.

SERVES 4

450g/1lb salmon fillet
475ml/16fl oz/2 cups near-boiling
  vegetable stock
4 shallots, very finely chopped
1 garlic clove, crushed
2.5cm/1in piece fresh galangal or ginger,
  finely chopped
1 lemon grass stalk, finely chopped
2.5ml/½ tsp dried chilli flakes
15ml/1 tbsp Thai fish sauce
5ml/1 tsp palm sugar or light muscovado
  (brown) sugar

COOK'S TIP
Allow the fish to return to room temperature before adding to the stock, so that the temperature of the liquid doesn't fall below simmering point.

1 Wrap the salmon fillet in clear film (plastic wrap) and place in the freezer for 30–40 minutes to firm up slightly.

2 Unwrap the fish, and carefully remove and discard the skin. Using a sharp knife, cut the fish into 2.5cm/1in cubes and remove any stray bones with your fingers or a pair of tweezers.

3 Place the cubed fish in a bowl, cover with clear film (plastic wrap) and leave to stand at room temperature.

4 Meanwhile, pour the hot vegetable stock into the ceramic cooking pot and switch the slow cooker to high.

GREEN FISH CURRY

Fresh-tasting, spicy curries made with coconut milk are a classic of Thai cuisine. This slow-cooker version of green curry uses desiccated coconut and cream to give a really rich taste and texture, which is offset by the generous use of spices, chilli and fragrant herbs.

SERVES 4

1 onion, chopped

1 large fresh green chilli, halved, seeded and chopped, plus extra slices to garnish

1 garlic clove, crushed

50g/2oz/½ cup cashew nuts

2.5ml/½ tsp fennel seeds

30ml/2 tbsp desiccated (dry unsweetened shredded) coconut

150ml/¼ pint/⅔ cup water

30ml/2 tbsp vegetable oil

1.5ml/¼ tsp cumin seeds

1.5ml/¼ tsp ground coriander

1.5ml/¼ tsp ground cumin

150ml/¼ pint/⅔ cup double (heavy) cream

4 white fish fillets, such as cod or haddock, skinned

1.5ml/¼ tsp ground turmeric

30ml/2 tbsp lime juice

salt

45ml/3 tbsp chopped fresh coriander (cilantro), plus extra to garnish

boiled rice, to serve

1 Place the onion, chilli, garlic, cashew nuts, fennel seeds and desiccated coconut in a food processor with 45ml/ 3 tbsp of the water and blend to make a smooth paste. Alternatively, work the dry ingredients to a paste in a mortar with a pestle, then stir in the water.

2 Heat the oil in a frying pan and fry the cumin seeds for 1 minute, until they give off their aroma. Add the coconut paste and fry for 5 minutes, then stir in the ground coriander, cumin and remaining water. Bring to the boil, then let the mixture bubble for 1 minute.

3 Transfer the mixture to the ceramic cooking pot. Stir in the cream, cover with the lid and switch the slow cooker to high. Cook for 1½ hours.

COOK'S TIP
Do not leave the fish to marinate for longer than 15 minutes because the texture will be spoilt.

4 Towards the end of cooking time, prepare and marinate the fish. Cut the fillets into 5cm/2in chunks and put them in a glass bowl. Combine the turmeric, lime juice and a pinch of salt in a separate bowl and pour it over the fish. Use your hands to rub it into the fish. Cover with clear film (plastic wrap) and leave to marinate for 15 minutes.

5 Stir the fish into the sauce, re-cover and cook for 30 minutes–1 hour, or until the fish flakes easily. Stir in the coriander. Spoon the curry into a warmed bowls. Garnish with chopped coriander and sliced green chilli, and serve with rice.

Nutritional information per portion: Energy 511Kcal/2118kJ; Protein 36.1g; Carbohydrate 6.4g, of which sugars 3.9g; Fat 37.9g, of which saturates 18.8g; Cholesterol 132mg; Calcium 50mg; Fibre 2g; Sodium 153mg.

POULTRY AND GAME

The slow cooker is perfect for making all manner of stews, casseroles and curries, and this chapter is packed with fantastic, healthy recipe ideas using poultry and game as the basis. Chicken is always a firm favourite, and the versatility of the slow cooker means that there is something here for everyone. In addition, there are plenty of other poultry and game dishes to whet the appetite, using turkey, guinea fowl and rabbit. All of these recipes draw their inspiration from favourite cuisines around the world, giving a wonderful choice of dishes for every occasion. Try Mexican drunken chicken, Indian korma, Creole jambalaya or French duck stew.

TURKEY and TOMATO HOT-POT

Often reserved for festive meals, turkey makes a great choice for any occasion. Here the meat is shaped into balls and simmered with rice in a richly flavoured tomato sauce.

SERVES 4

white bread loaf, unsliced
30ml/2 tbsp milk
1 garlic clove, crushed
2.5ml/½ tsp caraway seeds
225g/8oz minced (ground) turkey
1 egg white
350ml/12fl oz/1½ cups near-boiling
   chicken stock
400g/14oz can chopped tomatoes
15ml/1 tbsp tomato purée (paste)
90g/3½oz/½ cup easy-cook
   (converted) rice
salt and ground black pepper
15ml/1 tbsp chopped fresh basil, to garnish
courgette (zucchini) ribbons, to serve

1 Using a serrated knife, remove the crusts and cut the bread into cubes.

2 Place the bread in a mixing bowl and sprinkle with the milk, then leave to soak for about 5 minutes.

3 Add the garlic clove, caraway seeds, turkey, and salt and pepper to the bread and mix together well.

4 Whisk the egg white until stiff, then fold, half at a time, into the turkey mixture. Chill in the refrigerator.

5 Pour the stock into the ceramic cooking pot. Add the tomatoes and tomato purée, then switch to high, cover with the lid and cook for 1 hour.

6 Meanwhile, shape the turkey mixture into 16 small balls. Stir the rice into the tomato mixture, then add the turkey balls. Cook on high for a further hour, or until the turkey balls and rice are cooked. Serve with the courgettes.

Nutritional information per portion: Energy 187Kcal/797kJ; Protein 18.2g; Carbohydrate 26.6g, of which sugars 3.9g; Fat 1.7g, of which saturates 0.5g; Cholesterol 32mg; Calcium 44mg; Fibre 1g; Sodium 212mg.

LAYERED CHICKEN and MUSHROOM BAKE

*This rich, creamy dish makes a hearty winter supper. The thick sauce combines with
juices from the mushrooms and chicken during cooking to make a well-flavoured gravy.*

SERVES 4

15ml/1 tbsp olive oil
4 large chicken breast portions,
  cut into chunks
40g/1½oz/3 tbsp butter
1 leek, finely sliced into rings
25g/1oz/¼ cup plain (all-purpose) flour
550ml/18fl oz/2½ cups milk
5ml/1 tsp Worcestershire sauce (optional)
5ml/1 tsp wholegrain mustard
1 carrot, finely diced
225g/8oz/3 cups button (white)
  mushrooms, thinly sliced
900g/2lb potatoes, thinly sliced
salt and ground black pepper

1 Heat the olive oil in a large pan. Add
the chicken and fry gently until beginning
to brown. Remove the chicken from the
pan using a slotted spoon, leaving any
juices behind. Set aside.

2 Add 25g/1oz/2 tbsp of the butter to
the pan and heat gently until melted.
Stir in the leek and fry gently for about
minutes. Sprinkle the flour over the
leeks, then turn off the heat and
gradually blend in the milk until smooth.
Slowly bring the mixture to the boil,
stirring all the time, until thickened.

3 Remove the pan from the heat and
stir in the Worcestershire sauce, if using,
mustard, diced carrot, mushrooms and
chicken. Season generously.

4 Arrange enough potato slices to cover
the base of the ceramic cooking pot.
Spoon one-third of the chicken mixture
over the top, then cover with another
layer of potatoes. Repeat layering,
finishing with a layer of potatoes. Dot
the remaining butter on top.

5 Cover and cook on high for 4 hours,
or until the potatoes are cooked and
tender when pierced with a skewer.
If you like, place the dish under a
moderate grill (broiler) for 5 minutes
to brown, then serve.

Nutritional information per portion: Energy 461Kcal/1943kJ; Protein 42.4g; Carbohydrate 43.8g, of which sugars 5.2g; Fat 14.1g, of which saturates 6.4g; Cholesterol 126.3mg; Calcium 49mg; Fibre 4.3g; Sodium 351mg.

APRICOT and ALMOND STUFFED CHICKEN

Couscous makes a delicious and simple base for this sweet-and-sour stuffing flavoured with dried apricots and crunchy toasted almonds. A couple of spoonfuls of orange jelly marmalade adds tanginess to the sauce, as well as thickening it slightly.

3 Put the couscous in a bowl and spoon over 50ml/2fl oz/¼ cup of the stock. Leave to stand for 2–3 minutes, or until all the stock has been absorbed.

4 Drain the apricots, reserving the juice, then stir them into the couscous along with the chopped almonds and tarragon. Season with salt and black pepper, then stir in just enough egg yolk to bind the mixture together.

5 Divide the stuffing equally between the chicken portions, packing it firmly into the pockets, then securing with wooden cocktail sticks (toothpicks). Place the stuffed chicken portions in the base of the ceramic cooking pot.

6 Stir the orange marmalade into the remaining hot stock until dissolved, then stir in the orange juice. Season with salt and pepper and pour over the chicken. Cover the pot and cook on high for 3–5 hours, or until the chicken is cooked through and tender.

7 Remove the chicken from the sauce and keep warm. Tip the sauce into a wide pan and boil rapidly until reduced by half. Carve the chicken into slices on the diagonal and arrange on serving plates. Spoon over the sauce and serve immediately with basmati and wild rice.

COOK'S TIP

Sautéed spinach or steamed green vegetables make a great accompaniment to this dish. They go particularly well with the sweet, fruity stuffing.

SERVES 4

50g/2oz/¼ cup dried apricots
150ml/¼ pint/⅔ cup orange juice
4 skinned boneless chicken breast portions
50g/2oz/⅓ cup instant couscous
150ml/¼ pint/⅔ cup boiling chicken stock
25g/1oz/¼ cup chopped toasted almonds
1.5ml/¼ tsp dried tarragon
1 egg yolk
30ml/2 tbsp orange jelly marmalade
salt and ground black pepper
boiled or steamed basmati and wild rice,
   to serve

1 Put the dried apricots in a small bowl and pour over the orange juice. Leave to soak at room temperature while you prepare the remaining ingredients.

2 Using a sharp knife, cut a deep pocket horizontally in each chicken breast portion, taking care not to cut all the way through. Put the chicken portions between two sheets of oiled baking parchment or clear film (plastic wrap), then gently beat with a rolling pin or mallet until slightly thinner.

Nutritional information per portion: Energy 379Kcal/1604kJ; Protein 40.2g; Carbohydrate 38g, of which sugars 27g; Fat 8.5g, of which saturates 1.3g; Cholesterol 155mg; Calcium 61mg; Fibre 1.6g; Sodium 117mg.

HEN in a POT with PARSLEY SAUCE

Although harder to find nowadays, a boiling fowl will feed a family well. A large chicken could replace the boiling fowl. Serve with potatoes boiled in their jackets and cabbage.

SERVES 6

1.6–1.8kg/3½–4lb boiling fowl or
    whole chicken
½ lemon, sliced
small bunch of parsley and thyme
675g/1½lb carrots, cut into large chunks
12 shallots or small onions, left whole

For the sauce
50g/2oz/½ cup butter
50g/2oz/½ cup plain (all-purpose) flour
15ml/1 tbsp lemon juice
60ml/4 tbsp chopped flat leaf parsley
150ml/½ pint/⅔ cup milk
salt and ground black pepper
sprigs of flat leaf parsley, to garnish

VARIATION
A small joint of ham or bacon can also be added to the pot if available. Soak it overnight in cold water before cooking and do not add any extra salt without tasting first. A boiling fowl with a small joint of bacon, weighing 900g–1kg/2–2¼lb in total, should feed 8–10 people. Red cabbage makes a tasty accompaniment.

1 Remove any trussing string and loose pieces of fat from inside the boiling fowl or chicken, then rinse under cold water and place in the ceramic cooking pot. Add the lemon, parsley and thyme, carrots and onions and season well.

2 Pour in near-boiling water to just cover the fowl and vegetables. Cover with the lid, switch the slow cooker to high and cook for 1 hour.

3 Skim off any scum and fat using a slotted spoon. Re-cover the pot and cook for 2–2½ hours, or until the fowl is cooked and tender. Using a slotted spoon, lift the fowl on to a warmed serving dish, arrange the vegetables around it and keep warm.

4 Strain the cooking liquid into a pan and boil uncovered to reduce by a third. Strain and leave to settle for 2 minutes, then skim the fat off the surface.

5 Melt the butter in a saucepan, add the flour and cook, stirring, for 1 minute. Gradually stir in the stock (there should be about 600ml/1 pint/2½ cups) and bring to the boil.

6 Add the lemon juice, parsley and milk to the pan. Season with salt and ground black pepper and simmer the sauce for another 1–2 minutes.

7 To serve, pour a little of the sauce over the fowl and add the carrots and onions, then garnish with a few sprigs of fresh parsley, and take to the table for carving. Pour the rest of the sauce into a warmed sauceboat and serve separately.

Nutritional information per portion: Energy 509Kcal/2114kJ; Protein 36.2g; Carbohydrate 20.1g, of which sugars 12.2g; Fat 32g, of which saturates 11.4g; Cholesterol 195mg; Calcium 109mg; Fibre 4g; Sodium 214mg

CHICKEN FRICASSÉE

Traditionally made with chicken, rabbit or veal, this fricassée dish has a wonderfully rich and flavoursome sauce that is further enhanced with cream and fresh herbs. The meat is first seared in fat, then braised in stock with vegetables until tender. It is a perfect dish for entertaining because you can prepare it in advance and then simply leave it to simmer while you enjoy the company of your guests.

SERVES 4

20 small even-size button (pearl) onions or
    shallots
1.2–1.3kg/2½–3lb chicken, cut into pieces
25g/1oz/2 tbsp butter
30ml/2 tbsp sunflower oil
45ml/3 tbsp plain (all-purpose) flour
250ml/8fl oz/1 cup dry white wine
600ml/1 pint/2½ cups boiling chicken stock
1 bouquet garni
5ml/1 tsp lemon juice
225g/8oz/3 cups button (white) mushrooms
75ml/2½fl oz/⅓ cup double (heavy) cream
45ml/3 tbsp chopped fresh parsley
salt and ground black pepper
mashed potatoes and steamed seasonal
    vegetables, to serve

1 Put the onions or shallots in a bowl, add just enough boiling water to cover them, and leave to soak.

2 Meanwhile, rinse the chicken pieces well in cold water, and pat dry with kitchen paper.

3 Melt half the butter with the oil in a large frying pan. Add the chicken pieces and cook, turning occasionally, until lightly browned all over. Using a slotted spoon or tongs, transfer the chicken pieces to the ceramic cooking pot, leaving the juices behind.

4 Stir the flour into the pan juices, then blend in the wine. Stir in the stock and add the bouquet garni and the lemon juice. Bring the mixture to the boil, stirring all the time, until the sauce has thickened. Season well and pour over the chicken. Cover the pot with the lid and switch the slow cooker to high.

5 Drain and peel the onions or shallots. (Soaking them in boiling water loosens the skins, making them easy to peel.) Trim the stalks from the mushrooms.

6 Clean the frying pan, then add the remaining butter and heat gently until melted. Add the mushrooms and onions or shallots and cook for 5 minutes, turning frequently until they are lightly browned. Tip into the ceramic cooking pot with the chicken.

7 Re-cover the slow cooker with the lid and cook on high for 3–4 hours, or until the chicken is cooked and tender. (To test that the chicken is cooked through, pierce the thickest part of one of the portions with a skewer or thin knife; the juices should run clear.)

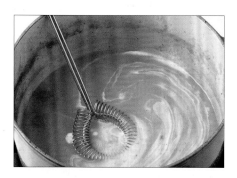

8 Using a slotted spoon, remove the chicken and vegetables to a warmed serving dish. Add the cream and 30ml/ 2 tbsp of the parsley to the sauce and whisk to combine. Check the seasoning and adjust if necessary, then pour the sauce over the chicken and vegetables.

9 Sprinkle the fricassée with the remaining parsley and serve with mashed potatoes and seasonal vegetables.

COOK'S TIP
A classic bouquet garni is made up of parsley stalks, a sprig of thyme and a bay leaf. You can tie these together with a piece of string, or tie the herbs in a small square of muslin (cheesecloth). Some people like to add rosemary as well.

Nutritional information per portion: Energy 613Kcal/2563kJ; Protein 53.1g; Carbohydrate 36.4g, of which sugars 17.9g; Fat 25g, of which saturates 11.1g; Cholesterol 196mg; Calcium 128mg; Fibre 5.3g; Sodium 396mg.

SPRING CHICKEN SLOW-BRAISED in SMOKY BACON SAUCE

Sweet, succulent and tangy with the flavour of apples and aromatic thyme, this delicious stew makes a great alternative to the classic roast. Baby spring chickens are also known as poussin and can weigh 350–500g/12oz–1¼lb. Be sure to buy large ones because the smaller birds are only big enough for a single serving.

SERVES 4

2 large spring chickens
25g/1oz/2 tbsp unsalted
    (sweet) butter
10ml/2 tsp sunflower oil
115g/4oz chopped bacon pieces
    or smoked streaky (fatty) bacon
2 leeks, washed and sliced
175g/6oz/2¼ cup small button (white)
    mushrooms, trimmed
120ml/4fl oz/½ cup apple juice,
    plus a further 15ml/1 tbsp
120ml/4fl oz/½ cup chicken stock
30ml/2 tbsp clear honey
10ml/2 tsp chopped fresh thyme
    or 2.5ml/½ tsp dried
225g/8oz crisp red apples
10ml/2 tsp cornflour (cornstarch)
salt and ground black pepper
creamy mashed potatoes and
    pan-fried or steamed baby leeks,
    to serve

1 Using a sharp, heavy knife or a meat cleaver, carefully split the spring chickens in half to make four portions. Rinse the portions well under cold running water, then pat dry using kitchen paper.

2 Heat the butter and sunflower oil in a large pan and add the spring chicken portions. Fry, turning the pieces over, until lightly browned on all sides. Transfer the chicken portions to the ceramic cooking pot, leaving the cooking fat in the pan.

3 Add the chopped bacon to the pan and cook for about 5 minutes, stirring occasionally, until beginning to brown.

4 Using a slotted spoon transfer the bacon to the ceramic cooking pot, leaving all the fat and juices behind.

5 Add the leeks and mushrooms to the pan and cook for a few minutes until they begin to soften and the mushrooms begin to release their juices.

6 Pour 120ml/4fl oz/½ cup apple juice and the chicken stock into the pan, then stir in the honey and thyme. Season well with salt and ground black pepper.

7 Bring the mixture almost to boiling point, then pour over the chicken and bacon. Cover the ceramic cooking pot with the lid, switch the slow cooker to high and cook for 2 hours.

8 Quarter, core and thickly slice the apples. Add them to the cooking pot, submerging them in the liquid to stop them turning brown. Cook for a further 2 hours, or until the chicken and vegetables are cooked and tender.

9 Remove the chicken from the cooking pot, place on a plate and keep warm.

10 Blend the cornflour with the 15ml/1 tbsp apple juice and stir into the cooking liquid until thickened. Taste and adjust the seasoning, if necessary.

11 Serve the chicken on warmed plates with sauce poured over the top. Accompany with mashed potatoes and pan-fried or steamed baby leeks.

COOK'S TIP
Always check that chicken is thoroughly cooked before serving to avoid any risk of salmonella. To test, pierce the thickest part of the meat with a skewer or thin knife; the juices should run clear.

Nutritional information per portion: Energy 465Kcal/1945kJ; Protein 32.8g; Carbohydrate 25.9g, of which sugars 20.7g; Fat 26.3g, of which saturates 9.5g; Cholesterol 172mg; Calcium 40mg; Fibre 3.3g; Sodium 632mg.

TARRAGON CHICKEN in CIDER

Aromatic tarragon has a distinctive flavour that goes wonderfully with both cream and chicken. This recipe is truly effortless, yet provides an elegant dish for entertaining or a special family meal. Serve with sautéed potatoes and a green vegetable.

SERVES 4

350g/12oz small button (pearl) onions
15ml/1 tbsp sunflower oil
4 garlic cloves, peeled
4 boneless chicken breast portions,
  skin on
350ml/12fl oz/1½ cups dry (hard) cider
1 bay leaf
200g/7oz/scant 1 cup crème fraîche
  or sour cream
30ml/2 tbsp chopped fresh tarragon
15ml/1 tbsp chopped fresh parsley
salt and ground black pepper

1 Put the button onions in a heatproof bowl and pour over enough boiling water to cover. Leave to stand for at least 10 minutes, then drain and peel off the skins. (They should come off very easily after soaking.)

2 Heat the oil in a frying pan, add the onions and cook gently for 10 minutes, or until lightly browned, turning them frequently. Add the garlic and cook for a further 2–3 minutes. Using a slotted spoon, transfer the onions and garlic to the ceramic cooking pot.

3 Place the chicken breast portions in the frying pan and cook for 3–4 minutes, turning once or twice until lightly browned on both sides. Transfer the chicken to the ceramic cooking pot.

4 Pour the cider into the pan, add the bay leaf and a little salt and pepper, and bring to the boil.

5 Pour the hot cider and bay leaf over the chicken. Cover the ceramic cooking pot with the lid and cook on low for 4–5 hours, or until the chicken and onions are cooked and very tender. Lift out the chicken breasts. Set aside while you finish preparing the cider sauce.

COOK'S TIP

When preparing and cooking poultry, always be sure to wash utensils, surfaces and hands afterwards to avoid risk of contamination or food poisoning. Use a plastic or glass chopping board when cutting all poultry, meat or fish because they are easier to wash and much more hygienic. Wooden boards are absorbant and should therefore be avoided.

6 Stir the crème fraîche or sour cream and the herbs into the sauce. Return the chicken breasts to the pot and cook for a further 30 minutes on high, or until piping hot. Serve the chicken immediately, with lightly sautéed potatoes and a green vegetable, such as cabbage.

VARIATIONS

• Guinea fowl and pheasant portions can also be cooked in this way. Try using white wine in place of the cider and serve with creamy mashed potatoes and steamed baby carrots drizzled with a little melted butter.
• Try using 1 or 2 sprigs of fresh thyme in place of the tarragon. It gives a very different flavour but is equally good. Serve with rice and roasted tomatoes.

Nutritional information per portion: Energy 520Kcal/2167kJ; Protein 36.9g; Carbohydrate 12.1g, of which sugars 9.2g; Fat 33.9g, of which saturates 12.9g; Cholesterol 184mg; Calcium 90mg; Fibre 1.5g; Sodium 138mg.

CHICKEN with CHIPOTLE SAUCE

Spicy-hot and deliciously rich and smoky, this dish of chicken cooked in a rich chilli sauce is great served with rice for a tasty, healthy supper. The purée can be prepared ahead of time, making this recipe ideal for casual entertaining.

SERVES 6

6 chipotle chillies
200ml/7fl oz/scant 1 cup boiling water
about 200ml/7fl oz/scant 1 cup chicken
   stock
45ml/3 tbsp vegetable oil
3 onions
6 boneless chicken breast portions
salt and ground black pepper
fresh oregano, to garnish

COOK'S TIP
Spicy-hot, wrinkled, dark red chipotle chillies are smoke-dried jalepeños and have a really rich taste. To really bring out their flavour, they need long, slow cooking – making them perfect for slow cooker casseroles.

1 Put the dried chillies in a bowl and cover with the boiling water. Leave to stand for about 30 minutes until very soft. Drain, reserving the soaking water in a measuring jug (pitcher). Cut off the stalk from each chilli, then slit the chilli lengthways and scrape out the seeds with a small, sharp knife.

2 Chop the chillies roughly and put in a food processor or blender. Add enough chicken stock to the soaking water to make it up to 400ml/14fl oz/1⅔ cups, then pour into the food processor or blender. Process until smooth.

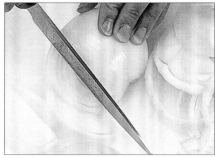

3 Heat the oil in a frying pan. Halve and slice the onions and add them to the pan. Cook, stirring, over a medium heat for 5 minutes, or until soft but not coloured.

4 Transfer the onions to the ceramic cooking pot and switch to high. Sprinkle the onion slices with a little salt and ground black pepper.

5 Remove the skin from the chicken breast portions and trim off any pieces of fat. Arrange in a single layer on top of the onion slices. Sprinkle with a little salt and several grindings of black pepper.

6 Pour the chilli purée over the chicken, making sure that each piece is evenly coated. Cover with the lid and cook for 3–4 hours, or until the chicken is cooked through but still moist and tender. Garnish with fresh oregano and serve.

Nutritional information per portion: Energy 235Kcal/989kJ; Protein 36.9g; Carbohydrate 5.9g, of which sugars 4.2g; Fat 7.3g, of which saturates 1.1g; Cholesterol 105mg; Calcium 26mg; Fibre 1.1g; Sodium 92mg.

DRUNKEN CHICKEN

Flavoured with a mixture of sherry and tequila, this rich, fruity casserole makes a great meal for any occasion. Serve with bowls of steamed or plain boiled rice to soak up the juices, or with warmed flour tortillas to scoop up the chicken and sauce.

SERVES 4

150g/5oz/1 cup raisins
120ml/4fl oz/½ cup sherry
115g/4oz/1 cup plain (all-purpose) flour
2.5ml/½ tsp salt
2.5ml/½ tsp ground black pepper
45ml/3 tbsp vegetable oil
8 skinless chicken thighs
1 onion, halved and thinly sliced
2 garlic cloves, crushed
2 tart eating apples
115g/4oz/1 cup flaked (sliced) almonds
1 slightly under-ripe plantain, peeled
   and sliced
300ml/½ pint/1¼ cups boiling
   chicken stock
120ml/4fl oz/½ cup tequila
chopped fresh herbs, to garnish

1 Put the raisins in a bowl and add the sherry. Set aside to soak.

2 Meanwhile, combine the flour, salt and pepper and spread the mixture out on a large plate. Heat 30ml/2 tbsp of the oil in a large frying pan. Coat each chicken thigh in the seasoned flour, then fry, turning, until browned all over. Drain well on kitchen paper.

3 Heat the remaining oil in the pan, add the onion and fry for 5 minutes, or until soft and beginning to brown. Stir in the garlic, then remove the pan from the heat. Tip the onions and garlic into the ceramic cooking pot and switch the slow cooker to high.

4 Peel, core and dice the apples. Add them to the ceramic cooking pot, then sprinkle with the almonds, plantain slices and raisins. Pour in the sherry, chicken stock and tequila and stir to combine.

5 Add the chicken pieces to the fruit and vegetable mixture, pressing them down into the stock so that they are completely covered. Cover with the lid and cook for 3 hours, or until the chicken thighs are very tender.

6 Check the chicken is cooked: pierce the thickest part with a sharp knife or skewer; the juices should run clear. Cook for a little longer, if necessary.

7 Taste the sauce and add a little more salt and ground black pepper if necessary. Serve the chicken piping hot, sprinkled with chopped fresh herbs.

Nutritional information per portion: Energy 529Kcal/2227kJ; Protein 23.1g; Carbohydrate 63.7g, of which sugars 34.1g; Fat 11.5g, of which saturates 1.8g; Cholesterol 94.5mg; Calcium 76mg; Fibre 2.9g; Sodium 401mg.

CARIBBEAN PEANUT CHICKEN

Peanut butter adds a delicious richness and depth of flavour to this spicy rice dish.
It is a classic ingredient used in many slow-cooked Caribbean curries and stews.

3 Meanwhile, heat the remaining oil in a frying pan, add the onion and fry for 10 minutes until soft. Transfer to the ceramic cooking pot and switch the slow cooker to high. Add the chopped tomatoes and chilli and stir to combine.

4 Put the peanut butter into a bowl, then blend in the stock, adding a little at a time. Pour the mixture into the ceramic cooking pot, season and stir. Cover with the lid and cook for 1 hour.

5 About 30 minutes before the end of cooking time, remove the chicken from the refrigerator and leave it to come to room temperature.

6 Add the chicken and the marinade to the ceramic cooking pot and stir to mix. Re-cover and cook for 1 hour.

7 Sprinkle the rice over the casserole, then stir to mix. Cover and cook for a final 45 minutes–1 hour, or until the chicken and rice are cooked and tender. Serve straight away, garnished with lemon or lime wedges for squeezing over, and sprigs of fresh parsley.

SERVES 4

4 skinless, boneless chicken
    breast portions
45ml/3 tbsp groundnut (peanut) or
    sunflower oil
1 garlic clove, crushed
5ml/1 tsp chopped fresh thyme
15ml/1 tbsp curry powder
juice of half a lemon
1 onion, finely chopped
2 tomatoes, peeled, seeded and chopped
1 fresh green chilli, seeded and sliced
60ml/4 tbsp smooth peanut butter
750ml/1¼ pints/3 cups boiling
    chicken stock
300g/10oz/1½ cups easy-cook (converted)
    white rice
salt and ground black pepper
lemon or lime wedges and sprigs of fresh
    flat leaf parsley, to garnish

1 Cut the chicken breast portions into thin strips. In a bowl, mix together 15ml/1 tbsp of the oil with the garlic, thyme, curry powder and lemon juice.

2 Add the chicken strips to the ingredients in the bowl and stir well to combine. Cover with clear film (plastic wrap) and leave to marinate in the refrigerator for 1½–2 hours.

Nutritional information per portion: Energy 635Kcal/2677kJ; Protein 45.8g; Carbohydrate 70.7g, of which sugars 4.4g; Fat 20.8g, of which saturates 4.1g; Cholesterol 105mg; Calcium 65mg; Fibre 2.1g; Sodium 354mg.

JAMAICAN JERK CHICKEN

The word "jerk" refers to the herb and spice seasoning traditionally used to marinate
meat in Jamaica. It was originally used only for pork, but jerked chicken is just as good.

SERVES 4

8 chicken pieces, such as thighs and legs
15ml/1 tbsp sunflower oil
15g/½ oz/1 tbsp unsalted (sweet) butter

For the sauce
1 bunch of spring onions (scallions),
    trimmed and finely chopped
2 garlic cloves, crushed
1 hot red chilli pepper, halved, seeded
    and finely chopped
5ml/1 tsp ground allspice
2.5ml/½ tsp ground cinnamon
5ml/1 tsp dried thyme
1.5ml/¼ tsp freshly grated nutmeg
10ml/2 tsp demerara sugar
15ml/1 tbsp plain (all-purpose) flour
300ml/½ pint/1¼ cups chicken stock
15ml/1 tbsp red or white wine vinegar
15ml/1 tbsp lime juice
10ml/2 tsp tomato purée (paste)
salt and ground black pepper
salad leaves or rice, to serve

VARIATION
For jerked pork, sauté 4 pork loin steaks
(each about 90g/3½oz) in oil for 30 seconds
on each side. Make the jerk sauce as above,
using vegetable instead of chicken stock.
Cook in the same way as the chicken recipe
above, and serve with plain boiled rice and
chargrilled pineapple wedges.

1 Wipe the chicken pieces, then pat dry
on kitchen paper. Heat the oil and butter
in a frying pan until melted, then add the
chicken, in batches if necessary, and cook
until browned on all sides. Remove with
a slotted spoon, leaving the fat in the
pan, and transfer to the ceramic cooking
pot. Switch the slow cooker to high.

2 Add the spring onions, garlic and chilli
to the frying pan and cook gently for
4–5 minutes, or until softened, stirring
frequently. Stir in the allspice, cinnamon,
thyme, nutmeg and sugar. Sprinkle in the
flour and stir to mix, then gradually add
the chicken stock, stirring until the
mixture bubbles and thickens. Remove
the pan from the heat.

3 Stir the vinegar, lime juice, tomato
purée and some salt and ground black
pepper into the sauce. Pour over the
chicken pieces, cover with a lid and cook
on high for 3–4 hours, or until the
chicken is cooked and very tender.

4 Remove the chicken from the sauce
and place on a serving dish. Taste the
sauce and adjust the seasoning, then
serve separately, with salad leaves or
rice as an accompaniment.

COOK'S TIP
There are many recipes for jerk seasoning,
but all include chillies, allspice and thyme.
The spicy sauce not only flavours the
meat, it also tenderizes it.

Nutritional information per portion: Energy 189Kcal/794kJ; Protein 21g; Carbohydrate 7g, of which sugars 3.1g; Fat 8.8g, of which saturates 3.1g; Cholesterol 107mg; Calcium 24mg; Fibre 0.5g; Sodium 238mg.

SPICY CHICKEN JAMBALAYA

This classic Creole dish is great for a family supper, served with a simple salad. Spicy red Spanish chorizo sausage gives the stew a real flavour boost. It is available from most large supermarkets, or from specialist Mediterranean stores and delicatessens.

SERVES 6

225g/8oz skinless, boneless chicken
    breast portions
175g/6oz piece raw smoked gammon
    or bacon
30ml/2 tbsp olive oil
1 large onion, peeled and chopped
2 garlic cloves, crushed
2 sticks celery, diced
5ml/1 tsp chopped fresh thyme or
    2.5ml/½ tsp dried thyme
5ml/1 tsp mild chilli powder
2.5ml/½ tsp ground ginger
10ml/2 tsp tomato purée (paste)
2 dashes of Tabasco sauce
750ml/1¼ pints/3 cups boiling
    chicken stock
300g/10oz/1½ cups easy-cook
    (converted) rice
115g/4oz chorizo sausage (cooked), sliced
30ml/2 tbsp chopped fresh flat leaf parsley,
    plus extra, to garnish
salt and ground black pepper

1 Cut the chicken into 2.5cm/1in cubes and season with salt and pepper. Trim any fat off the gammon or bacon, then cut the meat into 1cm/½in cubes.

2 Heat 15ml/1 tbsp of the olive oil in a pan, add the onion and fry gently for about 5 minutes, until beginning to colour. Stir in the garlic, celery, thyme, chilli powder and ginger and cook for about 1 minute. Transfer the mixture to the ceramic cooking pot and turn the slow cooker to high.

3 Heat the remaining 15ml/1 tbsp olive oil in the pan, add the chicken pieces and fry briefly until lightly browned. Add the chicken to the ceramic cooking pot with the gammon or bacon cubes.

4 Add the tomato purée and Tabasco sauce to the stock and whisk together. Pour into the slow cooker, cover with the lid and cook on high for 1½ hours.

5 Sprinkle the rice into the pot and stir to mix. Cover and cook on high for 45 minutes–1 hour, or until the rice is almost tender and most of the stock has been absorbed. Check towards the end of cooking time and add a little extra hot stock or water if the mixture is dry.

6 Stir in the chorizo and cook on high for a further 15 minutes, or until heated through. Stir in the chopped parsley, then taste and adjust the seasoning. Turn off the slow cooker and leave to stand for 10 minutes. Stir with a fork to fluff up the rice, then serve garnished with chopped fresh parsley.

Nutritional information per portion: Energy 384Kcal/1617kJ; Protein 21.2g; Carbohydrate 48.6g, of which sugars 2.9g; Fat 13g, of which saturates 3.6g; Cholesterol 43mg; Calcium 57mg; Fibre 1.1g; Sodium 630mg.

DOROWAT

The long-simmered stews eaten in Ethiopia are known as wats *and are traditionally served with a pancake-like flatbread called* injera. *Hard-boiled eggs are added to the sauce towards the end of cooking, so that they soak up the flavour of the spices.*

SERVES 4

30ml/2 tbsp vegetable oil
2 large onions, chopped
3 garlic cloves, chopped
2.5cm/1in piece peeled and finely
    chopped fresh root ginger
175ml/6fl oz/3/4 cup chicken
    or vegetable stock
250ml/8fl oz/1 cup passata (bottled
    strained tomatoes) or 400g/14oz
    can chopped tomatoes
seeds from 5 cardamom pods
2.5ml/1/2 tsp ground turmeric
large pinch of ground cinnamon
large pinch of ground cloves
large pinch of grated nutmeg
1.3kg/3lb chicken, cut into 8–12 portions
4 hard-boiled eggs
cayenne pepper or hot paprika, to taste
salt and ground black pepper
roughly chopped fresh coriander (cilantro)
    and onion rings, to garnish
flatbread or rice, to serve

1 Heat the oil in a large pan, add the onions and cook for 10 minutes until softened. Add the garlic and ginger and cook for 1–2 minutes.

2 Add the stock and the passata or chopped tomatoes to the pan. Bring to the boil and cook, stirring frequently, for about 10 minutes, or until the mixture has thickened, then season.

COOK'S TIP
Check the sauce just before you add the hard-boiled eggs. If it seems too thick, add a little more stock.

3 Transfer the mixture to the ceramic cooking pot and stir in the cardamom, turmeric, cinnamon, cloves and nutmeg. Add the chicken in a single layer, pushing the pieces down into the sauce.

4 Cover with the lid and cook on high for 3 hours. Remove the shells from the eggs, then prick the eggs a few times with a fork or very fine skewer. Add to the sauce and cook for 30–45 minutes, or until the chicken is cooked through and tender. Season to taste with cayenne pepper or hot paprika. Garnish with coriander and onion rings and serve with flatbread or rice.

Nutritional information per portion: Energy 388Kcal/1629kJ; Protein 54.6g; Carbohydrate 13g, of which sugars 9.6g; Fat 13.4g, of which saturates 2.8g; Cholesterol 13mg; Calcium 81mg; Fibre 2.5g; Sodium 311mg.

FRAGRANT CHICKEN CURRY

Lentils are used to thicken the sauce in this mild, fragrant curry, and fresh coriander gives the dish a really distinctive, fresh taste. The generous quantities of spinach mean that you won't need an additional vegetable dish to balance the meal.

2 Add the chicken to the lentil mixture, pressing it down in a single layer. Cover and cook on high for 3 hours, or until the chicken is just tender.

3 Add the spinach to the pot, pressing it down into the hot liquid. Cover and cook for a further 30 minutes until wilted. Stir in the chopped coriander.

4 Season the curry with salt and pepper to taste, then serve garnished with fresh coriander sprigs and accompanied with basmati rice and poppadums.

COOK'S TIP
You will need a large slow cooker to accomodate all the spinach in this recipe. It will shrink down during cooking, but the initial volume is large. If you have a small slow cooker, use thawed, well-drained frozen spinach instead.

SERVES 4

75g/3oz/scant ½ cup red lentils
30ml/2 tbsp mild curry powder
10ml/2 tsp ground coriander
5ml/1 tsp cumin seeds
350ml/12fl oz/1½ cups boiling vegetable
   or chicken stock
8 chicken thighs, skinned
225g/8oz fresh shredded spinach
15ml/1 tbsp chopped fresh
   coriander (cilantro)
salt and ground black pepper
sprigs of fresh coriander,
   to garnish
white or brown basmati rice
   and poppadums, to serve

1 Place the lentils in a sieve (strainer) and rinse under cold running water. Drain well, then put in the ceramic cooking pot with the curry powder, ground coriander, cumin seeds and stock. Cover and cook on high for 2 hours.

Nutritional information per portion: Energy 591Kcal/2490kJ; Protein 75.5g; Carbohydrate 38.2g, of which sugars 3.9g; Fat 16.1g, of which saturates 3.9g; Cholesterol 171mg; Calcium 426mg; Fibre 9.4g; Sodium 880mg.

CHICKEN in a CASHEW NUT SAUCE

The Moguls had a profound impact on the Indian cuisine, and the resulting style of cooking is known as Mughlai food. One of their legacies is the use of nut paste, which is used here to give the curry a rich yet delicately flavoured sauce.

SERVES 4

I large onion, roughly chopped
I clove garlic, crushed
15ml/1 tbsp tomato purée (paste)
50g/2oz/½ cup cashew nuts
7.5ml/1½ tsp garam masala
5ml/1 tsp chilli powder
1.5ml/¼ tsp ground turmeric
5ml/1 tsp salt
15ml/1 tbsp lemon juice
15ml/1 tbsp natural (plain) yogurt
30ml/2 tbsp vegetable oil
450g/1lb chicken breast fillets, skinned
    and cubed
175g/6oz/2¼ cups button (white)
    mushrooms
15ml/1 tbsp sultanas (golden raisins)
300ml/½ pint/1¼ cups chicken
    or vegetable stock
30ml/2 tbsp chopped fresh coriander
    (cilantro), plus extra to garnish
rice and fruit chutney, to serve

I Put the onion, garlic, tomato purée, cashew nuts, garam masala, chilli powder, turmeric, salt, lemon juice and yogurt in a food processor and process to a paste.

2 Heat the oil in a large frying pan or wok and fry the cubes of chicken for a few minutes, or until just beginning to brown. Using a slotted spoon, transfer the chicken to the ceramic cooking pot, leaving the oil in the pan.

3 Add the spice paste and mushrooms to the pan, lower the heat and fry gently, stirring frequently, for 3–4 minutes. Tip the mixture into the ceramic pot.

4 Add the sultanas to the pot and stir in the chicken or vegetable stock. Cover with the lid and switch the slow cooker to high. Cook for 3–4 hours, stirring halfway through the cooking time. The chicken should be cooked through and very tender, and the sauce fairly thick.

5 Stir the chopped coriander into the sauce, then taste and add a little more salt and pepper, if necessary. Serve the curry from the ceramic cooking pot, or transfer to a warmed serving dish, and garnish with a sprinkling of chopped fresh coriander. Serve with rice and a fruit chutney, such as mango.

Nutritional information per portion: Energy 239Kcal/1006kJ; Protein 31.6g; Carbohydrate 10.7g, of which sugars 7.6g; Fat 8.1g, of which saturates 1.7g; Cholesterol 78.9mg; Calcium 39mg; Fibre 1.9g; Sodium 696mg.

CHICKEN KORMA

The use of ground almonds to thicken the sauce gives this mild, fragrant curry a beautifully creamy texture. Its mild taste makes it particularly popular with children.

SERVES 4

75g/3oz/¾ cup flaked (sliced) almonds
15ml/1 tbsp ghee or butter
675g/1½lb skinless, boneless chicken
    breast portions, cut into bitesize
    pieces
about 15ml/1 tbsp sunflower oil
1 onion, chopped
4 green cardamom pods
2 garlic cloves, crushed
10ml/2 tsp ground cumin
5ml/1 tsp ground coriander
pinch of ground turmeric
1 cinnamon stick
good pinch of chilli powder
250ml/8fl oz/1 cup coconut milk
120ml/4fl oz/½ cup boiling chicken stock
5ml/1 tsp tomato purée (paste) (optional)
75ml/5 tbsp single (light) cream
15–30ml/1–2 tbsp fresh lime
    or lemon juice
10ml/2 tsp grated lime or lemon rind
5ml/1 tsp garam masala
salt and ground black pepper
saffron rice and poppadums, to serve

1 Dry-fry the flaked almonds in a frying pan until pale golden. Transfer about two-thirds of the almonds to a plate and continue to dry-fry the remainder until they are slightly deeper in colour. Put the darker almonds on a separate plate and set them aside to use for the garnish. Leave the paler almonds to cool, then grind them until fine in a spice grinder or coffee mill used for the purpose.

2 Heat the ghee or butter in the frying pan and gently fry the chicken pieces until evenly brown. Transfer to a plate.

3 Add a little sunflower oil to the fat in the pan, if necessary, then fry the onion for 8 minutes. Stir in the cardamom pods and garlic and fry for a further 2 minutes, until the onion is soft and just starting to colour.

4 Add the ground almonds, cumin, coriander, turmeric, cinnamon stick and chilli powder to the frying pan and cook for about 1 minute. Transfer the mixture to the ceramic cooking pot and switch the slow cooker to high.

5 Add the coconut milk, stock and tomato purée, if using, to the pot and stir in. Add the chicken and season with salt and pepper. Cover with the lid and cook on high for 3 hours, or until the chicken is cooked and very tender.

6 Stir the cream, citrus juice and rind and the garam masala into the curry and cook on high for 30 minutes. Check the seasoning, garnish with the reserved almonds, and serve immediately with saffron rice and poppadums.

Nutritional information per portion: Energy 410Kcal/1714kJ; Protein 45.7g; Carbohydrate 7.8g, of which sugars 6.4g; Fat 22g, of which saturates 6g; Cholesterol 136mg; Calcium 98mg; Fibre 1.9g; Sodium 202mg.

CHICKEN and SPLIT PEA KORESH

A traditional Persian Koresh – a thick saucy stew served with rice – is usually made with lamb, but here chicken is used to create a lighter, lower-fat dish.

SERVES 4

50g/2oz/¼ cup green split peas
45ml/3 tbsp olive oil
1 large onion, finely chopped
450g/1lb boneless chicken thighs
350ml/12fl oz/1½ cups boiling
   chicken stock
5ml/1 tsp ground turmeric
2.5ml/½ tsp ground cinnamon
1.5ml/¼ tsp grated nutmeg
30ml/2 tbsp dried mint
2 aubergines (eggplant), diced
8 ripe tomatoes, diced
2 garlic cloves, crushed
salt and ground black pepper
fresh mint, to garnish
plain boiled rice, to serve

1 Put the split peas in a large bowl. Pour in cold water to cover and leave to soak for at least 6 hours or overnight.

2 Tip the split peas into a sieve (strainer) and drain well. Place in a large pan, cover with fresh cold water and bring to the boil. Boil rapidly for 10 minutes, then rinse, drain and set aside.

3 Heat 15ml/1 tbsp of the oil in a pan, add the onion and cook for about 5 minutes. Add the chicken and cook until golden on all sides, then transfer to the ceramic cooking pot. Add the split peas, hot chicken stock, turmeric, cinnamon, nutmeg and mint and season well with salt and black pepper.

4 Cover the pot with the lid and cook on high or auto for 1 hour. Switch the slow cooker to low or leave on auto and cook for a further 3 hours, or until the chicken is just cooked and the split peas are nearly tender.

5 Heat the remaining 30ml/2 tbsp of oil in a frying pan, add the diced aubergines and cook for about 5 minutes until lightly browned. Add the tomatoes and garlic and cook for a further 2 minutes.

6 Transfer the aubergines to the ceramic cooking pot, stir to combine, then cook for about 1 hour. Sprinkle with fresh mint leaves to garnish and serve with plain boiled rice.

Nutritional information per portion: Energy 298Kcal/1251kJ; Protein 29.1g; Carbohydrate 18.5g, of which sugars 10.2g; Fat 12.5g, of which saturates 2.3g; Cholesterol 118mg; Calcium 48mg; Fibre 4.5g; Sodium 206mg.

BRAISED GUINEA FOWL with RED CABBAGE

The slightly gamey flavour of guinea fowl is complemented perfectly by the sweet, fruity flavour of red cabbage, braised in apple juice and scented with juniper berries.

SERVES 4

15ml/1 tbsp unsalted (sweet) butter
½ red cabbage, weighing
    about 450g/1lb
1.3kg/3lb oven-ready guinea
    fowl, jointed
15ml/1 tbsp sunflower oil
3 shallots, very finely chopped
15ml/1 tbsp plain (all-purpose) flour
120ml/4fl oz/½ cup chicken stock
150ml/¼ pint/⅔ cup apple juice
15ml/1 tbsp soft light brown sugar
15ml/1 tbsp red wine vinegar
4 juniper berries, lightly crushed
salt and ground black pepper

VARIATIONS

• Other mild-tasting poultry or game such as chicken or pheasant can be used in place of the guinea fowl, if preferred.
• Add to the fruity flavour of the cabbage by adding 15ml/1tbsp sultanas (golden raisins) to the pot before cooking.

1 Use half the butter to grease the ceramic cooking pot. Cut the cabbage into wedges, removing any tough outer leaves and the central core. Shred the cabbage finely, then place in the ceramic cooking pot, packing it down tightly.

2 Rinse the guinea fowl portions and pat dry with kitchen paper. Heat the remaining butter and the oil in a pan and brown the guinea fowl on all sides. Lift from the pan, leaving the fat behind, and place on top of the red cabbage.

3 Add the shallots to the frying pan and cook gently for 5 minutes. Sprinkle with the flour, cook for a few seconds, then gradually stir in the stock followed by the apple juice. Bring to the boil, stirring continuously, until thickened. Remove from the heat, stir in the sugar, vinegar and juniper berries, and season.

4 Pour the sauce over the guinea fowl, cover and cook on high for 4 hours, or until the meat and cabbage are tender. Check the seasoning and serve.

Nutritional information per portion: Energy 456Kcal/1907kJ; Protein 44.5g; Carbohydrate 20g, of which sugars 15g; Fat 22.5g, of which saturates 6.7g; Cholesterol 225mg; Calcium 96mg; Fibre 3.1g; Sodium 15mg.

GUINEA FOWL and SPRING VEGETABLE STEW

Resembling a well-flavoured chicken stew, this tasty dish of guinea fowl cooked with spring vegetables and flavoured with mustard and herbs is a sure winner.

SERVES 4

1.6kg/3½lb guinea fowl
45ml/3 tbsp plain (all-purpose) flour
45ml/3 tbsp olive oil
115g/4oz pancetta, cut into tiny cubes
1 onion, chopped
3 cloves garlic, chopped
200ml/7fl oz/scant 1 cup white wine
225g/8oz baby carrots
225g/8oz baby turnips
6 baby leeks, cut into 7.5cm/3in lengths
sprig of fresh thyme
1 bay leaf
10ml/2 tsp Dijon mustard
150ml/¼ pint/⅔ cup boiling chicken
    or vegetable stock
225g/8oz shelled peas
30ml/2 tbsp chopped fresh parsley
15ml/1 tbsp chopped fresh mint
salt and ground black pepper

1 Joint the guinea fowl into eight pieces. Wipe or lightly rinse them, then pat dry on kitchen paper. Season the flour with salt and pepper and toss the guinea fowl portions in it. Set aside any leftover flour.

2 Heat 30ml/2 tbsp of the oil in a large frying pan, add the pancetta and fry over a medium heat until lightly browned, stirring occasionally. Using a slotted spoon, transfer the pancetta to the ceramic cooking pot, leaving any fat and juices in the frying pan.

3 Add the guinea fowl portions to the pan and fry, turning, until browned on all sides. Arrange the guinea fowl portions in a single layer in the cooking pot on top of the pancetta.

4 Add the remaining 15ml/1 tbsp oil to the frying pan, add the onion and cook for 3–4 minutes, until just beginning to soften. Add the garlic and cook for about 1 minute, then stir in the reserved flour. Gradually stir in the wine and bring to the boil. Pour over the guinea fowl.

5 Add the carrots, turnips and leeks to the cooking pot with the thyme and bay leaf. Blend the mustard with the stock, season with salt and pepper and pour over. Cover with the lid and cook on high for 3–4 hours, or until the guinea fowl and vegetables are tender.

6 Add the peas to the stew and cook for a further 45 minutes. Taste and adjust the seasoning, then stir in most of the fresh herbs. Divide the stew among four warmed serving plates, sprinkle the remaining fresh herbs over the top and serve immediately.

COOK'S TIPS
• To save time on preparation, ask your butcher to joint the guinea fowl for you.
• Rabbit has a delicate flavour that goes well with the tender spring vegetables and herbs used in this stew. Try using eight rabbit joints in place of the guinea fowl.

Nutritional information per portion: Energy 581Kcal/2425kJ; Protein 50.5g; Carbohydrate 29.1g, of which sugars 11.2g; Fat 26.5g, of which saturates 7.4g; Cholesterol 224mg; Calcium 109mg; Fibre 6.9g; Sodium 668mg.

DUCK STEW with OLIVES

This method of cooking duck with olives, onions and wine has its roots in Provence in France. The sweetness brought out by slow-cooking the onions balances the saltiness of the olives beautifully. Simple, creamy mashed potatoes make a perfect accompaniment.

SERVES 4

4 duck quarters or breast portions
225g/8oz baby (pearl) onions, peeled
2.5ml/½ tsp caster (superfine) sugar
30ml/2 tbsp plain (all-purpose) flour
250ml/8fl oz/1 cup dry red wine
250ml/8fl oz/1 cup duck or chicken stock
1 bouquet garni
115g/4oz/1 cup pitted green or black
    olives, or a combination
salt and ground black pepper

1 Put the duck skin side down in a large frying pan and cook for 10–12 minutes, turning to colour evenly, until browned on both sides. Lift out with a slotted spoon and place skin side up in the ceramic cooking pot. Switch the slow cooker to high.

2 Pour off most of the fat from the pan, leaving about 15ml/1 tbsp behind. Add the onions and cook over a medium-low heat until beginning to colour. Sprinkle over the sugar and cook for 5 minutes until golden, stirring frequently. Sprinkle with the flour and cook, uncovered, for 2 minutes, stirring frequently.

3 Gradually stir the red wine into the onions, followed by the stock. Bring to the boil, then pour over the duck. Add the bouquet garni to the pot, cover with the lid and cook on high for 1 hour.

4 Turn the slow cooker to low and cook for a further 4–5 hours, or until the duck and onions are very tender.

5 Put the olives in a heatproof bowl and pour over very hot water to cover. Leave to stand for about 1 minute, then drain thoroughly. Add the olives to the casserole, re-cover with the lid and cook for a further 30 minutes.

6 Transfer the duck, onions and olives to a warm serving dish or individual plates. Skim all the fat from the cooking liquid and discard the bouquet garni. Season the sauce to taste with black pepper and a little salt, if needed, then spoon over the duck and serve immediately.

COOK'S TIPS
• Taste the stew before adding more salt; if the olives were salty, the stew will not need any more.
• The skin may be removed from the duck before cooking, if you prefer, and the duck pieces cooked in 15ml/1 tbsp oil for a few minutes to brown them.

Nutritional information per portion: Energy 414Kcal/1736kJ; Protein 47.3g; Carbohydrate 8.2g, of which sugars 2.3g; Fat 18.5g, of which saturates 5.2g; Cholesterol 257mg; Calcium 67mg; Fibre 1.6g; Sodium 917mg.

PAPPARDELLE with RABBIT

This rich-tasting dish comes from northern Italy, where rabbit sauces are very popular.
It is ideal for entertaining as the sauce can be kept warm in the slow cooker until needed.

SERVES 4

15g/½oz dried porcini mushrooms
150ml/¼ pint/⅔ cup warm water
1 small onion
½ carrot
½ celery stick
2 bay leaves
25g/1oz/2 tbsp butter or 15ml/1 tbsp
    olive oil
40g/1½oz pancetta or rindless streaky
    (fatty) bacon, chopped
15ml/1 tbsp roughly chopped fresh flat leaf
    parsley, plus extra to garnish
250g/9oz boneless rabbit meat
60ml/4 tbsp dry white wine
200g/7oz can chopped Italian plum
    tomatoes or 200ml/7fl oz/scant 1 cup
    passata (bottled strained tomatoes)
300g/11oz fresh or dried pappardelle
salt and ground black pepper

1 Put the dried mushrooms in a bowl,
pour over the warm water and leave to
soak for 15 minutes. Finely chop the
vegetables, either in a food processor or
by hand. Make a tear in each bay leaf, so
that they will release their flavour when
added to the sauce.

2 Heat the butter or oil in a large frying
pan until just sizzling. Add the chopped
vegetables, pancetta or bacon and the
parsley and cook for about 5 minutes.

3 Add the rabbit pieces and fry on both
sides for 3–4 minutes. Transfer the
mixture to the ceramic cooking pot and
switch to the high or auto setting. Add
the wine and tomatoes or passata.

4 While the mixture is starting to heat
through, drain the mushrooms and strain
the soaking liquid into the slow cooker
through a fine sieve (strainer). Chop the
mushrooms and add to the mixture,
with the bay leaves. Season to taste with
salt and black pepper. Stir well, cover
with the lid and cook for 1 hour. Reduce
the setting to low or leave on auto, and
cook for a further 2 hours, or until the
meat is tender.

5 Lift out the rabbit pieces, cut them
into bite-size chunks and stir them back
into the sauce. Remove and discard the
bay leaves. Taste the sauce and season,
as necessary. The sauce is now ready to
serve, but can be kept hot in the slow
cooker for 1–2 hours.

6 About 10 minutes before serving,
cook the pasta according to the
instructions on the packet. Drain the
pasta, add to the sauce and toss well to
mix. Serve immediately, sprinkled with
fresh parsley.

VARIATION
If you prefer, or if rabbit is not available,
this dish can be made with chicken instead.

Nutritional information per portion: Energy 393Kcal/1653kJ; Protein 23g; Carbohydrate 46g, of which sugars 4.9g; Fat 13.3g, of which saturates 5g; Cholesterol 46mg; Calcium 80mg; Fibre 1.1g; Sodium 128mg.

RABBIT CASSEROLE with JUNIPER

Because rabbit is such a lean meat, casseroling is an ideal way to cook it, helping to keep it really moist and juicy. Using a well-flavoured marinade improves both the taste and texture of the meat. Chicken leg portions make an excellent alternative to rabbit if you prefer. Serve with steamed new potatoes and whole baby carrots.

SERVES 4

900g/2lb prepared rabbit pieces
1 onion, roughly chopped
2 garlic cloves, crushed
1 bay leaf
350ml/12fl oz/1½ cups fruity red wine
2 sprigs of fresh thyme
1 sprig of fresh rosemary
15ml/1 tbsp juniper berries
30ml/2 tbsp olive oil
15g/½oz dried porcini mushrooms
30ml/2 tbsp chopped fresh parsley
25g/1oz/2 tbsp chilled butter
salt and ground black pepper

1 Put the rabbit pieces in a glass or ceramic dish with the onion, garlic, bay leaf and wine. Bruise the thyme and rosemary to release their flavour and lightly crush the juniper berries and add them to the dish. Toss to combine. Cover and marinate in the refrigerator for at least 4 hours or overnight, turning the pieces once or twice, if possible.

2 Remove the rabbit from the marinade, reserving the marinade, and pat dry with kitchen paper. Heat the oil in a frying pan, add the rabbit pieces and fry for 3–5 minutes, turning to brown all over. Transfer the meat to the ceramic cooking pot.

3 Pour the marinade into the frying pan and bring to boiling point. Pour over the rabbit, cover the ceramic cooking pot with the lid and switch the slow cooker to high. Cook for about 1 hour.

4 Meanwhile, put the mushrooms in a heatproof bowl and pour over 150ml/¼ pint/⅔ cup boiling water. Leave to soak for 1 hour, then drain, reserving the soaking liquid, and finely chop the mushrooms. Put the mushrooms in a small bowl and cover with clear film (plastic wrap) to keep them moist.

5 Pour the soaking liquid from the mushrooms into the ceramic cooking pot. Cook for a further 2 hours. Lift out the rabbit pieces with a slotted spoon and strain the cooking liquid, discarding the vegetables, herbs and juniper berries. Wipe the ceramic cooking pot clean, then return the rabbit and cooking liquid. Add the mushrooms and season.

6 Cover and cook for a further hour, or until the meat and mushrooms are cooked and tender. Stir in the chopped parsley, then lift out the rabbit pieces and arrange on a warmed serving dish. Cut the chilled butter into small cubes and whisk it into the sauce, one or two pieces at a time, to thicken. Spoon the sauce over the rabbit and serve.

Nutritional information per portion: Energy 356Kcal/1483kJ; Protein 32g; Carbohydrate 3.2g, of which sugars 2.3g; Fat 17.5g, of which saturates 6.3g; Cholesterol 163mg; Calcium 30mg; Fibre 0.6g; Sodium 66mg.

HARE POT PIES

The full, gamey flavour of hare is perfect for this dish, but boneless rabbit, venison, pheasant or any other game meat can be used instead. The meat filling is cooked in the slow cooker until tender and succulent – this can be done the day before if you like – before being topped with pastry and finished in the oven.

SERVES 4

45ml/3 tbsp olive oil
1 leek, sliced
225g/8oz parsnips, sliced
225g/8oz carrots, sliced
1 fennel bulb, sliced
675g/1½lb boneless hare, diced
30ml/2 tbsp plain (all-purpose) flour
60ml/4 tbsp Madeira
300ml/½ pint/1¼ cups game
    or chicken stock
45ml/3 tbsp chopped fresh parsley
450g/1lb puff pastry, thawed
    if frozen
beaten egg yolk, to glaze

VARIATION
You can make one large single pie, instead of four individual ones, if you like.

1 Heat 30ml/2 tbsp of the oil in a large pan. Add the leek, parsnips, carrots and fennel and cook for about 10 minutes, stirring frequently, until softened.

2 Using a slotted spoon, transfer the vegetables to the ceramic cooking pot. Cover with the lid and switch the slow cooker to the high or auto setting.

3 Heat the remaining oil in the pan and fry the hare in batches until well browned. When all the meat has been cooked, return it to the pan. Sprinkle over the flour and cook, stirring, for a few seconds, then gradually stir in the Madeira and stock and bring to the boil.

4 Transfer the hare mixture to the ceramic cooking pot and cook for 1 hour. Switch the slow cooker to low or leave on auto and cook for a further 5–6 hours, until the meat and vegetables are tender. Stir in the chopped parsley, then set aside to cool.

5 To make the pies, preheat the oven to 220°C/425°F/Gas 7. Spoon the hare mixture into four individual pie dishes. Cut the pastry into quarters and roll out on a lightly floured work surface to make the pie covers. Make the pieces larger than the dishes. Trim off any excess pastry and use the trimmings to line the rim of each dish.

6 Dampen the pastry rims with cold water and cover with the pastry lids. Pinch the edges together to seal in the filling. Brush each pie with beaten egg yolk and make a small hole in the top of each one to allow steam to escape.

7 Stand the pies on a baking tray and bake for 25 minutes, or until the pastry is well risen and dark golden. If the pastry is browning too quickly, cover with foil after 15 minutes to prevent it from overbrowning.

Nutritional information per portion: Energy 906Kcal/3784kJ; Protein 45g; Carbohydrate 60.4g, of which sugars 10g; Fat 53.7g, of which saturates 15.9g; Cholesterol 107mg; Calcium 180mg; Fibre 7.6g; Sodium 553mg.

MEAT DISHES

Slow cooking is suitable for all kinds of meat, but it works its magic best on less tender cuts, helping to improve and enhance their flavour and texture. Although beef and pork are great for robust dishes, such as beef and mushroom pudding, they can also be used to make lighter modern meals, like spicy pork casserole with dried fruit. Most lamb cuts are naturally tender and succulent and the slow cooker ensures they stay that way. Whatever meat you choose and whether you are looking for a simple supper or an impressive dinner, you will find plenty of recipes here for delicious pot roasts, braised dishes, casseroles and stews.

STEAK and KIDNEY PIE with MUSTARD GRAVY

Peppery mustard gravy flavoured with bay leaves and parsley complements the tasty chunks of succulent beef and kidney in this classic pie. Cooking the puff pastry topping separately from the filling ensures it remains perfectly crisp – and is a perfect technique to use when making the pie using a slow cooker.

SERVES 4

675g/1½lb stewing steak
225g/8oz ox or lamb's kidney
45ml/3 tbsp oil
15g/½oz/1 tbsp unsalted (sweet) butter
2 onions, chopped
30ml/2 tbsp plain (all-purpose) flour
300ml/½ pint/1¼ cups beef stock
15ml/1 tbsp tomato purée (paste)
10ml/2 tsp English mustard
2 bay leaves
375g/13oz puff pastry
beaten egg, to glaze
15ml/1 tbsp chopped fresh parsley
salt and ground black pepper
creamed potatoes and green vegetables,
    to serve

1 Using a sharp knife, cut the stewing steak into 2.5cm/1in cubes. Remove all fat and skin from the kidney and cut into cubes or thick slices.

2 Heat 30ml/2 tbsp of the oil in a frying pan and brown the beef on all sides. Remove from the pan with a slotted spoon and place in the ceramic cooking pot. Switch the slow cooker on to high.

3 Add the kidney to the frying pan and brown for 1–2 minutes before adding to the beef. Add the remaining oil and the butter to the pan, add the onions and cook for 5 minutes, until just beginning to colour. Sprinkle with the flour and stir in, then remove the pan from the heat.

4 Gradually stir the stock into the pan, followed by the tomato purée and mustard. Return to the heat and bring to the boil, stirring constantly, until thickened. Pour the gravy over the meat, then add the bay leaves and season. Stir well and cover with the lid. Reduce the cooker to low and cook for 5–7 hours, or until the meat is very tender.

VARIATION
To make a richer version, use half the quantity of stock and add 150ml/¼ pint/⅔ cup stout or red wine.

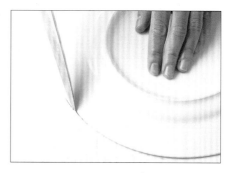

5 While the beef is cooking, roll out the pastry and, using a dinner plate as a guide, cut out a 25cm/10in round. Transfer the pastry round to a baking sheet lined with baking parchment.

6 Using a sharp knife, mark the pastry into quarters, cutting almost but not quite through it. Decorate with pastry trimmings, then flute the edge. Cover with clear film (plastic wrap) and place in the refrigerator until ready to cook.

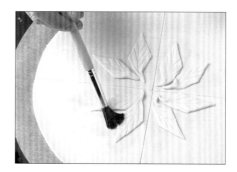

7 Towards the end of the beef's cooking time, preheat the oven to 200°C/400°F/Gas 6. Brush the pastry all over with beaten egg to glaze, then bake for about 25 minutes, or until well risen, golden-brown and crisp.

8 To serve, stir the chopped parsley into the steak and kidney stew and spoon on to warmed serving plates. Cut the baked pie crust into four, using the markings as a guide, and top each portion of stew with a wedge of pastry. Serve immediately with rich, creamed potatoes and green vegetables.

Nutritional information per portion: Energy 637Kcal/2652kJ; Protein 18.7g; Carbohydrate 46.2g, of which sugars 5.2g; Fat 43.4g, of which saturates 13.1g; Cholesterol 259mg; Calcium 99mg; Fibre 2.7g; Sodium 578mg.

PROVENÇAL BEEF STEW

Known in France as daube de boeuf à la Provençal, *after the earthernware pot it was originally cooked in, this deliciously rich, fruity stew makes a perfect winter supper dish. Serve with mashed or boiled new potatoes and green vegetables.*

SERVES 4

45ml/3 tbsp olive oil
115g/4oz lean salt pork or
    thick-cut bacon, diced
900g/2lb stewing steak cut into
    4cm/1½in pieces
1 large onion, chopped
2 carrots, sliced
2 ripe tomatoes, peeled, seeded
    and chopped
10ml/2 tsp tomato purée (paste)
2 garlic cloves, very finely chopped
250ml/8fl oz/1 cup fruity red wine
150ml/¼ pint/⅔ cup beef stock
1 bouquet garni
1 small onion, studded with 2 cloves
grated zest and juice of ½ unwaxed orange
15ml/1 tbsp chopped fresh parsley
salt and ground black pepper

1 Heat 15ml/1 tbsp of the oil in a large heavy frying pan, then add the salt pork or bacon and cook over a medium heat for 4–5 minutes, stirring frequently, until browned and the fat is rendered.

2 Using a slotted spoon, transfer the pork or bacon to the ceramic cooking pot and switch the slow cooker to high.

3 Working in batches, add the beef to the pan in a single layer (do not overcrowd the pan, or the meat will stew in its own juices and not brown). Cook for 6–8 minutes until browned, turning to colour all sides.

4 Transfer the beef to the ceramic cooking pot and continue browning the rest of the meat in the same way, adding more oil when needed.

5 Pour the wine and stock over the beef in the ceramic cooking pot, then add the bouquet garni and the onion. Add the remaining oil and the onion to the frying pan and cook gently for 5 minutes. Stir in the carrots and cook for a further 5 minutes, until softened. Stir in the tomatoes, tomato purée and garlic, then transfer to the ceramic cooking pot.

6 Cover with the lid and switch the slow cooker to low. Cook for 5–7 hours, or until the beef and vegetables are very tender. Uncover and skim off any fat. Season, discard the bouquet garni and clove-studded onion, and stir in the orange zest and juice and the parsley.

Nutritional information per portion: Energy 547Kcal/2286kJ; Protein 55.8g; Carbohydrate 8.7g, of which sugars 7.2g; Fat 27.8g, of which saturates 8.9g; Cholesterol 170mg; Calcium 43mg; Fibre 2g; Sodium 682mg.

BRAISED BEEF in a RICH PEANUT SAUCE

Like many dishes brought to the Philippines by the Spanish, this slow-cooking Estofado,
renamed by the Philippinos as Kari Kari, retains much of its original charm. Peanuts are
used to thicken the juices, yielding a rich, sweet, glossy sauce.

SERVES 4

900g/2lb stewing (braising) chuck,
   shin or blade steak
45ml/3 tbsp vegetable oil
2 onions, chopped
2 cloves garlic, crushed
5ml/1 tsp paprika
pinch of ground turmeric
225g/8oz celeriac or swede (rutabaga),
   peeled and cut into 2cm/¾in dice
425ml/15fl oz/1¾ cups boiling beef stock
15ml/1 tbsp fish or anchovy sauce
30ml/2 tbsp tamarind sauce (optional)
10ml/2 tsp soft light brown sugar
1 bay leaf
1 sprig thyme
30ml/2 tbsp smooth peanut butter
45ml/3 tbsp easy-cook (converted)
   white rice
5ml/1 tsp white wine vinegar
salt and ground black pepper

1 Using a sharp knife, cut the beef into 2.5cm/1in cubes. Heat 30ml/2 tbsp of the oil in a pan and fry the beef, turning until well browned all over.

2 Transfer the meat and any juices to the ceramic cooking pot and switch the slow cooker to high.

3 Add the remaining 15ml/1 tbsp oil to the frying pan, add the onions and fry gently for 10 minutes until softened.

4 Add the garlic, paprika and turmeric to the pan and cook for 1 minute. Transfer the mixture to the ceramic pot and add the celeriac or swede.

5 Pour in the stock, fish or anchovy sauce and taramind sauce, if using, and add the sugar, bay leaf and thyme. Cover with the lid, then reduce the heat to low and cook for 4 hours, or until the beef and vegetables are just tender.

6 Turn the slow cooker up to high, then remove about 60ml/4 tbsp of the cooking juices to a bowl and blend with the peanut butter. Stir the mixture into the casserole, sprinkle with the rice, and stir again to combine.

7 Cover the pot and cook for about 45 minutes, or until the rice is cooked and the sauce has thickened slightly. Stir in the wine vinegar and season to taste.

COOK'S TIP
This stew makes a meal in itself so needs no accompaniments. However, a simple green salad served on the side makes a refreshing palate cleanser.

Nutritional information per portion: Energy 577Kcal/2408kJ; Protein 48.9g; Carbohydrate 14.1g, of which sugars 8.9g; Fat 36.8g, of which saturates 12.2g; Cholesterol 141mg; Calcium 70mg; Fibre 2.4g; Sodium 561mg.

BEEF and MUSHROOM PUDDING

Based on a great British classic, this steamed savoury pudding has a light herb pastry crust made with a mixture of suet and butter for both taste and colour. A mouthwatering mixture of dried porcini and chestnut mushrooms gives the filling an intense flavour.

SERVES 4

25g/1oz/½ cup dried porcini mushrooms
475ml/16fl oz/2 cups near-boiling
   beef stock
675g/1½lb stewing (braising) steak
60ml/4 tbsp plain (all-purpose) flour
45ml/3 tbsp sunflower oil
1 large onion, finely chopped
225g/8oz chestnut or flat mushrooms,
   thickly sliced
1 bay leaf
15ml/1 tbsp Worcestershire sauce
75ml/2½fl oz/⅓ cup port or red wine
salt and ground black pepper

For the pastry
275g/10oz/2½ cups self-raising
   (self-rising) flour
2.5ml/½ tsp baking powder
2.5ml/½ tsp salt
15ml/1 tbsp each chopped parsley
   and fresh thyme
75g/3oz/1½ cups beef or vegetable suet
   (chilled, grated shortening)
50g/2oz/¼ cup butter, frozen and grated
1 egg, lightly beaten
about 150ml/¼ pint/⅔ cup cold water

1 Put the dried mushrooms in a bowl and pour over the stock. Leave to soak for about 20 minutes.

2 Meanwhile, trim the meat and cut into 2cm/¾in pieces. Place the flour in a bowl, season, then add the meat and toss to coat. Heat the oil in a frying pan and fry the meat in batches until browned on all sides. Transfer to the ceramic cooking pot.

3 Add the onion to the pan and cook gently for 10 minutes, or until softened. Transfer to the ceramic cooking pot, then add the chestnut mushrooms and the bay leaf.

4 In a bowl or jug (pitcher), combine the Worcestershire sauce with the port or wine, then pour into the ceramic cooking pot. Drain the soaked porcini mushrooms, pouring the stock into the pot, then chop them and add to the pot.

5 Stir the ingredients together, then cover with the lid and cook on high or auto for 1 hour. Reduce the heat to low and cook for a further 5–6 hours, or until the meat and onions are tender. Remove the bay leaf, then leave the mixture to cool completely.

6 To make the pastry, butter a deep 1.7 litre/3 pint/7½ cup heatproof pudding basin. Sift the flour, baking powder and salt into a mixing bowl and stir in the herbs followed by the suet and butter. Make a well in the centre, add the egg and enough cold water to mix, and gather into a soft dough.

7 Lightly knead the dough for a few seconds on a floured surface until smooth. Cut off a quarter of the dough and wrap in clear film (plastic wrap). Shape the rest into a ball and roll out into a round large enough to line the basin or bowl. Lift up the pastry and carefully place in the basin, pressing it against the sides and allowing the excess to fall over the sides. Roll out the reserved pastry to make a round large enough to use as a lid for the pudding.

8 Spoon in the cooled filling and enough of the gravy to come to within 1cm/½in of the rim. (Reserve the remaining gravy to serve with the pudding.) Brush the top edge of the pastry with water and place the lid on top. Press the edges together to seal and trim off any excess.

9 Cover the pudding basin with a pleated, double thickness layer of baking parchment and secure under the rim using string. Cover with pleated foil to allow the pudding to rise.

10 Put an inverted saucer or metal pastry ring in the base of the cleaned ceramic cooking pot and place the pudding basin on top. Pour in enough near-boiling water to come just over halfway up the sides of the basin. Cover with the lid and cook on high for 3 hours.

11 Carefully remove the pudding from the slow cooker, then take off the foil, string and greaseproof paper. Loosen the edges of the pudding and invert on to a warmed serving plate.

Nutritional information per portion: Energy 1061Kcal/4444kJ; Protein 70g; Carbohydrate 75.1g, of which sugars 4.8g; Fat 54.3g, of which saturates 24.5g; Cholesterol 265mg; Calcium 319mg; Fibre 4.4g; Sodium 941mg.

BRAISED BEEF with HORSERADISH

This dark rich beef with a spicy kick makes an ideal alternative to a meat roast. The meat slowly tenderizes in the slow cooker and all the flavours blend together beautifully. It is also a great dish for entertaining because it can be prepared in advance and then simply left to simmer on its own until you are ready to serve.

SERVES 4

30ml/2 tbsp plain (all-purpose) flour
4 × 175g/6oz braising steaks
30ml/2 tbsp sunflower oil
12 small shallots, peeled and halved
1 garlic clove, crushed
1.5ml/¼ tsp ground ginger
5ml/1 tsp curry powder
10ml/2 tsp dark muscovado (molasses)
    sugar
475ml/16fl oz/2 cups near-boiling beef stock
15ml/1 tbsp Worcestershire sauce
30ml/2 tbsp creamed horseradish
225g/8oz baby carrots, trimmed
1 bay leaf
salt and ground black pepper
30ml/2 tbsp chopped fresh chives,
    to garnish
roast vegetables, to serve

1 Place the flour in a large, flat dish and season with salt and black pepper. Toss the steaks in the flour to coat.

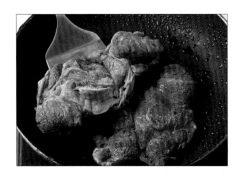

2 Heat the oil in a pan and quickly brown the steaks on both sides. Transfer them to the ceramic cooking pot.

3 Add the halved shallots to the pan and cook gently for 10 minutes, or until golden and beginning to soften. Stir in the garlic, ginger and curry powder and cook for 1 minute more, then remove the pan from the heat.

4 Tip the shallot mixture into the ceramic cooking pot, spreading it over the meat, and sprinkle with the sugar.

5 Pour the beef stock over the shallots and meat, then add the Worcestershire sauce, horseradish, baby carrots and bay leaf. Stir to combine, then season with salt and black pepper. Cover with the lid and cook on high or auto for 1 hour.

6 Reduce the slow cooker to low, or leave on auto, and continue to cook the stew for a further 5–6 hours, or until the beef and vegetables are very tender.

7 Remove the bay leaf from the stew and sprinkle with the chopped chives before serving with roast vegetables.

COOK'S TIPS

• Choose a medium curry powder for flavouring the stew. There is already plenty of bite from the horseradish, so you don't want to overpower the meat flavours entirely with a very strong, spicy curry powder.
• To give the stew a really robust flavour, replace 175ml/6fl oz/¾ cup of the stock with red wine.
• The sweet flavour of roasted parsnips and butternut squash goes particularly well with the spicy bite of horseradish. Cook plenty of roast potatoes too – they are the perfect accompaniment to braised beef, and are great for mopping up the delicious gravy.

Nutritional information per portion: Energy 478Kcal/2010kJ; Protein 62.5g; Carbohydrate 17.7g, of which sugars 9.6g; Fat 18.1g, of which saturates 7.4g; Cholesterol 176mg; Calcium 65mg; Fibre 2.5g; Sodium 423mg.

HUNGARIAN CHOLENT

A traditional Sabbath dish of the Ashkenazi Jews, cholent is a long-simmered dish of beans, grains, meat and vegetables. The addition of whole boiled eggs is a classic feature. Don't forget to start soaking the beans the day before; they need at least 8 hours.

SERVES 4

250g/9oz/1⅓ cups dried haricot (navy) beans
30ml/2 tbsp olive oil
1 onion, chopped
4 garlic cloves, finely chopped
50g/2oz pearl barley
15ml/1 tbsp ground paprika
pinch of cayenne pepper
1 celery stick, chopped
400g/14oz can chopped tomatoes
3 carrots, sliced
1 small turnip, diced
2 baking potatoes, peeled and cut into chunks
675g/1½lb mixture of beef brisket, stewing beef and smoked beef, cut into cubes
1 litre/1¾ pints/4 cups boiling beef stock
30ml/2 tbsp easy-cook (converted) white rice
4 eggs, at room temperature
salt and ground black pepper

3 Meanwhile, heat the oil in a pan, add the onion and cook gently for about 10 minutes, or until soft. Transfer the onions to the ceramic cooking pot.

4 Add the garlic, beans, barley, paprika, cayenne pepper, celery, tomatoes, carrots, turnip, potatoes, beef and stock to the onions and stir to combine.

5 Cover the pot with the lid and cook on low for 5–6 hours, or until the meat and vegetables are tender. Add the rice, stir, and season with salt and pepper.

6 Rinse the eggs in tepid water, then lower them, one at a time, into the hot stock. Cover and cook for a further 45 minutes, or until the rice is cooked. Serve hot, making sure each portion contains a whole egg.

1 Place the beans in a large bowl. Pour over plenty of cold water to cover and leave to soak for at least 8 hours, or overnight if you like.

2 Drain the beans well, then place them in a large pan, cover with fresh cold water and bring to the boil. Boil them steadily for about 10 minutes, skimming off any froth that rises to the surface, then drain well and set aside.

Nutritional information per portion: Energy 860Kcal/3607kJ; Protein 58.9g; Carbohydrate 74.2g, of which sugars 13.7g; Fat 38.8g, of which saturates 12.7g; Cholesterol 341mg; Calcium 164mg; Fibre 10.9g; Sodium 639mg.

SPICED BEEF

This is a classic Irish dish, although it is a modern version of the traditional recipe, as it omits the initial pickling stage and takes only three or four days to cure in comparison with ten days for the older method. Serve on thinly sliced brown bread, with chutney.

SERVES 6

15ml/1 tbsp coarsely ground
   black pepper
10ml/2 tsp ground ginger
15ml/1 tbsp juniper berries, crushed
15ml/1 tbsp coriander seeds, crushed
5ml/1 tsp ground cloves
15ml/1 tbsp ground allspice
45ml/3 tbsp soft dark brown sugar
2 bay leaves, crushed
1 small onion, finely chopped
1.8kg/4lb corned beef, silverside or tail end
300ml/½ pint/1¼ cups Guinness
fruit chutney and brown bread, to serve

COOK'S TIP
• As a first course, serve the beef thinly sliced with home-made brown bread and a fruit chutney, such as apple and sultana.
• Spiced beef is excellent as finger food for parties, sliced thinly and served with sour cream lightly flavoured with horseradish and black pepper.

3 When the joint is cooked, leave it to cool in the cooking liquid. Wrap in foil and keep in the refrigerator until required, then slice thinly to serve. It will keep for about 1 week.

1 First, spice the beef: blend the pepper, spices and sugar thoroughly, then mix in the bay leaves and onion. Rub the mixture into the meat, then put it into a suitable lidded container and refrigerate for 3–4 days, turning and rubbing with the mixture daily.

2 Put the meat into the ceramic cooking pot and barely cover with cold water. Cover with the lid and switch on to auto or high. Cook for 3 hours, then leave on auto or reduce to low and cook for a further 3–4 hours, until the meat is very tender. For the last hour add the Guinness.

Nutritional information per portion: Energy 309Kcal/1301kJ; Protein 53.6g; Carbohydrate 2g, of which sugars 2g; Fat 9.7g, of which saturates 3.6g; Cholesterol 137mg; Calcium 15mg; Fibre 0g; Sodium 140mg

HOT and SOUR PORK

This has all the flavour of a stir-fry without the hassle of last-minute cooking. Using lean pork fillet and reducing the temperature to low after an hour means that the meat remains wonderfully moist and tender, while the vegetables retain their crunchy texture.

SERVES 4

15ml/1 tbsp dried Chinese mushrooms
150ml/¼ pint/⅔ cup boiling
   vegetable stock
350g/12oz pork fillet
115g/4oz baby corn kernels
1 green (bell) pepper
225g/8oz pineapple chunks
   in natural juice
20ml/4 tsp cornflour (cornstarch)
15ml/1 tbsp sunflower oil
115g/4oz water chestnuts
2.5cm/1 in piece root ginger, grated
1 red chilli, seeded and finely chopped
5ml/1 tsp Chinese five-spice powder
15ml/1 tbsp sherry vinegar
15ml/1 tbsp dark soy sauce
15ml/1 tbsp hoisin sauce
plain boiled or fried rice, to serve

1 Put the mushrooms in a heatproof bowl, then pour over the hot stock and leave to soak for 15–20 minutes.

2 Trim away any visible fat from the pork and cut into 1cm/½ in slices. Slice the baby corn kernels lengthways. Halve, seed and slice the green pepper. Drain the pineapple chunks, reserving the juice. Drain the mushrooms, reserving the stock, and slice any large ones.

3 In a bowl, blend the cornflour with a little of the reserved pineapple juice, then slowly stir in the remainder.

4 Heat the oil in a non-stick frying pan. Add the pork and sear for 30 seconds on each side, or until lightly browned. Transfer to the ceramic cooking pot and add the vegetables, pineapple chunks and water chestnuts.

5 In a bowl, combine the ginger, chilli and five-spice powder with the vinegar, soy sauce, hoisin sauce and reserved stock. Pour in the pineapple juice mixture, then tip into the frying pan and bring to the boil, stirring constantly. As soon as the mixture thickens, pour over the pork and vegetables.

6 Cover with the lid and switch the slow cooker to high. Cook for 1 hour, then reduce the temperature to low and cook for 1–2 hours, or until the pork is cooked and the vegetables retain some crispness. Serve with rice.

Nutritional information per portion: Energy 358Kcal/1509kJ; Protein 19.9g; Carbohydrate 49.4g, of which sugars 36.3g; Fat 10.3g, of which saturates 2.8g; Cholesterol 60.4mg; Calcium 43mg; Fibre 2.7g; Sodium 405mg.

BOSTON BAKED BEANS

*The slow cooker was actually invented for making baked beans. Molasses gives the beans
a very rich flavour and dark colour, but you can replace it with maple syrup if you prefer.*

SERVES 8

450g/1lb/2½ cups dried haricot
   (navy) beans
4 whole cloves
2 onions, peeled
1 bay leaf
90ml/6 tbsp tomato ketchup
30ml/2 tbsp molasses
30ml/2 tbsp dark brown sugar
15ml/1tbsp Dijon-style mustard
475ml/16fl oz/2 cups unsalted
   vegetable stock
225g/8oz piece of salt pork
salt and ground black pepper

1 Rinse the beans, then place in a large
bowl. Cover with cold water and leave
to soak for at least 8 hours or overnight.

2 Drain and rinse the beans. Place them
in a large pan, cover with plenty of cold
water and bring to the boil. Boil gently
for about 10 minutes, then drain and tip
into the ceramic cooking pot.

3 Stick 2 cloves in each of the onions.
Add them to the pot with the bay leaf,
burying them in the beans.

4 In a bowl, blend together the ketchup,
molasses, sugar, mustard and stock, and
pour over the beans. Add more stock,
or water, if necessary, so that the beans
are almost covered with liquid. Cover
with the lid and switch the slow cooker
to low. Cook for 3 hours.

5 Towards the end of the cooking time,
place the salt pork in a pan of boiling
water and cook for 3 minutes.

6 Using a sharp knife, score the pork
rind in deep 1.5cm/½in cuts. Add the
salt pork to the ceramic cooking pot,
pushing it down just below the surface
of the beans, skin side up. Cover the
pot with the lid and cook for a further
5–6 hours, until the beans are tender.

7 Remove the pork from the beans and
set aside until cool enough to handle,
Using a sharp knife, slice off the rind and
fat and finely slice the meat.

8 Using a spoon, skim off any fat from
the top of the beans, then stir in the
pieces of meat. Season to taste with salt
and black pepper, and serve hot.

COOK'S TIPS

• Be sure to taste the beans before adding
any more salt. The salt pork will have
already added plenty, so you may only
need to season with black pepper.
• To make a vegetarian version of these
beans, simply leave out the salt pork.
They are just as good cooked without.

Nutritional information per portion: Energy 228Kcal/968kJ; Protein 13.4g; Carbohydrate 43.9g, of which sugars 19.4g; Fat 1g, of which saturates 0.1g; Cholesterol 0mg; Calcium 140mg; Fibre 9.5g; Sodium 334mg.

ITALIAN PORK SAUSAGE STEW

This hearty casserole, made with spicy sausages and haricot beans, is flavoured with fragrant fresh herbs and dry Italian wine. Serve with Italian bread for mopping up the delicious juices. Remember to leave time for the beans to soak before cooking.

SERVES 4

225g/8oz/1¼ cups dried haricot
    (navy) beans
2 sprigs fresh thyme
30ml/2 tsp olive oil
450g/1lb fresh Italian pork sausages
1 onion, finely chopped
2 sticks celery, finely diced
300ml/½ pint/1¼ cups dry red or white
    wine, preferably Italian
1 sprig of fresh rosemary
1 bay leaf
300ml/½ pint/1¼ cups boiling
    vegetable stock
200g/7oz can chopped tomatoes
¼ head dark green cabbage such as cavolo
    nero or Savoy, finely shredded
salt and ground black pepper
chopped fresh thyme, to garnish
crusty Italian bread, to serve

1 Put the haricot beans in a large bowl and cover with cold water. Leave to soak for at least 8 hours, or overnight.

2 Drain the beans and place in a pan with the thyme sprigs and at least twice their volume of cold water. Bring to the boil and boil steadily for 10 minutes, then drain and place in the ceramic cooking pot, discarding the thyme.

3 Meanwhile, heat the oil in a pan and cook the sausages until browned all over. Transfer to the ceramic cooking pot and tip away all but 15ml/1 tbsp of the fat in the frying pan.

4 Add the onion and celery to the pan and cook gently for 5 minutes until softened but not coloured. Add the wine, rosemary and bay leaf and bring to the boil. Pour over the sausages, add the stock and season with salt and pepper. Cover with the lid, switch the slow cooker to high and cook for 5–6 hours, until the beans are tender.

5 Stir the chopped tomatoes and the shredded cabbage into the stew. Cover and cook for 30–45 minutes, or until the cabbage is tender but not overcooked. Divide between warmed plates, garnish with a little chopped fresh thyme and serve with crusty Italian bread.

COOK'S TIP
The tomatoes are added towards the end of cooking because their acidity would prevent the beans from becoming tender if added earlier.

PORK and POTATO HOT-POT

Long, slow cooking makes the pork chops meltingly tender and allows the potato slices to soak up all the delicious juices from the meat. Perfect for a family meal or casual supper with friends, simply serve with lightly cooked green vegetables.

SERVES 4

25g/1oz/2 tbsp butter
15ml/1 tbsp oil
1 large onion, very thinly sliced
1 garlic clove, crushed
225g/8oz/generous 3 cups button (white)
   mushrooms, sliced
1.5ml/¼ tsp dried mixed herbs
900g/2lb potatoes, thinly sliced
4 thick pork chops
750ml/1¼ pints/3 cups vegetable
   or chicken stock
salt and ground black pepper

1 Use 15g/½oz/1 tbsp of the butter to grease the base and halfway up the sides of the ceramic cooking pot.

2 Heat the oil in a frying pan, add the sliced onion and cook gently for about 5 minutes, until softened and translucent.

3 Add the garlic and mushrooms to the pan and cook for a further 5 minutes until softened. Remove the pan from the heat and stir in the mixed herbs.

4 Spoon half the mushroom mixture into the base of the ceramic cooking pot, then arrange half the potato slices on top and season with salt and ground black pepper.

5 Using a sharp knife, trim as much fat as possible from the pork chops, then place them on top of the potatoes in a single layer. Pour about half the stock over the top to cover the potatoes and prevent them discolouring.

6 Repeat the layers of the mushroom mixture and potatoes, finishing with a layer of neatly overlapping potatoes. Pour over the remaining stock; it should just cover the potatoes, so use a little more or less if necessary. Dot the remaining butter on top of the potatoes and cover with the lid.

7 Cook the stew on high for 4–5 hours, or until the potatoes and meat are tender when pierced with a thin skewer. If you like, place the hot-pot under a medium grill (broiler) for 5–10 minutes to brown before serving.

Nutritional information per portion: Energy 511Kcal/2132kJ; Protein 17.9g; Carbohydrate 41.5g, of which sugars 6.5g; Fat 31.5g, of which saturates 12.1g; Cholesterol 67mg; Calcium 40mg; Fibre 3.7g; Sodium 529mg.

POTATO and SAUSAGE CASSEROLE

There are many variations of this traditional Irish supper dish, known as Irish coddle, but the basic ingredients are the same wherever you go – potatoes, sausages and bacon.

SERVES 4

15ml/1 tbsp vegetable oil
8 large pork sausages
4 bacon rashers (slices), cut into 2.5cm/
   1in pieces
1 large onion, chopped
2 garlic cloves, crushed
4 large baking potatoes, peeled
   and thinly sliced
1.5ml/¼ tsp fresh sage
300ml/½ pint/1¼ cups vegetable stock
salt and ground black pepper

COOK'S TIPS
• For an authentic Irish feel, serve this delicious, hearty casserole with braised green cabbage.
• Choose good-quality sausages because it will make all the difference to the final result. Many Irish artisan butchers export quality Irish sausages, so it is well worth keeping an eye out for them.

1 Heat the oil in a frying pan. Gently fry the sausages for about 5 minutes, turning frequently until they are golden but not cooked through. Remove from the frying pan and set aside. Tip away all but about 10ml/2 tsp of fat from the pan.

2 Add the bacon to the pan and fry for 2 minutes. Add the onion and fry for about 8 minutes, stirring frequently until golden. Add the garlic and fry for a further 1 minute, then turn off the heat.

3 Arrange half the potato slices in the base of the ceramic cooking pot. Spoon the bacon and onion mixture on top. Season well with salt and ground black pepper, and sprinkle with the fresh sage. Cover with the remaining potato slices.

4 Pour the stock over the potatoes and top with the sausages. Cover with the lid and cook on high for 3–4 hours, or until the potatoes are tender and the sausages cooked through. Serve hot.

Nutritional information per portion: Energy 717Kcal/2984kJ; Protein 20.5g; Carbohydrate 49.9g, of which sugars 6.1g; Fat 49.8g, of which saturates 18.1g; Cholesterol 78.1mg; Calcium 73mg; Fibre 4g; Sodium 1322mg.

PORK FILLETS with PRUNE STUFFING

The sweet flavour and rich texture of dried fruit, such as prunes, goes particularly well
with pork. If you want to ring the changes, dried apricots or figs can be used instead.

SERVES 4

15g/½oz/1 tbsp butter
1 shallot, very finely chopped
1 stick celery, very finely chopped
finely grated rind of ½ orange
115g/4oz/½ cup (about 12) stoned
   (pitted), ready-to-eat prunes, chopped
25g/1oz/½ cup fresh white breadcrumbs
30ml/2 tbsp chopped fresh parsley
pinch of grated nutmeg
two 225g/8oz pork fillets, trimmed
6 slices Parma ham or prosciutto
15ml/1 tbsp olive oil
150ml/¼ pint/⅔ cup dry white wine
salt and ground black pepper
mashed root vegetables and wilted pak
   choi (bok choy), to serve

1 Melt the butter in a frying pan, add the shallot and celery, and fry gently until soft. Tip into a bowl and stir in the orange rind, prunes, breadcrumbs, parsley and nutmeg. Season and leave to cool.

2 Slice down the length of each fillet, cutting three-quarters of the way through.

3 Open out each pork fillet and lay it out on a board. Cover the meat with a piece of oiled clear film (plastic wrap), then gently bash with a rolling pin until the meat is about 5mm/¼in thick.

4 Arrange 3 slices of the ham on a board and place one pork fillet on top. Repeat with the remaining ham and fillet.

5 Divide the prune and breadcrumb stuffing between the pork fillets, then fold over to enclose the filling.

6 Wrap the ham around one stuffed pork fillet, and secure with one or two wooden cocktail sticks (toothpicks). Repeat with the remaining ham and fillet.

7 Heat the oil in the clean frying pan and quickly brown the wrapped pork fillets all over, taking care not to dislodge the cocktail sticks, before transferring them to the ceramic cooking pot.

8 Pour the white wine into the frying pan and bring almost to the boil, then pour over the pork.

9 Cover the ceramic cooking pot with the slow cooker lid and cook on high for 1 hour, then reduce the temperature to low and cook for a further 2–3 hours, or until the pork is cooked completely through and tender.

10 Remove the cocktail sticks from the meat and cut the pork into slices. Arrange on warmed plates and spoon over some of the cooking juices. Serve with mashed root vegetables and wilted pak choi leaves.

Nutritional information per portion: Energy 245Kcal/1027kJ; Protein 17.3g; Carbohydrate 14.6g, of which sugars 11.3g; Fat 10.8g, of which saturates 4g; Cholesterol 59mg; Calcium 34mg; Fibre 2g; Sodium 378mg.

SPICY PORK CASSEROLE with DRIED FRUIT

Inspired by the South American mole – a paste of chilli, shallots and nuts – this casserole is thickened and flavoured with a similar mixture, which really brings out the taste of the onions, meat and sweet dried fruit. Part of the mole is added at the end of cooking to retain its fresh flavour. Serve the casserole with rice and a green salad.

SERVES 6

25ml/1½ tbsp plain (all-purpose) flour
1kg/2¼lb shoulder or leg of pork,
   cut into 4cm/1½in cubes
30ml/2 tbsp olive oil
450ml/¾ pint/scant 2 cups fruity
   white wine
150ml/¼ pint/⅔ cup vegetable stock
   or water
115g/4oz/1½ cups ready-to-eat prunes
115g/4oz/1½ cups ready-to-eat dried
   apricots
grated rind and juice of 1 small orange
pinch of muscovado sugar
30ml/2 tbsp chopped fresh parsley
1 fresh green or red chilli, seeded
   and finely chopped
salt and ground black pepper
plain boiled rice, to serve

For the *mole*
3 ancho chillies and 2 pasilla chillies
   (or other varieties of large,
   medium-hot dried red chillies)
30ml/2 tbsp olive oil
2 large onions, finely chopped
3 garlic cloves, chopped
1 fresh green chilli, seeded and
   chopped
10ml/2 tsp ground coriander
5ml/1 tsp mild Spanish paprika
   or pimenton
50g/2oz/½ cup blanched almonds,
   toasted
15ml/1 tbsp chopped fresh oregano
   or 2.5ml/½ tsp dried oregano

1 Make the *mole* paste first. Toast the dried chillies in a dry frying pan over a low heat for 1–2 minutes, stirring, until they are aromatic. Remove the chillies from the heat, place in a small bowl and pour over warm water to cover. Leave to soak for about 30 minutes.

2 Drain the chillies, reserving the soaking water, then remove and discard the woody stalks and seeds.

3 Heat the oil in a frying pan and fry the onions over a low heat for about 10 minutes until soft. Remove two-thirds of the onions from the pan and set aside. Add the garlic, fresh green chilli and ground coriander to the pan and cook for a further 5 minutes.

4 Transfer the onion mixture to a food processor and add the drained chillies, paprika or pimenton, almonds and oregano. Process the mixture, adding 45–60ml/3–4 tbsp of the chilli soaking liquid to make a workable paste.

5 Place the flour in a shallow dish and season with salt and black pepper. Add the pork and toss well to coat.

6 Wipe the frying pan clean with kitchen paper and heat the olive oil. Fry the pork in two batches over a high heat for 5–6 minutes, stirring frequently, until it is sealed on all sides. Transfer the pork to the ceramic cooking pot with a slotted spoon and switch the slow cooker to high.

7 Add the reserved fried onions to the pan. Pour in the wine and stock or water and simmer for 1 minute. Stir in half the *mole* paste, bring back to the boil and bubble for a few seconds before pouring over the pork. Stir to mix, then cover with the lid and cook for 2 hours.

8 Stir the fruit, orange juice and sugar into the stew. Switch the slow cooker to low and cook for a further 2–3 hours, or until the pork is very tender.

9 Stir in the remaining *mole* paste and cook for 30 minutes. Serve sprinkled with orange rind, parsley and fresh chilli.

Nutritional information per portion: Energy 477Kcal/1999kJ; Protein 40.7g; Carbohydrate 25.6g, of which sugars 21g; Fat 19.1g, of which saturates 3.8g; Cholesterol 105mg; Calcium 86mg; Fibre 4.1g; Sodium 149mg.

CIDER-GLAZED GAMMON

This is a classic buffet centrepiece, which is ideal for Christmas or Thanksgiving. A fresh cranberry sauce provides the perfect foil to the richness of the meat and can be made in the slow cooker the day before if you want to serve the gammon hot, rather than cold. Soaking smoked gammon overnight helps to remove the excess salts.

SERVES 8

2kg/4½lb middle gammon joint, soaked
　　overnight, if smoked
2 small onions
about 30 whole cloves
3 bay leaves
10 black peppercorns
150ml/¼ pint/⅔ cup medium-dry
　　(medium-hard) cider
45ml/3 tbsp soft light brown sugar

For the cranberry sauce
350g/12oz/3 cups cranberries
175g/6oz/scant 1 cup caster (superfine)
　　sugar
grated rind and juice of 2 clementines
30ml/2 tbsp port

1 Drain the gammon joint, if soaked overnight, then place it in the ceramic cooking pot. Stud the onions with 6 of the cloves and add to the cooking pot with the bay leaves and peppercorns.

2 Pour over enough cold water to just cover the gammon. Switch the slow cooker to high, cover with the lid and cook for 1 hour. Skim off any scum from the surface, re-cover and cook for a further 4–5 hours. Check once during cooking and skim the surface, if necessary.

COOK'S TIP
The gammon should remain barely covered with water during cooking. There should be little evaporation from the slow cooker, but if necessary, top up with a small amount of boiling water.

3 Carefully lift the gammon joint out of the slow cooker using large forks or slotted spoons, and place it in a roasting tin (pan) or ovenproof dish. Leave to stand for about 15 minutes until cool enough to handle.

4 Meanwhile, make the glaze. Pour the cider into a small pan, add the soft brown sugar and heat gently, stirring, until dissolved. Simmer for 5 minutes to make a sticky glaze, then remove from the heat and leave to cool for a few minutes so that it thickens slightly.

5 Preheat the oven to 220°C/425°F/ Gas 7. Using a pair of scissors, snip the string off the gammon then carefully slice off the rind, leaving a thin, even layer of fat over the meat.

6 Using a sharp knife, score the fat into a neat diamond pattern. Press a clove into the centre of each diamond, then spoon over the glaze. Bake for about 25 minutes, or until the fat is brown, glistening and crisp. Remove from the oven and set aside until ready to serve.

7 Meanwhile, make the cranberry sauce. Wash the ceramic cooking pot, then add all the ingredients for the cranberry sauce to it. Switch the slow cooker to high and cook uncovered for 20 minutes, stirring continuously, until the sugar has dissolved completely.

8 Cover the pot with the lid and cook on high for 1½–2 hours, or until the cranberries are tender. Transfer the sauce to a jug (pitcher) or bowl, or keep warm in the slow cooker until ready to serve with the gammon. (The sauce can be served hot or cold.)

COOK'S TIPS
• If serving hot, cover the gammon with foil and leave to rest for 15 minutes before carving.
• If you prefer, serve the ham with redcurrant sauce or jelly. You can also use honey in place of the soft brown sugar for the glaze, if you like.

Nutritional information per portion: Energy 404Kcal/1689kJ; Protein 44.1g; Carbohydrate 15.2g, of which sugars 14.8g; Fat 18.8g, of which saturates 6.3g; Cholesterol 57mg; Calcium 25mg; Fibre 1g; Sodium 220mg.

VEAL STEW with TOMATOES

This classic French dish is traditionally made with lean and mildly flavoured veal.
Pork fillet makes an excellent, and economical, alternative.

SERVES 4

30ml/2 tbsp plain (all-purpose) flour
675g/1½lb boneless veal shoulder,
　　trimmed and cut into cubes
30ml/2 tbsp sunflower oil
4 shallots, very finely chopped
300ml/½ pint/1¼ cups boiling vegetable
　　or chicken stock
150ml/¼ pint/⅔ cup dry white wine
15ml/1 tbsp tomato purée (paste)
225g/8oz tomatoes, peeled, seeded
　　and chopped
115g/4oz mushrooms, quartered
grated zest and juice of 1 small
　　unwaxed orange
bouquet garni
salt and ground black pepper
30ml/2 tbsp chopped fresh parsley,
　　to garnish

1 Put the flour in a small plastic bag and season with salt and pepper. Drop the pieces of meat into the bag a few at a time and shake to coat with the flour.

2 Heat 15ml/1 tbsp of the oil in a pan, add the shallots and cook gently for 5 minutes. Transfer to the ceramic cooking pot and switch to high or auto.

3 Add the remaining 15ml/1 tbsp oil to the pan and fry the meat in batches until well browned on all sides, then transfer to the ceramic cooking pot.

4 Pour the stock and white wine into the pan. Add the tomato purée and bring to the boil, stirring. Pour the sauce over the meat. Add the tomatoes, mushrooms, orange zest and juice, and bouquet garni to the pot and stir briefly to mix the ingredients. Cover with the lid and cook for about 1 hour.

5 Reduce the temperature to low or leave on auto and cook for 3–4 hours, or until the meat and mushrooms are very tender. Remove the bouquet garni, check the seasoning and add more salt and ground black pepper if necessary. Garnish with fresh parsley and serve.

Nutritional information per portion: Energy 323Kcal/1358kJ; Protein 38.2g; Carbohydrate 13.8g, of which sugars 5.4g; Fat 10.6g, of which saturates 2.3g; Cholesterol 141mg; Calcium 47mg; Fibre 1.7g; Sodium 314mg.

GREEK MEATBALLS in RICH TOMATO SAUCE

There are many versions of these sausage-shaped meatballs, known as yiouvarlakia or soudzoukakia. These are made with lamb, but beef makes an excellent alternative.

SERVES 4

50g/2oz/1 cup fresh white breadcrumbs
1 egg, lightly beaten
finely grated rind of ½ small orange
2.5ml/½ tsp dried oregano
450g/1lb minced (ground) lamb
1 small onion, peeled and grated
2 cloves garlic, crushed
15ml/1 tbsp plain (all-purpose) flour
30ml/2 tbsp olive oil
salt and ground black pepper
flat leaf parsley, to garnish

For the sauce
1 onion, very finely chopped
400g/14oz can chopped tomatoes
150ml/¼ pint/⅔ cup hot lamb or beef
  stock
1 bay leaf

1 Put the breadcrumbs, beaten egg, orange rind and oregano in a bowl and stir together. Add the lamb, onion and garlic and season with salt and pepper. Mix together until thoroughly combined.

2 Using dampened hands, so that the mixture doesn't stick, press the meat mixture into small sausage-shapes, about 5cm/2in long, and roll them in flour. Place in the refrigerator for 30 minutes to firm up slightly.

COOK'S TIP
Serve these meatballs with a refreshing salad and plenty of fresh, country-style crusty bread for mopping up the juices. Alternatively, serve with pitta bread so that guests can stuff the breads with meatballs and fresh green salad.

3 Heat the oil in a large frying pan and add the meatballs, working in batches if necessary. Cook for 5–8 minutes, turning the meatballs, until evenly browned all over. Transfer to a plate and set aside, leaving the fat and juices in the pan.

4 To make the sauce, add the onion to the pan and cook for 3–4 minutes, until beginning to soften. Pour in the chopped tomatoes, bring to the boil and cook gently for 1 minute.

5 Transfer the sauce to the ceramic cooking pot and stir in the stock. Add the bay leaf and season with salt and ground black pepper.

6 Arrange the meatballs in a single layer in the sauce. Cover with the lid and cook on high or auto for 1 hour. Reduce the temperature to low or leave on auto and cook for a further 4–5 hours. Serve garnished with sprigs of fresh parsley.

Nutritional information per portion: Energy 363Kcal/1515kJ; Protein 26.1g; Carbohydrate 15g, of which sugars 5.3g; Fat 22.5g, of which saturates 8.3g; Cholesterol 141mg; Calcium 68mg; Fibre 1.5g; Sodium 239mg.

LANCASHIRE HOT-POT

This dish is traditionally made without browning the lamb or vegetables, and relies on long, slow cooking to develop the flavour. You can brown the top under the grill, if you like.

SERVES 4

8 middle neck or loin lamb chops, about 900g/2lb in total weight
900g/2lb potatoes, thinly sliced
2 onions, peeled and sliced
2 carrots, peeled and sliced
1 stick celery, trimmed and sliced
1 leek, peeled and sliced
225g/8oz/generous 3 cups button (white) mushrooms, sliced
5ml/1 tsp dried mixed herbs
small sprig of rosemary
475ml/16fl oz/2 cups lamb or beef stock
15g/½oz/1 tbsp butter, melted
salt and ground black pepper

3 Pour the meat stock into the ceramic cooking pot, then cover with the lid and switch the slow cooker to high or auto. Cook for 1 hour, then reduce the temperature to low or leave on auto and cook for 6–8 hours or until tender.

4 Brush the top layer of potatoes with melted butter. Place under a preheated grill (broiler) and cook for 5 minutes, or until the potatoes are lightly browned. Serve immediately.

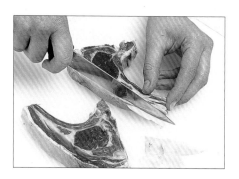

1 Trim the lamb chops of excess fat. Place a layer of sliced potatoes in the base of the ceramic cooking pot, and top with some sliced vegetables and a sprinkling of dried herbs, salt and black pepper. Place four of the chops on top.

2 Repeat the layers of sliced potato, vegetables, dried herbs and meat, tucking the rosemary sprig down the side of the pot. Continue layering up the remaining vegetables, finishing with a neat layer of potatoes on the top.

Nutritional information per portion: Energy 850Kcal/3544kJ; Protein 44.7g; Carbohydrate 45.3g, of which sugars 10.1g; Fat 55.8g, of which saturates 26.5g; Cholesterol 186mg; Calcium 72mg; Fibre 4.3g; Sodium 274mg.

LAMB PIE with MUSTARD THATCH

Here, a traditional shepherd's pie is given a contemporary twist with a tangy topping of mashed potato flavoured with peppery mustard. Serve with vegetables.

SERVES 4

450g/1lb lean minced (ground) lamb
1 onion, very finely chopped
2 celery sticks, thinly sliced
2 carrots, finely diced
15ml/1 tbsp cornflour (cornstarch)
    blended into 150ml/¼ pint/⅔ cup
    lamb stock
15ml/1 tbsp Worcestershire sauce
30ml/2 tbsp chopped fresh rosemary,
    or 10ml/2 tsp dried
800g/1¾lb floury potatoes, diced
60ml/4 tbsp milk
15ml/1 tbsp wholegrain mustard
25g/1oz/2 tbsp butter
salt and ground black pepper

1 Heat a non-stick frying pan, then add the lamb, breaking it up with a wooden spoon, and cook until lightly browned all over. Add the onion, celery and carrots to the pan and cook for 2–3 minutes, stirring frequently.

2 Stir the stock and cornflour mixture into the pan. Bring to the boil, stirring constantly, then remove from the heat. Stir in the Worcestershire sauce and rosemary, and season well with salt and ground black pepper.

3 Transfer the mixture to the ceramic cooking pot and switch the slow cooker to high. Cover and cook for 3 hours.

4 Towards the end of the cooking time, cook the potatoes in a large pan of boiling salted water until tender. Drain well, mash, and stir in the milk, mustard and butter. Season to taste.

5 Spoon the mashed potatoes on top of the lamb, spreading the mixture out evenly. Cook for a further 45 minutes. Brown the topping under a pre-heated grill (broiler) for a few minutes, if you like, then serve immediately.

Nutritional information per portion: Energy 458Kcal/1920kJ; Protein 26.5g; Carbohydrate 42.2g, of which sugars 8.1g; Fat 21.5g, of which saturates 10.6g; Cholesterol 101mg; Calcium 84mg; Fibre 3.5g; Sodium 264mg.

MOUSSAKA

This classic Greek dish topped with a light egg and cheese sauce is delicious in summer or winter, served with a crisp leafy salad. Try to find small, sweet aubergines with firm, shiny skins because they have much the best flavour. For an authentic touch, look out for Kefolotiri cheese in delicatessens and specialist food stores – although if you can't find it, Cheddar cheese will give equally good results.

SERVES 6

900g/2lb small or medium aubergines
   (eggplant), thinly sliced
60ml/4 tbsp olive oil
1 onion, finely chopped
2 garlic cloves, crushed
450g/1lb lean minced (ground) lamb
400g/14oz can chopped tomatoes
5ml/1 tsp dried oregano
pinch of ground cinnamon
salt and ground black pepper

For the topping
50g/2oz/¼ cup butter
50g/2oz/½ cup plain (all-purpose) flour
600ml/1 pint/2½ cups milk
pinch of freshly grated nutmeg
75g/3oz/¾ cup grated Kefolotiri or
   mature Cheddar cheese
1 egg yolk
30ml/2 tbsp fresh white breadcrumbs

1 Layer the aubergine slices in a sieve (strainer) or colander, sprinkling each layer with salt. Place the sieve over a bowl and leave to drain for 20 minutes. Rinse the aubergine slices thoroughly under cold running water and pat dry with kitchen paper.

VARIATION

You can use courgettes (zucchini) in place of the aubergines, if you prefer. Simply slice the courgettes, brush with olive oil and grill as before. There is no need to salt the courgette slices.

2 Lightly brush the aubergine slices with about half the oil, then arrange the slices in a single layer on a baking sheet. Place the baking sheet under a medium grill (broiler) and cook, turning once, until the aubergine slices are softened and golden brown on both sides.

3 Arrange half the aubergine slices in the bottom of the ceramic cooking pot and switch the slow cooker to high. Set aside the remaining slices.

4 Heat the remaining olive oil in a heavy pan, add the onion and fry gently for about 10 minutes, or until softened. Add the garlic and lamb and cook, stirring and breaking up the meat with a wooden spoon, until the meat is evenly browned.

5 Stir the tomatoes, oregano and cinnamon into the meat mixture, season generously with salt and ground black pepper and slowly bring to the boil over a gentle heat.

6 Spoon the lamb mixture into the slow cooker, covering the aubergine slices. Arrange the remaining aubergine slices on top, cover and cook for 2 hours.

7 Meanwhile, make the cheese topping. Melt the butter in a pan, stir in the flour and cook for one minute. Gradually stir in the milk, bring to the boil over a low heat, stirring constantly, and cook until thick and creamy. Lower the heat and simmer for 1 minute. Remove from the heat, season, then stir in the nutmeg and two-thirds of the cheese.

8 Leave the sauce to cool for 5 minutes, then beat in the egg yolk. Pour the sauce over the aubergine slices. Cover and cook for a further 2 hours, or until the topping is lightly set.

9 Sprinkle the remaining cheese and the breadcrumbs over the top and cook under a grill (broiler) for 3–4 minutes, or until golden brown. Leave to stand for 5–10 minutes before serving.

Nutritional information per portion: Energy 444Kcal/1850kJ; Protein 24.1g; Carbohydrate 1.5g, of which sugars 11.2g; Fat 31g, of which saturates 14g; Cholesterol 93.5mg; Calcium 268mg; Fibre 4.1g; Sodium 266mg.

MOROCCAN LAMB with HONEY and PRUNES

This classic dish of the Moroccan Jews is eaten at Rosh Hashanah – the Jewish New Year – when sweet foods are served in anticipation of a sweet new year to come.

SERVES 6

130g/4½oz/generous ½ cup stoned (pitted) prunes
350ml/12fl oz/1½ cups hot tea
1kg/2¼lb stewing or braising lamb, such as shoulder
30ml/2 tbsp olive oil
1 onion, chopped
2.5ml/½ tsp ground ginger
2.5ml/½ tsp curry powder
pinch of freshly grated nutmeg
10ml/2 tsp ground cinnamon
1.5ml/¼ tsp saffron threads
30ml/2 tbsp hot water
75ml/5 tbsp clear honey
200ml/7fl oz/scant 1 cup near-boiling lamb or beef stock
salt and ground black pepper
115g/4oz/1 cup blanched almonds, toasted
30ml/2 tbsp chopped fresh coriander (cilantro) and 3 hard-boiled eggs, cut into wedges, to garnish

1 Put the prunes in a heatproof bowl, then pour over the tea and leave to soak. Meanwhile, trim the lamb and cut into chunky pieces, no larger than 2.5cm/1in. Heat the oil in a frying pan and sauté the lamb in batches for 5 minutes, stirring frequently, until well-browned. Remove with a slotted spoon and transfer to the ceramic cooking pot.

2 Add the onion to the frying pan and cook for 5 minutes, until starting to soften. Stir in the ginger, curry powder, nutmeg, cinnamon, salt and a large pinch of black pepper, and cook for 1 minute. Add to the ceramic cooking pot with the meat and their juices.

3 Drain the prunes, adding the soaking liquid to the lamb. Cover the prunes.

4 Soak the saffron in the hot water for 1 minute, then add to the cooking pot with the honey and stock. Cover with the lid and cook on high or auto for 1 hour. Reduce the temperature to low and cook for a further 5–7 hours, or until the lamb is very tender.

5 Add the prunes to the cooking pot and stir to mix. Cook for 30 minutes, or until warmed through. Serve sprinkled with the toasted almonds and chopped coriander, and topped with the wedges of hard-boiled egg.

Nutritional information per portion: Energy 490Kcal/2051kJ; Protein 43.6g; Carbohydrate 23.8g, of which sugars 23.4g; Fat 25.2g, of which saturates 10.3g; Cholesterol 279mg; Calcium 41mg; Fibre 1.4g; Sodium 197mg.

LAMB in DILL SAUCE

In this recipe, the lamb is cooked with vegetables to make a clear well-flavoured broth,
which is then thickened with an egg and cream mixture to make a smooth delicate sauce.

SERVES 6

1.3kg/3lb lean boneless lamb
1 small onion, trimmed and quartered
1 carrot, peeled and thickly sliced
1 bay leaf
4 sprigs of fresh dill, plus 45ml/3 tbsp
  chopped
1 thinly pared strip of lemon rind
750ml/1¼ pints/3 cups near-boiling lamb
  or vegetable stock
225g/8oz small shallots
15ml/1 tbsp olive oil
15g/½oz/1 tbsp unsalted (sweet) butter
15ml/1 tbsp plain (all-purpose) flour
115g/4oz frozen petits pois, defrosted
1 egg yolk
75ml/2½fl oz/⅓ cup single (light) cream, at
  room temperature
salt and ground black pepper
new potatoes and carrots, to serve

1 Trim the lamb and cut into 2.5cm/1in
pieces. Place in the ceramic cooking pot
with the onion, carrot, bay leaf, sprigs of
dill and lemon rind. Pour over the stock,
cover and cook on high for 1 hour. Skim
off any scum, then re-cover and cook for
a further 2 hours on high or 4 hours on
low, until the lamb is fairly tender.

2 Meanwhile, put the shallots in a
heatproof bowl and pour over enough
boiling water to cover. Leave to cool,
then drain and peel off the skins.

3 Remove the meat from the pot. Strain
the stock, discarding the vegetables and
herbs. Clean the pot. Return the meat
and half the stock (reserving the rest),
cover and switch to high.

4 Heat the oil and butter in a pan, add
the shallots and cook gently, stirring, for
10–15 minutes, or until browned and
tender. Turn off the heat, then transfer
the shallots to the cooking pot, using a
slotted spoon.

5 Sprinkle the flour over the fat
remaining in the pan, then stir in the
reserved stock, a little at a time. Bring
to the boil, stirring all the time until
thickened, then stir into the lamb and
shallot mixture. Stir in the peas and
season with salt and pepper. Cook on
high for 30 minutes until piping hot.

6 Blend the egg yolk and the cream
together, then stir in a few spoonfuls
of the hot stock. Add to the casserole
in a thin stream, stirring until slightly
thickened. Stir in the chopped dill and
serve immediately, with steamed new
potatoes and carrots.

Nutritional information per portion: Energy 631Kcal/2629kJ; Protein 60.9g; Carbohydrate 7g, of which sugars 3.5g; Fat 40g, of which saturates 17.5g; Cholesterol 249mg; Calcium 123mg; Fibre 1.9g; Sodium 566mg.

TUSCAN POT-ROASTED SHOULDER of LAMB

*This delicious boned and rolled shoulder of lamb, studded with rosemary sprigs and garlic,
then cooked on a bed of vegetables, makes a perfect alternative to a traditional meat
roast. Check that the lamb will fit comfortably in the slow cooker before you start.*

SERVES 6

15ml/1 tbsp olive oil
1.3kg/3lb lamb shoulder, trimmed,
    boned and tied
3 large garlic cloves
12 small fresh rosemary sprigs
115g/4oz lean rinded smoked bacon,
    chopped
1 onion, chopped
3 carrots, finely chopped
3 celery sticks, finely chopped
1 leek, finely chopped
150ml/¼ pint/⅔ cup red wine
300ml/½ pint/1¼ cups lamb or vegetable
    stock
400g/14oz can chopped tomatoes
3 sprigs of fresh thyme
2 bay leaves
400g/14oz can flageolet (small cannellini)
    beans, drained and rinsed
salt and ground black pepper
potatoes or warm crusty bread, to serve

1 Heat the oil in a large frying pan and
brown the lamb on all sides. Remove
from the pan and leave to stand until it
is cool enough to handle.

2 Meanwhile, cut the garlic cloves into
quarters. When the lamb is cool enough,
make twelve deep incisions all over the
meat. Push a piece of garlic and a small
sprig of rosemary into each incision.

COOK'S TIP
Lamb can be quite a fatty meat, so ask
your butcher to trim off as much excess
fat as possible from the joint, before
boning, rolling and tying it.

3 Add the bacon, onion, carrot, celery
and leek to the pan and cook for about
10 minutes until soft, then transfer to
the ceramic cooking pot. Stir the red
wine into the cooking pot.

4 Add the stock and chopped tomatoes
to the pot and season with salt and
pepper. Add the thyme and bay leaves,
submerging them in the liquid. Place the
lamb on top, cover with the lid and cook
on high for 4 hours.

5 Lift the lamb out of the pot and stir
the beans into the vegetable mixture.
Return the lamb, re-cover and cook for
a further 1–2 hours, or until the lamb is
cooked and tender.

6 Remove the lamb from the ceramic
cooking pot using slotted spoons, cover
with foil to keep warm, and leave to rest
for 10 minutes.

7 Remove the string from the lamb and
carve the meat into thick slices. Remove
the thyme and bay leaves from the
vegetable and bean mixture and carefully
skim off any fat from the surface. Spoon
the vegetables on to warmed serving
plates and arrange the sliced lamb on
top. Serve with potatoes or warm bread.

VARIATIONS
• Flageolet beans have a delicate yet
distinctive flavour that goes particularly
well in this dish. However, you can use
other mildly flavoured beans instead,
such as butter beans or cannellini beans.
• Try using 15ml/1 tsp fresh oregano in
place of the thyme, if you prefer. This
classic Italian herb tastes just as good.

Nutritional information per portion: Energy 710Kcal/2958kJ; Protein 60.2g; Carbohydrate 13.7g, of which sugars 4.8g; Fat 44.6g, of which saturates 19.4g; Cholesterol 229mg; Calcium 58mg; Fibre 4.7g; Sodium 864mg.

LAMB and CARROT CASSEROLE with BARLEY

Barley and carrots make natural partners for lamb and mutton. In this convenient casserole the barley extends the meat and adds to the flavour and texture as well as thickening the sauce. This warming dish is comfort food at its very best.

SERVES 6

675g/1½lb stewing (braising) lamb
15ml/1 tbsp vegetable oil
2 onions
675g/1½lb carrots, thickly sliced
4–6 celery sticks, sliced
45ml/3 tbsp pearl barley, rinsed
600ml/1 pint/2½ cups near-boiling lamb or
    vegetable stock
5ml/1 tsp fresh thyme leaves or pinch of
    dried mixed herbs
salt and ground black pepper
spring cabbage and jacket potatoes,
    to serve

1 Trim all excess fat from the lamb, then cut the meat into 3cm/1¼in pieces. Heat the oil in a frying pan, add the lamb and fry until browned. Remove from with a slotted spoon and set aside.

2 Slice the onions and add to the pan. Fry gently for 5 minutes until golden. Add the carrots and celery and cook for a further 3–4 minutes or until beginning to soften. Transfer the vegetables to the ceramic cooking pot and switch the slow cooker to high.

3 Sprinkle the pearl barley over the vegetables in the cooking pot, then arrange the lamb pieces meat on top.

4 Lightly season with salt and ground black pepper, then scatter with the herbs. Pour the stock over the meat, so that all of the meat is covered.

5 Cover the slow cooker with the lid and cook on auto or high for 2 hours. Lift the lid and, using a large spoon, skim off any scum that has risen to the surface of the casserole.

6 Re-cover the pot and leave on auto or switch to low and cook for a further 4–6 hours or until the meat, vegetables and barley are tender. Serve with spring cabbage and jacket potatoes.

Nutritional information per portion: Energy 304Kcal/1263kJ; Protein 23.2g; Carbohydrate 13g, of which sugars 11.3g; Fat 18g, of which saturates 7.5g; Cholesterol 84mg; Calcium 53mg; Fibre 3.6g; Sodium 110mg

LAMB STEWED with TOMATOES and GARLIC

This simple rustic stew comes from the plateau of Puglia in Italy, where sheep graze beside the vineyards. Serve simply, with fresh crusty bread and a green leaf salad.

SERVES 4

1.2kg/2½lb stewing (braising) lamb
30ml/2 tbsp plain (all-purpose) flour, seasoned with ground black pepper
60ml/4 tbsp olive oil
2 large cloves garlic, finely chopped
1 sprig fresh rosemary
150ml/¼ pint/⅔ cup dry white wine
150ml/¼ pint/⅔ cup lamb or beef stock
2.5ml/½ tsp salt
450g/1lb fresh tomatoes, peeled and chopped, or 400g/14oz can chopped tomatoes
salt and ground black pepper

4 Season with salt and pepper and stir in the tomatoes. Cover the cooking pot with the lid and switch the slow cooker to high or auto. Cook for 1 hour.

5 Reduce the heat to low or leave on auto and cook for a further 6–8 hours, or until the lamb is tender. Taste and adjust the seasoning before serving.

VARIATION

For Lamb with Butternut Squash, sauté 675g/1½lb cubed lamb fillet in 15ml/1 tbsp oil, then transfer to the ceramic cooking pot. Fry 1 chopped onion and 2 crushed garlic cloves until soft, and add to the lamb with 1 cubed butternut squash, 400g/14oz can chopped tomatoes, 150ml/¼ pint/⅔ cup lamb stock and 5ml/1 tsp dried marjoram. Cover and cook on low for 5–6 hours.

1 Trim all fat and gristle from the lamb and cut into 2.5cm/1in cubes. Toss in the flour to coat. Set aside the excess flour.

2 Heat the oil in a pan and fry the lamb, in two batches for 5 minutes, stirring, until browned. Lift out the lamb and transfer to the ceramic cooking pot.

3 Add the garlic and cook for a few seconds before adding the rosemary, wine and stock. Bring almost to the boil, stirring, to remove any meat sediment from the pan. Pour over the lamb.

Nutritional information per portion: Energy 636Kcal/2656kJ; Protein 62.4g; Carbohydrate 11.5g, of which sugars 3.9g; Fat 35.5g, of which saturates 12.2g; Cholesterol 222mg; Calcium 62mg; Fibre 1.4g; Sodium 508mg.

VEGETARIAN AND SIDE DISHES

Just because you follow a vegetarian diet doesn't mean you need to miss out on fabulous-tasting food. This chapter makes use of all kinds of wonderful vegetables, beans and grains to make fabulous slow-cooked main meals that will appeal just as much to meat eaters as they do to vegetarians. Try rich and creamy rosemary risotto with borlotti beans, or aromatic vegetable kashmiri for a hearty main meal. Or if you are looking for something a little less substantial, try baked eggs with creamy leeks or spicy chickpeas. Whatever you are in the mood for, you are sure to find the perfect meat-free recipe in this chapter.

BAKED EGGS with CREAMY LEEKS

Enjoy these deliciously creamy eggs for a light lunch or supper with toast and a salad.
You can use other vegetables in place of the leeks, such as puréed spinach or ratatouille.

3 Melt the butter in a small frying pan and cook the leeks over a medium heat, stirring frequently, until softened.

4 Add 45ml/3 tbsp of the cream and cook gently for about 5 minutes, or until the leeks are very soft and the cream has thickened a little. Season with salt, black pepper and nutmeg.

5 Spoon the leeks into the ramekins or soufflé dishes, dividing the mixture equally. Using the back of the spoon, make a hollow in the centre of each pile of leeks, then break an egg into the hollow. Spoon 5–10ml/1–2 tsp of the remaining cream over each egg and season lightly with salt and pepper.

6 Cover each dish with clear film (plastic wrap) and place in the slow cooker. If necessary, pour in a little more boiling water to come halfway up the sides of the dishes. Cover and cook for 30 minutes, or until the egg whites are set and the yolks are still soft, or a little longer if you prefer the eggs firmer.

SERVES 4

15g/½oz/1 tbsp butter, plus extra
   for greasing
225g/8oz small leeks, thinly sliced
60–90ml/4–6 tbsp whipping or double
   (heavy) cream
freshly grated nutmeg
4 eggs
salt and ground black pepper

VARIATION

To make herb and cheese eggs, put 15ml/1 tbsp double (heavy) cream in each dish with some chopped herbs. Break in the eggs, add 15ml/1 tbsp double cream and a little grated cheese, then cook as before. This is the perfect recipe for a lazy weekend brunch.

1 Pour about 2.5cm/1in hot water into the ceramic cooking pot and switch the slow cooker to high.

2 Using a pastry brush, lightly butter the base and insides of four 175ml/6fl oz/¾ cup ramekins or individual soufflé dishes.

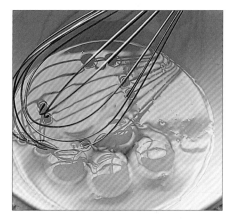

Nutritional information per portion: Energy 239Kcal/990kJ; Protein 8.5g; Carbohydrate 2g, of which sugars 1.6g; Fat 21.9g, of which saturates 11.4g; Cholesterol 266mg; Calcium 58mg; Fibre 1.2g; Sodium 110mg.

SAVOURY NUT LOAF

Ideal as an alternative to the traditional meat roast, this wholesome dish is perfect for special occasions. It is also particularly good served with a spicy fresh tomato sauce.

SERVES 4

30ml/2 tbsp olive oil, plus extra
  for greasing
1 onion, finely chopped
1 leek, finely chopped
2 celery sticks, finely chopped
225g/8oz/3 cups mushrooms, chopped
2 garlic cloves, crushed
425g/15oz can lentils, rinsed and drained
115g/4oz/1 cup mixed nuts, such as
  hazelnuts, cashew nuts and almonds,
  finely chopped
50g/2oz/½ cup plain (all-purpose) flour
50g/2oz/½ cup grated mature (sharp)
  Cheddar cheese
1 egg, beaten
45–60ml/3–4 tbsp chopped fresh
  mixed herbs
salt and ground black pepper
chives and sprigs of fresh flat leaf parsley,
  to garnish

1 Place an upturned saucer or metal pastry ring in the base of the ceramic cooking pot. Pour in about 2.5cm/1in hot water and switch the slow cooker to high.

2 Lightly grease the base and sides of a 900g/2lb loaf tin (pan) or terrine – first making sure it will fit in the slow cooker – and line the base and sides of the tin with baking parchment.

3 Heat the oil in a large pan, add the onion, leek, celery, mushrooms and garlic, then cook for 10 minutes, until the vegetables have softened. Do not let them brown.

4 Remove the pan from the heat, then stir in the lentils, mixed nuts and flour, grated cheese, beaten egg and herbs. Season well with salt and black pepper and mix thoroughly.

5 Spoon the nut mixture into the prepared loaf tin or terrine, pressing right into the corners. Level the surface with a fork, then cover the tin with a piece of foil. Place the loaf tin in the ceramic cooking pot and pour in enough near-boiling water to come just over halfway up the side of the dish.

6 Cover the slow cooker with the lid and cook for 3–4 hours, or until the loaf is firm to the touch.

7 Leave the loaf to cool in the tin for about 15 minutes, then turn out on to a serving plate. Serve the loaf hot or cold, cut into thick slices and garnished with fresh chives and sprigs of flat leaf parsley.

Nutritional information per portion: Energy 484Kcal/2019kJ; Protein 23.7g; Carbohydrate 34.1g, of which sugars 5.1g; Fat 29g, of which saturates 5.4g; Cholesterol 69mg; Calcium 238mg; Fibre 8.7g; Sodium 128mg.

MUSHROOM and FENNEL HOT-POT

Hearty and richly flavoured, this tasty stew makes a marvellous vegetarian main dish, but it can also be served as an accompaniment to meat dishes. Dried mushrooms swell up a great deal after soaking, so a little goes a long way in terms of both flavour and quantity.

SERVES 4

25g/1oz/½ cup dried shiitake mushrooms
1 small head of fennel
30ml/2 tbsp olive oil
12 shallots, peeled
225g/8oz/3 cups button (white)
    mushrooms, trimmed and halved
250ml/8fl oz/1 cup dry (hard) cider
25g/1oz/½ cup sun-dried tomatoes
30ml/2 tbsp/½ cup sun-dried
    tomato paste
1 bay leaf
salt and ground black pepper
chopped fresh parsley,
    to garnish

1 Place the dried shiitake mushrooms in a heatproof bowl. Pour over just enough hot water to cover them and leave to soak for about 15 minutes. Meanwhile, trim and slice the fennel.

2 Heat the oil in a heavy pan. Add the shallots and fennel, then sauté for about 10 minutes over a medium heat, until the vegetables are softened and just beginning to brown. Add the button mushrooms to the pan and cook for a further 2–3 minutes, stirring occasionally.

3 Transfer the vegetable mixture to the ceramic cooking pot. Drain the shiitake mushrooms, adding 30ml/2 tbsp of the soaking liquid to the cooking pot. Chop them and add them to the pot.

4 Pour the cider into the pot and stir in the sun-dried tomatoes and tomato paste. Add the bay leaf. Cover with the lid and cook on high for 3–4 hours, or until the vegetables are tender.

5 Remove the bay leaf and season to taste with salt and black pepper. Serve sprinkled with plenty of chopped parsley.

Nutritional information per portion: Energy 94Kcal/394kJ; Protein 2.1g; Carbohydrate 4.2g, of which sugars 4g; Fat 6g, of which saturates 0.9g; Cholesterol 0mg; Calcium 28mg; Fibre 2.4g; Sodium 17mg.

SWEET and SOUR MIXED-BEAN HOT-POT

This impressive-looking dish, topped with sliced potatoes, is incredibly easy, making the most of dried and canned ingredients from the kitchen cupboard and combining them with a deliciously rich and tangy tomato sauce.

SERVES 6

40g/1½oz/3 tbsp butter
4 shallots, peeled and finely chopped
40g/1½oz/⅓ cup plain (all-purpose)
    or wholemeal (whole-wheat) flour
300ml/½ pint/1¼ cups passata (bottled
    strained tomatoes)
120ml/4fl oz/½ cup unsweetened
    apple juice
60ml/4 tbsp soft light brown sugar
60ml/4 tbsp tomato ketchup
60ml/4 tbsp dry sherry
60ml/4 tbsp cider vinegar
60ml/4 tbsp light soy sauce
400g/14oz can butter beans
400g/14oz can flageolet (small cannellini)
    beans
400g/14oz can chickpeas
175g/6oz green beans, cut into 2.5cm/
    1in lengths
225g/8oz/3 cups mushrooms, sliced
450g/1lb unpeeled potatoes
15ml/1 tbsp olive oil
15ml/1 tbsp chopped fresh thyme
15ml/1 tbsp fresh marjoram
salt and ground black pepper
fresh herbs, to garnish

1 Melt the butter in a pan, add the shallots and fry gently for 5–6 minutes, until softened. Add the flour and cook for 1 minute, stirring all the time, then gradually stir in the passata.

2 Add the apple juice, sugar, tomato ketchup, sherry, vinegar and light soy sauce to the pan and stir in. Bring the mixture to the boil, stirring constantly until it thickens.

VARIATIONS
• You can vary the proportions and types of beans used, depending on what you have in the store cupboard (pantry). Kidney beans and borlotti beans would work well and can be either interchanged with any of the beans used here, or combined with them.
• Try using mangetout or sugar snap peas in place of the green beans, if you prefer.

3 Rinse the beans and chickpeas and drain well. Place them in the ceramic cooking pot with the green beans and mushrooms and pour over the sauce. Stir well, then cover with the lid and cook on high for 3 hours.

4 Meanwhile, thinly slice the potatoes and par-boil them for 4 minutes. Drain well, then toss them in the oil so that they are lightly coated all over.

5 Stir the fresh herbs into the bean mixture and season with salt and pepper. Arrange the potato slices on top of the beans, overlapping them slightly so that they completely cover them. Cover the pot and cook for a further 2 hours, or until the potatoes are tender.

6 Place the ceramic cooking pot under a medium grill (broiler) and cook for 4–5 minutes to brown the potato topping. Serve garnished with herbs.

Nutritional information per portion: Energy 483Kcal/2042kJ; Protein 18.5g; Carbohydrate 73.3g, of which sugars 24.8g; Fat 13.8g, of which saturates 4.5g; Cholesterol 14mg; Calcium 134mg; Fibre 10.9g; Sodium 826mg.

ROOT VEGETABLE CASSEROLE with CARAWAY DUMPLINGS

Stirring soft cheese into the cooking juices gives this incredibly easy casserole a wonderfully creamy richness, while thickening and flavouring it at the same time. Light courgette dumplings spiced with caraway complete the meal.

SERVES 3

300ml/½ pint/1¼ cups dry (hard) cider
175ml/6fl oz/¾ cup boiling vegetable stock
2 leeks
2 carrots
2 small parsnips
225g/8oz potatoes
1 sweet potato, weighing about 175g/6oz
1 bay leaf
7.5ml/1½ tsp cornflour (cornstarch)
115g/4oz full-fat soft cheese with garlic
    and herbs
salt and ground black pepper

For the dumplings
115g/4oz/1 cup self-raising
    (self-rising) flour
5ml/1 tsp caraway seeds
50g/2oz/½ cup shredded vegetable suet
    (chilled, grated shortening)
1 courgette (zucchini), grated
about 75ml/5 tbsp cold water

1 Reserve 15ml/1 tbsp of the cider and pour the rest into the ceramic cooking pot with the stock. Cover with the lid and switch the slow cooker to high.

2 Meanwhile, prepare the vegetables. Trim the leeks and cut into 2cm/¾in slices. Peel the carrots, parsnips, potatoes and sweet potato and cut into 2cm/¾in chunks.

3 Add the vegetables to the ceramic cooking pot with the bay leaf. Cover with the lid and cook for 3 hours.

4 In a small bowl, blend the cornflour with the reserved cider. Add the cheese and mix together until combined, then gradually blend in a few spoonfuls of the cooking liquid. Pour over the vegetables and stir until thoroughly mixed. Season with salt and black pepper. Cover and cook for a further 1–2 hours, or until the vegetables are almost tender.

5 Towards the end of the cooking time, make the dumplings. Sift the flour into a bowl and stir in the caraway seeds, suet, courgettes, salt and black pepper. Stir in the water, adding a little more if necessary, to make a soft dough. With floured hands, shape the mixture into 12 dumplings, about the size of walnuts.

6 Carefully place the dumplings on top of the casserole, cover with the lid and cook for a further hour, or until the vegetables and dumplings are cooked. Adjust the seasoning and serve in warmed deep soup plates.

VARIATION
To make a non-vegetarian version of this dish, add some fried chopped bacon or pancetta to the pot with the vegetables.

Nutritional information per portion: Energy 616Kcal/2584kJ; Protein 11.9g; Carbohydrate 74.9g, of which sugars 17.1g; Fat 28.9g, of which saturates 15.9g; Cholesterol 35mg; Calcium 256mg; Fibre 9.5g; Sodium 369mg.

SPICY-HOT MIXED-BEAN CHILLI with CORNBREAD TOPPING

Inspired by traditional Texan cooking, this chilli combines Tex-mex with classic Texan cornbread. The delicious topping offers the starch component of the dish, making this dish a filling one-pot meal with no need for accompaniments.

SERVES 4

115g/4oz/generous ½ cup dried red
    kidney beans
115g/4oz/generous ½ cup dried
    black-eyed beans
1 bay leaf
15ml/1 tbsp vegetable oil
1 large onion, finely chopped
1 garlic clove, crushed
5ml/1 tsp ground cumin
5ml/1 tsp chilli powder
5ml/1 tsp mild paprika
2.5ml/½ tsp dried marjoram
450g/1lb mixed vegetables such
    as potatoes, carrots, aubergines
    (eggplant), parsnips and celery
1 vegetable stock cube
400g/14oz can chopped tomatoes
15ml/1 tbsp tomato purée (paste)
salt and ground black pepper

For the cornbread topping
250g/9oz/2¼ cups fine cornmeal
30ml/2 tbsp wholemeal
    (whole-wheat) flour
7.5ml/1½ tsp baking powder
1 egg, plus 1 egg yolk lightly beaten
300ml/½ pint/1¼ cups milk

1 Put the dried beans in a large bowl and pour over at least twice their volume of cold water. Leave to soak for at least 6 hours, or overnight.

2 Drain the beans and rinse well, then place in a pan with 600ml/1 pint/2½ cups of cold water and the bay leaf. Bring to the boil and boil rapidly for 10 minutes. Turn off the heat, leave to cool for a few minutes, then tip into the ceramic cooking pot and switch the slow cooker to high.

3 Heat the oil in a pan, add the onion and cook for 7–8 minutes. Add the garlic, cumin, chilli powder, paprika and marjoram and cook for 1 minute. Tip into the ceramic cooking pot and stir.

4 Prepare the vegetables, peeling or trimming them as necessary, then cut into 2cm/¾ in chunks.

5 Add the vegetables to the mixture, making sure that those that may discolour, such as potatoes and parsnips, are submerged. It doesn't matter if the other vegetables are not completely covered. Cover with the lid and cook for 3 hours, or until the beans are tender.

6 Add the stock cube and chopped tomatoes to the cooking pot, then stir in the tomato purée and season with salt and ground black pepper. Replace the lid and cook for a further 30 minutes until the mixture is at boiling point.

7 To make the topping, combine the cornmeal, flour, baking powder and a pinch of salt in a bowl. Make a well in the centre and add the egg, egg yolk and milk. Mix, then spoon over the bean mixture. Cover and cook for 1 hour, or until the topping is firm and cooked.

Nutritional information per portion: Energy 613Kcal/2595kJ; Protein 29.6g; Carbohydrate 97.4g, of which sugars 15.8g; Fat 14.5g, of which saturates 3.4g; Cholesterol 112mg; Calcium 257mg; Fibre 13.4g; Sodium 413mg.

PASTA with MUSHROOMS

Slow-cooking a mixture of mushrooms, garlic and sun-dried tomatoes together with white wine and stock makes a rich and well-flavoured pasta sauce. Served with warm ciabatta, this makes a truly excellent vegetarian supper dish.

SERVES 4

15g/½oz dried porcini mushrooms
120ml/4fl oz/½ cup hot water
2 cloves garlic, finely chopped
2 large pieces drained sun-dried tomato
    in olive oil, sliced into thin strips
120ml/4fl oz/½ cup dry white wine
120ml/4fl oz/½ cup vegetable stock
225g/8oz/2 cups chestnut mushrooms,
    thinly sliced
1 handful fresh flat leaf parsley, roughly
    chopped
450g/1lb/4 cups dried short pasta shapes,
    such as ruote, penne, fusilli or eliche
salt and ground black pepper
rocket and/or fresh flat leaf parsley,
    to garnish

1 Put the dried porcini mushrooms in a large bowl. Pour over the hot water and leave to soak for 15 minutes.

2 While the mushrooms are soaking, put the garlic, tomatoes, wine, stock and chestnut mushrooms into the ceramic cooking pot and switch the slow cooker to high.

3 Tip the porcini mushrooms into a sieve (strainer) set over a bowl, then squeeze them with your hands to release as much liquid as possible. Reserve the soaking liquid. Chop the porcini finely. Add the liquid and the chopped porcini to the ceramic cooking pot, and cover the slow cooker with the lid. Cook on high for 1 hour, stirring halfway through cooking time to make sure that the mushrooms cook evenly.

4 Switch the slow cooker to the low setting and cook for a further 1–2 hours, until the mushrooms are tender.

5 Cook the pasta in boiling salted water for 10 minutes, or according to the instructions on the packet. Drain the pasta and tip it into a warmed large bowl. Stir the chopped parsley into the sauce and season to taste with salt and black pepper. Add the sauce to the pasta and toss well. Serve immediately, garnished with rocket and/or parsley.

VARIATIONS

Fresh wild mushrooms can be used instead of chestnut mushrooms, although they are seasonal and often expensive. A cheaper alternative is to use a box of mixed wild mushrooms, available from good supermarkets and delicatessens.

Nutritional information per portion: Energy 420Kcal/1787kJ; Protein 15.1g; Carbohydrate 84.9g, of which sugars 5.1g; Fat 2.6g, of which saturates 0.3g; Cholesterol 0 mg; Calcium 61mg; Fibre 4.8g; Sodium 14mg.

MUSHROOM AND COURGETTE LASAGNE

This is the perfect main-course lasagne for vegetarians. Adding dried porcini to fresh chestnut mushrooms intensifies the flavour. The dish can be made and assembled in the slow cooker early in the day, then left to cook. Serve with crusty Italian bread.

SERVES 6

For the tomato sauce
15g/½oz dried porcini mushrooms
120ml/4fl oz/½ cup hot water
1 onion
1 carrot
1 celery stick
30ml/2 tbsp olive oil
2 x 400g/14oz cans chopped tomatoes
15ml/1 tbsp sun-dried tomato paste
5ml/1 tsp granulated sugar
5ml/1 tsp dried basil or mixed herbs

For the lasagne
30ml/2 tbsp olive oil
50g/2oz/¼ cup butter
450g/1lb courgettes (zucchini), thinly sliced
1 onion, finely chopped
450g/1lb/6 cups chestnut mushrooms, thinly sliced
2 garlic cloves, crushed
6–8 non-pre-cook lasagne sheets
50g/2oz/½ cup freshly grated Parmesan cheese
salt and ground black pepper
fresh oregano leaves, to garnish
Italian-style bread, to serve (optional)

For the white sauce
40g/1½oz/3 tbsp butter
40g/1½oz/⅓ cup plain (all-purpose) flour
900ml/1½ pints/3¾ cups milk
freshly grated nutmeg

1 Put the dried porcini mushrooms in a bowl. Pour over the hot water and leave to soak for 15 minutes. Tip the porcini and liquid into a sieve (strainer) set over a bowl and squeeze the mushrooms with your hands to release as much liquid as possible. Chop the mushrooms finely and set aside. Strain the soaking liquid through a fine sieve and reserve.

2 Chop the onion, carrot and celery finely. Heat the olive oil in a pan and fry the vegetables until softened. Place in a food processor with the tomatoes, tomato paste, sugar, herbs, porcini and soaking liquid, and blend to a purée.

3 For the lasagne, heat the olive oil and half the butter in a large pan. Add half the courgette slices and season to taste. Cook over a medium heat, turning the courgettes frequently, for 5–8 minutes, until lightly coloured on both sides. Remove from the pan with a slotted spoon and transfer to a bowl. Repeat with the remaining courgettes.

4 Melt the remaining butter in the pan, and cook the onion for 3 minutes, stirring. Add the chestnut mushrooms, chopped porcini and garlic and cook for 5 minutes. Add to the courgettes.

5 For the white sauce, melt the butter in a large pan, then add the flour and cook, stirring, for 1 minute. Turn off the heat and gradually whisk in the milk. Bring to the boil and cook, stirring, until the sauce is smooth and thick. Season with salt, black pepper and nutmeg.

6 Ladle half of the tomato sauce into the ceramic cooking pot and spread out to cover the base. Add half the vegetable mixture, spreading it evenly. Top with about one-third of the white sauce, then about half the lasagne sheets, breaking them to fit the cooking pot. Repeat these layers, then top with the remaining white sauce and sprinkle with grated Parmesan cheese.

7 Cover the ceramic cooking pot with the lid and cook on low for 2–2½ hours or until the lasagne is tender. If you like, brown the top under a medium grill (broiler). Garnish with a sprinkling of fresh oregano leaves, and serve with fresh Italian-style bread.

Nutritional information per portion: Energy 421Kcal/1757kJ; Protein 15.5g; Carbohydrate 32.9g, of which sugars 15g; Fat 26.2g, of which saturates 12.4g; Cholesterol 49mg; Calcium 346mg; Fibre 3.8g; Sodium 310mg.

SWEET PUMPKIN and PEANUT CURRY

Rich, sweet, spicy and fragrant, the flavours of this delicious Thai-style curry really come together with long, slow cooking. Serve with rice or noodles for a substantial supper dish.

3 Add the lime leaves, galangal, pumpkin and sweet potatoes to the cooking pot. Pour the stock and 150ml/¼ pint/⅔ cup of the coconut milk over the vegetables, and stir to combine. Cover with the lid and cook on high for 1½ hours.

4 Stir the mushrooms, soy sauce and Thai fish sauce into the curry, then add the chopped peanuts and pour in the remaining coconut milk. Cover and cook on high for a further 3 hours, or until the vegetables are very tender.

5 Spoon the curry into warmed serving bowls, garnish with the pumpkin seeds and chillies, and serve immediately.

SERVES 4

30ml/2 tbsp vegetable oil
4 garlic cloves, crushed
4 shallots, finely chopped
30ml/2 tbsp yellow curry paste
400ml/14fl oz/1⅔ cups near-boiling
    vegetable stock
300ml/½ pint/1¼ cups coconut milk
2 kaffir lime leaves, torn
15ml/1 tbsp chopped fresh galangal
450g/1lb pumpkin, peeled, seeded
    and diced
225g/8oz sweet potatoes, diced
90g/3½oz/1½ cups chestnut
    mushrooms, sliced
15ml/1 tbsp soy sauce
30ml/2 tbsp Thai fish sauce
90g/3½ oz/scant 1 cup peanuts, roasted
    and chopped
50g/2oz/⅓ cup pumpkin seeds, toasted,
    and fresh green chilli flowers, to garnish

1 Heat the oil in a frying pan. Add the garlic and shallots and cook over a medium heat, stirring occasionally, for 10 minutes, until softened and beginning to turn golden.

2 Add the yellow curry paste to the pan and stir-fry over a medium heat for 30 seconds, until fragrant. Tip the mixture into the ceramic cooking pot.

COOK'S TIP
Fresh chilli flowers make an impressive garnish for a special occasion dinner, and will make the curry look authentically Thai. To make chilli flowers, hold each chilli by the stem and slit the chilli in half lengthways, keeping the stem end intact. Continue slitting the chilli in the same way to make thin strips. Put the chillies in a bowl of iced water and leave for several hours to curl up like flower petals.

Nutritional information per portion: Energy 337Kcal/1404kJ; Protein 10.3g; Carbohydrate 21.7g, of which sugars 10.8g; Fat 23.8g, of which saturates 4g; Cholesterol 0mg; Calcium 168mg; Fibre 5.1g; Sodium 554mg.

VEGETABLE KASHMIRI

Delicious vegetables cooked in a spicy and aromatic yogurt sauce make a lovely
vegetarian main meal. You can use any combination of your favourite vegetables.

SERVES 4

10ml/2 tsp cumin seeds
8 black peppercorns
2 green cardamom pods, seeds only
5cm/2in cinnamon stick
2.5ml/½ tsp grated nutmeg
45ml/3 tbsp vegetable oil
1 fresh green chilli, seeded and chopped
2.5cm/1in piece of fresh root ginger, grated
5ml/1 tsp chilli powder
2.5ml/½ tsp salt
2 large potatoes, cut into 2.5cm/
    1in chunks
225g/8oz cauliflower florets
400ml/14fl oz/1⅔ cups boiling
    vegetable stock
150ml/¼ pint/⅔ cup Greek (US strained
    plain) yogurt
225g/8oz okra, thickly sliced
toasted flaked (sliced) almonds and
    sprigs of fresh coriander (cilantro),
    to garnish

4 In a bowl, stir a few spoonfuls of the hot stock into the yogurt, then pour over the vegetable mixture, and stir until thoroughly combined.

5 Add the okra to the pot, stir, cover and cook for a further 1½–2 hours, or until all the vegetables are very tender.

6 Serve the curry straight from the ceramic cooking pot, or spoon into a warmed serving dish. Sprinkle with toasted almonds and fresh coriander sprigs to garnish.

1 Put the cumin seeds, peppercorns, cardamom seeds, cinnamon stick and nutmeg in a mortar or spice grinder, and grind to a fine powder.

2 Heat the oil in a frying pan, add the chilli and ginger and fry for 2 minutes, stirring all the time. Add the chilli powder, salt and ground spice mixture, and fry gently for 2–3 minutes, stirring constantly to prevent the spices from sticking to the pan.

3 Transfer the mixture to the ceramic cooking pot and stir in the potatoes and cauliflower. Pour in the stock, cover with the lid, and cook on high for 2 hours.

Nutritional information per portion: Energy 294Kcal/1231kJ; Protein 9g; Carbohydrate 35.5g, of which sugars 7g; Fat 13.8g, of which saturates 4g; Cholesterol 6mg; Calcium 161mg; Fibre 5.1g; Sodium 427mg.

VEGETABLE and CASHEW NUT BIRYANI

*Full of the flavours of India, this hearty supper dish is great for chilly winter evenings.
The nuts add protein, and the combination of aubergines and parsnips is delicious.*

SERVES 4

1 small aubergine (eggplant), sliced
3 onions
2 garlic cloves
2.5cm/1in piece of fresh root
 ginger, peeled
about 60ml/4 tbsp sunflower oil
3 parsnips, chopped into 2cm/¾in pieces
5ml/1 tsp ground cumin
5ml/1 tsp ground coriander
2.5ml/½ tsp chilli powder
750ml/1¼ pints/3 cups boiling
 vegetable stock
1 red (bell) pepper, seeded and sliced
275g/10oz/generous 1½ cups easy-cook
 (converted) basmati or white rice
175g/6oz/1½ cup unsalted cashew nuts
40g/1½oz/¼ cup sultanas (golden raisins)
salt and ground black pepper
2 hard-boiled eggs, quartered, and sprigs
 of fresh coriander to garnish

1 Layer the aubergine slices in a strainer or colander, lightly sprinkle with salt and leave to drain for 30 minutes. Rinse thoroughly under cold running water, pat dry and cut into bitesize pieces.

2 Roughly chop one of the onions and place in a food processor with the garlic and ginger. Add 45ml/3 tbsp cold water and process to a smooth paste.

3 Finely slice the remaining onions. Heat 30ml/2 tbsp of the oil in a large frying pan, add the onions and fry gently for 10–15 minutes until they are soft and golden. Add the aubergine and parsnips and cook for 3–4 minutes to soften. Transfer to the ceramic cooking pot.

4 Add 15ml/1 tbsp oil to the pan, add the onion paste and cook, stirring, for 3–4 minutes. Stir in the cumin, coriander and chilli powder and cook for 1 minute.

5 Gradually stir one-third of the stock into the pan, then transfer the mixture to the ceramic cooking pot and switch the slow cooker to high. Add the remaining stock and the pepper, then season and cover with the lid. Cook for 2–3 hours, or until the vegetables are almost tender.

6 Spoon the rice in a layer over the vegetables, then re-cover and cook for 45 minutes–1 hour until the rice is tender and most of the stock has been absorbed. If the rice becomes too dry, add an extra 30ml/2 tbsp stock.

7 Meanwhile, heat the remaining 15ml/ 1 tbsp of oil in a clean frying pan, add the cashew nuts and stir-fry for about 2 minutes. Add the sultanas and fry for a few seconds until they swell up. Remove the pan from the heat and drain the nuts and sultanas on kitchen paper.

8 Add half the cashew nuts and sultanas to the vegetable rice and gently fold in using a fork. Turn off the slow cooker, cover with the lid and leave the biryani to stand for 5 minutes to finish cooking.

9 Spoon the vegetable biryani on to a warmed serving dish and scatter with the remaining nuts and sultanas. Garnish with quartered eggs and fresh coriander, and serve immediately.

Nutritional information per portion: Energy 801Kcal/3360kJ; Protein 18.7g; Carbohydrate 103.4g, of which sugars 25.7g; Fat 37.6g, of which saturates 6.7g; Cholesterol 0mg; Calcium 129mg; Fibre 9.2g; Sodium 230mg.

PILAFF with SAFFRON and PICKLED WALNUTS

Fragrant saffron gives this lovely rice dish a warm, spiced flavour and glorious colour. The pickled walnuts, which are available in large supermarkets and delicatessens, have a strong, really distinctive flavour that goes well with the spices, pine nuts and dried fruit.

SERVES 4

5ml/1 tsp saffron strands
50g/2oz/½ cup pine nuts
45ml/3 tbsp olive oil
1 large onion, finely chopped
3 garlic cloves, crushed
1.5ml/¼ tsp ground allspice
4cm/1½in piece fresh root ginger, grated
750ml/1¼ pints/3 cups boiling
    vegetable stock
300g/10oz/generous 1½ cups easy-cook
    (converted) rice
50g/2oz/½ cup pickled walnuts, drained
    and roughly chopped
40g/1½oz/¼ cup raisins
45ml/3 tbsp roughly chopped fresh parsley
    or coriander (cilantro)
salt and ground black pepper
parsley or coriander (cilantro) leaves,
    to garnish
natural (plain) yogurt, to serve

1 Put the saffron strands in a heatproof bowl with 15ml/1 tbsp boiling water and leave to stand.

2 Meanwhile, heat a large frying pan and dry-fry the pine nuts until golden. Set them aside until needed.

COOK'S TIP
Saffron is the most expensive spice in the world because the stigmas of the saffron crocus have to be hand-picked. Ground turmeric makes a cheaper alternative and gives a similar golden yellow colour and warm flavour and aroma. Simply leave out step 1 and stir in 2.5ml/½ tsp ground turmeric with the allspice and the ginger.

3 Heat the oil in a pan, add the onion and fry gently for 8 minutes. Stir in the garlic, allspice and ginger and cook for 2 minutes, stirring constantly. Transfer the mixture to the ceramic cooking pot.

4 Pour the boiling vegetable stock into the cooking pot and stir to combine, then cover with the lid and switch the slow cooker to high. Cook for 1 hour.

5 Sprinkle the rice into the cooking pot, then stir to mix thoroughly. Re-cover with the lid and cook for 1 hour, or until the rice is almost tender and most of the stock has been absorbed. Add a little extra boiling stock or water to the pot if the mixture is already becoming dry.

6 Stir the saffron and soaking liquid into the rice, then add the pine nuts, pickled walnuts, raisins and parsley or coriander and stir well to combine. Season to taste with salt and ground black pepper.

7 Re-cover the ceramic cooking pot with the lid and cook for a further 15 minutes, until the rice is very tender and all the ingredients are completely warmed through. Garnish with fresh parsley or coriander leaves and provide a bowl of natural yogurt on the side for guests to serve themselves.

VARIATION
For a spicy mushroom pilaff, cook 3 sliced shallots in 15ml/1 tbsp oil until soft. Stir in 2.5ml/½ tsp ground turmeric and 5ml/1 tsp each cumin and coriander. Transfer to the ceramic cooking pot. Add 750ml/1¼ pints/3 cups hot vegetable stock. Cover with the lid and cook on high for 30 minutes. Stir in 300g/10oz/ generous 1½ cups easy-cook (converted) rice and cook for 30 minutes. Fry 225g/8oz mixed mushrooms in 25g/1oz butter until soft, then stir into the ceramic cooking pot and season to taste. Cook for a further 30 minutes, then serve.

Nutritional information per portion: Energy 585Kcal/2456kJ; Protein 10.2g; Carbohydrate 77.1g, of which sugars 11.1g; Fat 28.5g, of which saturates 3.1g; Cholesterol 0mg; Calcium 72mg; Fibre 2g; Sodium 222mg.

ROSEMARY RISOTTO with BORLOTTI BEANS

Using easy-cook Italian rice means that all the wine and stock can be added at the
same time, rather than ladleful by ladleful, as with a traditional risotto. The gentle,
constant heat of the slow cooker produces a delicious risotto that is still thick and creamy.

SERVES 3

400g/14oz can borlotti beans
15g/½oz/1 tbsp butter
15ml/1 tbsp olive oil
1 onion, finely chopped
2 garlic cloves, crushed
120ml/4fl oz/½ cup dry white wine
225g/8oz/generous 1 cup easy-cook
   (converted) Italian rice
750ml/1¼ pints/3 cups boiling
   vegetable stock
60ml/4 tbsp mascarpone cheese
5ml/1 tsp chopped fresh rosemary
65g/2½oz/¾ cup freshly grated
   Parmesan cheese, plus extra to
   serve (optional)
salt and ground black pepper

1 Drain the borlotti beans in a sieve, rinse well under cold running water and drain again. Place about two-thirds of the beans in a food processor or blender and process to a coarse purée. Tip the remaining beans into a bowl and set aside for later.

2 Heat the butter and oil in a pan, add the onion and garlic and fry gently for 7–8 minutes until soft. Transfer the mixture to the ceramic cooking pot and stir in the wine and bean purée. Cover with the lid and cook on high for 1 hour.

3 Add the rice to the pot, then stir in the stock. Re-cover with the lid and cook for about 45 minutes, stirring once halfway through cooking. The rice should be almost tender and most of the stock should have been absorbed.

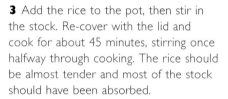

4 Stir the reserved beans, mascarpone and rosemary into the risotto. Cover again with the lid and cook for a further 15 minutes, until the rice is tender but still has a little bite.

5 Stir the Parmesan cheese into the risotto and season to taste with salt and ground black pepper. Turn off the slow cooker, cover and leave to stand for about 5 minutes, so that the risotto absorbs the flavours fully and the rice completes cooking.

6 Spoon the rice into warmed serving bowls and serve immediately, sprinkled with extra Parmesan, if you like.

VARIATIONS
• Try using different herbs to vary the flavour. Fresh thyme or marjoram would make a good alternative to rosemary.
• To make a lower-fat version of this dish, use Quark cheese in place of the mascarpone. It offers the same creamy texture with much less fat.

Nutritional information per portion: Energy 651Kcal/2740kJ; Protein 25g; Carbohydrate 87g, of which sugars 4.6g; Fat 22.2g, of which saturates 10.5g; Cholesterol 41.9mg; Calcium 357mg; Fibre 7.1g; Sodium 1462mg.

COUSCOUS-STUFFED SWEET PEPPERS

The peppers are softened in boiling water before filling to ensure really tender results. Choose red, yellow or orange peppers for this dish, but avoid green ones because they tend to discolour after a couple of hours of cooking and do not have such a sweet taste.

SERVES 4

4 (bell) peppers
75g/3oz/½ cup instant couscous
75ml/2½fl oz/⅓ cup boiling
   vegetable stock
15ml/1 tbsp olive oil
10ml/2 tsp white wine vinegar
50g/2oz dried apricots, finely chopped
75g/3oz feta cheese, cut into tiny cubes
3 ripe tomatoes, skinned, seeded
   and chopped
45ml/3 tbsp toasted pine nuts
30ml/2 tbsp chopped fresh parsley
salt and ground black pepper
flat leaf parsley, to garnish

1 Halve the peppers lengthways, then remove the core and seeds. Place the peppers in a large heatproof bowl and pour over boiling water to cover. Leave to stand for about 3 minutes, then drain thoroughly and set aside.

2 Meanwhile, put the couscous in a small bowl and pour over the stock. Leave to stand for about 5 minutes until all the water has been absorbed.

3 Using a fork, fluff up the couscous, then stir in the oil, vinegar, apricots, feta cheese, tomatoes, pine nuts and parsley, and season to taste with salt and ground black pepper.

COOK'S TIP
Be sure to taste the stuffing before adding any more salt. Feta cheese can be very salty already, so you may not need to add any extra.

4 Fill the peppers with the couscous mixture, gently packing it down using the back of a spoon.

5 Place the peppers, filling side up, in the ceramic cooking pot, then pour 150ml/¼ pint/⅔ cup near-boiling water around them.

6 Cover with the lid, switch the slow cooker to high and cook for 2–3 hours, or until the peppers are tender. Brown under a hot grill (broiler) for 2 minutes and serve garnished with fresh parsley.

Nutritional information per portion: Energy 303Kcal/1266kJ; Protein 33.7g; Carbohydrate 33.6g, of which sugars 17g; Fat 15.8g, of which saturates 3.9g; Cholesterol 13mg; Calcium 105mg; Fibre 4.3g; Sodium 285mg.

PARSNIPS and CHICKPEAS in GARLIC, ONION, CHILLI and GINGER PASTE

The sweet flavour of parsnips goes very well with the spices in this Indian-style vegetable stew. It makes an ideal meal for vegetarians, because chickpeas are high in protein. Complete the meal with warm Indian breads, such as chapati or naan.

SERVES 4

5 garlic cloves, finely chopped
1 small onion, chopped
5cm/2in piece fresh root ginger, chopped
2 green chillies, seeded and finely chopped
75ml/5 tbsp cold water
60ml/4 tbsp groundnut (peanut) oil
5ml/1 tsp cumin seeds
10ml/2 tsp coriander seeds
5ml/1 tsp ground turmeric
2.5ml/½ tsp chilli powder or mild paprika
50g/2oz/½ cup cashew nuts, toasted and
    ground
225g/8oz tomatoes, peeled and chopped
400g/14oz can chickpeas, drained
    and rinsed
900g/2lb parsnips, cut into
    2cm/¾in chunks
350ml/12 fl oz/1½ cups boiling
    vegetable stock
juice of 1 lime, to taste
salt and ground black pepper
chopped fresh coriander (cilantro) leaves,
    toasted cashew nuts and natural (plain)
    yogurt, to serve

1 Reserve 10ml/2 tsp of the garlic, then place the remainder in a food processor or blender with the onion, ginger and half the chilli. Add the water and process to make a smooth paste.

2 Heat the oil in a large frying pan, add the cumin seeds and cook for about 30 seconds. Stir in the coriander seeds, turmeric, chilli powder or paprika and the ground cashew nuts. Add the ginger and chilli paste and cook, stirring frequently, until the paste bubbles and the water begins to evaporate.

COOK'S TIPS
• Buy spices in small quantities and store them in a cool, dark place. Try to use them within a few months because they quickly lose their flavour.
• Frying spices before adding to the cooking pot intensifies their taste.

3 Add the tomatoes to the pan and cook for 1 minute. Transfer the mixture to the ceramic cooking pot and switch the slow cooker to high.

4 Add the chickpeas and parsnips to the pot and stir to coat in the spicy tomato mixture, then stir in the stock and season with salt and pepper. Cover with the lid and cook on high for 4 hours, or until the parsnips are tender.

5 Stir half the lime juice, the reserved garlic and green chilli into the stew. Re-cover and cook for 30 minutes more, then taste and add more lime juice if needed. Spoon on to plates and sprinkle with fresh coriander leaves and toasted cashew nuts. Serve immediately with a generous spoonful of natural yogurt.

Nutritional information per portion: Energy 453Kcal/1899kJ; Protein 14.8g; Carbohydrate 50.1g, of which sugars 16.6g; Fat 23g, of which saturates 4.3g; Cholesterol 0mg; Calcium 148mg; Fibre 15.8g; Sodium 394mg.

ONIONS STUFFED with GOAT'S CHEESE and SUN-DRIED TOMATOES

Long, slow cooking is the best way to get maximum flavour from onions, so the slow cooker is the natural choice for these delicious stuffed onions. Serve with a rice or cracked wheat pilaff to make a great vegetarian main course.

SERVES 4

2 large onions
30ml/2 tbsp olive oil (or use oil from
    the sun-dried tomatoes)
150g/5oz/⅔ cup firm goat's cheese,
    crumbled or cubed
50g/2oz/1 cup fresh white breadcrumbs
8 sun-dried tomatoes in olive oil, drained
    and chopped
1 garlic clove, finely chopped
2.5ml/½ tsp fresh thyme
30ml/2 tbsp chopped fresh parsley
1 small egg, beaten
45ml/3 tbsp pine nuts
150ml/¼ pint/⅔ cup near-boiling
    vegetable stock
salt and ground black pepper
chopped fresh parsley, to garnish

1 Bring a large pan of water to the boil. Add the whole onions in their skins and boil for 10 minutes.

2 Drain the onions and leave until cool enough to handle, then cut each onion in half horizontally and peel. Using a teaspoon, remove the centre of each onion, leaving a thick shell.

3 Very finely chop the flesh from one of the scooped-out onion halves and place in a bowl. Stir in 5ml/1 tsp of the olive oil or oil from the sun-dried tomatoes, then add the goat's cheese, breadcrumbs, sun-dried tomatoes, garlic, thyme, parsley, egg and pine nuts. Season with salt and pepper and mix well.

4 Divide the stuffing among the onions and cover each one with a piece of oiled foil. Brush the base of the ceramic cooking pot with 15ml/1 tbsp of the oil, then pour in the stock. Arrange the onions in the base of the cooking pot, cover with the lid and cook on high for 4 hours, or until the onions are very tender but still hold their shape.

5 Carefully remove the onions from the slow cooker and transfer them to a grill (broiler) pan. Remove the foil and drizzle the tops with the remaining 10ml/1 tsp oil. Brown under a medium grill for 3–4 minutes, taking care not to burn the nuts. Serve immediately, garnished with fresh chopped parsley.

VARIATIONS
• Try using feta cheese in place of the goat's cheese and add chopped fresh mint, currants and pitted black olives in place of the other flavourings.
• Alternatively, use 175g/6oz Roquefort or Gorgonzola in place of the goat's cheese and add about 75g/3oz/¾ cup chopped walnuts and 115g/4oz/1 cup very finely chopped celery in place of the sun-dried tomatoes and pine nuts.

Nutritional information per portion: Energy 330Kcal/1370kJ; Protein 13.8g; Carbohydrate 14.3g, of which sugars 11.3g; Fat 24.7g, of which saturates 8.4g; Cholesterol 83.7mg; Calcium 98mg; Fibre 1.9g; Sodium 349mg.

ORANGE CANDIED SWEET POTATOES

Candied sweet potatoes are the classic accompaniment to a traditional Thanksgiving dinner. For a really fresh, festive look, serve with extra orange segments.

SERVES 8

900g/2lb sweet potatoes
150ml/¼ pint/⅔ cup orange juice
30ml/2 tbsp maple syrup
5ml/1 tsp freshly grated ginger
2.5ml/½ tsp ground cinnamon
2.5ml/½ tsp ground cardamom
5ml/1 tsp salt
ground black pepper
orange segments, to serve (optional)

VARIATION
You can serve this rich vegetable dish as a purée if you prefer (but omit the orange segments). Transfer the cooked candied sweet potatoes to a food processor, adding a little of the sauce, and blend until smooth. You may need to add a little more of the sauce to make a soft, creamy, spoonable purée.

1 Peel the potatoes and cut them into 2cm/¾in cubes. Put them in a large heatproof bowl and pour over just enough boiling water to cover. Leave to stand for 5 minutes.

2 Meanwhile, put the orange juice, maple syrup, spices and salt in the ceramic cooking pot and stir to mix. Switch the slow cooker to high.

3 Drain the sweet potato cubes and add to the ceramic cooking pot. Gently stir to coat in the spicy orange mixture. Cover and cook for 4–5 hours, until tender, stirring twice during cooking.

4 Stir the orange segments, if using, into the sweet potatoes, and season to taste with pepper. Serve immediately.

Nutritional information per portion: Energy 53Kcal/226kJ; Protein 2.9g; Carbohydrate 13.7g, of which sugars 11.8g; Fat 0g, of which saturates 0g; Cholesterol 0mg; Calcium 5mg; Fibre 0.2g; Sodium 158mg.

POTATO, ONION and GARLIC GRATIN

This tasty side dish makes the perfect accompaniment to roasts, stews and grilled meat or fish. Cooking the potatoes in stock with onions and garlic gives them a really rich flavour.

3 Pour just enough of the stock into the pot to cover the potatoes. Cover with the lid and cook on low for 8–10 hours, or on high for 4–5 hours, until the potatoes are tender.

4 If you like, brown the potatoes under a hot grill (broiler) for 3–4 minutes. Serve sprinkled with a little salt and ground black pepper.

VARIATIONS
• To make this dish more substantial, sprinkle 115g/4oz/1 cup of grated Gruyère cheese over the top of the cooked potatoes and brown under a preheated grill (broiler) for 3–4 minutes until golden-brown and bubbling.
• Alternatively, crumble 165g/5½oz/scant 1 cup soft goat's cheese on the gratin 30 minutes before the end of cooking.
• To vary the flavour, try using chopped rosemary or sage in place of the thyme, or use crushed juniper berries instead.

SERVES 4

40g/1½oz/3 tbsp butter
1 large onion, finely sliced into rings
2–4 garlic cloves, finely chopped
2.5ml/½ tsp dried thyme
900g/2lb waxy potatoes, very finely sliced
450ml/¾ pint/scant 2 cups boiling
    vegetable, chicken, beef or
    lamb stock
sea salt and ground black pepper

1 Grease the inside of the ceramic cooking pot with 15g/½oz/1 tbsp of the butter. Spoon a thin layer of onions on to the base of the cooking pot, then sprinkle over a little of the chopped garlic, thyme, salt and pepper.

2 Carefully arrange an overlapping layer of potato slices on top of the onion mixture in the ceramic cooking pot. Continue to layer the ingredients in the pot until all the onions, garlic, herbs and potatoes are used up, finishing with a layer of sliced potatoes.

Nutritional information per portion: Energy 260Kcal/1092kJ; Protein 5.1g; Carbohydrate 41.9g, of which sugars 6.4g; Fat 9.1g, of which saturates 5.4g; Cholesterol 21mg; Calcium 31mg; Fibre 3.3g; Sodium 171mg.

BROWN RICE with LIME and LEMON GRASS

It is unusual to find brown rice given the Thai treatment, but the nutty flavour of the grains is enhanced by the fragrance of limes and lemon grass in this delicious dish.

3 Heat the oil in a large pan. Add the onion and cook over a low heat for 5 minutes. Stir in the ginger, coriander and cumin seeds, lemon grass and lime rind and cook for 2–3 minutes. Tip the mixture into the ceramic cooking pot.

4 Pour the stock into the pot, briefly stir to combine, then cover with the lid and switch the slow cooker to high. Cook for 1 hour.

5 Rinse the rice in cold water until the water runs clear, then drain and add to the ceramic cooking pot. Cook for 45 minutes–1½ hours, or until the rice is tender and has absorbed the stock.

6 Stir the fresh coriander into the rice and season with salt and pepper. Fluff up the grains with a fork and serve garnished with strips of spring onions and toasted coconut, and lime wedges.

SERVES 4

2 limes
1 lemon grass stalk
15ml/1 tbsp sunflower oil
1 onion, chopped
2.5cm/1in piece fresh root ginger, peeled
  and very finely chopped
7.5ml/1½ tsp coriander seeds
7.5ml/1½ tsp cumin seeds
750ml/1¼ pints/3 cups boiling
  vegetable stock
275g/10oz/1½ cups easy-cook (converted)
  brown rice
60ml/4 tbsp chopped fresh coriander
  (cilantro)
salt and ground black pepper
spring onions (scallion), toasted coconut
  strips and lime wedges, to garnish

1 Using a cannelle knife (zester) or fine grater, pare the rind from the limes, taking care not to remove any of the bitter white pith. Set the rind aside.

2 Cut off the lower portion of the lemon grass stalk, discarding the papery top end of the stalk. Finely chop the lemon grass and set aside.

Nutritional information per portion: Energy 308Kcal/1304kJ; Protein 5.6g; Carbohydrate 64g, of which sugars 5.1g; Fat 5.1g, of which saturates 0.9g; Cholesterol 0mg; Calcium 17mg; Fibre 2g; Sodium 129mg.

SPICY TAMARIND CHICKPEAS

Chickpeas make a good base for many vegetarian dishes. Here, they are tossed with sharp tamarind and spices to make a deliciously light vegetarian lunch or side dish.

SERVES 4

225g/8oz/1¼ cups dried chickpeas
50g/2oz tamarind pulp
45ml/3 tbsp vegetable oil
2.5ml/½ tsp cumin seeds
1 onion, very finely chopped
2 garlic cloves, crushed
2.5cm/1in piece of fresh root ginger,
    peeled and grated
1 fresh green chilli, finely chopped
5ml/1 tsp ground cumin
5ml/1 tsp ground coriander
1.5ml/¼ tsp ground turmeric
2.5ml/½ tsp salt
225g/8oz tomatoes, skinned
    and finely chopped
2.5ml/½ tsp garam masala
chopped fresh chillies and chopped
    onion, to garnish

1 Put the chickpeas in a large bowl and pour over cold water to cover. Leave to soak for at least 8 hours, or overnight.

2 Drain the chickpeas and put in a pan with at least double the volume of cold water. (Do not add salt to the water because this will toughen the chickpeas and spoil the final dish.)

3 Bring the water to the boil and boil vigorously for at least 10 minutes. Skim off any scum, then drain the chickpeas and tip into the ceramic cooking pot.

4 Pour 750ml/1¼ pints/3 cups of near-boiling water over the chickpeas and switch the slow cooker to high. Cover with the lid and cook for 4–5 hours, or until the chickpeas are just tender.

5 Towards the end of the cooking time, put the tamarind in a bowl and break up with a fork. Pour over 120ml/4fl oz/½ cup of boiling water and leave to soak for about 15 minutes.

6 Tip the tamarind into a sieve (strainer) and discard the water. Rub the pulp through, discarding any stones and fibre.

7 Heat the oil in a large pan, add the cumin seeds and fry for 2 minutes, until they splutter. Add the onion, garlic and ginger and fry for 5 minutes. Add the cumin, coriander, turmeric, chilli and salt and fry for 3–4 minutes. Add the tomatoes, garam masala and tamarind pulp and bring to the boil.

8 Stir the tamarind mixture into the chickpeas, cover and cook for a further 1 hour. Either serve straight from the ceramic cooking pot, or spoon into a warmed serving dish and garnish with chopped chilli and onion.

COOK'S TIP
To save time, make double the quantity of tamarind pulp and freeze in ice-cube trays. It will keep for up to 2 months.

Nutritional information per portion: Energy 277Kcal/1164kJ; Protein 12.8g; Carbohydrate 32.6g, of which sugars 5.3g; Fat 11.5g, of which saturates 1.3g; Cholesterol 0mg; Calcium 103mg; Fibre 7.1g; Sodium 274mg.

COCONUT, TOMATO and LENTIL DHAL with TOASTED ALMONDS

Richly flavoured and utterly moreish, this lentil dish makes a filling supper served with warm naan bread and plain yogurt. Split red lentils give the dish a vibrant colour, but you could use larger yellow split peas instead, although they will take a little longer to cook.

SERVES 4

30ml/2 tbsp vegetable oil
1 large onion, very finely chopped
3 garlic cloves, chopped
1 carrot, diced
10ml/2 tsp cumin seeds
10ml/2 tsp yellow mustard seeds
2.5cm/1in piece fresh root ginger, grated
10ml/2 tsp ground turmeric
5ml/1 tsp mild chilli powder
5ml/1 tsp garam masala
225g/8oz/1 cup split red lentils
400ml/14fl oz/1⅔ cup boiling
   vegetable stock
400ml/14fl oz/1⅔ cups coconut milk
5 tomatoes, peeled, seeded and chopped
juice of 2 limes
60ml/4 tbsp chopped fresh coriander
   (cilantro)
salt and ground black pepper
25g/1oz/¼ cup flaked (sliced) almonds,
   toasted, to garnish

1 Heat the oil in a pan. Add the onion and cook for 5 minutes, until softened, stirring occasionally.

2 Add the garlic, carrot, cumin, mustard seeds and ginger to the pan. Cook for 3–4 minutes, stirring, until the seeds begin to pop, the aromas are released and the carrot softens slightly.

COOK'S TIP
This dish reheats well, so it is worth making a double batch and freezing half. Thaw, then add a little water and reheat.

3 Add the ground turmeric, chilli powder and garam masala to the pan and cook, stirring, for 1 minute, or until the flavours begin to mingle.

4 Tip the mixture into the ceramic cooking pot. Add the lentils, stock, coconut milk and tomatoes and season with salt and pepper. Stir well and cover the pot with the lid.

5 Cook on high for 2 hours, or until the lentils are soft, stirring halfway through the cooking time to prevent the lentils sticking. Stir the lime juice and 45ml/ 3 tbsp of fresh coriander into the dhal.

6 Check the seasoning and cook for a further 30 minutes. To serve, sprinkle with the remaining fresh coriander and the toasted almonds.

Nutritional information per portion: Energy 335Kcal/1421kJ; Protein 16.6g; Carbohydrate 46.3g, of which sugars 14.3g; Fat 10.6g, of which saturates 1.4g; Cholesterol 0mg; Calcium 99mg; Fibre 5.5g; Sodium 230mg.

SPICED INDIAN RICE with SPINACH, TOMATOES and CASHEW NUTS

This all-in-one rice dish makes a delicious, nutritious vegetarian meal but can also be served as an accompaniment to a spicy meat curry. Ghee, the clarified butter used in much Indian cooking, is available in cans from large supermarkets and Asian stores.

SERVES 4

30ml/2 tbsp sunflower oil
15ml/1 tbsp ghee or unsalted
   (sweet) butter
1 onion, finely chopped
2 garlic cloves, crushed
3 tomatoes, peeled, seeded and chopped
275g/10oz/1½ cups easy-cook (converted)
   brown rice
5ml/1 tsp each ground coriander
   and ground cumin, or 10ml/2 tsp
   dhana jeera powder
2 carrots, coarsely grated
750ml/1¼ pints/3 cups boiling
   vegetable stock
175g/6oz baby spinach leaves, washed
50g/2oz/½ cup unsalted cashew nuts,
   toasted
salt and ground black pepper

1 Heat the oil and ghee or butter in a heavy-based pan, add the onion and fry gently for 6–7 minutes, until soft. Add the garlic and chopped tomatoes and cook for a further 2 minutes.

2 Rinse the rice in a sieve (strainer) under cold water, drain well and tip into the pan. Add the coriander and cumin or dhana jeera powder and stir for a few seconds. Turn off the heat and transfer the mixture to the ceramic cooking pot.

3 Stir in the carrots, then pour in the stock, season with salt and pepper and stir to mix. Switch the slow cooker on to high. Cover and cook for 1 hour.

4 Lay the spinach on the surface of the rice, replace the lid and cook for a further 30–40 minutes, or until the spinach has wilted and the rice is cooked and tender.

5 Stir the spinach into the rice and check the seasoning, adding a little more salt and pepper if necessary. Sprinkle the cashew nuts over the rice and serve.

COOK'S TIP
If baby spinach leaves are unavailable, use larger fresh spinach leaves instead. Remove any tough stalks and chop the leaves roughly before adding to the rice.

Nutritional information per portion: Energy 473Kcal/1989kJ; Protein 10.1g; Carbohydrate 72.1g, of which sugars 9.2g; Fat 18g, of which saturates 4.5g; Cholesterol 8mg; Calcium 111mg; Fibre 4.8g; Sodium 349mg.

DESSERTS AND CAKES

From baked custards and poached fruit to steamed puddings and luscious cakes, this tempting chapter is perfect for anyone with a sweet tooth. Try old-fashioned favourites such as poached pears, baked stuffed apples and tapioca pudding, or indulge yourself with a really wicked treat such as chocolate chip and banana pudding or Vermont baked maple custard. When you are looking for a little something to enjoy mid-afternoon with a cup of tea or coffee, try any one of the fabulous cakes – frosted carrot and parsnip cake, chocolate cheesecake brownies or moist golden ginger cake. One mouthful of any of these delights and you will be in heaven.

COCONUT CUSTARD

This classic Thai dessert, made with rich, creamy coconut milk, is often served with a selection of fresh fruit. Mangoes and tamarillos go particularly well.

2 Strain the mixture into a jug (pitcher), then pour into four individual heatproof glasses, ramekins or one single ovenproof dish. Cover the containers with clear film (plastic wrap).

3 Place the dishes in the slow cooker and, if necessary, pour a little more boiling water around them to reach just over halfway up their sides.

4 Cover the ceramic cooking pot with the lid, then cook for 3 hours, or until the custards are lightly set. Test with a fine skewer or cocktail stick (toothpick); it should come out clean.

5 Carefully lift the dishes out of the slow cooker and leave to cool. Once cool, chill in the refrigerator until ready to serve. Decorate the custards with a light dusting of icing sugar, and serve with sliced fruit.

SERVES 4

4 eggs
75g/3oz/generous ⅓ cup soft light brown
    sugar
250ml/8fl oz/1 cup coconut milk
5ml/1 tsp vanilla, rose or jasmine extract
icing (confectioners') sugar, to decorate
sliced fresh fruit, to serve

COOK'S TIP
Line the bases of individual ramekins with rounds of baking parchment, then lightly oil the sides. After cooking and chilling, run a knife around the insides of the custards and turn out on to individual dessert plates.

1 Pour about 2.5cm/1in of hot water into the base of the ceramic cooking pot and switch the slow cooker on to low. Whisk the eggs and sugar in a bowl until smooth. Gradually add the coconut milk and flavoured extract, and whisk well.

Nutritional information per portion: Energy 175Kcal/738kJ; Protein 7.5g; Carbohydrate 22.7g, of which sugars 22.7g; Fat 6.7g, of which saturates 2g; Cholesterol 227mg; Calcium 57mg; Fibre 0g; Sodium 151mg.

TAPIOCA PUDDING

Another Thai-style dessert, this version of the classic tapioca pudding is made from large pearl tapioca and coconut milk and is served warm. It is very good served with lychees.

SERVES 4

115g/4oz/⅔ cup large pearl tapioca
475ml/16fl oz/2 cups very hot water
115g/4oz/generous ½ cup caster
    (superfine) sugar
pinch of salt
250ml/8fl oz/1 cup coconut milk
250g/9oz prepared tropical fruits
shredded lime rind and shaved fresh
    coconut, to decorate (optional)

COOK'S TIP
This dish includes a lot of sugar – as it would in Thailand – but you may prefer to reduce the sugar according to taste.

1 Put the tapioca in a bowl and pour over enough warm water to cover generously. Leave the tapioca to soak for 1 hour until the grains swell, then drain well and set aside.

2 Pour the measured water into the ceramic cooking pot and switch the slow cooker to high. Add the sugar and salt and stir until dissolved. Cover with the lid and heat for about 30 minutes, until the water reaches boiling point.

3 Add the tapioca and coconut milk and stir well. Cover and cook for a further 1–1½ hours, or until the tapioca grains become transparent.

4 Spoon into one large dish or four individual bowls and serve warm with tropical fruits, decorated with the lime rind and coconut shavings, if using.

Nutritional information per portion: Energy 273Kcal/1164kJ; Protein 2.7g; Carbohydrate 66.7g, of which sugars 41.9g; Fat 1.3g, of which saturates 0.4g; Cholesterol 0mg; Calcium 43mg; Fibre 1.7g; Sodium 73mg.

POACHED PEARS in RED WINE

The pears take on a red blush from the wine and make a very pretty dessert. It works best in a small slow cooker, which ensures that the pears stay submerged during cooking.

SERVES 4

1 bottle fruity red wine
150g/5oz/¾ cup caster (superfine) sugar
45ml/3 tbsp clear honey
1 cinnamon stick
1 vanilla pod (bean), split lengthwise
large strip of lemon or orange rind
2 whole cloves
2 black peppercorns
4 firm ripe pears
juice of ½ lemon
mint leaves, to garnish
whipped cream or sour cream, to serve

1 Pour the red wine into the ceramic cooking pot. Add the sugar, honey, cinnamon stick, vanilla pod, lemon or orange rind, cloves and peppercorns. Cover with the lid and cook on high for 30 minutes, stirring occasionally.

2 Meanwhile, peel the pears using a vegetable peeler, leaving the stem intact. Take a very thin slice off the base of each pear so it will stand square and upright. As each pear is peeled, toss it in the lemon juice to prevent the flesh browning when exposed to the air.

3 Place the pears in the spiced wine mixture. Cover with the lid and cook for 2–4 hours, turning the pears occasionally, until they are just tender; be careful not to overcook them.

COOK'S TIP
The cooking time will depend on the size and ripeness of the pears. Small, ripe pears will cook quickly; large, hard pears will take longer.

4 Transfer the pears to a bowl using a slotted spoon. Continue to cook the wine mixture uncovered for a further hour, until reduced and thickened a little, then turn off the slow cooker and leave to cool. Alternatively, to save time, pour the cooking liquor into a pan and boil briskly for 10–15 minutes.

5 Strain the cooled liquid over the pears and chill for at least 3 hours. Place the pears in four individual serving dishes and spoon a little of the wine syrup over each one. Garnish with fresh mint and serve with whipped or sour cream.

Nutritional information per portion: Energy 87Kcal/367kJ; Protein 0.5g; Carbohydrate 16.6g, of which sugars 16.6g; Fat 0.2g, of which saturates 0g; Cholesterol 0mg; Calcium 19mg; Fibre 3.3g; Sodium 7mg.

WINTER FRUIT POACHED in MULLED WINE

*Poaching fresh apples and pears with dried apricots and figs in a spicy wine syrup makes
a delicious winter dessert. Serve on its own or with a generous spoonful of thick cream.*

SERVES 4

300ml/½ pint/1¼ cups fruity red wine
300ml/½ pint/1¼ cups fresh apple
   or orange juice
thinly pared strip of orange or
   lemon peel
45ml/3 tbsp clear honey
1 small cinnamon stick
4 whole cloves
4 cardamom pods, split
2 pears, such as Comice or William
8 ready-to-eat figs
12 ready-to-eat dried unsulphured apricots
2 eating apples, peeled, cored and thickly
   sliced

1 Pour the wine and apple or orange
juice into the ceramic cooking pot. Add
the citrus peel, honey, cinnamon stick,
cloves and cardamom pods. Cover with
the lid and cook on high for 1 hour.

2 Peel, core and halve the pears,
keeping the stalk intact if possible. Place
in the slow cooker with the figs and
apricots. Cook for 1 hour. Gently turn
the pears, then add the sliced apples
and cook for a further 1½–2 hours,
or until all the fruit is tender.

3 Using a slotted spoon, carefully
remove the fruit from the cooking pot
and place in a serving dish. Set aside
while you finish making the syrup.

4 Strain the syrup into a pan, discarding
the spices, then bring to the boil. Boil
vigorously for about 10 minutes, until
reduced by about one-third. Pour over
the fruit and serve hot or cold.

COOK'S TIP
Choose tart, well-tasting apples such as
Cox's Orange Pippin, Braeburn or Granny
Smith. They stand up particularly well
against the sweet dried fruits and spicy,
robust red wine syrup.

Nutritional information per portion: Energy 347Kcal/1476kJ; Protein 5g; Carbohydrate 78.1g, of which sugars 78.1g; Fat 1.9g, of which saturates 0g; Cholesterol 0mg; Calcium 284mg; Fibre 11.4g; Sodium 72mg.

BAKED STUFFED APPLES

Using Italian amaretti to stuff the apples gives a lovely almondy flavour, while dried cranberries and glacé fruit add sweetness and colour. Make sure that you choose a variety of apple that will remain firm during the long cooking time.

3 Add the nuts and dried cranberries or sour cherries and glacé fruit to the bowl and mix well, then set aside the filling while you prepare the apples.

4 Wash and dry the apples. Remove the cores using an apple corer, then carefully enlarge each core cavity to twice its size, using the corer to shave out more flesh. Using a sharp knife, score each apple around its equator.

5 Divide the filling among the apples, packing it into the hole, then piling it on top. Stand the apples in the cooking pot and cover with the lid. Reduce the temperature to low and cook for 4 hours, or until tender. Transfer the apples to warmed serving plates and spoon the sauce over the top. Serve with cream, crème fraîche or vanilla ice cream.

SERVES 4

75g/3oz/6 tbsp butter, softened
45ml/3 tbsp orange or apple juice
75g/3oz/scant ½ cup light muscovado (brown) sugar
grated rind and juice of ½ orange
1.5ml/¼ tsp ground cinnamon
30ml/2 tbsp crushed amaretti
25g/1oz/¼ cup pecan nuts, chopped
25g/1oz/¼ cup dried cranberries or sour cherries
25g/1oz/¼ cup luxury mixed glacé (candied) fruit, chopped
4 large cooking apples, such as Bramleys
cream, crème fraîche or vanilla ice cream, to serve

1 Grease the ceramic cooking pot with 15g/½oz/1 tbsp of the butter, then pour in the fruit juice and switch to high.

2 Put the remaining butter, the sugar, orange rind and juice, cinnamon and amaretti crumbs in a bowl and mix well.

COOK'S TIP

The cooking time will depend on the type and size of apples used.

Nutritional information per portion: Energy 347Kcal/1457kJ; Protein 1.6g; Carbohydrate 42.4g, of which sugars 41.3g; Fat 20.3g, of which saturates 10.3g; Cholesterol 40mg; Calcium 27mg; Fibre 3g; Sodium 131mg.

PAPAYA COOKED with GINGER

Spicy ginger enhances the delicate flavour of papaya perfectly. This recipe is excellent for busy people because it takes no more than 10 minutes to prepare and can then just be left to cook gently. Be careful not to overcook papaya or the flesh will become watery.

SERVES 4

150ml/¼ pint/⅔ cup hot water
45ml/3 tbsp raisins
shredded finely pared rind and juice
    of 1 lime
2 ripe papayas
2 pieces stem ginger in syrup, drained,
    plus 15ml/1 tbsp syrup from the jar
8 amaretti or other dessert biscuits
    (cookies), coarsely crushed
25g/1oz/¼ cup pistachio nuts, chopped
15ml/1 tbsp light muscovado
    (brown) sugar
60ml/4 tbsp crème fraîche, plus extra
    to serve

VARIATION
Try using chopped almonds and Greek
(US strained plain) yogurt in place of the
pistachio nuts and crème fraîche.

1 Pour the water into the base of the ceramic cooking pot and switch the slow cooker to high. Put the raisins in a small bowl and pour over the lime juice. Stir to combine, then leave to soak for at least 5 minutes, while preparing the remaining ingredients.

2 Cut the papayas in half and scoop out and discard their seeds using a teaspoon.

3 Finely chop the stem ginger and combine with the biscuits, raisins and lime juice, lime rind, two-thirds of the nuts, the sugar and crème fraîche.

4 Fill the papayas with the mixture and place in the cooking pot. Cover and cook for 1–1½ hours. Drizzle with the ginger syrup, sprinkle with the remaining nuts and serve with crème fraîche.

Nutritional information per portion: Energy 302Kcal/1272kJ; Protein 4.1g; Carbohydrate 45.6g, of which sugars 36.6g; Fat 12.8g, of which saturates 5.7g; Cholesterol 17mg; Calcium 70mg; Fibre 5.7g; Sodium 136mg.

VERMONT BAKED MAPLE CUSTARD

Maple syrup has a really distinctive flavour and gives these little baked custards a wonderfully rich taste. Try to find pure maple syrup – it will make all the difference.

SERVES 6

3 eggs
120ml/4fl oz/½ cup maple syrup
250ml/8fl oz/1 cup warm milk
150ml/¼ pint/⅔ cup warm single
   (light) cream
5ml/1 tsp vanilla essence (extract)
whole nutmeg, to grate

COOK'S TIP
Warming the milk and cream until tepid will help the custard cook and set more quickly. You can do this in a pan on the stovetop, or more simply, pour the milk and cream into a heatproof bowl or jug (pitcher) and place in the slow cooker filled with near-boiling water to a depth of about 5cm/2in. Switch the slow cooker to high and leave for 30 minutes. Remove the milk, then turn the slow cooker to low and use the hot water in the ceramic cooking pot to cook the custards.

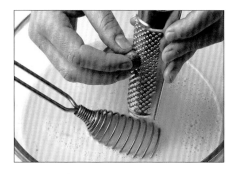

1 Beat the eggs in a large bowl, then whisk in the maple syrup, followed by the warm milk, cream and the vanilla essence. Grate in a little nutmeg.

2 Strain the custard mixture into six individual ramekins – first checking that the dishes will all fit inside the ceramic cooking pot in a single layer. Carefully cover each ramekin with a piece of kitchen foil, then place them in the ceramic cooking pot.

3 Pour very hot water around the dishes to come three-quarters of the way up their sides. Cover with the lid and cook on low for 2½–3 hours, or until set. To test, insert a skewer in the middle; it should come out clean.

4 Transfer the custards to a wire rack. Leave for 5 minutes and serve warm, or leave to cool completely, then chill. Remove from the refrigerator about 30 minutes before serving.

Nutritional information per portion: Energy 174Kcal/735kJ; Protein 8.6g; Carbohydrate 24.5g, of which sugars 18.7g; Fat 5.3g, of which saturates 1.6g; Cholesterol 116mg; Calcium 97mg; Fibre 9.1g; Sodium 120mg.

PETITS POTS de CRÈME au MOCHA

The name of these classic French baked custards comes from the baking cups, called pots de crème. *The addition of coffee gives the dessert an even richer, more indulgent flavour.*

SERVES 4

5ml/1 tsp instant coffee powder
15ml/1 tbsp soft light brown sugar
300ml/½ pint/1¼ cups milk
150ml/¼ pint/⅔ cup double (heavy) cream
115g/4oz plain (semisweet) chocolate
15ml/1 tbsp coffee liqueur (optional)
4 egg yolks
whipped cream and candied cake
    decorations, to decorate (optional)

1 Put the instant coffee and sugar in a pan and stir in the milk and cream. Bring to the boil over a medium heat, stirring constantly, until the coffee and sugar have dissolved completely.

2 Remove the pan from the heat and add the chocolate. Stir until the chocolate has melted, then stir in the coffee liqueur, if using.

3 In a bowl, whisk the egg yolks, then slowly whisk in the chocolate mixture until well blended. Strain the custard mixture into a large jug (pitcher) and divide equally among *pots de crème* or ramekins – first checking that they will all fit inside the ceramic cooking pot.

4 Cover each *pot de crème* or ramekin with a piece of foil, then transfer to the ceramic cooking pot. Pour enough hot water around the dishes to come just over halfway up their sides. Cover the slow cooker with the lid and cook on high for 2½–3 hours, or until they are just set and a knife inserted into the middle comes out clean.

5 Carefully remove the pots from the cooker and leave to cool. Cover and chill until ready to serve, then decorate with whipped cream and candied cake decorations, if you like.

Nutritional information per portion: Energy 443Kcal/1840kJ; Protein 8.3g; Carbohydrate 23.7g, of which sugars 23.7g; Fat 35.7g, of which saturates 20.2g; Cholesterol 264mg; Calcium 196mg; Fibre 0.2g; Sodium 74mg.

HOT BANANAS with RUM and RAISINS

These sticky, sweet baked bananas are utterly moreish and make a great dessert all year round. The rich sauce becomes almost toffee-like during cooking, and is irresistible.

3 Add the bananas to the melted butter and sugar mixture, cover with the lid and cook for about 30 minutes, or until the fruit is almost tender, turning over the bananas halfway through cooking time.

4 Sprinkle the nutmeg and cinnamon over the bananas, then pour in the rum and raisins. Stir very gently to mix, then re-cover and cook for 10 minutes.

5 Carefully lift the bananas out of the ceramic cooking pot and arrange on a serving dish or individual plates. Spoon over the sauce, then sprinkle with almonds, if using. Serve hot with whipped cream or vanilla ice cream.

COOK'S TIP

Choose almost-ripe bananas with even-coloured skins. Over-ripe bananas will not hold their shape during cooking, and will give mushy results.

SERVES 4

30ml/2 tbsp seedless raisins
45ml/3 tbsp dark rum
40g/1½oz/3 tbsp unsalted (sweet) butter
50g/2oz/¼ cup soft light brown sugar
4 slightly under-ripe bananas, peeled and
    halved lengthways
1.5ml/¼ tsp grated nutmeg
1.5ml/¼ tsp ground cinnamon
25g/1oz/¼ cup flaked (sliced) almonds,
    toasted (optional)
whipped cream or vanilla ice cream,
    to serve

1 Put the raisins in a bowl and spoon over 30ml/2 tbsp of the rum. Set aside and leave to soak.

2 Cut the butter into small cubes and place in the ceramic cooking pot with the sugar and remaining 15ml/1 tbsp rum. Switch the slow cooker to high and leave uncovered for 15 minutes, until the butter and sugar have melted.

VARIATION

If you don't like the taste of rum, try using an orange liqueur, such as Cointreau, instead. It makes a very good alternative and is a little less overpowering.

Nutritional information per portion: Energy 323Kcal/1355kJ; Protein 3g; Carbohydrate 47.1g, of which sugars 44.7g; Fat 12.1g, of which saturates 5.6g; Cholesterol 21mg; Calcium 33mg; Fibre 1.9g; Sodium 72mg.

CHOCOLATE CHIP and BANANA PUDDING

Rich, dense and sticky, this steamed pudding served with a glossy chocolate sauce is a great winter dessert. For an extra treat, serve with a scoop of vanilla ice cream.

SERVES 4

200g/7oz/1¾ cups self-raising
   (self-rising) flour
75g/3oz/6 tbsp unsalted (sweet) butter
2 ripe bananas
75g/3oz/6 tbsp caster (superfine) sugar
50ml/2fl oz/1¼ cups milk
1 egg, lightly beaten
75g/3oz/⅔ cup chocolate chips or
   chopped unsweetened chocolate

For the chocolate sauce
90g/3½oz/½ cup caster (superfine) sugar
50ml/2fl oz/¼ cup water
175g/6oz/1¼ cups plain (semisweet)
   chocolate chips or chopped
   unsweetened chocolate
25g/1oz/2 tbsp unsalted (sweet) butter
30ml/2 tbsp brandy or orange juice

1 Grease and line the base of a 1 litre/
1¾ pint/4 cup pudding basin with baking parchment. Put an inverted saucer in the bottom of the ceramic cooking pot and pour in about 2.5cm/1in of hot water. Turn the slow cooker to high.

2 Sift the flour into a large mixing bowl and rub in the butter until the mixture resembles coarse breadcrumbs. In a separate bowl, mash the bananas, then stir into the flour and butter mixture. Add the sugar and mix well.

3 In a clean bowl, whisk together the milk and egg, then beat into the banana mixture. Stir in the chocolate chips or chopped chocolate and spoon into the prepared pudding basin. Cover with a double thickness of buttered foil and place in the ceramic cooking pot. Pour enough boiling water around the basin to come just over halfway up the sides.

4 Cover the slow cooker and cook on high for 3–4 hours, or until the pudding is well risen and a skewer inserted in the middle comes out clean. Turn off the slow cooker and leave the pudding in the water while you make the sauce.

5 Put the sugar and water in a heavy pan and heat gently, stirring occasionally with a wooden spoon, until all the sugar has dissolved. Remove from the heat, add the chocolate and stir until melted, then add the butter in the same way. Stir in the brandy or orange juice.

6 Remove the pudding from the slow cooker and run a knife around the inside of the basin to loosen it. Turn it out on to a warmed serving dish and serve hot, with the sauce poured over.

Nutritional information per portion: Energy 926Kcal/3890kJ; Protein 11.1g; Carbohydrate 131.9g, of which sugars 93.2g; Fat 41.1g, of which saturates 24.6g; Cholesterol 118mg; Calcium 266mg; Fibre 3.3g; Sodium 378mg.

STICKY COFFEE and PEAR PUDDING

*This dark and moist fruity pudding is complemented with a tangy citrus-flavoured cream.
It is delicious served hot, but is equally good cold; serve at room temperature rather than
chilled to enjoy its rich flavour and wonderful texture at their best.*

SERVES 6

115g/4oz/½ cup butter, softened, plus
   extra for greasing
30ml/2 tbsp ground coffee
15ml/1 tbsp near-boiling water
50g/2oz/½ cup toasted skinned hazelnuts
4 small ripe pears
juice of ½ orange
115g/4oz/generous ½ cup golden caster
   (superfine) sugar, plus 15ml/1 tbsp for
   baking
2 eggs, beaten
50g/2oz/½ cup self-raising (self-rising) flour
45ml/3 tbsp maple syrup
fine strips of orange rind, to decorate

For the orange cream
300ml/½ pint/1¼ cups whipping cream
15ml/1 tbsp icing (confectioners') sugar,
   sifted
finely grated rind of ½ orange

1 Pour about 2.5cm/1in of hot water
into the ceramic cooking pot. Place an
upturned saucer or metal pastry ring in
the base, then turn on to high. Grease
and line the base of a deep 18cm/7in
fixed-base cake tin (pan) or soufflé dish.

COOK'S TIPS
• If you can't find ready-toasted skinned
hazelnuts, prepare your own. Toast the
nuts under a hot grill (broiler) for about
3 minutes, turning frequently until well
browned. Leave to cool and rub off the
skins before grinding.
• Many supermarkets and specialist food
stores sell flavoured coffees. Try using a
hazelnut-flavoured coffee for this dessert.

2 Put the ground coffee in a small bowl
and pour the water over. Leave to infuse
for 4 minutes, then strain through a fine
sieve. Place the hazelnuts in a coffee
grinder and grind until fine.

3 Peel, halve and core the pears. Thinly
slice across the pear halves part of the
way through, then brush them all over
with the orange juice.

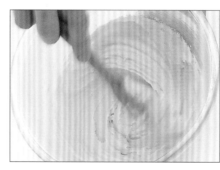

4 Beat the butter and the larger quantity
of caster sugar together in a bowl until
very light and fluffy. Gradually beat in
the eggs. Sift the flour, then fold into the
mixture in the bowl. Add the hazelnuts
and coffee. Spoon the mixture into the
tin or soufflé dish, and level the surface.

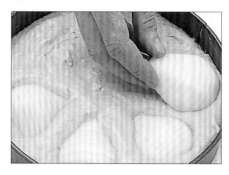

5 Pat the pears dry on kitchen paper
and arrange in a circle in the sponge
mixture, flat side down. Brush them with
some of the maple syrup, then sprinkle
with the 15ml/1 tbsp caster sugar.

6 Cover the top of the tin or soufflé
dish with kitchen foil and place in the
ceramic cooking pot. Pour enough
boiling water around the tin or dish to
come slightly more than halfway up the
sides. Cover with a lid and cook for
3–3½ hours, until firm and well risen.

7 Meanwhile, make the orange cream.
Whip the cream, icing sugar and orange
rind until soft peaks form. Spoon into
a serving dish and chill until needed.

8 Leave the sponge to cool in the tin
for about 10 minutes, then turn over
on to a serving plate. Lightly brush
with the remaining maple syrup, then
decorate with orange rind and serve
with the orange cream.

Nutritional information per portion: Energy 852Kcal/3571kJ; Protein 12.5g; Carbohydrate 107g, of which sugars 45g; Fat 44.5g, of which saturates 23.8g; Cholesterol 169mg; Calcium 362mg; Fibre 5.3g; Sodium 493mg.

STEAMED CHOCOLATE and FRUIT PUDDINGS

Drenched in a rich chocolate syrup, this wickedly indulgent steamed pudding makes a great alternative to a traditional Christmas pudding – although it is a fabulous treat at any time of year, the addition of cranberries gives it an unmistakably festive flavour.

SERVES 4

vegetable oil, for greasing
1 apple
25g/1oz/¼ cup cranberries, thawed
   if frozen
175g/6oz/¾ cup soft dark brown sugar
115g/4oz/½ cup soft margarine
2 eggs, lightly beaten
50g/2oz/½ cup self-raising (self-rising)
   flour, sifted
45ml/3 tbsp (unsweetened) cocoa powder

For the syrup
115g/4oz plain (semisweet) chocolate,
   chopped
30ml/2 tbsp clear honey
15g/½oz/1 tbsp unsalted (sweet) butter
2.5ml/½ tsp vanilla essence (extract)

1 Pour 2.5cm/1in of hot water into the cooking pot and switch the slow cooker to high. Grease four pudding basins with oil, then line with baking parchment.

2 Peel and core the apple, then dice the flesh. Place in a mixing bowl, then add the cranberries and 15ml/1 tbsp of the sugar. Mix well, then divide the fruit mixture among the prepared basins, gently patting it down into the base of each one.

3 Place the remaining sugar in a clean mixing bowl and add the margarine, eggs, flour and cocoa. Beat together with a wooden spoon until combined and smooth and creamy.

4 Spoon the mixture into the pudding basins and cover each with a double thickness of greased foil. Place the puddings in the ceramic cooking pot and pour in enough very hot water to come about two-thirds up the sides.

5 Cover with a lid and cook on high for 1½–2 hours, or until the puddings are well-risen and firm to the touch. Carefully remove from the slow cooker and leave to stand for 10 minutes.

6 Meanwhile, make the chocolate syrup. Put the chocolate, honey, butter and vanilla essence in a heatproof bowl and place in the hot water in the slow cooker. Leave for 10 minutes, until the butter has melted, then stir until smooth.

7 Run a knife around the edge of the puddings to loosen, then turn over on to warmed individual plates. Serve immediately with the chocolate syrup.

Nutritional information per portion: Energy 739Kcal/3094kJ; Protein 9.1g; Carbohydrate 88.3g, of which sugars 77.2g; Fat 41.3g, of which saturates 14.4g; Cholesterol 124mg; Calcium 103mg; Fibre 3.1g; Sodium 438mg.

HOT DATE PUDDINGS with TOFFEE SAUCE

Fresh dates make this pudding less rich than the classic dried date version, but it still makes an utterly indulgent dessert. Ideally, peel the dates because their skins can be tough. Squeeze them between your thumb and forefinger, and the skins will slip off.

3 Put the dates in a heatproof bowl, pour over the boiling water and mash well with a potato masher to make a fairly smooth paste.

4 Sift the flour and bicarbonate of soda over the creamed butter and sugar mixture, and fold in. Add the date paste and gently fold in.

SERVES 6

50g/2oz/¼ cup butter, softened
75g/3oz/½ cup light muscovado (brown) sugar
2 eggs, beaten
175g/6oz/generous 1 cup fresh dates, peeled, stoned (pitted) and chopped
75ml/5 tbsp boiling water
115g/4oz/1 cup self-raising (self-rising) flour
2.5ml/½ tsp bicarbonate of soda (baking soda)

For the sauce
50g/2oz/¼ cup butter, at room temperature
75g/3oz/½ cup light muscovado (brown) sugar
60ml/4 tbsp double (heavy) cream
30ml/2 tbsp brandy

1 Grease six individual pudding moulds or tins (pans) – first making sure that they will all fit in the slow cooker. Pour enough very hot water into the ceramic cooking pot to reach a depth of 2cm/¾in. Switch the slow cooker to high.

2 Put the butter and sugar in a mixing bowl and beat until pale and fluffy. Gradually beat in the eggs.

5 Spoon the mixture into the greased moulds or tins. Cover each with a piece of foil. Place in the ceramic cooking pot and pour enough boiling water around the puddings to come just over halfway up the sides. Cover with the lid and cook on high for 1½–2 hours, or until well risen and firm. Remove the puddings from the slow cooker.

6 Meanwhile, make the sauce. Put the butter, sugar, cream and brandy in a pan and heat very gently, stirring occasionally, until the mixture is smooth. Increase the heat and boil for 1 minute.

7 Turn the warm puddings out on to individual dessert plates. Spoon sauce over each one and serve immediately.

Nutritional information per portion: Energy 462Kcal/1932kJ; Protein 5.1g; Carbohydrate 50.3g, of which sugars 35.9g; Fat 26.9g, of which saturates 16g; Cholesterol 138mg; Calcium 109mg; Fibre 1.1g; Sodium 244mg.

FRESH FRUIT BREAD and BUTTER PUDDING

*Fresh currants add a tart touch to this scrumptious hot pudding. For the best results, use
a wide, shallow dish rather than a narrow, deep one, but make sure it fits comfortably in
the slow cooker. Serve drenched with a generous splash of fresh cream.*

SERVES 4

40g/1½oz/3 tbsp butter, softened,
    plus extra for greasing
6 medium-thick slices of day-old bread,
    crusts removed
115g/4oz/1 cup prepared redcurrants
    and raspberries
3 eggs, beaten
50g/2oz/¼ cup golden caster
    (superfine) sugar
300ml/½ pint/1¼ cups creamy milk
5ml/1 tsp vanilla essence (extract)
freshly grated nutmeg
30ml/2 tbsp demerara sugar
single (light) cream, to serve

1 Generously butter a 1 litre/1¾ pints/
4 cup round or oval baking dish – first
checking that it fits in your slow cooker.

2 Pour about 2.5cm/1in of very hot
water into the ceramic cooking pot.
Place an upturned saucer or metal
pastry ring in the base and switch the
cooker to high.

3 Spread the slices of bread generously
with the butter, then use a long serrated
knife to cut them in half diagonally.

VARIATIONS
• Try using slices of Italian panettone
in place of the white bread. It gives
a particularly rich, indulgent result.
• Use fresh blueberries or blackcurrants
in place of the fruit used here.
• When fresh berries and currants are
unavailable, use chopped ready-to-eat
dried apricots instead.

4 Arrange the buttered bread triangles
in the dish in neat layers, overlapping the
slices, with the buttered side facing up.

5 Scatter the fresh currants and berries
over the bread and between the slices,
ensuring that there is an even quantity of
fruit throughout the pudding.

6 Place the eggs and caster sugar in
a large mixing bowl and briefly beat
together. Gradually whisk in the milk,
vanilla essence and a large pinch of
freshly grated nutmeg until well mixed.

COOK'S TIP
Always buy whole nutmegs. Once grated,
the spice loses its flavour quickly.

7 Place the baking dish in the ceramic
cooking pot, then slowly pour the egg
and milk mixture over the bread, pushing
the bread slices down to submerge them
and making sure they are thoroughly
soaked. Scatter the demerara sugar and
a little nutmeg over the top, then cover
the dish with foil.

8 Pour near-boiling water around the
dish, so that the water level comes just
over halfway up the sides of the dish.
Cover with the lid and cook on high for
3–4 hours, or until a skewer inserted
into the centre comes out clean.

9 Carefully remove the dish from the
slow cooker and, if you like, briefly
brown the top of the pudding under
a hot grill (broiler). Cool slightly, then
serve with the single cream.

Nutritional information per portion: Energy 405Kcal/1700kJ; Protein 12.6g; Carbohydrate 53.7g, of which sugars 30.7g; Fat 16.9g, of which saturates 8.6g; Cholesterol 202mg; Calcium 234mg; Fibre 2.1g; Sodium 405mg.

RICH CHOCOLATE CAKE

This rich, dense steamed chocolate cake filled with a decadently creamy buttercream makes a perfect teatime treat. Serve with a big cup of strong coffee.

SERVES 8

115g/4oz plain (semisweet) chocolate,
   chopped into small pieces
45ml/3 tbsp milk
150g/5oz/10 tbsp butter, at room
   temperature
200g/7oz/scant 1 cup soft light
   brown sugar
3 eggs, lightly beaten
200g/7oz/1¾ cups self-raising
   (self-rising) flour
15ml/1 tbsp (unsweetened) cocoa powder
icing (confectioners') sugar and
   (unsweetened) cocoa powder,
   for dusting

For the chocolate buttercream:
75g/3oz/6 tbsp butter, at room
   temperature
115g/4oz/1 cup icing (confectioners') sugar
15ml/1 tbsp (unsweetened) cocoa powder
2.5ml/½ tsp vanilla essence (extract)

1 Grease and line a deep 18cm/7in fixed-base cake tin (pan) or soufflé dish with baking parchment. Pour about 5cm/ 2in very hot water into the ceramic cooking pot, then turn the slow cooker to high.

2 Put the chocolate and milk into a heatproof bowl and place in the cooking pot. Leave for about 10 minutes, until the chocolate softens, then stir until smooth. Remove and leave to cool for a few minutes.

3 Meanwhile, place the butter and sugar in a mixing bowl and beat together until light and fluffy. Beat in the eggs, a little at a time, then stir in the chocolate mixture until well mixed.

4 Sift the flour and cocoa over the chocolate mixture and fold in until evenly mixed. Spoon into the prepared tin or dish and cover the top with a piece of foil. Put a saucer in the bottom of the ceramic cooking pot, then rest the tin on top. If necessary, pour in more boiling water to come just over halfway up the sides of the tin.

5 Cover the slow cooker with the lid and cook for 3–3½ hours, or until firm to the touch and a fine skewer inserted into the middle comes out clean. Carefully lift the tin out of the cooking pot and leave to stand on a wire rack for 10 minutes. Turn out and leave to cool. Remove the lining paper.

6 To make the buttercream, put the butter in a large bowl and beat until very soft. Sift over the icing sugar and cocoa powder, then stir together. Add the vanilla essence and beat until the buttercream is light and fluffy.

7 Very carefully, cut the cake in half horizontally and spread a thick, even layer of the buttercream on one of the cut halves. Sandwich the cakes back together, then dust with a mixture of icing sugar and cocoa and serve.

Nutritional information per portion: Energy 564Kcal/2363kJ; Protein 6.6g; Carbohydrate 70g, of which sugars 51g; Fat 30.5g, of which saturates 18.2g; Cholesterol 146mg; Calcium 129mg; Fibre 1.5g; Sodium 321mg.

CHOCOLATE CHIP WALNUT CAKE

The tangy flavour of orange works well in this chocolate and nut loaf. It can be finished simply with a generous dusting of icing sugar, or as here with a zesty orange topping.

SERVES 8

115g/4oz/1 cup plain (all-purpose) flour
25g/1oz/¼ cup cornflour (cornstarch)
5ml/1 tsp baking powder
115g/4oz/½ cup butter, at room
    temperature
115g/4oz/½ cup golden caster (superfine)
    sugar
2 eggs, lightly beaten
75g/3oz/½ cup plain (semisweet), milk or
    white chocolate chips
50g/2oz/½ cup chopped walnuts
finely grated rind of ½ orange

For the topping
115g/4oz/1 cup icing (confectioners') sugar,
    sifted, plus 5ml/1 tsp for dusting
20–30ml/4 tsp–2 tbsp freshly squeezed
    orange juice
walnut halves, to decorate

1 Grease and line a 450g/1lb loaf tin (pan), with a capacity of 900ml/1½ pints/3¾ cups, with baking parchment. Place a metal pastry ring or upturned saucer in the base of the ceramic cooking pot and pour in about 2.5cm/1in very hot water. Switch the slow cooker to high.

2 Sift the flour, cornflour and baking powder together twice, so that the dry ingredients are well mixed and aerated, then set aside.

3 Place the butter in a large mixing bowl and beat until creamy. Add the golden caster sugar and continue beating until light and fluffy. Add the eggs a little at a time, beating well after each addition.

4 Gently fold about half of the sifted flour mixture into the creamed butter and sugar mixture, then add the rest with the chocolate chips, walnuts and orange rind. Fold in until just blended, taking care not to overmix.

5 Spoon the mixture into the prepared loaf tin and loosely cover with a piece of foil, allowing some space at the top for the cake to rise as it cooks.

6 Put the loaf tin on the pastry ring or saucer inside the ceramic cooking pot. Pour enough boiling water around the loaf tin to come two-thirds of the way up the sides.

7 Cover the slow cooker with a lid and cook for 2½–3 hours, or until a fine skewer pushed into the centre of the cake comes out clean. Carefully remove the cake from the slow cooker and stand it on a wire rack for 10 minutes, then turn out and leave to cool on the rack.

8 To decorate the cake, place the 115g/4oz/1 cup icing sugar in a mixing bowl. Stir in 20ml/4 tsp of the orange juice, adding a little more if needed to make the consistency of thick cream. Drizzle the mixture over the cake, then decorate with walnut halves dusted with the 5ml/1 tsp icing sugar. Leave the topping to set before serving.

Nutritional information per portion: Energy 395Kcal/1655kJ; Protein 4.7g; Carbohydrate 51g, of which sugars 36.9g; Fat 20.5g, of which saturates 9.9g; Cholesterol 87mg; Calcium 49mg; Fibre 0.9g; Sodium 171mg.

FROSTED CARROT and PARSNIP CAKE

A delicious twist on the classic plain carrot cake, this version is wonderfully light and crumbly. The grated vegetables help to keep it moist, and account for its excellent keeping qualities. Cooked meringue spread over the top makes a change from the usual cream cheese topping, and makes a stunning contrast to the wholesome, crumbly cake.

SERVES 8

oil, for greasing
1 orange or lemon
10ml/2 tsp caster (superfine) sugar
175g/6oz/¾ cup butter or margarine
175g/6oz/¾ cup soft light brown sugar
3 eggs, lightly beaten
175g/6oz carrots and parsnips, grated
50g/2oz/⅓ cup sultanas
   (golden raisins)
115g/4oz/1 cup self-raising
   (self-rising) flour
50g/2oz/½ cup self-raising (self-rising)
   wholemeal (whole-wheat) flour
5ml/1 tsp baking powder

For the topping
50g/2oz/¼ cup caster (superfine) sugar
1 egg white
pinch of salt

1 Put an upturned saucer or metal pastry cutter in the base of the ceramic cooking pot and pour in about 2.5cm/1in hot water. Turn the slow cooker to high. Lightly grease a deep 18cm/7in round fixed-based cake tin (pan) or soufflé dish with oil and line the base with baking parchment.

2 Finely grate the orange or lemon rind, taking care not to take off any of the white pith. Selecting the longest shreds, put about half the rind in a bowl and mix with the caster sugar. Arrange the sugar-coated rind on a sheet of greaseproof (waxed) paper and leave in a warm place to dry.

3 Put the butter or margarine and brown sugar in a large mixing bowl and beat together until pale and fluffy. Add the eggs a little at a time, beating well after each addition. Stir in the unsugared orange or lemon rind, grated carrots and parsnips and sultanas.

4 Sift the flours and baking powder together, adding any bran left in the sieve (strainer), then gradually fold into the carrot and parsnip mixture.

5 Transfer the mixture to the prepared tin and level the surface. Cover loosely with greased foil, then place in the ceramic cooking pot, on top of the saucer or pastry cutter. Pour sufficient boiling water around the tin to come just over halfway up the sides.

6 Cover the slow cooker with the lid and cook for 3–5 hours, or until a skewer inserted in the centre of the cake comes out clean. Carefully lift the tin out of the slow cooker and leave to stand for 5 minutes. Turn the cake out on to a wire rack and leave until cool.

7 To make the topping, place the caster sugar in a bowl over the near-simmering water in the slow cooker. Squeeze the juice from the orange or lemon and add 30ml/2 tbsp of the juice to the sugar. Stir over the heat until the sugar dissolves. Remove from the heat, add the egg white and salt, and whisk for 1 minute with an electric beater.

8 Return the bowl to the heat and whisk for about 6 minutes until the mixture becomes stiff and glossy, holding a good shape. Remove from the heat and allow to cool for about 5 minutes, whisking frequently.

9 Swirl the meringue topping over the cake and leave for 1 hour to firm up. To serve, sprinkle with the sugared orange or lemon rind.

VARIATION
If you do not like parsnips, you can make this cake with just carrots, or replace the parsnips with the same weight of grated courgettes (zucchini). Add a pinch of cinnamon and nutmeg to the mixture.

Nutritional information per portion: Energy 410Kcal/1718kJ; Protein 5.9g; Carbohydrate 53g, of which sugars 38.2g; Fat 20.8g, of which saturates 12.2g; Cholesterol 132mg; Calcium 98mg; Fibre 1.9g; Sodium 290mg.

CHOCOLATE CHEESECAKE BROWNIES

A very dense chocolate brownie mixture is swirled with creamy cheese to give a marbled effect. Cut into small squares for little mouthfuls of absolute heaven.

MAKES 9

50g/2oz dark (bittersweet) chocolate
  (minimum 70 per cent cocoa solids),
  chopped
50g/2oz/¼ cup unsalted (sweet) butter
65g/2½oz/5 tbsp light muscovado
  (brown) sugar
1 egg, beaten
25g/1oz/¼ cup plain (all-purpose) flour

For the cheesecake mixture
115g/4oz/½ cup full-fat cream cheese
25g/1oz/2 tbsp caster (superfine) sugar
5ml/1 tsp vanilla essence (extract)
½ beaten egg

1 Line the base and sides of a 15cm/6in square fixed-base cake tin (pan) with baking parchment. Pour about 5cm/2in of very hot water into the ceramic cooking pot and switch to high.

2 Put the chocolate and butter in a heatproof bowl and place in the slow cooker. Leave to stand for 10 minutes.

3 Meanwhile, make the cheesecake mixture. Put the cream cheese, sugar and vanilla essence in a clean mixing bowl and beat together. Gradually beat in the egg until the mixture is very smooth and creamy. Set aside.

4 Stir the chocolate and butter mixture until completely melted and smooth, then remove the bowl from the slow cooker. Add the muscovado sugar and stir to combine. Place an upturned saucer or metal pastry ring in the base of the ceramic cooking pot.

5 Add the beaten egg to the melted chocolate mixture a little at a time, and beat well until thoroughly mixed, then sift over the flour and gently fold in.

6 Spoon the chocolate mixture into the base of the tin. Drop small spoonfuls of the cheesecake mixture on top. Using a skewer, swirl the mixtures together.

7 Cover the tin with foil and place in the slow cooker. Pour in more boiling water around the tin to come just over halfway up the sides. Cook for 2 hours, or until just set in the centre. Remove the tin from the slow cooker and place on a wire rack to cool. Cut into squares.

Nutritional information per portion: Energy 174Kcal/727kJ; Protein 2.9g; Carbohydrate 16.2g, of which sugars 14g; Fat 11.3g, of which saturates 6.8g; Cholesterol 65mg; Calcium 25mg; Fibre 0.2g; Sodium 86mg.

LIGHT FRUIT CAKE

This incredibly easy all-in-one fruit cake has a crumbly texture. The combination of wholemeal flour and long slow cooking ensures that it stays beautifully moist.

SERVES 12

2 eggs
130g/4½oz/generous ½ cup butter,
    at room temperature
225g/8oz/1 cup light muscovado
    (brown) sugar
150g/5oz/1¼ cups self-raising
    (self-rising) flour
150g/5oz/1¼ cups wholemeal
    (whole-wheat) self-raising
    (self-rising) flour
pinch of salt
5ml/1 tsp mixed (apple pie) spice
450g/1lb/2½ cups luxury mixed
    dried fruit

1 Line the base and sides of a deep 18cm/7in round or 15cm/6in square fixed-base cake tin (pan) with baking parchment. Place an upturned saucer or metal pastry ring in the base of the ceramic cooking pot, then pour in about 2.5cm/1in of very hot water. Switch the slow cooker to high.

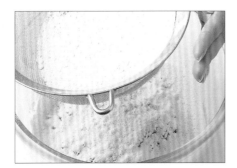

2 Crack the eggs into a large mixing bowl. Add the butter and sugar, then sift over the flours, salt and spice, adding any bran left in the sieve (strainer). Stir together with a wooden spoon until mixed, then add the dried fruit and beat for 2 minutes until the mixture is smooth and glossy.

COOK'S TIP
Choose a good-quality brand of luxury dried fruits. It should contain a good mix of currants, sultanas (golden raisins), mixed peel and glacé (candied) cherries, as well as other dried fruits.

3 Spoon the mixture into the prepared cake tin and level the surface. Cover the tin with a piece of buttered foil.

4 Put the tin in the slow cooker and pour in enough boiling water to come just over halfway up the sides of the tin. Cover with the lid and cook for 4–5 hours, or until a skewer inserted into the middle of the cake comes out clean.

5 Remove the cake from the slow cooker and place on a wire rack. Leave the cake to cool in the tin for about 15 minutes, then turn out and leave to cool completely. To store, wrap the cake in greaseproof (waxed) paper and then foil, and keep in a cool place.

Nutritional information per portion: Energy 351Kcal/1482kJ; Protein 4.9g; Carbohydrate 63g, of which sugars 46g; Fat 10.6g, of which saturates 6g; Cholesterol 60.8mg; Calcium 78.6mg; Fibre 2.3g; Sodium 148mg.

MARBLED SPICE CAKE

This cake can be baked in a fluted ring-shaped cake mould called a kugelhupf *or* gugelhupf, *which originates from Germany and Austria, or in a plain ring-shaped cake tin. The marbled effect looks particularly good when the cake is baked in a ring like this.*

SERVES 8

75g/3oz/6 tbsp butter, at room
    temperature, plus extra for greasing
130g/4½oz/generous 1 cup plain
    (all-purpose) flour, plus extra for
    dusting
115g/4oz/½ cup soft light brown sugar
2 eggs
few drops of vanilla essence (extract)
7.5ml/1½ tsp baking powder
45ml/3 tbsp milk
30ml/2 tbsp malt extract or black treacle
5ml/1 tsp mixed (apple pie) spice
2.5ml/½ tsp ground ginger
75g/3oz/¾ cup icing (confectioners') sugar,
    sifted, to decorate

1 Grease and flour a 1.2 litre/2 pint/
5 cup *kugelhupf* mould or ring-shaped
cake tin (pan). Put an inverted saucer
or large metal pastry cutter in the base
of the slow cooker and pour in about
5cm/2in hot water. Switch the slow
cooker to high.

2 Put the butter and sugar in a bowl
and beat together until light and fluffy.

3 In a separate bowl, beat together the
eggs and vanilla essence, then gradually
beat into the butter and sugar mixture,
adding a little at a time and beating well
after each addition.

COOK'S TIP
To make a marbled chocolate and vanilla
cake, stir 15ml/1 tbsp chocolate essence
into the cake mixture, in place of the malt
extract or treacle and spices.

4 Sift together the flour and baking
powder to combine, then fold the flour
into the butter and sugar mixture, adding
a little of the milk between each addition
until evenly combined.

5 Spoon about one-third of the mixture
into a small bowl and stir in the malt
extract or treacle, mixed spice and
ginger until just combined.

6 Drop a large spoonful of the light
mixture into the cake tin, followed by a
spoonful of the dark mixture. Continue
alternating spoonfuls of the light and
dark mixtures until all the mixture has
been used. Run a knife or skewer through
the mixtures to give a marbled effect.

7 Cover the tin with foil and place in
the ceramic cooking pot. Pour a little
more boiling water around the tin to
come just over halfway up the sides.
Cover the slow cooker with the lid and
cook for 3–4 hours. To test if it is done,
insert a skewer into the middle of the
cake; it should come out clean.

8 Carefully lift the cake out of the slow
cooker and leave in the tin for about
10 minutes before turning out on to
a wire rack to cool.

9 To decorate, place the icing sugar in
a bowl and add just enough warm water
to make a smooth icing (frosting) with
the consistency of single (light) cream.
Quickly drizzle the mixture over the
cake, then leave to set before serving
the cake in thick slices.

Nutritional information per portion: Energy 215Kcal/902kJ; Protein 2.8g; Carbohydrate 33g, of which sugars 20.3g; Fat 8.8g, of which saturates 5.2g; Cholesterol 49mg; Calcium 84mg; Fibre 0.5g; Sodium 172mg.

BLUEBERRY MUFFIN PUDDING

You can't cook traditional muffins in a slow cooker but this delicious alternative will satisfy your cravings. It's especially good served barely warm with custard or crème fraîche. Take the eggs and buttermilk out of the refrigerator at least an hour before you start mixing.

SERVES 4

75g/3oz/6 tbsp butter, plus extra
    for greasing
75g/3oz/6 tbsp soft light brown sugar
105ml/7 tbsp buttermilk, at room
    temperature
2 eggs, lightly beaten, at room temperature
225g/8oz/2 cups self raising
    (self-rising) flour
pinch of salt
5ml/1 tsp ground cinnamon
150g/5oz/¼ cup fresh blueberries
10ml/2 tsp demerara (raw) sugar,
    for sprinkling
custard or crème fraîche, to serve

1 Place an upturned saucer or metal pastry ring in the base of the slow cooker. Pour in about 5cm/2in of very hot water, then switch the slow cooker to high. Lightly grease a 1.5 litre/ 2½ pint/6¼ cup heatproof dish with butter – first making sure that it will fit the inside of your slow cooker.

2 Put the butter and sugar in a heatproof jug (pitcher) and place in the ceramic cooking pot. Leave uncovered for 20 minutes, stirring, until melted.

3 Remove the jug from the slow cooker and leave to cool until tepid, then stir in the buttermilk followed by the beaten egg, until well mixed.

COOK'S TIP
Because less liquid evaporates from the pudding in a slow cooker, the mixture is thicker than a conventional muffin batter.

4 Sift the flour, salt and cinnamon into a mixing bowl. Stir in the blueberries, then make a hollow in the middle. Pour in the buttermilk mixture and quickly stir until just combined. Do not overmix.

5 Spoon the mixture into the prepared dish, then sprinkle the top with the demerara sugar. Cover with a piece of buttered foil and place in the ceramic cooking pot. Pour in a little more boiling water around the dish, if necessary, to come halfway up the sides.

6 Cover the slow cooker with the lid and cook for 3–4 hours, until a skewer inserted in the middle comes out clean. Remove from the slow cooker and let the pudding cool slightly before serving with custard or crème fraîche.

Nutritional information per portion: Energy 499Kcal/2101kJ; Protein 10.1g; Carbohydrate 76.2g, of which sugars 34.4g; Fat 19.2g, of which saturates 10.7g; Cholesterol 153mg; Calcium 262mg; Fibre 2.2g; Sodium 367mg.

PUMPKIN and BANANA CAKE

Rather like a cross between a carrot cake and banana bread, this luscious cake is an
excellent way of using some of the scooped-out pumpkin flesh after making Hallowe'en
lanterns. A cream cheese topping provides a delicious contrast with the dense moist cake.

SERVES 12

225g/8oz/2 cups self-raising
   (self-rising) flour
7.5ml/1½ tsp baking powder
2.5ml/½ tsp ground cinnamon
2.5ml/½ tsp ground ginger
pinch of salt
125g/5oz/10 tbsp soft light brown sugar
75g/3oz/¾ cup pecans or walnuts,
   chopped
115g/4oz pumpkin flesh, coarsely grated
2 small bananas, peeled and mashed
2 eggs, lightly beaten
150ml/¼ pint/⅔ cup sunflower oil

For the topping
50g/2oz/¼ cup butter, at room
   temperature
150g/5oz/⅔ cup soft cheese
1.5ml/¼ tsp vanilla essence (extract)
115g/4oz/1 cup icing (confectioners') sugar
pecan halves, to decorate

1 Line the base and sides of a deep
20cm/8in round fixed-base cake tin (pan)
or soufflé dish with baking parchment.
Place an upturned saucer or metal
pastry ring in the base of the ceramic
cooking pot, then pour in about
2.5cm/1in of very hot water. Switch the
slow cooker to high.

2 Sift the flour, baking powder,
cinnamon, ginger and salt into a large
mixing bowl to combine. Stir in the
sugar, chopped pecans or walnuts and
grated pumpkin until thoroughly mixed.
Make a slight hollow in the middle of
the dry ingredients.

3 In a separate bowl, combine the
bananas, eggs and sunflower oil, then stir
into the dry ingredients. Turn into the
prepared tin and level the surface.

4 Cover the tin with a piece of buttered
foil and place in the slow cooker. Pour in
sufficient boiling water to come just over
halfway up the sides of the tin.

5 Cover the pot with the lid and cook
on high for 4–4½ hours, or until the
cake is firm and a skewer inserted into
the middle comes out clean.

6 Carefully remove the cake from the
slow cooker and stand the tin on a wire
rack to cool for 15 minutes. Turn out
and leave to cool completely, then peel
off the lining paper.

7 To make the topping, put the butter,
soft cheese and vanilla essence in a bowl
and beat until blended and smooth. Sift
in the icing sugar and beat again until
smooth and creamy. Thickly spread the
topping over the top of the cake and
decorate with pecan halves. Chill in the
refrigerator for at least 1 hour before
serving, to allow the topping to harden.

Nutritional information per portion: Energy 374Kcal/1567kJ; Protein 5.1g; Carbohydrate 43.2g, of which sugars 28.7g; Fat 21.3g, of which saturates 6.5g; Cholesterol 58mg; Calcium 101.7mg; Fibre 1g; Sodium 203mg.

MOIST GOLDEN GINGER CAKE

This is the ultimate ginger cake: instead of the traditional black treacle, a mixture of golden syrup and malt extract gives a really sticky, moist texture. Because of the long slow cooking, the cake matures sufficiently to eat straight away. However, the flavour improves and the texture becomes stickier if it is wrapped and kept for a day or two.

SERVES 10

175g/6oz/generous ¾ cup light muscovado
   (brown) sugar
115g/4oz/½ cup butter
150g/5oz/⅔ cup golden (light corn)
   syrup
25g/1oz malt extract
175g/6oz/1½ cups self-raising
   (self-rising) flour
50g/2oz/½ cup plain (all-purpose) flour
10ml/2 tsp ground ginger
pinch of salt
1 egg, lightly beaten
120ml/4fl oz/½ cup milk, at room
   temperature
2.5ml/½ tsp bicarbonate of soda
   (baking soda)

1 Line the base of a deep 18cm/7in round fixed-base cake tin (pan) or soufflé dish with baking parchment. Pour 5cm/2in of very hot water into the ceramic cooking pot. Switch to high.

2 Place the sugar, butter, golden syrup and malt extract in a heatproof bowl that will fit inside the slow cooker. Place in the ceramic cooking pot and leave for 15 minutes, or until melted.

3 Remove the bowl from the slow cooker and stir until smooth. Place an upturned saucer or metal pastry ring in the base of the ceramic cooking pot.

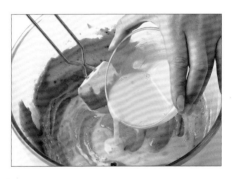

4 Sift the flours, ginger and salt into a separate mixing bowl. Pour the melted butter and sugar mixture into the flour and beat until smooth. Stir in the beaten egg until well mixed.

VARIATION
To turn this moist cake into a tempting treat for kids, try decorating it with plain lemon icing (frosting) and scattering with multi-coloured sugar sprinkles. To make the icing, put 75g/3oz/¾ cup icing sugar in a bowl and stir in just enough lemon juice to make a smooth icing with the consistency of single (light) cream. Drizzle over the cake and scatter with sprinkles.

5 Pour the milk in a jug (pitcher) and stir in the bicarbonate of soda. Pour the mixture into the ginger cake mixture and stir until combined.

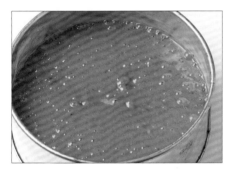

6 Pour the cake mixture into the prepared cake tin or soufflé dish, cover with foil and place in the cooking pot.

7 Pour a little more boiling water around the tin or dish to come just over halfway up the sides. Cover with the lid and cook for 5–6 hours, or until firm and a fine skewer inserted into the middle of the cake comes out clean.

8 Remove the cake from the slow cooker and place the tin or dish on a wire cooling rack. Leave to cool for 15 minutes, then turn out and leave to cool completely before serving in slices.

COOK'S TIP
Because this cake improves with keeping, it is the perfect choice when you are expecting guests because you can make it several days in advance.

Nutritional information per portion: Energy 289Kcal/1216kJ; Protein 3.4g; Carbohydrate 48g, of which sugars 31.1g; Fat 10.6g, of which saturates 6.4g; Cholesterol 48mg; Calcium 98mg; Fibre 0.7g; Sodium 211mg.

PRESERVES AND DRINKS

Although the slow cooker isn't suitable for fast-boiling jams, jellies and marmalades to setting point, it is perfect for making rich chutneys and relishes. The long, slow cooking develops their flavour to such an extent that long-maturation is unnecessary and many can be eaten immediately. It is particularly good for making textured preserves because the fruit and vegetables retain their shape well. Fruit curds, such as the traditional fresh lemon curd, are easier than those made conventionally because there is no need for constant stirring. You will also find a number of delicious drinks here: the slow cooker is great for infusing spices and keeping hot punches and drinks warm until you are ready to serve.

MANGO CHUTNEY

No Indian meal would be complete without this classic chutney. Its gloriously sweet, tangy flavour complements the warm taste of spices perfectly. It is also great served with chargrilled chicken or duck breasts, and will liven up cheese sandwiches a treat.

3 Stir the sugar, chilli, ginger, garlic, bruised cardamoms, bay leaf and salt into the mango mixture until the sugar has dissolved completely.

4 Cover and cook for 2 hours, then uncover and let the mixture cook for a further 1 hour, or until the chutney is reduced to a thick consistency and no excess liquid remains. Stir the chutney every 15 minutes during the last hour.

5 Remove and discard the bay leaf and the chilli. Spoon the chutney into hot sterilized jars and seal. Store for 1 week before eating and use within 1 year.

COOK'S TIP
To make a more fiery chutney, seed and slice two green chillies and stir into the chutney mixture with the other spices.

MAKES 450G/1LB

3 firm mangoes
120ml/4fl oz/½ cup cider vinegar
200g/7oz/scant 1 cup light muscovado (brown) sugar
1 small red finger chilli or jalapeño chilli, split
2.5cm/1in piece of fresh root ginger, peeled and finely chopped
1 garlic clove, finely chopped
5 cardamom pods, bruised
1 bay leaf
2.5ml/½ tsp salt

1 Peel the mangoes and cut out the stone, then cut the flesh into small chunks or thin wedges.

2 Put the chopped mango in the ceramic cooking pot. Add the cider vinegar, stir briefly to combine, and cover the slow cooker with the lid. Switch to high and cook for about 2 hours, stirring the chutney halfway through the cooking time.

Nutritional information (total): Energy 1045Kcal/4465kJ; Protein 4.1g; Carbohydrate 272.5g, of which sugars 271.1g; Fat 0.9g, of which saturates 0.5g; Cholesterol 0mg; Calcium 908mg; Fibre 11.7g; Sodium 1002mg.

BUTTERNUT, APRICOT and ALMOND CHUTNEY

Coriander seeds and turmeric add a slightly spicy touch to this rich golden chutney. It is delicious spooned on to little savoury canapés or with melting cubes of mozzarella cheese; it is also good in sandwiches – helping to spice up bland or run-of-the-mill fillings.

MAKES ABOUT 1.8KG/4LB

1 small butternut squash, weighing
   about 800g/1¾ lb
400g/14oz/2 cups golden granulated sugar
300ml/½ pint/1¼ cups cider vinegar
2 onions, finely chopped
225g/8oz/1 cup ready-to-eat dried
   apricots, chopped
finely grated rind and juice of 1 orange
2.5ml/½ tsp turmeric
15ml/1 tbsp coriander seeds
15ml/1 tbsp salt
115g/4oz/1 cup flaked (sliced) almonds

1 Halve the butternut squash and scoop out the seeds. Peel off the skin, then cut the flesh into 1cm/½in cubes.

2 Put the sugar and vinegar in the ceramic cooking pot and switch to high. Heat for 30 minutes, then stir until the sugar has dissolved.

3 Add the butternut squash, onions, apricots, orange rind and juice, turmeric, coriander seeds and salt to the slow cooker and stir well.

4 Cover with the lid and cook for 5–6 hours, stirring occasionally. After about 5 hours the chutney should be a fairly thick consistency with relatively little liquid. If it is still quite runny at this stage, cook uncovered for the final hour. Stir in the flaked almonds.

5 Spoon the chutney into warmed sterilized jars, cover and seal. Store in a cool, dark place and allow to mature for at least 1 month before eating. Use within 2 years. Once opened, store the chutney in the refrigerator and use within 2 months.

Nutritional information (total): Energy 2770Kcal/11723kJ; Protein 41.7g; Carbohydrate 532.6g, of which sugars 524.1g; Fat 67.3g, of which saturates 5.9g; Cholesterol 0mg; Calcium 807mg; Fibre 31.6g; Sodium 5967mg.

SWEET and HOT DRIED-FRUIT CHUTNEY

This rich, thick and slightly sticky preserve of spiced dried fruit is a wonderful way to enliven cold roast turkey left over from Christmas or Thanksgiving dinner.

MAKES ABOUT 1.5KG/3LB 6OZ

350g/12oz/1½ cups ready-to-eat
    dried apricots
225g/8oz/1½ cups dried dates,
    stoned (pitted)
225g/8oz/1⅓ cups dried figs
50g/2oz/⅓ cup glacé (candied) citrus peel
150g/5oz/1 cup raisins
50g/2oz/½ cup dried cranberries
75ml/2½fl oz/⅓ cup cranberry juice
300ml/½ pint/1¼ cups cider vinegar
225g/8oz/1 cup caster (superfine) sugar
finely grated rind of 1 lemon
5ml/1 tsp mixed (apple pie) spice
5ml/1 tsp ground coriander
5ml/1 tsp cayenne pepper
5ml/1 tsp salt

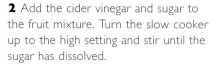

1 Roughly chop the apricots, dates, figs and citrus peel, then put all the dried fruit in the ceramic cooking pot. Pour over the cranberry juice, stir, then cover with the lid and switch the slow cooker on to low. Cook for 1 hour, or until the fruit has absorbed most of the juice.

2 Add the cider vinegar and sugar to the fruit mixture. Turn the slow cooker up to the high setting and stir until the sugar has dissolved.

3 Re-cover and cook for 2 more hours, or until the fruit is very soft and the chutney fairly thick (it will thicken further as it cools). Stir in the lemon rind, mixed spice, coriander, cayenne pepper and salt. Cook uncovered for 30 minutes, until little excess liquid remains.

4 Spoon the chutney into warmed sterilized jars, cover and seal. Store in a cool, dark place. Open within 10 months of making. Once opened, store in the refrigerator and use within 2 months.

VARIATIONS
Stoned dried prunes can be substituted for the dates, and dried sour cherries for the dried cranberries. Apple juice can be used instead of the cranberry juice.

Nutritional information (total): Energy 2873Kcal/12248kJ; Protein 32g; Carbohydrate 714.3g, of which sugars 703.5g; Fat 6.8g, of which saturates 0.2g; Cholesterol 0mg; Calcium 1075mg; Fibre 52.1g; Sodium 2358mg.

BEETROOT, DATE and ORANGE PRESERVE

*With its vibrant red colour and rich earthy flavour, this distinctive chutney is good with
salads as well as full-flavoured cheeses such as mature Cheddar, Stilton or Gorgonzola.*

MAKES ABOUT 1.4KG/3LB

300ml/½ pint/1¼ cups malt vinegar
200g/7oz/1 cup granulated sugar
350g/12oz raw beetroot (beets)
350g/12oz eating apples
225g/8oz red onions, very finely chopped
1 garlic clove, crushed
finely grated rind of 2 oranges
5ml/1 tsp ground allspice
5ml/1 tsp salt
175g/6oz/1 cup chopped dried dates

1 Put the vinegar and sugar in the
ceramic cooking pot. Cover with the
lid and switch the slow cooker to high.
Leave until steaming hot.

2 Meanwhile, scrub or thinly peel the
beetroot, then cut into 1cm/½in pieces.
Peel, quarter and core the apples and
cut into 1cm/½in pieces.

3 Stir the vinegar mixture with a
wooden spoon until the sugar has
dissolved. Add the beetroot, apples,
onions, garlic, orange rind, ground
allspice and salt. Stir everything together,
then re-cover and cook for 4–5 hours,
stirring occasionally until very tender.

4 Stir in the dates and cook for a
further hour until the mixture is really
thick. Stir once or twice during this time
to prevent the chutney catching on the
base of the ceramic cooking pot.

5 Spoon the chutney into warmed
sterilized jars, cover and seal. Store
in a cool, dark place and open within
5 months of making. Refrigerate after
opening and use within 1 month.

COOK'S TIP
For really speedy preparation and a
deliciously fine-textured chutney, put
the peeled beetroot through the coarse
grating blade of a food processor.
Alternatively, you can simply grate the
beetroot by hand.

Nutritional information (total): Energy 1632Kcal/6949kJ; Protein 16.8g; Carbohydrate 413.7g, of which sugars 406g; Fat 1.5g, of which saturates 0.2g; Cholesterol 0mg; Calcium 278mg; Fibre 23.1g; Sodium 2241mg.

CARROT and ALMOND RELISH

This Middle Eastern classic, usually made with long fine strands of carrot, is available from many supermarkets. This version, using coarsely grated carrots, is just as good.

3 Switch the slow cooker to high and cook for about 2 hours, or until the carrots and ginger are almost tender, stirring only if the mixture looks dry around the edges.

4 Stir in the lemon rind and cook for a further 1 hour, until the mixture is thick. Stir once towards the end of the cooking time to prevent the mixture from sticking to the base of the pot.

5 Put the almonds in a frying pan and toast over a low heat until just beginning to colour. Gently stir into the relish, taking care not to break the almonds.

6 Spoon the relish into warmed sterilized jars, cover and seal. Store in a cool, dark place and leave to mature for 1 week. The relish will keep unopened for up to 1 year. However, once the jars have been opened, store them in the refrigerator and use within 2 weeks.

MAKES ABOUT 675G/1½LB

15ml/1 tbsp coriander seeds
500g/1¼lb carrots, grated
50g/2oz fresh root ginger, finely shredded
200g/7oz/1 cup caster (superfine) sugar
120ml/4fl oz/½ cup white wine vinegar
30ml/2 tbsp clear honey
7.5ml/1½ tsp salt
finely grated rind of 1 lemon
50g/2oz/½ cup flaked (sliced) almonds

1 Crush the coriander seeds using a mortar and pestle. Put them in the ceramic cooking pot with the carrots, ginger and sugar, and mix well.

2 Put the vinegar, honey and salt in a jug (pitcher) and stir until the salt has dissolved completely. Pour the mixture over the carrots. Mix well, cover and leave for 1 hour.

Nutritional information (total): Energy 1407Kcal/5947kJ; Protein 13.7g; Carbohydrate 289.6g, of which sugars 285.8g; Fat 29.4g, of which saturates 2.7g; Cholesterol 0mg; Calcium 268mg; Fibre 15.7g; Sodium 2898mg.

PAPAYA and LEMON RELISH

This chunky relish is best made with a firm, unripe papaya. The slow, gentle cooking allows all the flavours to mellow. Serve with roast meats, or with cheese and crackers.

MAKES 450G/1LB

1 large unripe papaya
1 onion, very thinly sliced
175ml/6fl oz/generous ¾ cup red
    wine vinegar
juice of 2 lemons
165g/5½oz/¾ cup golden caster
    (superfine) sugar
1 cinnamon stick
1 bay leaf
2.5ml/½ tsp hot paprika
2.5ml/½ tsp salt
150g/5oz/1 cup sultanas (golden raisins)

1 Peel the papaya and cut it lengthways in half. Remove the seeds, then cut the flesh into small chunks.

2 Place the papaya in the ceramic cooking pot, add the onion slices and stir in the vinegar. Switch the slow cooker to high, cover and cook for 2 hours.

3 Add the lemon juice, sugar, cinnamon stick, bay leaf, paprika, salt and sultanas, and stir thoroughly until the sugar has completely dissolved.

4 Cook the chutney, uncovered, for a further 1 hour to allow the mixture to reduce slightly; the relish should be fairly thick and syrupy.

5 Ladle the chutney into hot sterilized jars. Seal and store for 1 week before using. Open within 1 year of making. Once opened, store in the refrigerator and use within 2 weeks.

Nutritional information (total): Energy 1294Kcal/5511kJ; Protein 8.4g; Carbohydrate 332.7g, of which sugars 332.7g; Fat 1.4g, of which saturates 0g; Cholesterol 0mg; Calcium 272mg; Fibre 16.1g; Sodium 1111mg.

CHRISTMAS MINCEMEAT

In many mincemeat recipes, the raw ingredients are simply mixed together. Here, gentle cooking develops and intensifies the flavour, so that the mincemeat may be used straight away without being left to mature. At the same time, heating it to simmering point helps prevent fermentation, and this allows a much longer shelf-life.

MAKES ABOUT 1.75G/4LB

450g/1lb cooking apples
115g/4oz/¾ cup glacé (candied) citrus peel
115g/4oz/½ cup glacé (candied) cherries
115g/4oz/½ cup ready-to-eat dried apricots
115g/4oz/1 cup blanched almonds
150ml/¼ pint/⅔ cup brandy
225g/8oz/1 cup currants
225g/8oz/1⅓ cups sultanas (golden raisins)
450g/1lb/3¼ cups seedless raisins
225g/8oz/1 cup soft dark brown sugar
225g/8oz/1⅔ cups suet (chilled, grated shortening) or vegetarian suet
10ml/2 tsp ground ginger
5ml/1 tsp ground allspice
5ml/1 tsp ground cinnamon
2.5ml/½ tsp grated nutmeg
grated rind and juice of 1 lemon
grated rind and juice of 1 orange

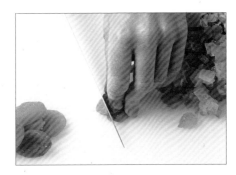

1 Peel, core and chop the cooking apples, then roughly chop the citrus peel, glacé cherries, apricots and blanched almonds.

2 Reserve half the brandy and put the rest into the ceramic cooking pot with all the other ingredients. Stir well until thoroughly mixed.

3 Cover the ceramic cooking pot with the lid and switch the slow cooker to high. Cook for 1 hour.

4 Stir the mixture well, then re-cover the pot and reduce the temperature to low. Cook for a further 2 hours, stirring halfway through cooking to prevent the mixture from overheating and sticking to the sides of the pot.

5 Remove the lid and leave the mixture to cool completely, stirring occasionally.

6 Stir the reserved brandy into the mincemeat and spoon the mixture into sterilized jars. Cover and store in a cool, dry place for up to six months. Once opened, store in the refrigerator and use within two weeks.

Nutritional information (total): Energy 7149Kcal/30087kJ; Protein 55.6g; Carbohydrate 1114g, of which sugars 1088.3g; Fat 267.7g, of which saturates 106.3g; Cholesterol 0mg; Calcium 1228mg; Fibre 47.3g; Sodium 774mg.

CONFIT of SLOW-COOKED ONIONS

This jam of slow-cooked, caramelized onions in sweet-sour balsamic vinegar will keep for several days in a sealed jar in the refrigerator. You can use red, white or yellow onions, but yellow onions will give the sweetest result. Shallots will also make an excellent confit.

2 Cover the pot with the lid, then place a folded dishtowel on top. Cook the onions for 5 hours, stirring the mixture several times during the cooking time to ensure the onions soften evenly.

3 Season well with salt and ground black pepper, then add the thyme, bay leaf, sugar, balsamic vinegar and red wine. Gently stir with a wooden spoon until the sugar has completely dissolved, then stir in the prunes.

4 Re-cover and cook for 1½–2 hours, or until the mixture is thick and sticky. Adjust the seasoning, adding more sugar and/or vinegar to taste. When cool, store the confit in the refrigerator. Serve either cold or warm.

SERVES 6

30ml/2 tbsp extra virgin olive oil
15g/½oz/1 tbsp butter
500g/1¼lb onions, thinly sliced
3–5 fresh thyme sprigs
1 bay leaf
30ml/2 tbsp light muscovado (brown)
    sugar, plus a little extra
30ml/2 tbsp balsamic vinegar,
    plus a little extra
120ml/4fl oz/½ cup red wine
50g/2oz/¼ cup ready-to-eat prunes,
    chopped
salt and ground black pepper

1 Put the oil and butter in the ceramic cooking pot and heat on high for about 15 minutes, until the butter has melted. Add the onions and stir to coat.

Nutritional information per portion: Energy 133Kcal/556kJ; Protein 1.2g; Carbohydrate 16.5g, of which sugars 14.6g; Fat 5.9g, of which saturates 1.8g; Cholesterol 5mg; Calcium 26mg; Fibre 1.6g; Sodium 20mg.

FRESH LEMON CURD

This classic tangy, creamy curd is still one of the most popular of all the curds. Delicious spread thickly over freshly baked white bread or served with American-style pancakes, it also makes a wonderfully rich, zesty sauce spooned over fresh fruit tarts.

3 Put the eggs and yolks in a bowl and beat together with a fork. Strain the eggs into the lemon mixture, and whisk well until combined. Cover the bowl with foil, then return it to the slow cooker.

4 Cook the lemon curd on low for 1–2 hours, stirring every 15 minutes, until thick enough to lightly coat the back of a wooden spoon.

5 Pour the curd into small warmed sterilized jars. Cover and seal. Store in a cool, dark place, ideally in the refrigerator, and use within 3 months. Once opened, store in the refrigerator.

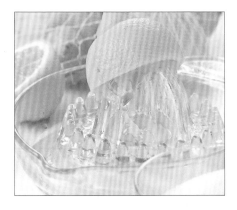

MAKES ABOUT 450G/1LB

finely grated rind and juice of 3 lemons (preferably unwaxed or organic)
200g/7oz/1 cup caster (superfine) sugar
115g/4oz/½ cup unsalted (sweet) butter, diced
2 large (US extra large) eggs
2 large (US extra large) egg yolks

COOK'S TIP
To make sharp, tangy lime curd, replace the lemons with the grated zest and juice of 4 large ripe, juicy limes. Lime curd has a lovely pale greenish hue.

1 Pour about 5cm/2in very hot water into the ceramic cooking pot. Switch the slow cooker to high. Put the lemon rind and juice, sugar and butter in the largest heatproof bowl that will fit inside the slow cooker.

2 Put the bowl into the slow cooker, then pour enough near-boiling water around it to come just over halfway up the sides. Leave for about 15 minutes, stirring occasionally, until the sugar has dissolved and the butter melted. Remove and allow to cool for a few minutes. Turn the slow cooker to low.

Nutritional information (total): Energy 1968Kcal/8224kJ; Protein 22.4g; Carbohydrate 215.3g, of which sugars 215.3g; Fat 118.9g, of which saturates 66.9g; Cholesterol 1102mg; Calcium 277mg; Fibre 0g; Sodium 895mg.

BLUSHING PEARS

As this pickle matures, the fruits absorb the colour of the vinegar, giving them a glorious
pink hue. Their deliciously spicy, sweet-and-sour flavour is especially good with cold turkey
at Christmas, or with game pie, well-flavoured cheese or paté.

MAKES ABOUT 1.3KG/3LB

1 small lemon
450g/1lb/2¼ cups golden granulated sugar
475ml/16fl oz/2 cups raspberry vinegar
7.5cm/3in cinnamon stick
6 whole cloves
6 allspice berries
150ml/¼ pint/⅔ cup water
900g/2lb firm pears

1 Using a sharp knife, thinly pare a few strips of rind from the lemon. Squeeze out the juice and add to the ceramic cooking pot with the strips of rind.

2 Add the sugar, vinegar, spices and water, and switch the slow cooker to high. Cover and leave to heat for about 30 minutes, then stir until the sugar has completely dissolved. Re-cover with the lid and heat for a further 30 minutes.

3 Meanwhile, prepare the pears. Peel and halve the pears, then scoop out the cores using a melon baller or small teaspoon. If the pears are very large, cut them into quarters rather than halves.

4 Add the pears to the slow cooker, cover and cook for 1½–2 hours, turning them occasionally to coat them in the syrup. Check the pears frequently; they should be tender and translucent but still retain their shape.

5 Using a slotted spoon, remove the pears from the slow cooker and pack into hot sterilized jars, adding the spices and strips of lemon rind.

6 Remove any scum from the surface of the syrup, then ladle it over the pears. Cover and seal. Store for a few days before eating, and use within 2 weeks.

Nutritional information (total): Energy 2133Kcal/9086kJ; Protein 5g; Carbohydrate 560.3g, of which sugars 560.3g; Fat 0.9g, of which saturates 0g; Cholesterol 0mg; Calcium 230mg; Fibre 19.8g; Sodium 50mg.

HOT SPICED WINE

On a cold winter evening, there is nothing more welcoming than a glass of warm spicy wine. The slow cooker is particularly useful when you are making the wine for guests: you can prepare the spiced wine up to four hours before your guests arrive, and the slow cooker will keep it at the ideal serving temperature until you are ready to serve.

SERVES 8

50g/2oz/¼ cup soft light brown sugar
150ml/¼ pint/⅔ cup near-boiling water
2 small oranges, preferably unwaxed
6 whole cloves
1 stick cinnamon
½ whole nutmeg
1½ bottles red wine, such as Bordeaux
150ml/¼ pint/⅔ cup brandy

1 Put the sugar in the ceramic cooking pot and pour in the near-boiling water. Stir until the sugar has dissolved, then switch the slow cooker to high.

COOK'S TIP
Use heatproof glasses with a handle so that guests can hold the hot wine easily.

2 Rinse the oranges, then press the cloves into one and add it to the slow cooker with the cinnamon, nutmeg and wine. Halve the remaining orange, then slice and set aside. Cover the slow cooker with the lid and cook on high or auto for 1 hour, then reduce to low or leave on auto and heat for 3 hours.

3 Stir the brandy into the spiced wine and add the orange slices. Heat for a further 1 hour.

4 Remove the whole orange and the cinnamon stick. The wine is now ready to serve and can be kept hot for up to 4 hours. Serve in heatproof glasses.

Nutritional information per portion: Energy 162Kcal/675kJ; Protein 0.2g; Carbohydrate 6.8g, of which sugars 6.8g; Fat 0g, of which saturates 0g; Cholesterol 0mg; Calcium 12mg; Fibre 0g; Sodium 10mg.

CRANBERRY and APPLE PUNCH

When you are throwing a party, it is good to have a non-alcoholic punch available. Here, the slow cooker extracts maximum flavour from fresh ginger and lime peel.

SERVES 6

1 lime
5cm/2in piece of fresh root ginger, peeled and thinly sliced
50g/2oz/¼ cup caster (superfine) sugar
200ml/7fl oz/scant 1 cup near-boiling water
475ml/16fl oz/2 cups cranberry juice
475ml/16fl oz/2 cups clear apple juice
ice and chilled sparkling mineral water or soda water, to serve (optional)

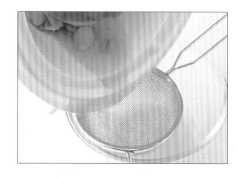

1 Pare the rind off the lime and place in the ceramic cooking pot with the ginger and sugar. Pour over the water and stir until the sugar dissolves. Cover with the lid and heat on high or auto for 1 hour, then reduce the temperature to low or leave on auto and heat for a further 2 hours. Switch off the slow cooker and leave the syrup to cool completely.

2 When cold, strain the syrup through a fine sieve (strainer) into a large serving jug (pitcher) or punch bowl and discard the lime rind and ginger.

3 Squeeze the juice from the lime and strain through a sieve into the syrup. Stir in the cranberry and apple juices. Cover and chill in the refrigerator for at least 3 hours or until ready to serve.

4 To serve, pour or ladle the punch over plenty of ice in tall glasses and top up with sparkling mineral water or soda water, if using.

COOK'S TIP
You can now buy all kinds of different apple juices made from specific varieties of apple. They have distinctive flavours, and it is well worth searching them out.

Nutritional information per portion: Energy 111Kcal/475kJ; Protein 0.1g; Carbohydrate 27.9g, of which sugars 16.5g; Fat 0.1g, of which saturates 0g; Cholesterol 0mg; Calcium 8mg; Fibre 0g; Sodium 2mg.

MEXICAN HOT CHOCOLATE

Blending or whisking the hot chocolate before serving gives it a wonderfully frothy texture. The slow cooker is particularly good for heating the milk in this recipe because the gentle heating process allows the cinnamon and cloves to infuse and flavour the hot chocolate with a deliciously warm and spicy flavour.

SERVES 4

1 litre/1¾ pints/4 cups milk
1 cinnamon stick
2 whole cloves
115g/4oz dark (bittersweet) chocolate, chopped into small pieces
2–3 drops of almond essence (extract)
whipped cream and cocoa powder or grated chocolate, to serve (optional)

COOK'S TIP
Traditional Mexican hot chocolate is always warmly spiced. It is a popular breakfast drink, often served with delicious deep-fried *churros*, which are Mexican sugared doughnuts.

1 Pour the milk into the ceramic cooking pot. Add the cinnamon stick and cloves, cover with the lid and switch the slow cooker to high. Leave to heat the milk and infuse the spices for 1 hour, or until the milk is almost boiling.

2 Add the chocolate pieces and almond essence to the milk and stir until melted. Turn off the slow cooker.

3 Strain the mixture into a blender (it may be necessary to do this in two batches) and whizz on high speed for about 30 seconds, until frothy. Alternatively, whisk the mixture in the ceramic cooking pot with a hand-held electric whisk or a wire whisk.

4 Pour or ladle the hot chocolate into warmed heatproof glasses. If you like, top each with a little whipped cream and a dusting of cocoa powder or grated chocolate. Serve immediately.

Nutritional information per portion: Energy 262Kcal/1102kJ; Protein 9.9g; Carbohydrate 30g, of which sugars 29.7g; Fat 12.3g, of which saturates 7.6g; Cholesterol 17mg; Calcium 309mg; Fibre 0.7g; Sodium 109mg.

NORMANDY COFFEE

The Normandy region of northern France is known for its abundant apple orchards, and its name is often given to dishes made with apple juice or apple sauce. This recipe combines the sweet-tart flavour of apples and spices to make a delicious, tangy coffee.

SERVES 4

475ml/16fl oz/2 cups apple juice
30ml/2 tbsp soft brown sugar, to taste
2 oranges, thickly sliced
2 small cinnamon sticks
2 whole cloves
pinch of ground allspice
475ml/16fl oz/2 cups hot, freshly brewed strong black coffee
halved cinnamon sticks, to serve (optional)

COOK'S TIPS
• For a good flavour, use strong coffee – espresso or filter-/plunger-brewed at 75g/3 tbsp/scant ½ cup coffee per 1 litre/1¾ pints/4 cups water.
• To make an alcoholic drink, replace a quarter of the apple juice with the French apple brandy, Calvados. Stir in the brandy after straining the spice-infused apple juice and removing the spices.

1 Pour the apple juice into the ceramic cooking pot and switch the slow cooker on to high.

2 Add the sugar, oranges, cinnamon sticks, cloves and allspice to the pot and stir. Cover and heat for 20 minutes.

3 Stir the mixture until the sugar has dissolved completely, then cover with the lid and heat for 1 hour.

4 When the juice is hot and infused with the spices, switch the slow cooker to low to keep warm for up to 2 hours.

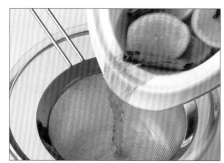

5 Strain the juice into a bowl, discarding the orange slices and spices.

6 Pour the hot coffee into the juice and stir. Quickly pour into warmed mugs or espresso-style cups, adding a halved cinnamon stick to each, if you like.

Nutritional information per portion: Energy 85Kcal/363kJ; Protein 0.2g; Carbohydrate 22.2g, of which sugars 22.2g; Fat 0.1g, of which saturates 0g; Cholesterol 0mg; Calcium 11mg; Fibre 0g; Sodium 3mg.

USEFUL ADDRESSES

MANUFACTURERS

Contact the following slow cooker manufacturers for retail advice, online orders and customer services, including parts and repairs.

UNITED KINGDOM

Lakeland Ltd
Customer Services Department
Alexandra Buildings
Windemere
Cumbria LA23 1BQ
Tel: (01539) 488100
www.lakeland.co.uk

Morphy Richards
Customer Services Department
Talbot Road
Mexborough
South Yorkshire
S64 8AJ
Tel: (01709) 582 402
www.morphyrichards.com

Prima
Contact shop.prima-international.com for online orders, retail advice and customer service centres in your area.

Russell Hobbs
Customer Services Department
Pifco Ltd
Failsworth
Manchester
M35 0HS
Tel: (0161) 681 8588
www.russell-hobbs.com

TEFAL
Contact www.tefal.co.uk for online orders, retail advice and customer service centres in your area.

UNITED STATES

Farberware Inc
Customer Services Department
Tel: (800) 253-9054
www.farberware.com

Hamilton Beach
Customer Services Department
55353 Lyon Industrial Drive
New Hudson
MI 48165
Tel: (1-800) 851-8900
www.hamiltonbeach.com

Kirby & Allen
Customer Services Department
1330 Livingstone Avenue
North Brunswick
NJ 08902
Tel: (732) 246-1460
Email: customerservice@kirby-allen.com
www.kirby-allen.com

Proctor Silex HB/PS
Customer Services Department
234 Springs Road
Washington, NC 27889
Tel: (US) (1-800) 851-8900
     (Can) (1-800) 267-2826
     (Mexico) (01-800) 71-16-100
www.proctor-silex.com

Rowecraft
Customer Services Department
24 Critchett Road
Raymond, NH 03077
www.rowecraft.com

Russell Hobbs
Customer Services Department
Myers Electric
416 Whalley Avenue
New Haven
CT 06511-3097
Tel: (toll free) 1-888-HOBBS-20
www.russell-hobbs.com

West Bend
Customer Services Department
PO Box 2780
West Bend
WI 53095
Tel: (262) 334-6949
www.west-bend.com

Windmere/Applica
Tel: (1-800) 557 9463
Contact applicaconsumeraffairs@fox-international.com for retail advice and customer service centers in your area.
www.windmere.com

AUSTRALIA

Morphy Richards
Contact www.morphyrichards.com for customer service centres in your area.

Russell Hobbs
Contact www.russell-hobbs.com for online orders, retail advice and customer service centres in your area.

TEFAL
Contact www.tefal.com for customer service centres in your area.

NEW ZEALAND

Morphy Richards
Contact www.morphyrichards.com for customer service centres in your area.

Russell Hobbs
Contact www.russell-hobbs.com for online orders, retail advice and customer service centres in your area.

TEFAL
Customer Services Department
PO Box 64-302
Botany Town Centre
East Tamaki
1730 Auckland
Tel: (0800) 700 711
www.tefal.com

INDEX

A

alcohol 29
 cider-glazed gammon 168–9
 drunken chicken 133
 hot bananas with rum and raisins 216
 hot spiced wine 248–9
 poached pears in red wine 210
 tarragon chicken in cider 130–1
 winter fruit poached in mulled wine 211
American frosting 55
anchovies
 cannelloni Sorrentina-style 102
 creamy anchovy and potato bake 98
apples
 apple chutney 62
 baked stuffed apples 26–7, 212
 cranberry and apple punch 248–9
apricot and almond stuffed chicken 124
apricot, butternut and almond chutney 239
Asian-style duck consommé 82
aubergines 23
 moussaka 174–5
avgolemono 77

B

bain-marie 50–5
baked egg custard 52–3
baked eggs with creamy leeks 184
baked stuffed apples 26–7, 212
banana and chocolate chip pudding 217
banana and pumpkin cake 233
bananas with rum and raisins 216
Basque-style tuna 113
beans 24, 25, 181
 Boston baked beans 161
 mushroom and bean pâté 90

rosemary risotto with borlotti beans 196
spicy hot mixed-bean chilli with cornbread topping 189
sweet and sour mixed-bean hot-pot 187
beef 12–13, 149
 beef and mushroom pudding 154–5
 braised beef in a rich peanut sauce 153
 braised beef with horseradish 156–7
 Hungarian cholent 158
 pot-roast brisket 47
 Provençal beef stew 152
 spiced beef 159
 steak and kidney pie with mustard gravy 150–1
beetroot, cabbage and tomato borscht 78
beetroot, date and orange preserve 241
beurre blanc 57
blueberry muffin pudding 232
blushing pears 247
Boston baked beans 161
bouillon powders 33
bouquet garni 28
braising 42–3
 braised beef in a rich peanut sauce 153
 braised beef with horseradish 156–7
 braised guinea fowl with red cabbage 142
 toppings 44–5
bread and butter pudding 53
bread toppings 45
brown rice with lime and lemon grass 202
butternut, apricot and almond chutney 239
butterscotch fondue 61
butterscotch sauce 59

C

cabbage 23
 braised guinea fowl with red cabbage 142
 braised red cabbage 43
 cabbage, beetroot and tomato borscht 78
cakes 54–5, 207, 224–235
canned vegetables 23
cannelloni
  smoked trout 101
  Sorrentina-style 102
caramel sauce 59
cardamom chicken mousselines 93
Caribbean peanut chicken 134

carrot and almond relish 242
carrot and coriander soup 69
carrot and lamb casserole with barley 180
carrot and parsnip cake 226–7
carrot dip 85
casseroles 38–41
 toppings 44–5
 lamb and carrot casserole with barley 180
 root vegetable casserole with caraway dumplings 188
 spicy pork casserole with dried fruit 166–7
cheese
 cheese and vegetable pudding 53
 cheese fondue 60
 cheese-stuffed pears 86
 chocolate cheesecake brownies 228
 French onion soup with cheese croûtes 68
 moussaka 172–3
 onions stuffed with goat's cheese and sun-dried tomatoes 199
 red lentil and goat's cheese pâté 91
chicken 16–17, 121
 apricot and almond stuffed chicken 124
 cardamom chicken mousselines 93
 Caribbean peanut chicken 134
 chicken and pistachio pâté 94–5
 chicken and split pea koresh 141
 chicken fricassée 126–7
 chicken in a cashew nut sauce 139
 chicken korma 140
 chicken soup with knaidlach 79
 chicken with chipotle sauce 132
 dorowat 137
 drunken chicken 133

fragrant chicken curry 138
hen in a pot with parsley sauce 125
Jamaican jerk chicken 135
layered chicken and mushroom bake 123
mousseline pâté 51
poaching 48
pot-roast 47
spicy chicken jambalaya 136
spring chicken slow-braised in smoky bacon sauce 128–9
stock 31–2
tarragon chicken in cider 130–1
chilled tomato and sweet pepper soup 71
chilli
 chicken with chipotle sauce 132
 parsnips and chickpeas in garlic, onion, chilli and ginger paste 198
 spicy hot mixed-bean chilli with cornbread topping 189
chocolate
 chocolate cheesecake brownies 228
 chocolate chip and banana pudding 217
 chocolate chip walnut cake 225
 chocolate fondue 61
 chocolate sauces 59
 dark chocolate cake 54–5
 Mexican hot chocolate 250–1
 rich chocolate cake 224
 steamed chocolate and fruit puddings 220
Christmas mincemeat 244
chutneys 237
 apple chutney 62
 butternut, apricot and almond chutney 239
 mango chutney 238
 sweet and hot dried fruit chutney 240
cider-glazed gammon 166–7
cobblers 27
coconut custard 208
coconut salmon 105
coconut, tomato and lentil dhal with toasted almonds 204
cod with caramelized onions 114
coffee
 Normandy coffee 250–1
 petits pots de crème au mocha 215
 sticky coffee and pear pudding 218–19
compôtes 27

confit of slow-cooked onions 245
cordial 63
coriander and carrot soup 69
cornbread topping with spicy hot mixed bean chilli 189
country-style terrine with leeks 92
courgette and mushroom lasagne 191
couscous-stuffed sweet peppers 197
cranberry and apple punch 248–9
creamy anchovy and potato bake 98
creamy chocolate sauce 59
crème brûlée 53
crumbles 27, 45
cucumber with salmon risotto 99
curry
  sweet pumpkin and peanut curry 192
  vegetable and cashew nut biryani 194
  vegetable kashmiri 193
custard 52–3, 58

D
dark chocolate cake 54–5
date puddings with toffee sauce 221
date, beetroot and orange preserve 241
decorating cakes 55
dippers 60, 61
dorowat 137
dried fruit sauce 58
drinks 237
drunken chicken 133
duck 17
  Asian-style duck consommé 82
  duck stew with olives 144
dumplings 44
  chicken soup with knaidlach 79
  root vegetable casserole with caraway dumplings 188

E
eggs
  avgolemeno 77
  baked egg custard 52–3
  baked eggs with creamy leeks 184
  dorowat 137
  Hungarian cholent 158
  Vermont baked maple custard 214
equipment 8–9, 10–11
essences (extracts) 29

F
fennel 23
  mushroom and fennel hot-pot 186
  red mullet braised on a bed of fennel 108–9
fish 20, 97
  Basque-style tuna 113
  braising 21
  cannelloni Sorrentina-style 102
  coconut salmon 105
  cod with caramelized onions 114
  creamy anchovy and potato bake 98
  fish terrine 87
  green fish curry 119
  haddock and smoked salmon terrine 88–9
  hoki balls in tomato sauce 107
  lemon sole and Parma ham roulades 112
  mixed fish jambalaya 106
  northern Thai fish curry 118
  poached fish in spicy tomato sauce 104
  poaching 21, 49
  red mullet braised on a bed of fennel 108–9
  salmon risotto with cucumber 99
  seafood chowder 76
  skate with tomato and olive sauce 111
  smoked trout cannelloni 101
  special fish pie 100
  spinach and nut stuffed herrings 116–17
  stock 32
  swordfish in barbecue sauce 115
  tuna lasagne 103
fondues 60–1
fragrant chicken curry 138
French onion soup with cheese croûtes 68
fresh fruit bread and butter pudding 222–3
fresh fruit sauce 58
fresh lemon curd 62–3, 246
fresh tomato sauce 56
frosted carrot and parsnip cake 226–7

frozen vegetables 23
fruit 26–7
  Christmas mincemeat 244
  fresh fruit bread and butter pudding 222–3
  fruit curds 62–3, 237
  light fruit cake 229
  Moroccan lamb with honey and prunes 175
  poaching 26, 49
  pork fillets with prune stuffing 165
  spicy pork casserole with dried fruit 162–3
  spicy tamarind chickpeas 203
  steamed chocolate and fruit puddings 220
  sweet and hot dried fruit chutney 240
  winter fruit poached in mulled wine 211
fudge frosting 55

G
Galician broth 75
game 16, 18–19
gammon
  Galician broth 75
  cider-glazed gammon 168–9
  poaching 49
garlic and tomatoes stewed with lamb 178
garlic, onion, chilli and ginger paste with parsnips and chickpeas 198
garlic, potato and onion gratin 201
Genoese minestrone 74
ginger cake 234–5
ginger cooked with papaya 213
ginger, garlic, onion and chilli paste with parsnips and chickpeas 198
glossy chocolate sauce 59
goose 17
grains 24–5, 41, 181
Greek meatballs in rich tomato sauce 171
green fish curry 119
grinding spices 29
guinea fowl 16, 121

braised guinea fowl with red cabbage 142
guinea fowl and spring vegetable stew 143

H
haddock and smoked salmon terrine 88–9
haddock with spicy Puy lentils 110
ham
  glazing 49
  lemon sole and Parma ham roulades 112
hare 19
  hare hot pies 147
hen in a pot with parsley sauce 125
herbs 28
  carrot and coriander soup 69
  hen in a pot with parsley sauce 125
  lamb in dill sauce 179
  root vegetable casserole with caraway dumplings 188
  rosemary risotto with borlotti beans 196
  tarragon chicken in cider 130–1
  tomato and fresh basil soup 70
herrings stuffed with spinach and nuts 116–17
hoki balls in tomato sauce 107
hollandaise sauce 56–7
honey and prunes with Moroccan lamb 176
hot and sour pork 160
hot and sour prawn soup 83
hot bananas with rum and raisins 216
hot date puddings with toffee sauce 221
hot spiced wine 248–9
Hungarian cholent 158

I
icings 55
Italian pork sausage stew 162

J
Jamaican jerk chicken 135

K
kidney
  steak and kidney pie with mustard gravy 150–1

L
lamb 14, 149
  boning 46
  braised lamb shanks 42
  Greek meatballs in rich tomato sauce 174
  lamb and carrot casserole with barley 180

lamb in dill sauce 177
lamb pie with mustard thatch
    173
lamb stewed with tomatoes
    and garlic 181
Lancashire hot-pot 172
Moroccan lamb with honey
    and prunes 176
moussaka 174–5
Tuscan pot-roasted shoulder
    of lamb 178–9
Lancashire hot-pot 172
lasagne, tuna 103
layered chicken and mushroom
    bake 123
leeks 22
baked eggs with creamy leeks
    184
country-style terrine with
    leeks 92
lemon and papaya relish 243
lemon curd 62–3, 246
lemon grass and lime with
    brown rice 202
lemon sole and Parma ham
    roulades 112
lentils 41
coconut, tomato and lentil
    dhal with toasted almonds
    204
haddock with spicy Puy lentils
    110
potage of lentils 80
red lentil and goat's cheese
    pâté 91
light fruit cake 229
lime and lemon grass with
    brown rice 202
lining cake tins 54

M
mango chutney 238
maple custard 214
marbled spice cake 230–1
marinades 18, 36–7
marmalade 63
meat 38, 149
basic meat stock 30
braising 42
brown meat stock 31
meat thermometers 11, 64–5
pot-roasting 46–7
Mexican hot chocolate 250–1
mincemeat 244
mixed fish jambalaya 106
mixed vegetable soup 34
moist golden ginger cake 234–5
Moroccan lamb with honey and
    prunes 176
moussaka 174–5
mousselines 51
cardamom chicken
    mousselines 93
mushrooms 22
beef and mushroom pudding
    154–5

layered chicken and
    mushroom bake 123
mushroom and bean pâté 90
mushroom and courgette
    lasagne 191
mushroom and fennel hot-pot
    186
pasta with mushrooms 190
wild mushroom soup 73
mustard gravy with steak and
    kidney pie 150–1
mustard thatch with lamb pie
    173

N
Normandy coffee 250–1
North African spiced soup 84
northern Thai fish curry 118
nuts 55
apricot and almond stuffed
    chicken 124
braised beef in a rich peanut
    sauce 153
butternut, apricot and almond
    chutney 239
Caribbean peanut chicken 134
carrot and almond relish 242
chicken and pistachio pâté
    94–5
chicken in a cashew nut sauce
    139
chicken korma 140
chocolate chip walnut cake
    225
coconut custard 208
coconut salmon 105
coconut, tomato and lentil
    dhal with toasted almonds
    204
pilaff with saffron and pickled
    walnuts 195
savoury nut loaf 185
spiced Indian rice with
    spinach, tomatoes and
    cashew nuts 205
spinach and nut stuffed
    herrings 116–17
sweet pumpkin and peanut
    curry 192
vegetable and cashew nut
    biryani 194

O
olive and tomato sauce with
    skate 111
olives with duck stew 111
onions 22
cod with caramelized onions
    114
confit of slow-cooked onions
    245
French onion soup with
    cheese croûtes 68
onions stuffed with goat's
    cheese and sun-dried
    tomatoes 199
parsnips and chickpeas in
    garlic, onion, chilli and
    ginger paste 198
potato, onion and garlic gratin
    201
orange candied sweet potatoes
    200
orange, date and beetroot
    preserve 241

P
papaya and lemon relish 243
papaya cooked with
    ginger 213
pappardelle with rabbit 145
parsnip and carrot cake 226–7
parsnips and chickpeas in garlic,
    onion, chilli and ginger
    paste 198
pasta 25, 41
cannelloni Sorrentina-style 102
Genoese minestrone 74
mushroom and courgette
    lasagne 191
pappardelle with rabbit 145
pasta with mushrooms 190
smoked trout cannelloni 101
tuna lasagne 103
pâtés 50–1, 67
chicken and pistachio pâté
    94–5
mousseline pâté 51
mushroom and bean pâté 90
red lentil and goat's cheese
    pâté 91
pears
blushing pears 247

cheese-stuffed pears 86
poached pears in red wine
    210
sticky coffee and pear pudding
    218–19
peas
chicken and split pea koresh
    141
parsnips and chickpeas in
    garlic, onion, chilli and
    ginger paste 198
spicy tamarind chickpeas 203
peppers see sweet peppers
petits pots de crème au mocha
    215
pilaff with saffron and pickled
    walnuts 195
poaching 21, 26, 48–9
poached fish in spicy tomato
    sauce 104
poached pears in red wine
    210
winter fruit poached in mulled
    wine 211
polenta toppings 45
pork 15, 149
Boston baked beans 161
cider-glazed gammon 168–9
Galician broth 75
glazed ham 49
hot and sour pork 160
Italian pork sausage stew 162
lemon sole and Parma ham
    roulades 112
pâté 50
poached gammon 49
pork and potato hot-pot 163
pork fillets with prune stuffing
    165
potato and sausage casserole
    164
spicy chicken jambalaya 136
spicy pork casserole with
    dried fruit 166–7
spring chicken slow-braised in
    smoky bacon sauce 128–9
pot-roasting 46–7
potage of lentils 80
potatoes
creamy anchovy and potato
    bake 98
orange candied sweet
    potatoes 200
pork and potato hot-pot 163
potato and sausage casserole
    164
potato, onion and garlic gratin
    201
toppings 44–5
poultry 16–17, 18, 38–9
poaching 48
pot-roasting 47
stock 31–2
prawns 21
hot and sour prawn soup 83
preserves 62–3

beetroot, date and orange
    preserve 241
Provençal beef stew 152
prune stuffing with pork fillets
    165
prunes and honey with
    Moroccan lamb 176
puddings 52, 53
pumpkins 23
    pumpkin and banana cake
        233
    spicy pumpkin soup 72
    sweet pumpkin and peanut
        curry 192

R
rabbit 19, 121
    pappardelle with rabbit 145
    rabbit casserole with juniper
        146
ready-made stocks 33
red lentil and goat's cheese pâté
    91
red mullet braised on a bed of
    fennel 108–9
reheating 43
relishes 237
    carrot and almond relish 242
    papaya and lemon relish 243
rice 24, 41
    avgolemono 77
    brown rice with lime and
        lemon grass 202
    pilaff with saffron and pickled
        walnuts 195
    rice pudding 53
    rosemary risotto with borlotti
        beans 196
    salmon risotto with cucumber
        99
    spiced Indian rice with
        spinach, tomatoes and
        cashew nuts 205
rich chocolate cake 224
root vegetable casserole with
    caraway dumplings 186
root vegetables 22, 81, 186
rosemary risotto with borlotti
    beans 196

S
sabayon sauce 57, 58–9
safety considerations 11, 64–5
saffron and pickled walnuts pilaff
    195
salmon
    coconut salmon 105
    haddock and smoked salmon
        terrine 88–9
    northern Thai fish curry 118
    salmon risotto with cucumber
        99
sauces 29
    savoury 56–7
    sweet 58–9
savoury dippers 60
savoury nut loaf 185
seafood chowder 76
shellfish 20, 21, 97
    hot and sour prawn soup 83
    mixed fish jambalaya 106
    seafood chowder 76
shrimp see prawns
skate with tomato and olive
    sauce 111
slow cookers 6–7, 8–9
    additional equipment 10–11
    bain-marie 50–5
    safety 64–5
smoked trout cannelloni 101
soups 34–5, 67
special fish pie 100
spiced beef 159
spices 28–9
    cardamom chicken
        mousselines 93
    haddock with spicy Puy lentils
        110
    hot spiced wine 248–9
    marbled spice cake 230–1
    North African spiced soup 84
    poached fish in spicy tomato
        sauce 104
    spiced carrot dip 85
    spiced Indian rice with
        spinach, tomatoes and
        cashew nuts 205
    spicy chicken jambalaya 136
    spicy hot mixed-bean chilli
        with cornbread topping
        189
    spicy pork casserole with
        dried fruit 162–3
    spicy pumpkin soup 72
    spicy tamarind chickpeas 203
spinach 23
    fragrant chicken curry 138
    spiced Indian rice with
        spinach, tomatoes and
        cashew nuts 205
    spinach and nut stuffed
        herrings 116–17
    spinach and root vegetable
        soup 81
spring chicken slow-braised in
    smoky bacon sauce 128–9

squashes 23
steak and kidney pie with
    mustard gravy 150–1
steamed chocolate and fruit
    puddings 220
steamed puddings 52
stewing fruit 26
stews 38–41
    Italian pork sausage stew 162
    veal stew with tomatoes 170
sticky coffee and pear pudding
    218–19
stock 30–3
studded terrine 51
sweet and hot dried fruit
    chutney 240
sweet and sour mixed-bean
    hot-pot 187
sweet dippers 61
sweet peppers 23
    chilled tomato and sweet
        pepper soup 71
    couscous-stuffed sweet
        peppers 197
sweet pumpkin and peanut
    curry 192
swordfish in barbecue sauce
    115

T
tamarind chickpeas 203
tapioca pudding 209
tarragon chicken in cider 130–1
terrines 50, 67
    country-style terrine with
        leeks 92
    fish terrine 87
    haddock and smoked salmon
        terrine 88–9
    studded terrine 51
toffee sauce with hot date
    puddings 221
tomatoes 23
    cabbage, beetroot and tomato
        borscht 78
    chilled tomato and sweet
        pepper soup 71
    coconut, tomato and lentil
        dhal with toasted almonds
        204

fresh tomato sauce 56
Greek meatballs in rich
    tomato sauce 171
hoki balls in tomato sauce 107
lamb stewed with tomatoes
    and garlic 181
onions stuffed with goat's
    cheese and sun-dried
    tomatoes 199
poached fish in spicy tomato
    sauce 104
skate with tomato and olive
    sauce 111
spiced Indian rice with
    spinach, tomatoes and
    cashew nuts 205
tomato and fresh basil soup
    70
turkey and tomato hot-pot
    122
veal stew with tomatoes 170
toppings 44–5
    spicy hot mixed bean chilli
        with cornbread topping
        187
trout cannelloni 101
tuna Basque-style 113
tuna lasagne 103
turkey 17, 121
    stock 32
    turkey and tomato hot-pot
        122
Tuscan pot-roasted shoulder of
    lamb 178–9

V
veal 13
    veal stew with tomatoes 170
vegetables 22–3, 39, 181
    cheese and vegetable pudding
        53
    Genoese minestrone 74
    guinea fowl and spring
        vegetable stew 143
    mixed vegetable soup 34
    North African spiced soup 84
    root vegetable casserole with
        caraway dumplings 188
    spinach and root vegetable
        soup 81
    stock 33
    vegetable and cashew nut
        biryani 194
    vegetable kashmiri 193
Vermont baked maple custard
    214

W
white chocolate sauce 59
white sauce 56
wild mushroom soup 73
winter fruit poached in mulled
    wine 211

Z
zucchini see courgettes